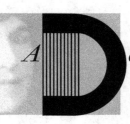

A Devil and a Good Woman, Too

A Devil and a Good Woman, Too

THE LIVES OF

Julia Peterkin

Susan Millar Williams

The University of Georgia Press

Athens & London

Second paperback edition, 2008
Paperback edition, 1999
© 1997 by the
University of Georgia Press
Athens, Georgia 30602
www.ugapress.org
All rights reserved
Designed by Richard Hendel
Set in Monotype Walbaum
by G&S Typesetters
Printed digitally in the United States of
America

The Library of Congress has cataloged
the hardcover edition of this book as
follows:
Library of Congress Cataloging-in-
Publication Data
Williams, Susan Millar.
   A devil and a good woman, too : the
lives of Julia Peterkin / Susan Millar
Williams.
   xx, 343 p. : ill. ; 25 cm.
   Includes bibliographical references
and index.
   ISBN 0-8203-1912-0 (alk. paper)
   1. Peterkin, Julia Mood, 1880–1961.
2. Authors, American—20th century—
Biography. 3. Women and literature—
South Carolina. 4. South
Carolina—Biography. I. Title.
PS3531.E77 Z97 1997
813′.52—dc21
[B]   97-13189

Second paperback edition
ISBN-13: 978-0-8203-3250-5
ISBN-10: 0-8203-3250-X

British Library Cataloging-in-Publication
Data available

FOR OLIVIA

Contents

Preface, *ix*

A Note on the Language, *xix*

1 Lang Syne, *1*

2 Cheating the Stillness, *21*

3 Cutting a Mouth, *35*

4 Poor Little Motherless, *50*

5 *Green Thursday, 62*

6 Cross Purposes, *83*

7 *Black April, 97*

8 *Scarlet Sister Mary, 121*

9 Gabriel's Harp, *139*

10 One Lovely, Tempting Place, *155*

11 A Stiff Masquerade, *175*

12 *Bright Skin, 186*

13 *Roll, Jordan, Roll, 202*

14 Smash-up, *226*

15 A Great White Column, *246*

Epilogue, *257*

Afterword: Searching for Julia, *259*

Key to Abbreviations, *267*

Notes, *269*

Bibliography, *307*

Index, *329*

Preface

eading Julia Peterkin for the first time was like discovering a room I never knew existed in the house where I had lived for many years. The shock sent a chill down the back of my neck, left me mesmerized, enraptured. Peterkin's Chekovian detachment, her gift for capturing character in a few words of dialogue, her deadpan humor, her spare, lyrical prose — these are the hallmarks of a great narrative voice, as powerful and true as any in literature.

Someone encountering Peterkin's novels and short stories without knowing who she was or when she lived would probably guess she is a black woman writing today. But Julia Peterkin was white, and her first book was published in 1924 — ten years before Zora Neale Hurston published her first novel, and long before Toni Morrison and Alice Walker were born. Along with Sherwood Anderson, Willa Cather, Sinclair

Lewis, Ernest Hemingway, F. Scott Fitzgerald, and Eugene O'Neill, Peterkin helped shape the sexual and racial attitudes of America between the two world wars. Her terse, economical style seems as fresh and arresting today as it must have seemed seventy years ago. Why, then, was Peterkin shoved under the carpet, and why has she resisted rediscovery?

Julia Peterkin began writing in 1921, at a time when the pundits of American culture, led by the irrepressible H. L. Mencken, were dismissing the South as a "gargantuan paradise of the fourth-rate," a place "as sterile, artistically, intellectually, culturally, as the Sahara desert." [1] Scornful as he was of the sentimental musings that passed for southern literature, Mencken foresaw a revolution: the lethargic South would be blasted awake by a new breed of writers, literary "anarchists" bent on purging its "mawkish," "mush-headed," and "idiotic" traditions.[2] Mencken had his eye on "several Southerners who show very high promise, including especially a lady in South Carolina." [3]

The lady was Julia Peterkin, the forty-year-old mistress of a cotton plantation who only recently had taken up writing "for a hobby." [4] Peterkin's first sketches and short stories, about the dangerous and difficult lives of rural blacks, were published in the fall 1921 issue of Mencken's popular magazine *Smart Set* and in a new little journal out of Richmond, Virginia, called the *Reviewer*. Within a year, Peterkin was receiving hate mail from white Southerners accusing her of betraying her race. In 1924, Alfred A. Knopf issued a slim collection of her short stories centered on the domestic life of a black farmer named Killdee. "Nothing so stark, taut, and poignant has come out of the white South in fifty years," wrote Joel Spingarn, the leading white academic authority on black culture.[5] Reviewers of both races uneasily confessed that they could not tell whether the author of *Green Thursday* was white or black, although W. E. B. Du Bois allowed that while it had been Julia Peterkin's misfortune to be born a southern white woman, she had somehow acquired "the eye and the ear to see beauty and know truth." [6]

Green Thursday sold poorly. In 1927, convinced that Alfred Knopf had failed to promote it properly, Peterkin jumped ship, taking her first novel, *Black April*, to the Bobbs-Merrill Company. Shrewdly appraising the psychology of the American book buyer, Bobbs-Merrill, unlike Knopf, proclaimed that Julia Peterkin was white. A blizzard of press releases identified her as "the mistress of Lang Syne plantation"; prominently placed on the dust jacket was an endorsement from the poet Carl

Sandburg lauding the novel as a remarkable evocation of black folk life while affirming that Julia Peterkin was "the fairest of Nordics."[7]

The Harlem renaissance was in full swing, yet no black fiction writer had ever reached the best-seller list or won more than scraps of praise from the critical establishment. "Wanted: A Negro Novelist," urged an article in the June 1924 *Independent.* Both the black middle class and the white intelligentsia were hungry for books that challenged racial stereotypes. *Black April* became a best-seller.

It is a characteristic American irony that a twentieth-century plantation mistress — a well-to-do white woman playing a role that was a throwback to the days of slavery — had more interest in and access to African American folk life than did educated blacks. Outsiders to the plantation culture because of their education and upbringing, African American writers such as Jessie Fauset, Nella Larsen, Wallace Thurman, and Walter White, who are now regarded as among the most important black novelists of the 1920s, were far more interested in the anxieties of middle-class blacks than in the struggles of illiterate farmhands. City dwellers all, they were eager to distance themselves from the backwardness of the rural South. When, like Walter White, they did portray southern blacks in fiction, they wrote about refined, well-educated professional people battling violent white supremacists.

Plowing, hog killing, revival meetings, and conjure bags — evidence of a world dominated by hard work, religion, and magic — drive the plot of Julia Peterkin's powerful first novel, *Black April.* The classic theme of a proud man confronting his own mortality is played out against the homely rituals of black country life. Donald Davidson, a founding editor of the *Fugitive,* the little magazine published at Vanderbilt University often credited with launching the southern renaissance, assessed *Black April*'s significance: it was both a gold mine of "superstitions and sayings" and an invaluable record of a primitive culture unaltered by civilization. More than that, however, *Black April* was a literary milestone, "the first genuine novel in English of the Negro as a human being."[8] A missing piece of the American puzzle fell into place. *The Negro as a human being.* Today the very phrase sounds preposterous, but in 1927 such an attitude was fresh, unprecedented, a revelation. The reviewers were bewildered: here was a white writer who didn't seem to realize that the people in her stories were black.

Julia Peterkin knew her stories would shock. White South Carolinians saw themselves as a besieged minority and put their children to bed with hair-raising tales about the Civil War and the atrocities of Radical Reconstruction. Julia's father, Julius Mood, and her grandparents, Henry and Laura Mood, were living in Columbia when General Sherman torched the city in February 1865. Laura and her young son Julius fled to the grounds of the insane asylum while Henry, the president of Columbia Female College, evacuated his students (the college buildings were used as a hospital).[9] Ten years later, as a member of Wade Hampton's Redshirts — terrorists on horseback whose self-appointed task was to restore white supremacy — Julius Mood held members of the Freedmen's Bureau at gunpoint to prevent black men from voting.[10] "The issues upon which every political struggle is fought are honesty versus vice; ignorance versus intelligence; Africanism versus Americanism," he wrote to the editor of the *New York Times* in 1882.[11]

In 1903, Julia Mood married W. G. Peterkin and moved to Lang Syne plantation. She had not been raised to preside over a great estate; it was a role she had to learn bit by bit, under the tutelage of a charismatic servant named Lavinia Berry. For the first fifteen years of her marriage Peterkin studied the part, acquiring traditional forms of power and influence. By 1920 she was an active member of the United Daughters of the Confederacy and the Daughters of the American Revolution, a dutiful housewife who played bridge and gave tea parties.[12] What unleashed the mysterious surge of creativity that transformed this circumspect white Southerner into one of the most famous "black" writers of the 1920s? Why would a white woman choose to write in a black voice when she had been brought up to believe that black people were violent, stupid, promiscuous, and dirty?

The community of people at Lang Syne plantation in 1900 consisted of five hundred blacks and five whites. The black women Peterkin knew pursued their lovers openly and changed them at will. By and large they were not financially dependent on their husbands. They spoke openly about their feelings of lust, jealousy, and betrayal, subjects forbidden to genteel white women. When provoked, they did not sit on their anger but lashed out, verbally and physically. Peterkin wished she could act that way, too. "These black friends of mine . . . live more in one Saturday night than I do in five years," she wrote to Mencken in 1921. "I envy them, and I guess as I cannot be them, I seek satisfaction in trying to record them." [13]

Raised to believe that women should not express strong emotions, Peterkin never could write candidly about herself. Yet many of her stories are veiled autobiography, confirming Toni Morrison's observation

that certain white writers invent black characters to express their deepest fears and desires.[14] At the same time, her novels and short stories are
a near-factual account of the lives of people at Lang Syne plantation.

Scarlet Sister Mary, for example, is in part the fictionalized biography of Mary Weeks, the woman who cultivated Julia Peterkin's garden
and washed her clothes. Like Weeks, the heroine of *Scarlet Sister Mary*
is abandoned by her husband. She takes many lovers, loses her firstborn
son, and eventually "finds peace" as a church member, though she refuses to give up her love charm and her gold hoop earrings. In other respects, Mary Pinesett is not Mary Weeks at all, but a projection of the
woman Julia Peterkin wanted to be. Sexy, independent, and outspoken,
she lives to please herself. Even in the Roaring Twenties such a heroine
raised eyebrows. *Scarlet Sister Mary* was banned in Boston, and one
member of the Pulitzer Prize selection committee objected that a book
about a promiscuous black woman violated Joseph Pulitzer's directive
that the winner represent the "wholesome best of American manhood."
The committee changed the rules.[15]

Julia Peterkin's third and last novel appeared in 1932. *Bright Skin*,
the story of a mulatto girl named Cricket who forsakes the plantation, is
Peterkin's most sophisticated treatment of African American experience. Several characters in the book flee to Harlem and become black
separatists, echoing the anger of Marcus Garvey and foreshadowing the
rise of Malcolm X. Such developments marked a radical departure, for
Julia Peterkin as well as for her characters. The plantation landscape
might be beautiful, and the old ways picturesque, but the way to get
ahead was to get away.

The agrarian way of life is dying in *Bright Skin*. New technologies
are sweeping inefficient labor off the plantation, and the descendants of
slaves have begun to resent their poverty. A stunning dissection of social
upheaval, *Bright Skin* was nevertheless scorned by leftists of the 1930s,
who considered it too complicated and too sympathetic to blacks who
opted to stay on the plantation. Nor did it suit those who had relished
the archaic, pastoral qualities of Peterkin's earlier work. *Bright Skin* did
not even make enough money to pay back the advance.[16]

Restless herself in the early 1930s, Julia Peterkin was faced with a
choice: should she leave her husband and her plantation to strike out on
her own, supporting herself by writing? Should she follow the people of
Lang Syne into the next phase of their lives? Or should she stay put, retreat into the past, and hold onto what she had? She knew best the ways
of the former slaves and the generations that followed — the country

people who had not yet fled the farm. Her public was losing interest, her defiance was fading, and the vocation of recording and analyzing the lives of poor people was being appropriated by "social scientists" — anthropologists and sociologists, folklorists and linguists.

In 1933, Peterkin wrote the text for a collection of photographs by her friend Doris Ulmann. An uneasy hybrid of fiction and nonfiction, *Roll, Jordan, Roll* was one of those projects writers take on hoping for a quick, easy book, and Julia Peterkin's heart was never in it. Old *Reviewer* sketches written from a black point of view were printed alongside new essays in Peterkin's own, increasingly paternalistic, voice. Readers whose racial consciousness had been raised by *Green Thursday, Black April, Scarlet Sister Mary,* and *Bright Skin* did not know what to make of this new Julia Peterkin, who turned on fieldworkers as "pitifully improvident and wasteful" and remarked that the "hysterical emotions" displayed during black church services "have little to do with salvation." [17] Regressing to an earlier role — the tea-drinking lady in the Big House — Peterkin had lost her genius.

The trade edition of *Roll, Jordan, Roll* garnered a few admiring reviews but otherwise fell flat. The publisher, Robert O. Ballou and Company, was soon out of business, and Bobbs-Merrill bought out the remaining stock.[18] Then, only a dozen years after she taught herself to write, Julia Peterkin simply stopped writing. For a few years more she was hailed as the grande dame of southern literature, consulted as an expert on "the Negro problem," and invited to speak at conferences, writers' colonies, and book fairs. By 1940 she had vanished from the literary scene.

Peterkin retired from writing in the hope that she could escape from controversy and regain her privacy. It was not to be. When her daughter-in-law committed suicide in 1941, Julia was blamed for it. Unwilling to defend herself for fear of subjecting the family to further scandal, Peterkin withdrew from society and turned her attention to mothering her grandson, gardening, and raising exotic fowl. Her retreat from public life was widely interpreted as an admission of guilt, and even today, some elderly South Carolinians remember her not as a Pulitzer Prize–winning novelist but as a dictatorial old crone who drove her son's wife to alcohol and drugs. One day in 1943, when her grandson was six years old, he came home from school and asked, "Grandmother, were you a writer?" "Yes," she replied, "but that was in another life." [19]

Over the past thirty years, as many black and female writers have been resurrected and appreciated, Julia Peterkin has been shunned.

Even among scholars who specialize in southern literature, very few know who she was or what she wrote. The standard literary histories allot her a sentence or two, tagging her as a sentimentalist, a local colorist, or a lurid sensationalizer.[20]

Peterkin's fiction is radiant, and her life story unforgettable — so why has she been forgotten? Why has her work, once recognized as revolutionary, been disparaged for so long? Perhaps one reason is that at a time when most of her contemporaries were moving toward the left, Peterkin abruptly and vocally returned to the conservative values of her childhood. In 1927, she accurately described her audience as "sophisticated and radical," people who read magazines like *American Mercury, New Masses, New Republic, Opportunity,* and *Nation.*[21] By 1933 she was selling stories to the *Ladies' Home Journal* and declaring that the Old South embodied the only real civilization America had ever known. Aristocratic Southerners were the childlike Negro's best friend, slavery had been beneficial to the slaves as well as their masters, and blacks and whites must never mix. In the South Carolina of the 1930s, as in the Arkansas of the 1950s and 1960s, where I grew up, such beliefs were always beckoning, a siren song calling white people to unite. Question them and you might be ridiculed, ostracized, or even physically attacked; embrace them and you could count on being embraced in return, welcomed as part of a larger community. After the publication of *Bright Skin,* Peterkin made a conscious decision to fit in. "One reason I've avoided writing for a time is that I found myself becoming too detached from the sense of being a part of my social group," she mused in 1937, "as if I looked on and had no part in the scene passing in front of my eyes. It gave me a queer feeling that I was not being entirely normal but was in danger of slipping into a world of my own making, something like those in which my insane acquaintances live."[22]

On the one hand, writing from the black point of view was deeply satisfying, a way of dramatizing herself, achieving fame, and shocking the bourgeoisie. On the other, it meant repudiating her social class, nullifying her individual identity. "I shall never write of white people," she informed a journalist in 1927.[23] From that point on, she never did, at least not for publication.

The truth is that Julia Peterkin *wanted* to write about white people, especially white people like herself. But when she tried, her vision dimmed and the strong, sure voice turned pompous. In the mid-1920s, she spent almost two years working on a book about the tormented life of a plantation mistress. The novel was never published, and for good reason: Peterkin had written herself into a quandary. The financial fears and angst-ridden love affairs of affluent whites seemed petty and trivial next to the life-and-death struggles of poor blacks. Yet when whites were in the picture, she was unable to identify with blacks or to lead her readers to empathize with them; in the presence of whites, her black characters came across as servile, artificial, and less than fully human. White writers normally "solved" such problems by keeping blacks in the background or using them as comic relief. Peterkin's approach was different. Only by showing blacks alone could she escape the strait-jacket of racism.

As it happened, Julia Peterkin knew a plantation community that provided the historical reality in which she could base her all-black fictions. Along the rivers of coastal South Carolina were scores of defunct rice plantations where large-scale farming had been abandoned and the black inhabitants left to their own devices for all but a few weeks of every year, when the wealthy owners returned to hunt. Peterkin's father briefly owned a share in one of the largest, Brookgreen, a cluster of estates on the Waccamaw River that had been converted to a hunting club in the early 1920s. Brookgreen plantation provided a solution to Peterkin's dilemma: instead of setting her novels on a midlands cotton estate like Lang Syne, where whites remained firmly in control, she transplanted her stories to the coastal, black-dominated "Blue Brook" plantation.

The characters in *Black April* and *Scarlet Sister Mary* share a naive folk tradition that centers on the plantation. The characters in *Bright Skin* have glimpsed other worlds and developed a sense of grievance. White supremacy is portrayed as malevolent—and transitory. A country minister thanks God for sending war and poverty to cleanse Blue Brook of white people. Now, he says, the plantation is "the peaceful home of those born in slavery. They enjoy the fruits of fields and rivers and seas. They reap the harvest of their own labor."[24]

Far from sharing this Afrocentric wish, Julia Peterkin lived much of her life in fear that what had occurred at Brookgreen would repeat itself on Lang Syne, that her family would lose the place to debt and the boll weevil. It never happened. The Peterkins held onto their land, and the workers did not "reap the harvest of their own labor." "Julia was not the great emancipator," I was told by an elderly white woman who knew her well.[25] She meant that Peterkin remained a plantation mistress until the day she died. Besides picking her cotton, black servants drew her bath, combed her hair, lit her fires, and mixed her drinks. The thought of redistributing the wealth or initiating other changes that might undermine her family's position at Lang Syne never occurred to her. She spoke out against lynching, persuaded Eleanor Roosevelt to put up the money for a new black school on the plantation, and encouraged certain young people to go north in search of opportunities. Otherwise, she did little to alter the status quo.

Inevitably, change did come to Lang Syne, in the form of tractors, cultivators, and mechanical cotton pickers — machinery designed to replace men and mules. By the mid-1940s it was technically possible to raise cotton without a lot of workers. "Robot Field Hands Successfully Invade Southland," announced the *Memphis Commercial Appeal* in October 1944.[26] Julia Peterkin and her son Bill continued providing work for people whose jobs were becoming obsolete, but human hands simply could not keep pace with motorized equipment.

Instead of whites abandoning the plantation to the blacks, as they had at Brookgreen, it was the blacks who went away. The cabins emptied. People had been leaving Lang Syne ever since Emancipation, though not in numbers large enough to disrupt society. During World War I people left in small groups; World War II sparked a larger migration. Before 1950, many of those who left eventually returned, whether to live out their lives, to die, or to be buried. After that, the exodus was permanent, and nearly total. The black settlement forged by slavery dissolved, leaving behind a handful of old people to claim the last meager benefits of paternalism. Julia Peterkin, the first American novelist to chronicle this gradual dissolution of the plantation, was gradually shut out, left behind, no longer able to share, even vicariously, in the African American community that had given her life structure, language, and meaning.

One fine spring day in 1992, I introduced Mary Weeks's great-great-nephew to Julia Peterkin's grandson. Jackie Whitmore, a twenty-two-year-old college student, accompanied me to Lang Syne, where fifty-four-year-old William Peterkin III still raises cotton. Thinking about their families' shared history, I was edgy about bringing the two men together. To my relief and delight, they launched into a boisterous reminiscence about mutual friends and relatives, a conversation so intense that they seemed to forget I was there. There and then, the contradictions between Julia Peterkin's personal life and her literature did not seem so bizarre after all.

Jackie and William and I strolled around the yard of the Big House, looking for traces of the old slave graveyard where, as Peterkin had written, "the pines rose tall and dark over graves that sheltered so many homeless bones." It was like stepping into the pages of *Scarlet Sister Mary.* "Yellow jessamines in full blossom made treetops gay and fragrant as new leaves pushed the old ones off the boughs and the wind scattered them in brown showers over the new grass. The old oaks tasseled out; pines sowed their winged seed. The whole earth was full of birthing and growing." [27] But something was missing. While the land remains, the people who once moved across it are gone.

As we drove the forty miles from Columbia to Lang Syne, Jackie had pointed out dozens of small, neat houses ranged along our route. They were, he said, the homes of folks who had once inhabited Lang Syne. In 1920, almost five hundred people lived at Lang Syne, all but four of them black. Today, the plantation is home to three small families, two black and one white. The cotton gin is covered with ivy; William Peterkin hauls his cotton ten miles to the county seat for ginning. The cabins that once lined the slave street have long since turned to dust; the last, Mary Weeks's, was blown down by Hurricane Hugo in 1989.

At Lang Syne you listen in vain to hear the beat of a drum calling people to a birth-night supper, the wail of a baby, the thunder of a sermon. Gone, too, are the crows of roosters, the chatter of guinea hens, the chopping of hoes, the creak of wagons, and the tinkle of trace chains on plodding mules. Yet the voices of the people live on, preserved in the amber of Julia Peterkin's fiction.

A Note on the Language

he characters in Julia Peterkin's fictional world speak Gullah, a creole language created by slaves in the seventeenth and eighteenth centuries in the southeastern United States. In the 1920s, it was commonly believed that Gullah was simply bad English, its speakers too thick-lipped to pronounce words correctly and too lazy to distinguish between male and female personal pronouns. As late as 1940, Mason Crum, a professor of history at Duke University, labeled Gullah "an abbreviated and mutilated English." [1] Since then, linguists have determined that Gullah combines an English vocabulary with grammatical forms from various West African languages. [2]

Far from being exclusive to black speakers in Peterkin's day, Gullah was often the first language of affluent whites raised by black servants. In rural communities along the South Carolina coast, where a diluted form of the language is still spoken, Gullah is stigmatized in middle-class circles as the dialect of poverty and ignorance, although black Americans searching for links to Africa have lately adopted historian Charles Joyner's view that the language is "a potent symbol of cultural unity."[3]

Early in her career, following the lead of other white writers, Peterkin attempted a more or less phonetic transcription of the dialect spoken at Lang Syne. But pure Gullah is a foreign tongue to most Americans. "We might do for Gullah all we can," lamented Charleston writer John Bennett in 1918, "but never what [Thomas Nelson] Page has done for Virginia, [Joel Chandler] Harris for Upper Georgia or [George Washington] Cable for New Orleans; for nobody can read Gullah in the great outside world."[4] Peterkin proved that it could be done, devising a literary version of the language that is intelligible to speakers of Standard English while respectful of Gullah's rhythms, expressions, and flavor.

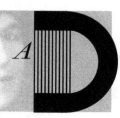

A **D***evil and a Good Woman, Too*

CHAPTER 1

Lang Syne

he rain showed no sign of stopping. Julia Mood stood at the window, searching the line of stretchers for a glimpse of her father's red hair. Her wedding gown, a cloud of chiffon, billowed on the bed behind her. Dr. Mood had been gone since mid-morning, called to the scene of a train derailment eight miles west of town. Rushing water had undermined a section of track, and the resultant cave-in had pitched an engine, a baggage car, and three coaches into a deep ravine. Five people were dead and dozens injured, all but one of them black.[1]

It was June 3, 1903, in Sumter, South Carolina, and Julia was about to wed William George Peterkin, the heir to Lang Syne plantation. Eight excited bridesmaids crowded the room. Laura, her beloved older sister, was not among them. She was living in the Latin Quarter of Paris, singing and posing for artists. Julia's mother had died when she was a toddler; she despised her stepmother. Most of her twenty-one years had been spent trying to get her father's attention, mainly by making him angry. Now she was finally doing something that Julius Mood approved of, and instead of playing the doting father he was off tending to the needs of strangers.

Born on Halloween with a caul over her head, Julia had been told by her black nurse, Maum Patsy, that she was gifted with the second sight, the ability to see spirits and predict the future. With a master's degree in comparative religions, she was hardly a superstitious woman.[2] But she had always heard that storms on a couple's wedding day foretold quarrels and infidelity, that every drop of rain that fell was a tear she would one day shed.[3]

As Julia peered through the streaming windowpane, a buzz ran through the house: the infirmary next door was full. Dr. Mood was bringing patients into his own home. The nine girls and all their finery were hustled into buggies. They would have to finish dressing somewhere else.

The roads ran like rivers. Water spilled over ditch banks; flooded creeks swept farm animals and fences downstream. By the next morning the flood would have swept away houses and cotton mills, drowned crops and people, and washed out bridges. But the Methodist church was filled with candlelight and greenery. The pews were packed with well-wishers. Julius Mood left his patients long enough to give his daughter away.[4] Julia, according to the newspaper account, wore a beatific smile.

Compulsive storyteller that she became, Julia never talked or wrote about her wedding day. Rain or no rain, she had reason to worry that her married life might be rocky. Before meeting William, she had been engaged to marry the illegitimate son of a textile baron, but she broke the engagement at her father's insistence.[5] Now, her family was relieved to be marrying her off. While living in her father's house after graduation from college, she had locked horns with her stepmother, quarreled with her father, brooded about the "bastard lover" she had been forced to give up, and blamed her family for everything that ailed her. Julius had strict notions about how his daughters should behave, and each time Julia hinted at mutiny, he lectured her about duty and reputation. Having lost control of Laura, he clamped down all the harder on Julia, the daughter who had been named after him and was most like him in looks and temperament.

When the teachers' registry in the state capital matched Julia with a position, she went off to teach in the hamlet of Fort Motte, in the midlands of South Carolina. Her workplace was a one-room schoolhouse where the children of planters, separated from their black playmates, learned to read, write, and "act white."[6] Slight, dark Willie Peterkin, sent by his older sister to pick up the new teacher, had met Julia at the train station, begrudging every minute it took to drive into town and fetch her. After delivering Miss Mood and her luggage to his sister's home, where she would board, he pulled Lizzie aside to ask, "Why on earth did you send me to meet that red-headed schoolteacher?"[7] Willie apparently suspected that Lizzie was playing matchmaker. If so, her efforts succeeded. Within a year, Willie Peterkin was engaged to marry Julia Alma Mood.

Willie managed the family plantation for his father, James Alexander Peterkin, who was famous for breeding a distinctive variety of upland cotton. James Peterkin had bought Lang Syne after the Civil War and moved there in 1877 from Marlboro County, in the northeastern part of the state.[8] It was said that "Captain" Peterkin was fleeing his enemies. During the war, he served as commander of a Marlboro County cavalry unit; one day, word arrived that General Wade Hampton needed his horses but not his men. Suspecting that his soldiers would not freely give up their mounts and accept a demotion from cavalry to infantry, Peterkin locked the men in an underground stockade while the horses were led away. They never forgave him, even though he had supplied most of the horses and equipment in the first place. After the war, they vandalized his property and threatened his family.[9] So he sold the place. His wife, Agenora, sold another plantation she had inherited, and they used the money to finance the move to Amelia Township, where the family could make a fresh start.[10] The Peterkins bought Lang Syne from the McCords, who had recovered it from the United States government after the war by taking the loyalty oath. Faced with the loss of their wealth and power, unwilling to endure the privations of daily life in Reconstruction South Carolina, the McCords sold Lang Syne, hoping to make a fresh start of their own — in Hawaii.[11]

The plantation comprised some fifteen hundred acres of high ground situated between swamps that feed the Congaree River and Buckhead Creek.[12] It was very large for a midlands plantation, and supported, in addition to its white owners, about five hundred black people who worked in the cotton fields. Like most plantations, Lang Syne fused a profitable commercial enterprise with a subsistence economy. Profits earned by the staple crop went to the owners, who were able to buy goods from the outside world while the laborers formed a self-sustaining work-force with highly skilled craftsmen who took care of everything from blacksmithing to butchering to barn building.

Julia was accustomed to depending on black domestics. In turn-of-the-century South Carolina, few white people who were not poor did without servants; cooks and maids were considered essential to middle-class existence. At Lang Syne the first language of the servants and field hands was Gullah. Julia had grown up hearing and even speaking some Gullah, but at Lang Syne the sense of being in a foreign country went beyond language. People still put their faith in roots and charms and feared spirits called "hags" and "plat-eyes." They had strange-sounding African names like Cudjoe and Anniker, or unusual English names like Earth and Champagne. Many lived in the same cabins their grandparents had occupied as slaves; they were issued rations once a week. Those who drew wages were expected to spend them at the Peterkins' store.

Most white people who had grown up in the South would have taken all this in stride. That was the way things were done on plantations. If living conditions for blacks were primitive, they believed, it was because black people were lazy and shiftless, not because white people kept them that way. Long before she married and moved to Lang Syne, Julia was accustomed to viewing her world though the flattering lens of white supremacy. Her father's mother's people, the Alstons, had been among the wealthiest planters in South Carolina and had owned hundreds of slaves. Whenever the subject of ancestors came up, as it constantly did in South Carolina, Julia could hold her head high. Her ties to the aristocratic slaveholding Alstons opened doors, and she adopted many of the old slaveholders' attitudes.

But there was another, stronger influence at work, one that would later surface in Julia's fiction. Julius Mood's father's clan, the Moods, insisted that blacks were human beings and that exploiting them was wrong. But slavery was ingrained in antebellum Charleston, and the Moods' idealism led to some strange compromises. In one of Julia's favorite tales, her grandfather Henry Mood was a small boy in Charleston, strolling with his father near a slave market off King Street. John Mood noticed a handsome black man on the auction block making the Masonic sign of distress. He sent young Henry running through the city to find two friends who could help him buy the slave.[13] Did they set him free or keep him as a servant? Julia never said, but we know that little Henry Mood grew up to own several slaves himself. A Methodist minister, he refused to raise his own hand against them but would hire someone else to whip them when they were troublesome.[14] John Mood's father-in-law, Alexander McFarlane, was said to have died on the West Coast of Africa while on a mission to return freed slaves. McFarlane was a sea captain, and Julia's father always suspected that his motives were not strictly humanitarian — that when his ships returned to America their holds may have been filled with fresh slaves, in defiance of the ban on the importation of Africans.[15] However, McFarlane was also a Methodist minister, one of the first in the city, and the early Methodist church was widely known, especially in Charleston, to be hostile to slavery.

The Moods were German Lutherans who had converted to Methodism in America. John Mood made exquisite silver tableware for the Charleston elite, but he was a poor manager and easily duped; his business was always on the brink of collapse.[16] When Henry, his eldest son, approached college age, Mood cast about for a job for the boy that would support him while he attended classes. Because he taught a Sunday school for blacks, John Mood was approached by the Brown Fellowship Society, a group of free mulattoes who wanted to establish a school for their children. Well-to-do, ambitious for their offspring, and literate themselves, these men could afford to rent a building and pay teachers. But the South Carolina legislature had recently passed laws forbidding blacks to assemble without white supervision, and they needed to hire a white principal.

John Mood accepted the position on behalf of his son. Henry could attend classes at the College of Charleston in the morning and teach and administer at the school in the afternoon. The position paid too well to refuse. The freemen put Henry through college, and when he graduated, his younger brother took over his post. A parade of Mood brothers, sisters, and cousins worked at the school while they attended college, and four of the five boys eventually became Methodist circuit riders. (The fifth became a physician.)[17] Over the years the Mood boys made enough extra money to buy their hapless father out of bankruptcy not once but twice. A new generation of black parents begged the family to continue teaching their children, at higher salaries and in improved facilities, but the Moods declined on the grounds that running the school would take them away from the work of spreading the gospel.[18]

At the start of the Civil War, the Mood family gathered in Columbia to pray. After asking God to guide them through the coming conflict, they decided that it would be sinful for them to fight.[19] Julia's maternal ancestors, the Archers, reached the same conclusion.[20] Neither family, however, felt that it would be wrong to provision the troops. The Moods stamped and burnished thousands of silver spurs and uniform buttons, just as they had manufactured slave badges. (The city of Charleston required slaves to carry metal identity passes when hired out by their masters.) The Archers expanded their harness-making enterprise to provide tack for the cavalry.[21] Both families negotiated contracts with the Confederate government and realized handsome profits.

When Julia and Willie arrived home from their honeymoon, the people of Lang Syne presented them with gifts of strawberries, peaches, eggs, and chickens. Some wished them joy, "a gal and a boy." Others hoped that "Miss" and the "Young Cap'n" would live together happily.[22] Since old Captain Peterkin and Willie's brother Preston occupied the sprawling farmhouse, Willie and his bride moved into a tiny cottage close by.[23]

Julia had looked forward to keeping house, but the servants objected when she tried to work; neither did they like being told what to do. Julia set tasks for the maids only to find that her instructions were ignored. She asked for toast; the cook served waffles.[24] Julia felt unwelcome in her own home. Then, almost at once, she discovered that she was pregnant. For the next nine months, her role in the plantation economy was clear.

Unlike his wife, Willie Peterkin did not question his purpose in life: he was destined to grow cotton and make money. He and his bachelor brother Preston owned almost every commercial enterprise in Fort Motte, including a bank, a drugstore, and a grocery. They operated a cotton gin and a cottonseed oil mill, cashing in on the expanding market for cotton by-products as well as the world demand for cotton fiber. Two of Willie's older brothers had gambled and drunk themselves into debt. Two others had died young. Preston suffered from Bright's disease, a crippling kidney disorder that would soon kill him. The girls, Lizzie and Mary Belle, had married and settled down on the plantation, but Lizzie's husband had died, leaving her with small children. Willie was the family hope, a nondrinker who shouldered the responsibilities of Lang Syne, assumed the mortgage, and supported his widowed sister and sisters-in-law even after they remarried. Willie had both James Alexander Peterkin's practicality and drive and his fascination with machinery and agricultural research. His acquisitiveness helped him provide for the large plantation community that depended on him for shelter and food. All he lacked was a son to carry on his name.[25]

Instead of sending for a midwife or a local doctor to deliver her baby, Julia traveled to Sumter so that her father could do the honors.[26] Dr. Mood had delivered hundreds of babies. When the time arrived, he quickly realized that Julia's child was presenting itself feet first and was wedged in her narrow pelvis. Hours passed; his daughter writhed and moaned, but no amount of pushing could dislodge the baby and end her ordeal. Julius administered an anesthetic and tried to rotate the baby so that he could ease it through the birth canal. Julia, now unconscious, stopped pushing. Horrified at the thought that his child and grandchild might die under his hands, Julius resorted to forceps. After thirty-one agonizing hours, William George Peterkin Junior was wrested into the world.[27]

Another delivery like this might kill Julia, Julius told Willie. She was still unconscious, and there was a simple surgical technique that could save her from future pain. As long as he was repairing her injuries, why not spare Julia a second operation? Julius was asking Willie's permission to remove Julia's ovaries, and Willie was not sure what to do. He understood that the operation would leave his wife unable to bear more children, but now that he had an heir, he could face that. He told Julius to go ahead.[28]

Bilateral oophorectomy—also called Battey's operation or female castration—was a fairly routine procedure. Since its introduction thirty years before, doctors had performed it on more than 150,000 American women.[29] The operation was widely touted as a panacea for melancholy, epilepsy, depression, and a host of other vaguely defined mental disorders, including nymphomania and neurosis. It was frequently used to stabilize (and sterilize) women in insane asylums. By 1904, however, the operation was falling into disrepute, even before the disquieting long-term consequences of oophorectomy were fully known.[30] Five years later, Battey's operation would be roundly condemned as a "mutilating" operation by reformers armed with new information about "the hormone theory."[31] But the tide of professional opinion turned too late for Julia.

For two years after the birth of her child, Julia refused to get out of bed.[32] The family treated her as an invalid long after her physical injuries had healed. Her postpartum depression was compounded by the psychological effects of premature menopause, but it was anger that paralyzed Julia. She hated her father for sterilizing her, she hated Willie for sanctioning him, and she hated baby William for tearing her apart. These men, she insisted some fifty years later, had "ruined" her.[33]

In 1904, Julia was unable to think these words, much less to say them out loud. Over the years she would find ways to punish her father, her husband, and her son, using her fiction as a form of revenge. Her fame would push them to the fringes of her life, chipping away at their claims to power. But in the months following Bill's birth and her own castration, Julia shut herself down.

In another time, another place, Julia might have pulled herself together to care for her child, but at Lang Syne she wasn't even needed for that. Her servants were more experienced than she at changing diapers, cooking meals, washing clothes, and scrubbing floors. There were no visitors to entertain, no fine rooms to decorate. No one needed her, or so she felt. She seemed, at age twenty-three, to have lived out her useful life. With nothing to do, she retreated into the prison of her infirmity.

Lavinia Berry had "come with the place" when the Peterkins bought it in 1877.[34] Born into slavery, she had cared for Willie when he was a baby; now she was nurse to both William and Julia. "Maum Vinner," as her people called her,[35] loved to talk about the good old days, before the war, when the Big House stood proud and white.[36] Sometime after Lang Syne changed hands, the Peterkin boys had done by accident what General Sherman had left undone a dozen years before—they, or possibly one of their guests, burned the mansion to the ground.[37] Vinner had long since given up any idea of civilizing the Peterkins and resigned herself to their ways. But she had high hopes for Julia. Long ago, she explained, before white men came, an old Indian woman had ruled the land. Since then, she said, "Some 'oman ever did dominize Lang Syne, an' eber will."[38] Julia had a job to do. She must learn to be Lang Syne's Miss.

Willie and his father were hard workers, but Vinner and the other old-timers claimed that things had changed for the worse since the Peterkins came to Lang Syne. They lacked the benevolent ways of "high-bredded folks."[39] In the old days, people "*had.*"[40] They had fine food, fine clothes, and fine homes. Everybody who lived at Lang Syne, even the lowliest servant, was downright pampered. The Peterkins provided food, clothing, and shelter. The hands expected something more, and they looked for it to come from Julia. As the plantation mistress, she must take it upon herself to settle arguments, help people who were in trouble with the law, provide medical care, and give everyone gifts of money, clothing, and furniture. In return, Vinner said, the people would treat her like a queen. Vinner warned Julia that many white women had come to Lang Syne, and those too weak or too fearful to "dominize" had either been crushed or taken away.[41]

Julia heeded Lavinia Berry. "Don' shut up tings too tight een you' heart," Vinner urged her. "Ef you hol' you Mad, e would kill eby Glad. An' Sorrow — E kin bus' you heart open." God had given Julia a mouth to talk about what bothered her. Such trials as hers came to every woman. "Boy-chillen brings mos' o' de misery dat's een dis worl'," Vinner declared. "Eby 'oman hab joy when e buth one. Eby gal hab joy when e love one. None ain' see how misery duh hide behime joy. Da misery gwine grow, grow big tell he choke de joy; tell de 'oman heart mos' bus' open, tell e open wide same like book." Julia should let go of her grudges and get on with life, Vinner said. "You breat' come an' go mighty sweet when e free. But you try fo' hol' em — e bitter!" [42]

The more Vinner talked, the more Julia wanted to learn. The mules, the chickens, the wild birds, and even the crops had "sense like people." Every creature on God's earth felt joy and pain. The footsteps of a pine beetle beneath the bark of a tree were as weighty as those of a weary man on a dusty road. Men and women were ruled by the laws of nature just as surely as the rooster in the barnyard or the water in a puddle.[43] Vinner related the doings of snakes and pigs, lamp shades and axes, in the same tones she used to talk about church deacons and jilted lovers.

Slowly Julia's depression lifted, and at last she got out of bed. Vinner counseled her to act like a lady — to get out into society. Julia already possessed most of the skills required to enter what passed for society in Calhoun County. Striving to become a "fine lady," she devoted herself to cards, teas, and meetings of the Daughters of the American Revolution. As her social orbit widened, she put pressure on Willie to make improvements at Lang Syne. When old Captain Peterkin and Preston both died, leaving the farmhouse empty, Julia and Willie moved into it. But Julia aspired to something grander, and she convinced Willie to hire an architect and build her a stately white house with pillars, a library, and a parlor. When it was finished, Vinner sorrowfully remarked that the whole thing could have fit into the ballroom of the old Big House.[44]

Cultivating a tiny garden helped her regain her strength, and watching things grow gave Julia something to look forward to. If she could not bear more babies, she could produce peas and lettuce, tomatoes and onions. Before long she was laying out new flower beds and transplanting bushes. Vinner's son Champagne protested that gardening was *his* job. When Julia deferred to his authority, Champagne taught her how to lime the soil with ashes and plant by the moon. Soon he was encouraging her to try her hand at poultry. She bought some ducks, turkeys, and guinea hens. Maum Anaky, Maum Martha, and Maum Vinner taught her the secrets of wine-making, pickling, and preserving. Other hands taught her to ride and fish and shoot straight, to bake and sew and season sausage.[45]

As she infiltrated the kitchen, the barnyard, and the garden at Lang Syne, Julia eavesdropped on the people gossiping about their lives in the Quarters, the old slave cabins clustered along a narrow street. She heard about women seducing each other's men, about people settling quarrels with razors and knives. The many "outside" children testified to the shifting sexual relationships that bound and divided the community by turns. Most of the women shared Lavinia Berry's opinion that "a man is a some-time ting."[46] Vinner's own husband had outside children, and Julia was astonished to hear her refer to the other woman's girl as "my best daughter."[47] Bastard children — those who had never seen their father's faces — were prized in the Quarters because people believed they could cure certain ailments and bring good luck.[48]

Mary Weeks, Vinner's niece, had a houseful of luck. Her husband, James "Bully" Bryant — Maum Anaky's son — had long since left the plantation. "My chillen daddy," said Mary, "ain' nobody een particular." Two of her offspring, Bessie and Essie, were "bright-skinned" — half white. And far from being nobody in particular, their daddies were Peterkins, Willie's brothers John and Jimmy. Bessie, four years younger than Julia, lived in a little house in Lizzie and Robert Adams's backyard and earned her keep as their maid. Lizzie was solicitous toward Mary's children, who were, after all, her nieces. Mary herself had a white grandfather, Jabez Weeks, who had been an overseer on Lang Syne before the Civil War.[49]

The deed to Lang Syne was originally in old Agenora Peterkin's name, supposedly because her husband had filed for bankruptcy after the Civil War. Agenora was angry about Bessie and Essie and afraid that her older sons might gamble the plantation away. Before she died in 1901, she willed everything to her youngest sons, Willie and Preston, charging them to support the rest of the family.[50]

Julia had boarded with the Adamses before her marriage, so Bessie must have lived under her very nose from the moment she arrived in Fort Motte. Perhaps by talking to Mary herself, Julia eventually discovered that the Peterkin boys had conceived Bessie and Essie in their own bedrooms, when Mary brought them hot water for shaving. Old Miss had banished Mary to the fields after the birth of the second mulatto child, but "Si May-e" had stayed on the place, outlived Agenora, and faced down everybody, black and white, who tried to shame her.[51] Julia took a liking to Mary and gave her a job in the garden. Mary had a charm, she told Julia, that could catch and hold any man for as long as she wanted him — but she seldom wanted the same one for long. "No man is wuth a drop of water that dreans from a woman's eye," she liked to declare.[52]

In the story "Finding Peace," written some twenty years after the two women met, Julia recorded a conversation between herself and Mary Weeks.[53] The sketch opens with Mary telling Julia that three girls have come to the back door to see her. They have all "found peace" and been cleared for baptism the next Sunday, and they have come to ask her to "he'p 'em out a little wid dey clo'es." Carry, Janie, and Cooch have each dreamed of carrying a heavy load, Mary reports. Something or someone white took the burden away, and each received a piece of gold jewelry. But another girl, Bina, has recounted an unconventional dream. "Now Bina, she say she been d' carry a scamlin. Fo' Gawd's sake, wha' you t'ink is a scamlin?" asks Mary. "Lessen she mean one dem boa'd lak de cyarpenter buil' house wid, enty?"

Mary digresses. She admits that she has been turned out of the church several times by "dem deacons" for bearing children out of wedlock. She has just seen a movie of Hell that scared her into praying — almost. She plans to seek peace before cold weather sets in, because sinners have to sit in the back of the church, far away from the fire. Sometimes she wonders if the deacons "be's so straight deyse'f," but she has no proof that they are sinners — "I ain' nebber fool roun wid none of em myse'f. I ain' nebber care bout no man bein' so Christian-like. Dey don' seem natch-el, somehow, lessen dey be's kinder wil' like, enty?"

Then she returns to the day's gossip: "But all de people is a talkin' 'bout dat scan'lous Bina. She say de wi'te man wha' tek de scamlin offer she, gi' her all two han' full o' gol'. Now all dem udder one been say eeder a ring, or a necklace, or a breas' pin, or somet'ing o' nudder lak dat, but Bina, she try fo' out-do all, an say he been gi' she all two han' full o' gol'. Bina oughta be shame. She ever did been a brazen t'ing."

The point of Mary's story, entertaining as it is, is that Julia should give her girls "a stockin' or a petticoat, or eeder clot' to mek [a] baptizin' robe." The point of Julia's story is that Mary is every bit as brazen as

Bina. Mary openly manipulates Julia, while Julia, less obviously, uses Mary for her own purposes — as the subject of a tale. Instead of the voices of mistress and servant, we hear the intimate tones of two friends happily dissecting the outrageous behavior of a third party. Mary expects Julia to share her puzzlement over what a "scamlin" might be, and to agree that men don't seem quite normal unless they're a little wild. Julia obliges.

Julia envied her black friends for their apparent freedom from inhibitions. "Love, Birth, Death, Joy, Sorrow, all walk stark in the open [in the Quarters at Lang Syne] with an arrant frankness," she would later write.[54] While Julia fantasized about attracting the admiration of her son's live-in tutor, a shy young man named Robin Carter, Bina lured Ellis Sanders, the plantation foreman, into running away with her, leaving his wife, Nannie, alone for "three long years."[55] Soon after Ellis returned to the fold, Nannie went off on an excursion with the new preacher and came home in disgrace, nursing a mysterious bullet wound in her behind.[56]

In Julia's circle, white people were almost as secretive about anger and discord as they were about sex. She and Willie rarely argued, and when they did they kept their voices down. When Hester Cheseboro quarreled with her husband, Jake, she hurled a month's rations out her cabin window and smashed iron pots with an ax.[57]

"Chances are I never would have written at all if when I married I had gone to live where there were plenty of people to talk to," Julia later reflected.[58] Of course, she meant *white* people. Willie was not a talkative man. Gentle, taciturn, and something of a workaholic, he saw no point in debating questions of race, sex, or human behavior with his wife or anyone else. No doubt Willie had opinions, but no one alive today seems to have any idea what they were. In public, he and Julia were unfailingly polite and respectful toward each other. Yet some relatives insist that Julia never loved Willie, and that sex played little part in their relationship.[59]

Like most long marriages, the union between Julia and Willie Peterkin was a tangle of private compromises and unresolved conflicts. No one can say exactly what these were, but everyone agrees about one thing — Willie was an exemplary provider. He farmed efficiently, kept up with the latest agricultural research, and invested his profits shrewdly. And cotton prices rose and rose again. Julia admired Willie's industry, valued his protection. She considered him a perfect father for little William, now called Bill. Still, she seized every opportunity to get away from the man who maintained her in style.

By 1909, Julia's widowed sister Laura was living in New York City, working as a Reader in the Christian Science Church.[60] Julia visited Laura at least once a year, reveling in the opportunity to shop, eat exotic food, attend plays, listen to concerts, and take in museums.[61] But soaking up culture was not her only enjoyment. On the long train trip north, she sometimes flirted with strangers. One man, led by her suggestive remarks to believe that he would be welcome, crept into her Pullman berth wearing nothing but his "BVD's." Julia ejected him. Thinking about what might have been, she tossed and turned all night. The next morning, as the man was about to get off the train, Julia threw her arms around his neck and kissed him.[62] Another man with whom she struck up a conversation pursued her from the train to her hotel room, begging her to spend the night with him. To her sister's horror, Julia agreed to go for a walk with this tall, dark stranger. She kissed him on the street, and then — according to her own account — sent him away.[63] To Julia, the goal of seduction was to make conquests, not to make love.

Unsure of her father's love and a permanent guest in her grandfather's household, Julia grew up striving to make men desire her. The epitome of the red-headed stepchild, hovering at the fringes of the family circle, she never could conquer the drive to seduce. The family she wanted into was fractured by the death of her mother, Alma Mood. Raised by her paternal grandparents, Julia shuttled from town to town as the minister Henry Mood was transferred by the Methodist Conference. Julius Mood stayed in Sumter with his second wife, Janie, Julia's two older sisters, and their half-brother Ashleigh. Julia couldn't stand to be in the same room with her stepmother, and chances are that if Julius had invited her to live with him, she would have refused.[64] It had not been her father's idea to turn her over to his parents: the dying Alma had made him promise to let the elder Moods raise her baby. Yet even in adulthood Julia was tortured by the conviction that she had been "given away" because her father did not love her.[65]

Julia idolized her grandfather, Henry Mood, and spent her childhood trying to be like him. By the time she was four, Henry had taught her to read by using flash cards cut from newspaper headlines; a bit later, he cured her of falling down stairs by spanking her whenever she stumbled.[66] Henry Mood insisted that all his grandchildren learn to speak clearly, practice good manners, and exercise self-discipline. He himself had led a rough-and-tumble childhood, his parents preoccupied by the demands of their silversmithing business and their passion to save souls. When Henry was a little boy, he is supposed to have sneaked into his parents' attic and unsheathed a saber that had belonged to some military ancestor. Henry knew that he was forbidden to play with the sword, but left unsupervised, he couldn't resist the temptation to flourish it. Somehow he fell on the point, running the blade through his side. Henry nursed his terrible wound in secret, convinced that it was justice for having disobeyed his parents.[67]

In old age, Henry dictated his memoirs to Julia, paying her by the page to transcribe them.[68] He recalled that in his father's day, it was not uncommon for thugs to disrupt Methodist services by throwing turkey buzzards into the sanctuary, where they would "fly at the lighted lamps, breaking them and scattering the oil and debris on the heads of the audience." In those days, he explained, Methodists were always under attack in Charleston because of their outspoken opposition to slavery.

Henry admired a fellow clergyman who, having been warned to watch his tongue since the congregation he would be preaching to was "highly refined and cultivated," pointed to a row of mulattoes sitting in the gallery and thundered, "Where did these people come from? What country claims them? Their mothers are here among you, but where are their fathers? You are a highly-cultivated people and very refined! The Lord have mercy on your souls." His own mother and father, Henry said, had been threatened with a coat of tar and feathers for teaching the black Sunday school, and he himself had been vilified as a "negro preacher." According to Henry, when the Methodist church eventually bowed to pressure and sought to distance itself from the black race, the Mood family did not.[69]

Julius Mood had not lived up to his father's high-minded example. As a college student, Julius's idea of fun was to pipe foul-smelling gas into a black church during services, laughing uproariously as the congregation scrambled for the doors.[70] In his youth, he was notorious for playing practical jokes, for womanizing, and for "blaspheming." Julia remembered her father beating a weary horse almost to death when it balked at pulling his carriage; later in life he was apt to spit on his car when it broke down.[71]

Predictably enough, Julius and his family often differed over the correct way to bring up Julia and her siblings. When Julius gave his children a quarter to go and see the circus, his sister offered a second quarter to each child who would resist temptation and stay home. Julia's sister Marian, normally the most compliant of the lot, once passed up the extra quarter and went to the circus. Her grandfather wrote her a yard-long letter on a roll of newsprint, explaining exactly why it was wicked to go to the circus.[72]

To Henry's distress, Julia grew more like her father with every passing day. She had Julius's hot temper and willful nature; she was more interested in her father's hair-raising, off-color anecdotes than in her grandfather's tales from the Bible and classical mythology. By age eight, Julia had begun to doubt the existence of God. Brought up to believe that she would be reunited with her loved ones in Heaven, the little girl sometimes dreamed of arriving at the pearly gates, glimpsing her mother, and kneeling at the throne of God, only to be turned away with the damning words, "You doubted."[73] Even as a small child, she felt torn between her grandfather's faith and her father's skepticism.

Henry Mood died of congestive heart failure on May 2, 1897, when Julia was sixteen years old. "You don't love your father," he accused Julia from his deathbed. Julius, he said, tried hard to be a good father, and Julia should look for the good in him. Julia promised to try.[74] She did learn to love her father, but she continued to hate him, too; the gentle affection Henry Mood had in mind was foreign to Julia's makeup. For as Carl Sandburg would later observe, her "range of love and hate [was] something vast."[75]

Reviews and feature stories would later paint a convincing picture of Julia Peterkin as a courageous white woman living alone amid a sea of black faces. In truth, she was surrounded by white people, most of whom bored and irritated her. There was always a crowd of relatives for Sunday supper, always at least one person staying in the spare room at Lang Syne. All of Willie's surviving sisters and brothers lived nearby at one time or another, and when Julia's sister Marian and her husband, Plumer Burgess, fell on hard times, Willie built a house for them on the plantation and hired Burgess to run his drugstore and keep the books for the general store. Friends frequently dropped by to play cards or gossip.[76] The men talked about politics and cotton, the women about clothes and club meetings. At some point, Julia simply stopped hearing them, the better to listen to Mary Weeks and Lavinia Berry.

After 1909, Julia lived within shouting distance of many white neighbors — one of them Julius Mood — for at least three months out of every year. Planters and their families traditionally fled to the mountains or the seashore during the hot summer months, and as soon as he was able, Willie bought a summer cottage in a rustic seaside resort called Sunnyside, on Murrells Inlet, where Julia and Bill could ride out the malaria season.

Willie seldom stayed there long, preferring the red clay of the midlands to the gray sand of the seacoast,[77] but Julius Mood loved the swimming, boating, hunting, fishing, drinking, and talking that went on at the inlet. He bought a house a few doors down from Julia and Willie's, and on lazy summer afternoons he would sprawl on his wide front porch, drink in hand, swapping stories with his friends. He liked to tell about the time he was met at the train station by a poor old woman who begged him to hurry. A young girl, she said, was having a baby. Something in the woman's manner made Julius rush to her cabin in spite of bad roads and flooded streams. When he arrived, he found that the girl had given birth prematurely. Shock and grief had sent her into labor, she said. Her mother had died several hours earlier. Julius asked to see the body, and there lay the corpse of the old woman who had waylaid him at the station. He had been summoned by her ghost.[78] Julius told other tales — about the time he caught a bootlegger and then let him go, about seeing Mr. Bigham murder his wife a few hundred yards away from where they sat, about some tobacco he raised and tried to smoke, not realizing that it had to be cured first — and Julia and Bill often formed part of his rapt audience.[79]

Julia's summer house was a tiny, ramshackle cottage built around the remains of a kitchen that had washed up on the spot during the hurricane of 1893. With no glass in its windows and no indoor plumbing, the cottage Julia dubbed "Pretend" resembled the cabins in the Quarters at Lang Syne. The people who summered at Murrells Inlet liked to say they lived by the tides, retreating from their stressful lives to a simpler, more primitive world. They did not retreat without servants, however. Like her neighbors, Julia always hired a black "creekboy" to harvest fish, shrimp, and crabs, as well as a cook to prepare them.[80]

Before the Civil War, Murrells Inlet and Waccamaw Neck — a long, narrow slice of land sandwiched between the Waccamaw River and the Atlantic Ocean — were linked to the rest of the world by rice and water. Huge fortunes had been made by planters who used slave labor to cultivate rice in the fertile lowlands along the river. Ships took the rice away and brought back fine furniture, silks, horses, tea, and medicines. After the war, the planter aristocrats dispersed, leaving behind overgrown rice fields, broken dikes, and opulent antebellum mansions. Some sold their estates to wealthy Northerners, who showed up once or twice a year to shoot ducks and deer. The rest of the time, the former slaves and their descendants had the plantations all to themselves. Many owned small farms and homesteads on marginal lands in the pinewoods. When Julia began summering on Waccamaw Neck, its days of international commerce were long past and the area had returned to nature. The few sandy roads leading into Murrells Inlet were almost impassable; to get there, the Peterkins took a train to Georgetown, spent the night in a hotel, boarded a steamboat the next morning for the trip up the Waccamaw River, and rode the last few miles to their summer house in an oxcart. Mail and other supplies came in once a week, by boat.[81]

Julia was fascinated to discover remote settlements of black people who no longer seemed bound by the ritual relationships of paternalism.[82] Still, she could see that life along the neck was far from idyllic for blacks. Lacking year-round jobs, many were even poorer than the hands at Lang Syne. Blacks competed for seasonal work with poor whites, and racial violence was commonplace. Yet it was not only the poor whites who made trouble.

Julia once caught a group of drunks torturing Wallace Heyward, a crippled black teenager who worked for her. Telling him that they had a machine that could straighten his crooked spine, the men had forced Wallace to take hold of two wires attached to a live battery. When Julia happened by, Wallace was having convulsions. Her neighbors, all prominent men, lounged nearby, laughing at the boy's gullibility. Julia cursed them and set their victim free. She and her father took Wallace to see a specialist, only to be told that nothing could be done to correct his deformity.[83]

Back at Lang Syne that fall, Lucy Leacey, the cook, left to start a restaurant in Charleston. Julia wrote to Wallace's sister Noonie, who cooked for her at Murrells Inlet, asking her to take over Lucy's duties. Wallace wrote back that Noonie had gone up North, but he would be glad to help her out. The crippled man and his letter arrived simultaneously. Julia took him in, even though she had never known him to cook anything. Determined to make good, Wallace memorized the directions for all of Julia's favorite dishes. Though he couldn't operate a can opener or read a recipe, he knew how to tell a tale, and Wallace Heyward soon joined Lavinia Berry and Mary Weeks as one of Julia's favorite people.[84]

Trying to live up to Vinner's expectations, Julia went on doing her duty as a plantation mistress. She bound wounds, gave hungry families a little extra to tide them over to the next paycheck, and encouraged their children to attend the "free school," a tiny cabin where seventy pupils recited lessons for a single teacher while seventy more were turned outside for recess.[85] Was this what it meant to "dominize" Lang Syne—doling out candy under the plantation Christmas tree, procuring a comfortable crutch for a little boy who had lost his leg, granting Wallace Heyward a job in her kitchen?[86] These acts of charity seemed to satisfy the servants, and they gave Julia a lofty sense of purpose. Yet as the years went by, she began to sense the irony of her position.

In some ways, treating the sick was the most gratifying of her duties. After almost four decades of practicing medicine in Sumter, Julius Mood was revered as a god by his patients, and Julia tried to imitate her father; whenever someone on the place was sick, she hastened to the sickbed with her bag of remedies. Her patients were usually grateful, the more so since few of them could afford to see a real doctor. But there were exceptions to the rule. Some people grew resentful when her pills and ointments failed to work. Faced with a host of contagious diseases including smallpox, influenza, tuberculosis, and syphilis, in addition to the chronic ailments caused by hard labor, malnutrition, and crowded conditions, Julia could seldom provide a cure. And sometimes it seemed that the more she tried to do for people, the more they blamed her for their misfortunes.

One day Julia walked over to check on Frank Hart, who was married to Vinner's daughter Charity. Hart's feet had abruptly stopped working, refusing to bear his weight. Charity had brewed tea of beargrass and violet leaves, prepared poultices, and bought charms. Nothing helped. Frank's feet had turned to stone. No one had ever seen a complaint like his before; people said that he must have been conjured. He couldn't stand, couldn't work, couldn't go out visiting. When Julia arrived, he sat hunched by his fireplace; while she talked about teaching him to read, he reached out his foot and held it against a live coal on the hearth. The smell of cooking meat filled the air, but Hart did not flinch. His foot had lost all feeling.

At a loss for what to do, Julia offered to bathe Hart's feet. Charity heated the water and watched while Julia added a drop of carbolic acid as a disinfectant, hoping the man would take courage from the idea that he was being treated. When she stood up to say goodbye, she glanced into the tub and saw five toes bobbing in the water.

How could a man's toes come loose from their moorings? Charity and Frank blamed Julia's medicine. Julia called her father to the plantation, as much to exonerate herself as to treat Hart. Could a man's toes really come off without warning, without pain? Dr. Mood assured everyone that they could. He diagnosed Frank Hart's trouble as senile gangrene — the toes had rotted away because of poor circulation. The disinfectant had nothing to do with it. And unless Hart's legs were treated immediately, the gangrene would kill him. "Treated" meant "amputated." Accompanied by his son, young Frank, Hart was carried to the train station on a stretcher. At the Mood Infirmary in Sumter, Julius Mood cut off his legs.[87]

As long as he stayed in the hospital, Hart's spirits were high. Nurses rushed to his bedside when he rang a bell, bringing hot food and clean linens. The staff catered to his whims. But after he went home to Lang Syne, he fell into a depression. Without legs a man might as well be dead. Children laughed in his face. His wife slipped out at night to visit other men. Hart wanted to die. Dr. Mood offered to fit him up with a pair of mechanical legs, but his family refused further treatment for him. Frank Hart did ask for one thing. "Bury me in a man-sized box," he said. "I kept money for it, hid it from Charity in the Bible. You'll find it where he said about the mansions. . . . I been six foot fo'." [88]

Julius Mood had mutilated Frank Hart to save his life. The episode would torment Julia Peterkin for the rest of her days, for it seemed a cruel repetition of what had been done to her after Bill's birth; but this time she was the perpetrator, not the victim. Perhaps she should have let nature take its course, yet that, too, would have seemed wrong. Whether she wanted to or not, Julia exercised power over Frank Hart. In the end she fulfilled his last wish by having the legless man buried in a full-sized coffin.

Ten years later, Julia would cast Hart as April Locust, the hero of her first novel, *Black April.* In the interval she would tell, write, and revise his story dozens of times until she had converted the helpless victim into a tyrant. The real Frank Hart "never doubted up to the day he died that the medicine in the water [robbed him of his toes]," she later confessed. "He almost made me believe it." [89] Searching Frank Hart's death for meaning, testing its dramatic possibilities, Julia would finally portray him not as one of her wards, but as a powerful leader feared and admired by his fellows. Her April is a man who can halt a brawl, banish an enemy, or seduce a woman with a look, yet in the end he is forced to "bend his neck under" the "galling, hellish yoke" of his own mortality.[90] As a plantation mistress, Julia wanted to believe that the force that oppressed people like Frank Hart was an impersonal one. As the descendant of men and women who had risked tar and feathers to educate slaves, she suspected otherwise. She had profited by the plantation system and so had consented to deprive Frank Hart of more than just his toes.

CHAPTER 2

Cheating the Stillness

y 1914, Lang Syne was flourishing under the hand of a strong woman, just as Lavinia Berry had prophesied. During most of Bill's childhood, cotton prices were high, the crops were good, and the plantation was a crowded, bustling, cheerful place. Yet trouble was never far away. Some money disappeared from the drugstore till in 1914, and Willie accused Plumer Burgess, Julia's sister Marian's husband, of taking it. Burgess blamed James Crouch, Willie's sister's husband, a handsome Yale-educated lawyer who shared responsibility for the book-keeping. Willie took Crouch's side. Outraged, Burgess packed up his wife and children and moved them to Summerton. Marian stopped speaking to Julia, a painful breach that would last for many years. Rather than hire another druggist, Willie shut down the drugstore.[1]

The bank of Fort Motte, another of Willie's businesses, suddenly failed when the cotton bales in which it had invested were struck by lightning.[2] The killer influenza epidemic of 1918 swept through Lang Syne. Then came a devastating bout of hog cholera that left the red hillsides littered with dead pigs.[3]

In the world outside Lang Syne, blacks were pushing for more rights, and whites were pushing them back. Woodrow Wilson, elected president in 1912, set about resegregating the government and removing blacks from federal offices. When Wilson's close friend D. W. Griffith produced his twelve-reel cinematic tribute to the Ku Klux Klan, *Birth of a Nation* (based on Thomas Dixon's novel *The Clansman*), Wilson and his entire cabinet, the Supreme Court, and the Congress attended private — but widely publicized — screenings. The film was first shown in Columbia, South Carolina, in October 1915, its arrival heralded by huge ads. Audiences often grew hysterical, throwing eggs at the screen as they watched a filthy black man try to rape an angelic white girl, played by Mae Marsh. Many people wept with relief at the end of the film, when the attacker was lynched. As one historian observed, white South Carolinians greeted *The Birth of a Nation* as "Christmas morning, circus day, and victory over the home team . . . all rolled into one."[4] Unreconstructed Southerners regarded the film as a belated recognition of the horrors they had endured since 1861, as well as a rousing vindication of the violent methods they had used to regain control.

Across the South, segregation was intensifying. Restrooms, public transportation, theaters, restaurants, and waiting rooms were officially designated for "white" and "colored." In the summer of 1919, bloody race riots erupted, first in Charleston and then in St. Louis, Memphis, Chicago, Tulsa, and other cities, as blacks who had served in the armed forces in Europe during the Great War demanded better treatment at home. In New York City's Harlem, Marcus Garvey preached that great civilizations had been formed by the colored races when white men were little more than barbarians and savages.[5]

The number of lynchings in the South skyrocketed. Rumors of a black uprising in Columbia sent whites scurrying to arm themselves. Though both the *Charleston News and Courier* and the *Columbia State* decried lynching and mob violence, their editorializing carried far less weight than the pronouncements of local dignitaries like former governor Coleman Blease, who praised lynching as "necessary and good" and boasted of having planted a black man's severed finger in his garden.[6]

Liberal white Southerners were sensitive to charges that the South was hostile to the black man. Josiah Morse, a professor at the University of South Carolina, optimistically summed up the "Outlook for the Negro" in 1920 by assuring his readers that "the heart of the South is warm and big, as human hearts go." The white South was still determined to "remain distinct" in "all things racial and social," he said, but Southerners were increasingly inclined to "give the Negro equal public facilities and service for equal pay." Morse proudly pointed out that "when the state legislature of South Carolina appropriated $100,000 for a memorial to the white soldiers, it appropriated an equal amount for a memorial for the negro soldiers." This generosity showed, he said, that "in all things material the ideal of the white South is to be at least mathematically honest."[7] The reality was that the white South was anything *but* "mathematically honest" in its dealings with blacks, who had to make do with grossly substandard housing, schools, and transportation.

If blacks were being pushed out of the South by Jim Crow and racial violence, for a decade or more they had also been feeling the pull of opportunity. Lured by the promise of higher wages and better treatment, thousands of people left the fields and headed north to seek work in the cities. At first, this mass migration seemed a blessing to large landowners like the Peterkins. The advent of gasoline motors, electricity, commercial canned goods, and various other labor-saving devices had sharply reduced the need for manual laborers; further, the exodus promised to shrink the black population so that whites would no longer feel so outnumbered. Yet, as the trend continued, and as some of the hands who stayed behind began to defy white authority, the planters began to wonder who was going to hoe their cotton.

The arrival of the boll weevil heightened the tensions. For twenty years, weevils had been working their way north from Mexico, laying waste to cotton crops in their path. The pests hollowed out the cotton buds, or "squares," preventing the plant from producing bolls. Weevils were first detected near Lang Syne in 1917. The infestation was light, and the cotton crop was relatively unaffected. But everybody knew what was coming — farmers had already seen it happen in Louisiana, Mississippi, Alabama, and Georgia. Agents from the Department of Agriculture advised local farmers to burn or plow under the dead stalks at the end of the season, to diversify into livestock and other crops, and to plant short staple cotton varieties that would mature rapidly and outrun the weevil. Willie Peterkin followed this prescription to the letter; but like many of his neighbors, he also looked for a chemical miracle. Hoping to salvage his crop, Willie laid in a good supply of calcium arsenate, a high-powered pesticide, and purchased equipment for spreading it. His farmhands refused to handle the green dust; it was dangerous and wrong, they said, to poison the land. Julia overheard people murmuring that someone was liable to conjure or even kill "Cap'n" Peterkin to halt his meddling.

Willie induced some of the laborers to spread the arsenic anyway. Day after day, men and mules trudged down the long furrows in a haze of green dust.[8] Years later, Julia would describe the experience in the words of a field hand:

> At night. . . , when de cotton is wet wid dew, a pizen dust'll stick to you' feets. When I look out o' my door at night and see dat pizen dust a-floatin' over de cotton fields in dem big white cl[o]uds, an' dat machine a'singin' like a locust, a-creepin' up and down de rows, th'owin' out pizen I git too scared to look. No wonder de mens hates to take part in it. Dem pizened blossoms is done killed all de bees on de place, an' a lot o' de turkeys and de guineas died from eatin' de pizened evils.[9]

Birds, wild animals, and insects died by hundreds and thousands, leaving an eerie silence over the once-teeming fields and forests. The weevils adapted and multiplied.

Willie Peterkin's fields produced more than a thousand bales of cotton in 1920; in 1921, he would harvest only sixteen.[10] In early 1920, with the market still inflated by wartime demands, the price of cotton was 40 cents a pound; six months later it had plunged to 13.5 cents.[11] Lang Syne was heavily mortgaged. Willie played the cotton futures market and lost, then continued to invest money while the figures from "Liverfool," as Vinner called it, plummeted. As Julia remembered it, "he borrowed and borrowed and held on, and the market went down and down. He could not sleep. . . . He ate little." He considered cashing in his life insurance.[12]

While Willie Peterkin hurtled toward bankruptcy, Julius Mood continued to prosper. In 1920 he purchased a partnership in a six-thousand-acre tract near his vacation home in Murrells Inlet, an estate once owned by his aristocratic ancestors, the Alstons. Julius Mood and his friends bought Brookgreen, The Oaks, and Laurel Hill (known collectively as Brookgreen) as a hunting preserve, although Julius fondly hoped to reclaim some of the acreage for rice, the crop that had built the Alstons' antebellum empire.[13] To Julia, frantic about the fate of Lang Syne, Brookgreen represented a plantation that had defeated its white masters. The house she and her father occupied while duck hunting was fully furnished, its walls adorned with the glassy-eyed heads of deer and boar. Books, magazines, and personal letters lay open on the tables, as though the former owners had gone out for a walk and would be coming back soon. Pondering her own troubles, Julia paced the neglected gardens, once so carefully manicured, now tangled and run wild.

The most famous mistress of the Brookgreen plantations was Theodosia Burr Alston, daughter of Aaron Burr. Complimented as "the best educated woman of her time and country," Theodosia had a reputation for wit and vivacity. She disappeared at sea in 1812, when she was only twenty-nine years old, and her body was never recovered. Stories were told that her ship was wrecked and all hands lost, that pirates had forced her to walk the plank, that she swam to shore and lived out her life on the Outer Banks of North Carolina.

Before she disappeared, Theodosia and her domineering father wrote hundreds of letters to each other on subjects ranging from politics to plantation management. Though these letters had been published in several editions, most of what Julia knew about Theodosia came from reading the works of later writers nostalgic for the old order. To them, Theodosia was a "fair young queen" ruling over "an empire in the South." She was also a selfless, voiceless, and sexless being. "Submission and obedience are the lessons of her life, and peace and happiness are her reward," wrote J. A. Groves in 1901. "The tongue of the licentious is dumb in her presence, the awe of her virtue keepeth him silent. When scandal is busy, and the fame of her neighbor is tossed from tongue to tongue, charity and good nature open not her mouth." [14] Julia loved the idea of being a fair young queen. But if being a plantation mistress meant modeling herself on the saintly Theodosia, she thought she might be better off as something else.

Julia's most famous predecessor at Lang Syne, Louisa McCord, was anything but a silent, selfless woman. The daughter of statesman Langdon Cheves, she inherited Lang Syne from her aunt in 1830. McCord believed that a woman ought to write, for only by writing could she "make mankind her heir." [15] In the course of her lifetime she published two books, a collection of lyric poems, and a tragedy called *Caius Gracchus;* she translated Bastiat's "Sophisms of the Protective Policy" and contributed articles to the *Southern Quarterly Review, DeBow's Review,* and the *Southern Literary Messenger.*[16] Louisa McCord is remembered today less for her own writing than as a character in the wartime diary of another plantation mistress, Mary Boykin Chesnut.[17]

McCord sometimes described herself as "a woman with over two hundred children," and visitors to Lang Syne praised her for taking such good care of her slaves.[18] She established a day nursery to care for the infants of slave women and provided medical care to all her hands. Most of Louisa McCord's articles on "social and economic issues" are impassioned defenses of slavery, although she complained privately that the plantation system was an emotional and financial drain. "I would prefer to have $25,000 in good bank stock rather than $100,000 in negroes and plantations," she once confided to a guest.[19]

After the war, Louisa McCord was surprised and hurt when her former slaves cut up her damask tablecloths and lace curtains to make underwear. She was horrified when they mounted "an attack on the potato hills," shouting that they had raised the potatoes and that "Mr. Smythe [her son-in-law] didn't hab nuttin to do wid 'em anyhow."[20] The "children" had turned against her.

By the time Julia came to Lang Syne, the planters had regained a good deal of their power and prosperity. Men like Willie Peterkin were again able to demand that their hands put in a year's worth of work in return for food, clothing, and shelter. Now, however, because of forces outside their control, that power was eroding once more. Facing huge financial losses, the planters resented their many dependents, a number of whom were unable or unwilling to work. The hands' refusal to poison boll weevils sent much the same message as the ex-slaves' attack on the potato hills. The planters held power only as long as the political system worked in their favor, the plantation made a profit, and the labor force saw no alternative to obedience. In short, a plantation mistress was neither a goddess nor a queen.

Contemplating the overgrown graveyards at Brookgreen and Lang Syne, Julia considered the generations of white women who lay underground there. With half her life already behind her, she swore an oath that she would somehow learn to live before she died.[21] What were the options for a forty-year-old woman who had spent the last twenty years teaching herself how to be an anachronism? Julia had no idea. She simply resolved not to be numbered among the many plantation mistresses who had been fooled by wealth and power into thinking that "fine damask curtains an' tester beds could hinder death from layin his hand on dey hearts." [22]

Bill Peterkin grew up big-boned and fair, and with a striking resemblance to Julius Mood. He had the Mood temperament, too; even as a little boy he was talkative, gregarious, and charming. When Bill was entering his teens, Julia acquired another child by a gradual and informal process of adoption. Willie's sister Mary Belle was widowed in 1917. One day shortly afterward her daughter Belle, a plain, meek little girl, rode up on her horse and announced that she had come to stay with Julia and Willie. When Mary Belle remarried and moved to Spartanburg with her seven other children, Belle stayed put. She flattered her Aunt Julia, took her part in arguments, and agreed with everything she said. Belle made herself indispensable by adoring both Julia and Bill, whom she always addressed as "Darling." Belle was not adored in return, but she did manage to create a permanent place for herself in the Peterkin household. [23]

The few years when Bill, Belle, and other nieces and nephews filled her house with laughter may have been among the happiest in Julia's long life. But children grow up, and in Julia's day the sons and daughters of well-to-do planters were usually packed off to boarding school at about age twelve. Bill and Belle were no exception. Once again, Julia faced an empty house and a hollow life.

One fateful day in 1920, her friend Blanche Kaminer, who lived on a plantation nearby, happened to mention that she had been taking piano lessons at Chicora College in Columbia. As a girl, Julia had dreamed of becoming a concert pianist. Columbia was less than an hour away by train. Caught up in a pleasant fantasy, Julia contacted the dean of the School of Fine Arts, Henry Bellamann, and asked him to give her private piano lessons. She wanted to learn all the sonatas of Beethoven in order to "cheat the stillness" of the country. [24]

Henry Bellamann was handsome, bright, and cultured. As she auditioned for him, Julia realized with dismay that she played the piano badly. Trying to distract him from her poor performance, she started telling tales about her life at Lang Syne. Before the first lesson was over she had poured out the story of Frank Hart's toes. As the weeks wore on, she quoted Lavinia Berry, described Mary Weeks, and reminisced about Dukkin, whose mother had "marked him on a cow" when she was pregnant. Dukkin chewed his cud, poisoned farm animals, and talked nonsense, but Julia speculated that he was the only truly happy person she had ever seen. Bellamann was mesmerized.[25]

Bellamann's wife, Katherine, a former opera singer, was also a professor in the music department at the college. She kept a watchful eye on her husband, especially when he was teaching pretty females.[26] Julia struck Katherine Bellamann as even more dangerous than the smitten girls who trotted at Henry's heels. Mrs. Bellamann warned Julia to stop "upsetting" her husband with her dreadful plantation talk.[27] Behind Katherine's back, however, Henry encouraged Julia to write down more tales between her lessons.[28]

Soon the keyboard might as well have been a desktop. Instead of giving Julia piano lessons, Henry — who had recently published a book of verse — was teaching her to write. "Mary Weeks was born the third year of freedom," begins one of Julia's early attempts. "She is lithe and straight, wears gold earrings. Bully married her when she was a girl. Within a year, he left her with a baby girl. She was heartbroken. She had to make a living, came to the Big House to carry water. All day she went and came, bringing water from the spring, a bucket on her head, one in each hand. In the morning she took hot water to the gentlemen for shaving. When Bessie was born, she was a pretty yellow baby; then Essie, pretty and yellow, too. After this, Mary was put to work in the field. Every other year a baby came, each different, all strong — for Mary chose virile men." [29]

This was racy stuff, especially for a southern lady. "Brother Bob was Vinner's husband," Julia wrote. "Paul was their oldest son, the image of his father. Big Rachel had children for him too. Hagar was her oldest daughter, the image of her mother. Paul married Hagar. Vinner says Hagar is her best daughter." [30] Henry liked what he read but thought it undeveloped. "Tell me more," he seems to have urged. "Set the scene. Let your characters speak for themselves."

Henry and Katherine Bellamann ran with a crowd of would-be bohemians who called themselves the Columbia Stage Society, a loose-knit group of students, college professors, art lovers, and leisured women directed by Daniel Reed.[31] Veterans of big-city playhouses, Reed and his wife, Isadora Bennett, had recently acquired an old house and converted it into an auditorium where they dreamed of presenting plays, concerts, and lectures by famous people.

Before she married Dan Reed, Isadora Bennett had worked as a reporter for the *Chicago Daily News*. One of her co-workers was the poet Carl Sandburg, who now hustled for a living as a traveling troubadour.

For several months each year he sang, played American folk songs, strummed the guitar, and recited a little poetry in culture-hungry cities across the country. The Reeds invited Sandburg to appear in Columbia on February 17, 1921, the day after he was to perform for the South Carolina Poetry Society in Charleston.[32]

Isadora was sure that Lang Syne would interest Sandburg as a rich vein of "negro material," and she suggested to Julia that the poet might like to visit her plantation. Seizing on the idea, Julia studied Sandburg's *Smoke and Steel* and *Chicago Poems*. Without consulting Henry Bellamann, she mailed a packet of manuscripts to him. "Dear Sir," she wrote, "My new year's resolution is to do what I do not dare to do. . . . I wish you'd come here to Lang Syne Plantation where five hundred of us are black and six are white, and learn about us and with your remarkable idiom, make us immortal." "P.S.," she added, "I neglected to say I am one of the six who are white."[33] Sandburg laid this peculiar letter aside to answer later. By January 25, Julia had grown testy over his failure to respond. "Dear Sir," she wrote again. "In South Carolina we'd let nothing short of sudden death prevent our answering a polite invitation."[34] That got his attention.

"Dear Mrs. Peterkin," Sandburg replied. "And when an invitation is to an event of great simplicities and dark intangibles — and a man understands it as a privilege — and does not know whether it will be months or years before he can go — he may be addedly slow as well as naturally always slow about writing."[35] He thanked her for letting him see the manuscripts and added that he would wait to comment on them until he reached Lang Syne.

After she grew famous, Julia loved to tell the story of how she had been discovered. It would become one of her most convincing fictions. Bellamann, she said, brought Sandburg to meet her. Sandburg insisted on seeing her manuscripts, read them right there in her living room, and announced that they should be published. Julia resisted the idea, accusing him of flattery. She asked for the name of the toughest critic in America and promised to send the sketches to him. Sandburg said Henry Mencken was the best critic in America, so Julia "reluctantly" mailed off a batch of sketches. Mencken embraced them and announced that they should be published. Suddenly, Julia Peterkin was a writer.

It is a lovely story, but false. Julia was far from diffident about meeting Sandburg. As soon as she discovered that he would be staying in Charleston, with then-unknown DuBose Heyward, the insurance agent and sometime poet who had arranged his southern tour, she fired off a telegram: "If you go to Columbia Thursday morning by the Southern railroad you pass Fort Motte at midday. Please look for me . . . on the train as I go to Columbia that morning too." [36]

Whether or not they first met on the train to Columbia, Julia Peterkin and Carl Sandburg clearly liked each other on sight. Furthermore, he admired her sketches. On the surface, it was an unlikely attraction. Sandburg was a socialist who had recently completed a series of investigative reports on the Chicago race riots, and in spite of her newfound ambition to be almost anything else, Julia was a plantation mistress still. What she saw in him, at first, was opportunity. What he saw in her was intelligence, a sharp tongue, and a bawdy sense of humor. The very qualities she had been warned to hide from men were the ones that made Sandburg grin. Julia drove him around the plantation and introduced him to Mary Weeks and Lavinia Berry. After dinner, when Willie had retired to bed, Julia sent to the Quarters for a man who played the guitar and sang spirituals and "reels" — secular, often raunchy songs that church members were forbidden even to hum. [37] The evening was a huge success.

For years afterward, Julia would observe the anniversary of Sandburg's first visit as her "birth-day," the day she "came to [her]self." [38] Henry Bellamann, delightful as he was, had served his purpose; now Julia was eager to move on. She was elated to realize that there were men in the world she could talk to. These men, by and large, were artists and writers, and they moved in a world she knew very little about. They did not belong to the elite Vinner had had in mind when she encouraged Julia to get out in society, but they belonged to an elite nonetheless.

Sandburg left, promising to keep in touch. He mailed Julia a pair of inexpensive Japanese prints, and she spent weeks happily fretting over how to frame them. [39] In the months that followed, she made sure that Sandburg would not forget his promise, sending letter after letter even when he failed to answer. "I wish I could discover in some way that you're my cousin or something, a sort of kinship that would be a tie so you could not forget that we are here and we think about you and want you to come back," she told him. [40] By "we," she meant not "Willie and me" but "Mary and Vinner and me," a distinction she clarified by telling him that her two black friends sent their regards and hoped, like her, that he would find time to visit again soon. In another letter, Julia revealed that on the day after Sandburg left, "a well-developed epidemic of small-pox was discovered in the quarter." She had decided not to worry about him, she said, because "we [by which, in this instance, she meant 'we white people'] rarely suffer from these diseases."[41] Sandburg, who like Julia had no doubt been vaccinated against smallpox, was preoccupied with illness of a different kind. Just before he left for South Carolina, his nine-year-old daughter, Margaret, had suffered several mysterious attacks. She had more convulsions during his absence, and more after his return home. Years later, she would be diagnosed as epileptic.[42]

After her heady encounter with Carl Sandburg, Julia was determined to meet any other literary celebrities who might show up in Columbia. The next lecturer in the Town Theater series was Harriet Monroe, the editor of *Poetry* magazine and the person who had discovered and promoted Sandburg. On March 1, Monroe was driven out to Lang Syne and handed a stack of manuscripts, Julia's plantation sketches arranged as free verse. Miss Monroe politely encouraged her hostess to keep writing and to make more effort, as she put it, to "express beauty." Julia's tales struck her as too "revolting" to appear in *Poetry*.[43]

Then, again without telling Bellamann, Julia shipped off a packet of sketches to H. L. Mencken, the editor of *Smart Set* magazine. "No evangelist had ever given me so strong a conviction of guilt and general worthiness to be damned as your second series of 'Prejudices,'" she wrote, "yet I brave your scorn and send you a manuscript."[44] H. L. Mencken replied with a short note of encouragement.

Mencken was a formidable figure, idolized by half his audience and despised by the other half, who read him anyway. His scathing columns, written for the *Baltimore Sun,* were reprinted in newspapers all around the country. Ridicule was his medium, and the South was one of his favorite targets. To Julia, Mencken's outrageous tirades were like a bracing gust of wind. Drawing a bead on hypocrisy and pretension, he mocked everything she had ever despised about her native state. Mencken denounced the South as a country barren of literature, music, painting, and the dramatic arts. "The Sahara of the Bozart," he called it, and the epithet stuck.

Never one to miss an opportunity for name-dropping, Julia soon fired off another batch of sketches to Mencken, mentioning that both Carl Sandburg and Harriet Monroe had recently paid her a visit and "approv[ed]" of her pieces, "stark, undressed as they are."[45] They had come to see her; why shouldn't he?

Julia begged Mencken to bring culture to Lang Syne. "There's not an opinion in reach of me that's worth having," she announced, apparently discounting Henry Bellamann's.[46] She apologized for her own forwardness, then berated herself for apologizing. "I don't know why I give what a wicked woman would call 'a damn' about your opinion but for some reason I do," she confessed.[47] Three months later, she was still worried about seeming pushy. "I know it's downright bad taste to be persistent as I've been," she told Mencken.[48] But the alternative was invisibility. "A woman who has self-control remains undiscovered, unseen by men," Julia mused in one of her notes for future stories. "She does not try to charm or fascinate as the common woman does. Mary Weeks has a lurid past, but nevertheless she has had every adventure a woman can have with men, and today she is the strongest, straightest, happiest woman. Her children adore her." [49]

Julia Peterkin felt ready to emulate Mary Weeks, to do whatever it took to be discovered, to be *seen*, by men, preferably powerful men. Men like Carl Sandburg and H. L. Mencken, who derived their power from words. To Julia, aware that the power of cotton and guns was evaporating, words suddenly seemed more dependable. But there was a problem: Julia felt that writing was really a male activity. She urged Mencken to come and "write some things here that need to be written." [50] Her invitation to Sandburg was similar: she hoped he would see fit to "make us immortal." [51] Even while she was struggling to make herself into a writer, she wanted famous men to write *about* her.

Julia had plenty of competition for Mencken's attention. As the co-editor of *Smart Set,* he received scores of letters and manuscripts every day. "A hundred thousand secondhand Coronas rattle and jingle in ten thousand remote and lonely towns," he once remarked to a friend; his mail was "as heavy as the mail of a get-rich-quick stockbroker." Though he groused that unsolicited manuscripts were "mostly crap," Mencken almost always replied kindly when beginners like Julia asked stupid questions.[52] "I live pretty far away from things and people," she wrote to him. "Here, one needs no vocabulary nor imagination. How can I best acquire them? I mean this seriously." Julia flattered Mencken shamelessly. For her, she said, he was "something on the order of God," though he answered her prayers "more directly." [53] Years later, looking back over her letters, Mencken would observe that Julia "showed a good deal of the traditional Southern blarney in her dealings with men." [54] Certainly she played on Mencken's notions about what a southern writer should be. When he blustered that Reconstruction had put "white trash in the saddle," she offered herself as one of the few aristocrats who had survived the chaos.[55]

Lang Syne was "only" eighteen hours from New York, if there were no delays on rail or road. "If you were here," she wrote to Mencken when he complained of feeling poorly, "we'd rub the soles of your feet with suet and tie a collard leaf on your head." [56] The "we" was Julia and Mary and Vinner. Mencken was blasé about city women who drank themselves blind and ended up in his bed, yet the thought of traveling to the hinterlands to have his feet massaged gave him pause. He consulted with friends about whether to accept Julia's invitations and, after deliberating, "declined on the advice of counsel." [57]

It would have been easy enough for Julia to get on the train and meet Henry Mencken on his own turf, but she feared that New York or Baltimore might make her betray her ignorance of what she called "the rules." [58] Feeling incapable of carrying on a conversation about the business of writing, she quietly purchased a practical literary education in the same way she shopped for seeds, exotic fowl, cookbooks, and magazines — by mail order. Julia signed up with the Home Correspondence School in Springfield, Massachusetts, and began absorbing the basics of plot and character. Galloping through lessons on themes, complications, and settings, she wrote notes on little scraps of paper, reminding herself to "learn a new word every day." She imitated the styles of other writers and invented characters from all walks of life. Much of what the Home Correspondence School taught her was formulaic. "Have heroine opposite, in every way, to hero," she dutifully noted. "There must be a *coincidence*, meeting. She must object to him, he resent her." [59]

Before she sent them to Mencken, most of Julia's manuscripts had already been edited by her Home Correspondence instructor, J. Berg Esenwein, who showed her, among other things, where a title should appear on the page. One of the many exercises Julia submitted to Esenwein was a grim little story called "Nancy."

Nancy and Monroe, who are first cousins, fall in love. Everyone on the plantation warns them that marrying is sure to bring bad luck. Insisting that love is stronger than luck, they marry anyway. Nancy bears two children, both of them deaf. The crops fail. Just when Nancy is about to give up and admit that luck is stronger than love, a perfect baby girl arrives. Things get better — the curse seems to have lifted. But then, one day, a rooster wanders up to the baby's little low bed and pecks out her eye. The baby lives, and at the end of the story is "sixteen now, and always wears a hat. When a stranger looks at her, she pulls it down a little on one side." [60]

Esenwein pronounced the plot "sordid" and advised Julia to "tear this story to pieces and rebuild it, showing . . . that the case of Nancy and her husband is much less hopeless." The baby's blinding was so repellent that it overwhelmed the rest of the story. If the reader could identify with Nancy before being confronted with her baby's gaping eye socket, the horror might have some point. A lighter version of "Nancy," he added, might even sell to one of the popular magazines.[61] Julia would no more have tacked on a happy ending than she would have offered Nancy and Monroe her guest room. Still, she was shrewd enough to see that Esenwein had a point. After all, even Mencken was warning that many of her stories were too gruesome for publication and that most readers who encountered her phonetic renderings of the Gullah dialect would find them incomprehensible.

As advice trickled into her mailbox at the little post office in Fort Motte, Julia pretended to her relatives that her writing was just another hobby, like raising fowl or making fig preserves. By the end of the year, however, she was admitting to herself — and to Mencken — that she hoped it would make her rich and famous. Mencken advised her to be patient, to write and rewrite. "I do wish instead of saying 'Patience' and 'there's plenty of time,' you'd say 'Strive harder! Hurry up!'" she fumed. "When one is old, what good is success? I want it now. Now!" [62]

CHAPTER 3

Cutting a Mouth

ne of H. L. Mencken's few enthusiasms in the great southern wasteland was a little magazine called the *Reviewer*. Promising writers not yet sophisticated enough for his urbane *Smart Set* could be showcased in the *Reviewer* while they were still in training. During the summer of 1921, Mencken wrote to Emily Clark, the *Reviewer*'s editor, advising her to get in touch with Julia. Clark wrote at once asking to see some manuscripts.[1] Wary of sending "negro sketches" to a publication in Richmond, Julia asked for Mencken's help. "I have friends in Richmond," she worried. "Worse, cousins. I know ladies who are probably like Miss Clark. I fear she will find what I write revolting."[2] Mencken selected several sketches and made suggestions for their revision; by the end of the summer a group of Julia's short tales had been accepted for publication in the *Reviewer*.

No money changed hands — the magazine warned that contributors would be paid in fame, not in "specie."

The October issue, in which Julia was scheduled to make her debut, kicked off the second volume of the *Reviewer*. The first had come out as a fortnightly pamphlet that received good notices in the national press and then promptly ran out of cash. Julia's first submission arrived at a moment when publication had been suspended and the editors feared the magazine would fold. Trusting that a benefactor would appear, Clark had continued accepting manuscripts. That fall, enough money was found to resume publication, and the magazine was reborn as a monthly. Its mission was "to develop young Southern writers, unhampered by provincialism or commercial requirements." The editorial staff, Clark avowed, "felt themselves totally unable to cope with politics, either Southern or national," and simply required pieces to be "honest and interesting." [3] The *Reviewer* shied away from experimental fiction, preferring traditional narratives with an ironic slant. James Branch Cabell, author of the notorious novel *Jurgen*, who had recently been prosecuted for obscenity, offered to edit the first three monthly issues, giving the magazine a certain cachet. Mencken weighed in with an essay called "Morning Song in C Major," ridiculing southern fiction as "treacley and insignificant." [4]

Julia's three sketches appeared under the title "From Lang Syne Plantation," and no one could accuse them of being treacly. One is about a little boy named Mose who is sent to get something to ease his grandmother's indigestion. By the time he reaches the Big House he has forgotten why he came. He falls asleep by the side of the road. When he wakes up it is too late to go back to the house on his errand, though he now remembers what he was supposed to get there — soda. Mose recalls hearing the field hands talk about the big sacks of soda they are spreading on the corn, so he goes to the fertilizer shed and fills his can. His grandmother, who has been waiting all day for relief, swallows a dose, convulses, and dies. No one realizes that Mose has poisoned his grandmother; the story ends with two women enumerating all the random bad luck they have experienced in the past year. "People dying so quick like this with a misery, and boll weevils eatin' the cotton everywhere," says Mary Weeks. "Charity, yo' cow dead quick too las' week, enty?" "Yes," says Charity, "them chillen tied her out by that house where they keeps that soda what they puts on corn. She licked a little o' it an' it killed her dead as a wedge. Jesus! tha' soda sho' a pisen thing." [5]

In another sketch, a father teaches his son to avoid fire by handing him a burning coal. In the third, a little boy is so moved by a preacher's sermon that he rushes forward to the altar, only to be snatched back by a relative. If he gets saved, she says, he won't be able to play ball with Young Cap'n on Sundays. Parents inflict pain and deprivation on their children under the guise of protecting them from harm, a motif reflecting Julia's rage at her father that would resurface in her more mature fiction. Each piece packed a punch; none was fully developed as a short story.

These "thumbnail sketches" were ideal for the *Reviewer*, but Mencken wanted to publish something more substantial. Already he had sent several of Julia's "grim and impressive" stories to his coeditor at *Smart Set*, George Jean Nathan. Mencken was always on the lookout for material that would help the magazine slough off its turn-of-the-century skin, a format that still included cloying "candy-box covers" and regular installments of the society novelettes he referred to as "trade goods." So far, 1921 had been an especially dry year; Julia Peterkin's tales from the black South would surely dispel the perception that *Smart Set* leaned toward the "fluffy and inconsequential." Nathan disliked all dialect stories on principle, and the two editors had a long-standing agreement that if one of them objected to a piece, it was out. Yet Mencken was adamant that *Smart Set* should publish Julia Peterkin. Breaking his own rule, he talked his partner into buying a story called "The Merry-Go-Round."[6] A "beautiful check" for one cent a word, engraved with red devils and cherubs, appeared in Julia's mailbox.[7]

In "The Merry-Go-Round," an itinerant white carousel barker, called Collins in the original draft, tries to seduce a black girl named Meta.[8] Cheered on by a crowd of other black men, Meta's boyfriend, Jesse Weeks, beats up Collins. In the middle of the night, Collins comes to Weeks's cabin and shoots him. Weeks is gravely wounded but not killed, and the news of the shooting spreads quickly. By dawn, hundreds of black men and women fill the village street, brandishing "hoes and rakes, axes and guns." Collins is nowhere to be found.[9]

The clerk at the general store calls for help from "all the gentlemen around here" to get Collins onto the eight o'clock train. Men arrive on horseback to help escort Collins to the station. The train leaves without incident, the white men mount their horses, and the black policeman who assisted them deliberately walks away after whispering with the crowd of black people. There is a shout, and Collins's merry-go-round goes up in flames.

We haven't seen the last of Collins. He gets off the train at the next big station, cases the town, and finds work in a revival tent. Putting his carnival training to a new use, Collins plays the organ, lights the gaslights, and gives "a remarkable testimony of his salvation from sin." Soon he is promoted to preaching, "a steadier business than his former one; more exciting, too."

Meanwhile Jesse Weeks, crippled by Collins's bullet, "makes baskets and fish traps and chair bottoms out of split hickory." Meta and her mother take in washing, and "all together they make a living." No matter how little they have, Meta's mother always takes part of their earnings to give to the church, because preachers, she says, are the servants of God, and without them the world would get "too full of sin."

"The Merry-Go-Round" is a tight, wry short story, perfectly attuned to the sensibilities of the 1920s. The Fort Motte "riot," the incident that inspired the story, was far less neatly structured. In late September 1896, after a hot, dry summer and a crop failure, George Collins shot Jessie Gooden, paralyzing him below the waist. Collins was white; Gooden black. The owner of the store where Collins clerked was also the commander of the local militia unit, and he took Collins into "protective custody." Word quickly spread that Gooden's friends and relatives were planning to lynch Collins. A crowd of black men and women gathered on the main street in Fort Motte and refused to disperse. There was a rumor that they planned to burn the town. A deputy sheriff sent out to arrest the leader of the blacks, Frank Cheseboro, ended up killing another man who was at Cheseboro's house.

Could this be the dreaded black uprising white South Carolinians had feared since the inception of slavery? The Fort Motte Guard was mobilized. Reinforcements were brought in from all over the state. Realizing that they were outnumbered and outgunned, the Fort Motte "rioters" quietly dispersed. "This is a white man's government, and, by the grace of God, we intend to hold it," proclaimed Dr. Charles Taber the next day to a large crowd of blacks. "By doing so we protect the rights of you colored people." [10]

White South Carolina had a long tradition of terrorist activity designed to keep unruly blacks in line. As early as 1721, a local militia's principal duty in South Carolina had been the "police supervision of slaves." [11] During Reconstruction, Julia's father had belonged to a band of night riders that intimidated blacks who wanted to exercise their rights. [12] Her father-in-law, James Alexander Peterkin, was a member of the Fort Motte Guard. The McCords resolved their "potato troubles" after the war by assembling a posse. All the whites in their neighborhood donned uniforms, shouldered their guns, and surrounded the Quarters until the blacks gave up a share of the stored crop.[13]

As men like Julius Mood and James Alexander Peterkin saw it, beleaguered white aristocrats had no choice but to ally themselves with people like Collins. The vastly outnumbered whites had to stand united against the menacing black horde. As Mary Weeks and Lavinia Berry saw it, however, the blacks had been right to rise up in anger. Julia was inclined to agree.

H. L. Mencken had coached Julia to provide a sophisticated frame for her sketches, to write as a detached observer who grasps the irony of the situation. "The Merry-Go-Round" suited his taste, not least because he understood how much it would infuriate white Southerners. Julia, on the other hand, could hardly imagine what it would be like to see her work in print and hadn't yet thought about how other people would react to it. She seldom bothered to make up names for her characters, and so had used the real first name of the victim and the real last name of his assailant. The black man was in no position to object, but the white one and his relatives were.

"Many of the nearest whites are Ku Klux, I hear," she wrote to Mencken. "Occasionally one gets drunk and expresses himself. I'd hate to wake up some fine morning and find white crosses on my door step." [14] Mencken, she said, must change the name of the main character. Either change the name or kill the story.

Mencken found it hard to believe that Julia was in any danger.[15] Still, he agreed to change the name of the merry-go-round man from Collins to Carson.[16] No crosses were burned on the steps of Lang Syne. And when the December *Smart Set* hit the newsstands before the October *Reviewer*, Julia wound up making her literary debut in Mencken's magazine.[17]

Emily Clark was determined to carve out a bigger niche for the *Reviewer*, both by emphasizing its progressive "southernness" and by soliciting manuscripts from famous nonsouthern writers. Carping privately to novelist Joseph Hergesheimer that "Mr. Mencken's Southern talk . . . won't fill the magazine — with much but slush," Clark pursued "a large Southern correspondence, which bores me horribly, in order to have a good report" for Mencken.[18] "Mr. Mencken continues to write me about unknown Southern authors, but I shan't encourage them unless they are rolling in money," she informed Hergesheimer. "If the *Reviewer* ever gets on its feet I shall . . . refuse to be either threatened or bought." [19] The January 1922 issue featured articles by best-selling novelists Hergesheimer and John Galsworthy. It also contained a group of five dramatic monologues by the nearly unknown Julia Peterkin titled "Imports from Africa."

Gullah stories, both spoken and written, were much beloved by white South Carolinians, but Julia's sketches broke with tradition by taking their black subjects seriously. In "Cooch's Premium," Mary Weeks shows off her daughter's baby, bragging that "he's a good kinder chile to hab here in de quarter. You know, he ain' nebber look on e' daddy face, an' a chile lak dat kin cure all kinder sickness; fever an' rheumatism, an' t'rash in babies' mout'; mos' any kinder ailment." In "Cat-Fish," a black man explains what happened when a strange white man told him that "wher' he come f'om de fa'mers buys grineup fish to put to dey corn." The white man suggested that he fertilize his fields by burying a catfish in every hill of corn. It sounded like a fine idea, and the farmer put his whole family to work catching and burying catfish. But the ploy did not have its intended effect. The smell of rotting fish drew dogs, which dug up the fish, and with it the seed corn, leaving the field in ruins. In "The Ortymobile," a white man has just hit a horse with his car. Without actually accusing the driver of the automobile, the black man who owns the horse manages to strike a good bargain for a replacement. In "The Plat-Eye," the speaker describes how spirits can change shape, from dog to horse to man to fog. "Den you run," he says. "A cowardly man don' tote no break bones." And in "Betsy," a woman clings to her dead baby. "Lemme feel his lil han's jus' one mo' time! Gawd! His lil mout'! An' me wid all two breas' full o' milk!" [20]

A touching sketch about a mother's grief was alien to the tradition of white Gullah storytellers. Ambrose Gonzales, the editor of the *Columbia State*, had won local acclaim with his most recent collection of Gullah stories, *The Black Border*. In a typical tale called "Sam Dickerson," Gonzales described a black lawyer as "monkey-like" and "simian," his well-thumbed law books as "tawdry and greasy," and his gestures as "grotesque antics." Reading out an indictment in court, Sam Dickerson "mouthed and slobbered over it as one mouths the pit of a clingstone peach." [21]

Though virtually incomprehensible to the average reader, Gonzales's rendering of Gullah is more phonetic than Julia's, and arguably more accurate. "Uh gone Wadmuhlaw fuh dig Irish tettuh, en' w'en middleday come, me en' all dem todduh man en' 'ooman gone to de Jew fuh buy bittle fuh eat, en' him yeddy suh we come f'um Swintun place," says Bina, a witness for the defense. (I went to Wadmalaw to dig Irish potatoes, and when noon came, I and all the other men and women went to the Jew to buy food to eat, and he asked if we came from the Swinton place.)[22]

Like most of his white contemporaries, Gonzales regarded all black dialects as a hilarious mangling of the King's English. Sam Dickerson tries to ape the speech and mannerisms of white lawyers when he declares to the court, "Dis man bin chaa'ge', yo' onnuh, wid laa'ceny! He bin chaa'ge' wid laa'ceny! W'at am laa'ceny, yo' onnuh?"[23] In fact, Sam Dickerson's pronunciation was probably not very different from his white counterpart's, yet Gonzales would never have thought to render an educated white man's speech phonetically.

Unlike Gonzales, who deliberately used dialect to set himself apart from blacks, Julia experimented with ways to dignify her characters without losing the tang of their distinctive language. Her early efforts were not always successful. In "Green Walnuts," a sketch that appeared in the March 1922 *Reviewer* as one of two "Studies in Charcoal," Maum Nellie calls Miss to come check on her grandson Breeze, who has a bad stomachache. Nellie is at her wits' end, having done everything she can think of to relieve the pain. "I done gi' em eby bit de medicine I had een de house an' I had plenty too. E mammy who stay to Char'ston, eby time 'e come, e fetch me all kin o sample and t'ing wha' de people een town gi' way," she says. Sure enough, Miss spies a whole collection of empty medicine bottles on a table. This alone would be enough to account for the stomachache, yet she sets out to extract a full confession from Breeze. The child first claims that he "ain' ate nuttin a'tall oncommon." Under pressure he admits to snacking on a little sugarcane, a raw sweet potato, a handful of sparkleberries, raw peanuts, windfall persimmons, mush and greens, canned salmon, and some leftover clabber. Miss is relentless. "And what else?" she keeps asking. At last Breeze reveals that he tasted a few green walnuts in the woods. His grandmother flies into a rage: "My Gawd, Breeze! you would do sich a t'ing? Much as I tol' you to lef dem green wa'nuts lone? Ain' I raise you to know dey's de wus t'ing eber was to mek lice een you haid?" Miss has pushed Breeze into a confession when she knew all along what had caused the problem. She uses the incident to put Nellie in her place. "You aren't going to have any lice," she proclaims, giving Breeze a dose of oil.[24]

"Green Walnuts" marks the first time Julia gave herself a speaking part in a story, and her appearance sets a tone of condescension that the earlier sketches lack. By comparison with Miss, the black characters appear backward and stupid. All Nellie wants is for her grandson to make a good impression on Miss; she forgets his pain. Breeze would rather die than admit he has eaten green walnuts. Miss alone acts sensibly. If Julia could have admitted that Miss's "nursing" was self-serving, "Green Walnuts" might have been brilliant. But she couldn't.

"Roots Work," which appeared with "Green Walnuts," follows Julia's earlier pattern of keeping Miss quiet. Long ago Katy's husband ran off with Nettie, a sixteen-year-old girl the two had taken in to help tend the children and do the housework. Her husband "took [the girl] away an' . . . lived wid her twenty-three years. Twenty-three years. She had eight childern by him." As Katy sees it, "Somebody worked a root on him. It wain't him. He wain't to blame." Katy noticed that something was passing between Jim and Nettie, and Jim came to say "he had to go wid her. Him a man wid standin', an' edication, an' mos white too, he had to go wid dat black gyurl, an' he'd he'p raise her." Katy got through the bad years by smoking and praying. "But I tell you," she says, "I know. *Roots work.*"[25]

Both Sandburg and Mencken were pressing Julia to write a novel based on the short pieces she had already done. In January 1922, Julia sent a sheaf of manuscripts to Sandburg's publisher, Alfred Harcourt. She addressed the package to Joel Spingarn, cofounder and editor at Harcourt and an authority on black culture. Though white, Spingarn had served for six years as the national chairman of the National Association for the Advancement of Colored People. He was out of the office when Julia's manuscripts arrived, and one of his assistants returned them with a rejection slip. Harcourt was interested in publishing stories of Negro life, he said, but Julia's sketches contained far too much dialect.[26]

When Carl Sandburg learned that his publisher had given Julia the brush-off, he took matters into his own hands and mailed an example of her work to Harcourt along with a ringing endorsement. Harcourt did not respond. Sandburg dispatched yet another letter: Julia, he said, would someday be hailed as "a sort of Turgenev of the plantation niggers." Her best work, he claimed, was "as good as the best in American literature, some of it subtle and simple as good Chinese poetry."[27] Harcourt finally took the bait and wrote to Julia asking for sample stories, which he then passed on to Sinclair Lewis, whose novel *Main Street* he had published in 1920.

H. L. Mencken was also pitching Julia's work. Since 1916 he had been scouting manuscripts for Alfred A. Knopf, and if Julia was going to make a book, he wanted her to do it with Knopf.[28] By the end of April 1922, Julia had produced about two hundred pages of material, but even to her it seemed "a very confused, chopped-up lot."[29] She begged Mencken, "Please, *please* see me through this book business. It is so out of my line. Of course I'll omit whatever you say. There's a surfeit of stuff in that manuscript but I don't know what is intelligible and what isn't."[30] Lewis, Harcourt, Spingarn, Mencken, and Knopf all agreed that the sketches could be turned into a marketable book, but only if the dialect were removed and the stories interwoven.

"It's hard to avoid dialect in presenting these black people," Julia wrote to Sandburg in discouragement. "Their very coined words are so right. . . . Wallace the cook says 'A 'oman name is *ficklety.*' Who can beat 'ficklety'?"[31] She was equally perplexed over how to bind the stories together. Seeing herself as the unifying thread, she thought about putting in a plantation mistress who turned into a sycamore tree and stood at the fork of the road between the Big House and the Quarters, watching over everyone. The tree's roots, working deep into the soil, would be black. "They live in darkness and among worms," she told Mencken, laboring to provide the tree with "beautiful leaves and golden balls."[32] Sandburg and Mencken were appalled — the romantic, fanciful image clashed with the brutal realism they valued. Sensing that no one was very interested in her struggles as a white woman, Julia complained to Sandburg that "writing a novel seems like moving a mountain to me. I'm in terrible danger, the danger that is most paralyzing. Being sorry for myself. . . . Shall I go on?" she asked.[33]

After several false starts, Julia hit on an acceptable plan for unifying the *Reviewer* pieces. What if "I make all the man experiences happen to one man," she asked Mencken, "the child's to one child?"[34] Try it and see, he advised her.

Mencken continued recommending Julia's stories to George Jean Nathan at *Smart Set*, but Nathan didn't like them. "Don't worry Mr. Nathan with these," Julia directed. "Why persecute him with my stuff? He would never 'get it' in a thousand years. It's too crude, raw, never 'Smart Set' material. Never!" Yet Julia admitted that Nathan might have other grounds to reject her stories: "Even I know I've not written anything yet that's worth — well, a damn."[35]

Both Bill and Willie Peterkin fell ill in the spring of 1922. Joking to Mencken that she was getting more experience as a nurse than as a writer, Julia accompanied them to Richmond for treatment. Family members do not recall what was wrong with the two men, how they came to be sick at the same time, or why they were transported four hundred miles to be hospitalized, although Julius Mood's friend Shelton Horsely practiced in Richmond. Julia's letters from the period do not reveal any details. What *is* clear is that Julia Peterkin was elated to be in Virginia. In fact, she seems to have been energized by the fact that Willie and Bill were confined to bed, as if their loss of power were her gain. Complaining about her patients' ill temper, she dashed off to meet her editors and their circle.[36]

Julia had been on the lookout for an opportunity to meet James Branch Cabell, the dean of the Richmond literati and a distant relation of Julius Mood's through the Alston line.[37] When she finally cornered him at a party, she talked shop, asking for advice on turning her sketches into a coherent whole. Cabell suggested expanding "Roots Work" into a novel.[38] Katy's story spanned a lifetime of betrayals and disappointments. Her husband's story, and the other woman's, might be equally moving.

Julia also hoped to meet Joseph Hergesheimer, who had recently been voted "best contemporary novelist" in a poll conducted by *Literary Digest*. Emily Clark knew him well and claimed him as a personal mentor.[39] Hergesheimer and Mencken privately agreed that Clark was the homeliest woman they had ever seen, though she had, as Hergesheimer put it, "a very graceful, a very ingratiating coastline" and a perfect pair of legs.[40] The combination was unsettling, the more so since Clark fancied herself a southern belle and could turn on her charm like a floodlight. Sitting at her desk in Richmond, Clark had envisioned Julia Peterkin as a stodgy matron — no competition in the coastline department. Instead, she met a slim, flirtatious redhead, "eager and vibrant as a girl."[41] Hergesheimer was not in Richmond, and after watching Julia operate, Clark was determined to keep the two apart. She shrewdly informed Hergesheimer that Julia had "tired [Cabell] to death" and advised him not to go and see her.[42]

Back at Lang Syne, Julia still was determined to write herself into a story. In May, "The Right Thing" appeared in the *Reviewer*. Like "Green Walnuts," it portrays Miss as the only sensible person on the plantation. In this version, Julia contrasted her own behavior with her husband's. "The Right Thing" opens with a crap game. Jim accuses John of cheating and goes off to get a gun. Paul Berry (Vinner's son) hears the commotion and joins the crowd. John Green returns, mistakes Paul for

Jim, and shoots him in the arm. Somebody runs to tell Cap'n, who roars away to the Quarters. As soon as his taillights fade into the distance, Miss hears John calling her from the entry hall. He tells her that he has accidentally killed Paul, his best friend. Now he is afraid to go back to the Quarters, where Jim and his friends will be laying for him. "Jim uncle been cut my daddy heart out, an' Jim ain' gwine ceasted tell he cut out mine lessen I cut out him own," he explains. Miss advises John to hide in the barn until morning. When Cap'n gets home, he vows to call the sheriff. "These niggers devil the life out of me," he remarks.

The plot is propelled by a thinly veiled antagonism between the boorish husband and the tactful wife. Cap'n is crass and self-absorbed. He dismisses Paul's injury with the observation, "There's not much work to do on the farm now so it doesn't matter especially." [43] Miss convinces her husband to get a good night's sleep before taking any action. In the morning, she gives him a big breakfast, lets him talk to John, and then suggests that "the right thing" would be to handle the matter on the plantation, without involving the law. John Green agrees to pay Paul's doctor bill and to feed his family until he gets well. Everyone is satisfied, but the story itself falls lifeless, bled dry by the presence of Miss.

Julia gave herself all the best lines, while Willie came off as a lout. In real life, their roles were less clearly defined: Julia sometimes played the despot, and Willie usually followed his father's example in dealing with the hands. "Be candid, positive, and honest with the Negro," the older man wrote in 1888. "Never swear or drink in their presence, treat them so that they will learn to respect you and treat you well, and you will have little if any trouble with them. Be the first in the field and the last one to leave it." [44] Willie had no way of challenging his wife's unflattering portrait—if, in fact, he ever read it. He didn't much care what people thought of him outside the state; those in his orbit saw him as a generous patriarch, an honest trader, a man who always tried to do "the right thing."

Around Fort Motte, Julia was the one whose motives were suspect. In an effort to amuse Mencken, she began collecting anecdotes that fueled his prejudices. When Mencken complained that the president of the University of South Carolina had publicly praised the hayseed evangelist Billy Sunday, Julia protested that "poor Mr. Melton" was simply trying to preserve his reputation and his job. "It is far more significant," she proclaimed, "that in the state penitentiary today there are stocks where women prisoners are put after they are stripped to the waist, and where their beatings are administered by men. Billy Sunday's religion is a better grade than the kind that is current here now."[45] A few weeks later, Julia reported that she had denounced the whippings to the county sheriff. To her amazement, she said, the sheriff had retorted that some women *needed* whipping, offering as proof a fresh human bite on his shoulder inflicted by a "nigger woman." The sheriff feared that he had contracted blood poisoning from the wound. "I may die," he announced, adding that he had "slapped this one silly" when she bit him.[46]

As Julia had deduced, one sure way to keep Mencken's attention was to provide him with evidence of the South's degeneracy. Her face-to-face encounter with the county sheriff was a brilliant stroke of one-upmanship. Mencken fought his battles from behind a desk; she was a brave soldier in the field. "Perhaps you are right," she concluded. "A flood should come, or the Japs, and destroy us all, and let a new race take charge here."[47]

In an article called "The Usual Buncombe," published in the January 1922 *Smart Set,* Mencken blamed "poor white trash" for the sad state of southern culture.[48] "Of course it's flattering to think you're right, and for the first time I believe you're wrong," Julia wrote to him. "You are encouraging the very feeling in the real South that is our greatest curse, putting the blame for our failure on somebody else." Southerners' limitations, she felt, resulted from living in the past and romanticizing the Old South. "The trouble is we're too satisfied," she continued, "because some old grandfather did something that sounds fine to us now, or some grandmother was a famous belle."[49]

Although Julia may have sounded radical in her letters to Mencken, she continued to blend in with her conservative neighbors. She served as chapter historian for the United Daughters of the Confederacy in 1923, dutifully recording speeches about the heroism of Jefferson Davis.[50] She played bridge with the neighborhood women and entertained her relations every Sunday evening.[51] But this wasn't enough to keep her son, Bill, from worrying about the family's reputation and begging his mother to spin stories about beautiful ladies and gentlemen, "not niggers" — or so Julia reported to Mencken.[52]

Julia had lately discovered that mentioning the objections of her friends and relatives was a sure way to wring praise and encouragement from Mencken and Sandburg, especially when she also threatened to stop writing. Her correspondents would shoot back earnest letters proclaiming that her work promised great things, and that her family was too backward to appreciate it.

One afternoon in May, the mail brought a copy of Mencken's "Violets in the Sahara." The great southern desert was exhibiting signs of life, proclaimed Mencken, sending up a few tender buds that promised lusher growth. Among these violets was a writer named Julia Peterkin, whose few short stories were "worth more than all the poetry of the South."[53] Mencken's essay had appeared in the *Baltimore Evening Sun* and soon would be reprinted all over the country. Julia gloated. "Somehow I feel vindicated, and I shall go on with my original resolution to do what I don't dare to do," she wrote to him. "Even my friends who dislike it may go to hell!"[54]

Julia mailed Henry Bellamann a copy of "Violets in the Sahara," observing, quite needlessly, that Mencken had left Bellamann's name off his list of southern writers worth reading. Though a published poet, Bellamann was primarily a musician and had not achieved literary renown. Icily addressing Julia as "Mrs. Peterkin," Bellamann replied, "Please remember that I predicted [your success] from the first. That Mr. Mencken and Mr. Sandburg are helping to make it come quickly is fine. Had I been a noteworthy figure in the critical world I would have done even more than they. But try to understand that I can't be made uncomfortable by Mr. Mencken's jibes at poetry. I am at least above artistic jealousy."[55]

Mencken and Clark were not the only editors pushing southern literature at the time. The *Double Dealer* flourished in New Orleans, the *Fugitive* in Nashville. In April 1922, *Poetry* put out a "Southern Number," which was dominated by the South Carolina Poetry Society. In an article titled "Poetry South," Hervey Allen and DuBose Heyward noted that black culture had yet to make its way into southern poetry and wondered when poets would tap into "this immense fund of rich material . . . which Negro music, legends, and folk-lore hold in trust." Warning that "the southern muse must be careful how she handles the tar-baby," they accurately predicted that "the weird, the bizarre and the grotesque in Negro life and story, and the tone of the 'spiritual' will have to be reckoned with."[56] At the back of the magazine was a letter to the editor from Carl Sandburg calling attention to "Imports from Africa" in the *Reviewer*: "Mrs. Peterkin is listening in on some rich folklore," Sandburg observed.[57] If this was not quite the distinction Julia aspired to, it did get her name into print.

Most members of the South Carolina Poetry Society were indeed wary of the tar baby. Though they had joined together to prove Mencken wrong, much of what they produced was of a piece with the sentimental, nostalgic strain of southern literature he despised. Heyward and Allen proudly admitted that the Charleston Poets wrote songs of "magnolia and azalea gardens oriental in a polychromatic spring; of swamps and eerie live-oak forests where the Spanish moss hangs like stalactites in twilit caverns; of the miles of deserted rice-fields where turbaned blacks walk ruined dykes; and of the ancient baronies and manors, each with its legend, where the deer feed around the stately columned houses — shells of a life and an epoch which have passed away." [58]

Bill Peterkin once complained that H. L. Mencken had "flattered" his mother into "cussing the South." [59] "A Baby's Mouth," which appeared in the May *Reviewer*, suggests that something a good deal more complicated had been going on. The story begins when Maum Hannah attends a woman in labor, delivers the child, and discovers a terrible deformity — the baby has no mouth. It cannot eat, it cannot cry. A devastating truth dawns on Hannah: "Somebody got to cut a mout' fo' dat chile. . . . Dey got to. Ef dey don't, he gwine dead."

At first, Maum Hannah does not think of cutting the mouth herself. She considers asking various men who own sharp tools — Gip Ragin, the butcher; John Green, the barber; or Dunk Bruce, who pulls teeth. Doll, the child's mother, pleads with her to do the job — "You do em, Auntie," she says. "You kin do em better'n anybody." Doll is right. The butcher can't bear to hold the defective baby, much less cut a mouth for it. "Seem lak I rudder fo' em to dead dan fo stick em an cut em so," he groans. In the end, Doll holds her own child while Maum Hannah cuts. "I dunno des how big fo' cut em," Hannah muses, "but den, ef I don' git em big 'nough fus time, I kin cut em mo', enty?" The mother faints, the baby cries. "Listen how dis chile do holler!" says Maum Hannah. "He hongry too! Look at em how e leek e own blood!" [60] The story closes on an idyllic scene: mother, child, and midwife "sleeping soundly."

H. L. Mencken questioned whether such a thing really could happen. Julia took offense. "It was just as I wrote you, however stupid that may seem to you. I do not lie very often. It is troublesome and so often useless." [61] Much later, she told a reporter that the story was based on a real incident, and that "the negroes believed the lips were sealed by the silence of the baby's mother. She would not tell who the baby's father was." [62] Mary Weeks's niece, Ella Weeks Walker, disputes this story; she doesn't recall a baby without a mouth being born at Lang Syne, and she laughs at the idea of somebody trying to cut one with a razor.[63]

Whether or not the story is true, cutting the mouth had special significance for Julia. It dramatized the painful process of opening up, finding a voice, making noise. For the baby, the operation is a matter of crude survival: if it cannot eat, it will surely die. Voicelessness, on the other hand, is seldom fatal; generations of southern white women had lived out their lives under the same handicap. In a poem, Julia complained that she felt "shut up in this cell of flesh" with "a queer muscle, a tongue, my only means of letting others know what I inside am like, what I think." [64] Now she had another means — words on paper.

When she sent "A Baby's Mouth" to Mencken, Julia enclosed a note: "Read this and be glad you have a mouth." [65] White men like Bellamann, Sandburg, and Mencken, she felt, had all been born with "mouths." Without their assistance, she could never have reached an audience. Yet they did not comprehend why she felt gagged, or what it meant to be a southern white woman. Mary Weeks and Lavinia Berry did understand, and helped her burst her bonds.

"A Baby's Mouth" was Julia's first sustained narrative from a black point of view. She was leaving behind the omniscient narrator favored by Mencken; she had already abandoned the naive free-verse transcription urged on her by Sandburg. The new form was all her own, and the voices belonged to her servants. It took Carl Sandburg and H. L. Mencken to get Julia published, but it was Lavinia Berry and Mary Weeks who set her free to write.

CHAPTER 4

Poor Little Motherless

ulia started receiving hate mail in October 1922, after "Missy's Twins" appeared in the *Reviewer*. Even H. L. Mencken was startled by the harshness of the tale, branding it "effective but terrible." [1] An old black woman must leave her pregnant foster daughter behind when she accompanies her white "family" on their summer trek to the mountains, where they go to escape the malaria season. Mammy does not read and must depend on her employer for news of Missy. None ever reaches her. Late in the fall, the plantation owner, his young son, and Mammy return home. On the train, Mammy is so preoccupied that the little boy takes her face in his hands and asks, "Mammy, you gone off an' lef' me?" When they reach home, she bathes the boy and puts him to bed. Then the boy's father appears. "It sounds pretty bad," he begins. "I don't know who is to blame. Nobody meant to be careless." At last

Mammy breaks in. "Fo' Gawd's sake! Wha you gwine say?" Missy, he says, had twins. The babies were born dead. Hounds have dug up their shallow graves and eaten the corpses. Mammy's silence on hearing this is intense, "like a thing in the room."[2]

The black woman is as kind and devoted as any southern sentimentalist could paint her. The white man appreciates her for nurturing his son and wants to spare her feelings. But underneath the personal affection is an impersonal force, white supremacy. The white child sleeps in a clean white bed; black children are not safe even in their graves. No Marxist could have drawn a starker contrast between the privileged and the expendable.

Disgusted readers canceled their subscriptions to the *Reviewer*. One man wrote that Julia Peterkin knew nothing about the South. Colored people, he said, never bury their dead in the garden; furthermore, no hound had ever been known to dig up and devour a corpse.[3] It was accepted wisdom that black people led violent, sordid lives, but heresy to suggest that white people — or even their dogs — might be responsible. Julia was indignant. "The hounds did eat those twins," she wrote to Mencken. "Shouldn't I write what is even though it is unpleasant?"[4]

Julia's cousin, Mac Stubbs, claimed that "Missy's Twins" was based on events that followed a vacation the Peterkins took when Bill was a little boy. Lavinia Berry is "Mammy," and the man and his son are modeled on Willie and Bill.[5] But there is no plantation mistress in "Missy's Twins." The white man's wife is dead, his little boy motherless. If the hounds really did eat those twins, where was Julia when it happened? Possibly she was in bed, suffering from depression. More likely, it was she who brushed off Vinner's anxiety about her pregnant foster daughter.

It is easy enough to think of reasons why Julia chose to remove herself from the story. By killing off her privileged "white" self, she was able to dodge responsibility for the situation and shift the blame to the men. Like the women in "A Baby's Mouth," Missy and Mammy get no help from men. Instead of returning Mammy to the plantation where she could help with Missy's delivery, the white man keeps the old woman in the mountains to mother his own son. Mammy's mothering is far too valuable to waste on a pregnant black girl. The black men who dig the graves are lazy and slipshod. The baby's father is never mentioned. But taking away the white child's mother also serves to make the white man more forgivable. The little boy *needs* a mother. At the end of the story, Mammy gazes at the sleeping white boy and whispers, "Po lil Mudderless."[6] There are not enough mothers to go around.

Having no mother of her own, Julia prized Lavinia Berry's nurturing. In this she was no different from the thousands of other southern white women who were cared for by black women like Maum Vinner, and who told themselves that they treated their beloved mammies "just like one of the family." Yet Julia *was* different, for she was capable of admitting that although Lavinia Berry was much loved and desperately needed, she was certainly *not* treated like one of the family.

Julia liked to say that she had been raised by a black woman named Maum Patsy, and that she learned to speak Gullah before Standard English. Her sister's children, sensitive to the implication that their aunt had been neglected as a child, are quick to correct the story. Julia, they say, was actually brought up by her grandmother.[7] As was the case in many white southern households, Julia was mothered by two women, one white and one black. Maum Patsy, she recalled, controlled her with flattery, assuring her that she was the best child who ever lived.[8] Old Mrs. Mood dispensed hard-nosed advice. "You will never be beautiful," she told the little girl, "but you can *learn* to be charming." Grandmother Mood might be a minister's wife, but she preached a worldly sermon. "In her youth," she often said, "a woman needs looks. In middle age she needs charm. But in old age, she'd better have money!" Julia had taken most of these warnings to heart, but there was one she yearned to disobey. "A woman's name should appear in the newspapers only when she is born, when she is married, and when she dies."[9]

By the time "Missy's Twins" appeared in print, Julia had found a more direct way to dramatize her fears and fantasies and get her name in the papers. Dan Reed, now the head of the drama department at the University of South Carolina, cast her as the lead in a play by Gilda Varesi called *Enter, Madame*. If Missy was Julia's projection of herself as a powerless young woman, playing Madame was a way to confront the fear that she was on her way to becoming a powerless *old* woman.

Madame is Lisa Della Robbia, an aging Italian opera star married to an American, Gerald Fitzgerald. As the play opens, Gerald is seen romancing another woman, Flora Preston, a stout, corseted, matronly lady. Gerald likes Flora because she is punctual, sympathetic, motherly, and stupid — the opposite of his wife. In fact, Gerald has just written Lisa to ask for a divorce so that he can marry Flora. He is tired, he says, of carrying his wife's poodle "through all the capitals of Europe."[10]

When Madame arrives home, Gerald tells his soon-to-be-ex-wife that she has been "the most ideal mistress a man has ever had," but no wife at all. Lisa Della Robbia is "one of the highest-paid prima donnas in Europe," but she is growing old. In fact, she forbids her son to meet her when her ship docks for fear that her public will see his long legs and realize just *how* old she is. When Gerald accuses her of deserting the boy, she declaims, "I am Della Robbia. Love is my master and my slave. I am young as eternity, old as the moon, wise as the stars." Her husband ripostes, "You're a conceited middle-aged woman whose career is on the wane. You never were a beauty at any time in your life." Holding up a mirror, he goads her to admit that she is losing her appeal. "There's too much rouge here. Too much makeup, too much trouble to gain your effects," he jeers.

Through much of the play, Lisa seems ridiculous and pitiable, but she is ruthless as well. She will stop at nothing to get her way. Under the guise of "taking it well," Lisa invites Gerald and Flora to have supper with her one night, cooing to Flora that since they will be "wives-in-law" they should also be friends. After the dinner, Gerald lingers with Lisa to "talk business" while Flora goes home. Flora, justifiably suspicious, rings him up every few minutes, until at last he takes the phone off the hook and follows Lisa into the bedroom.

In the morning, the happy servants decorate the breakfast table with orange blossoms, beaming as Lisa declares that she has decided to retire from the opera and live quietly in America, with Gerald. Flora, leading a ravenous pack of tabloid journalists, bursts in and threatens to sue Gerald for breach of promise. Lisa's son, John, worries about "the dignity of the family." Gerald and Lisa make plans to catch a boat to Buenos Aires. In the rush for the ship, Lisa hands Gerald her little dog, Toto. Gerald hesitates, then takes the dog. Madame is entirely victorious.

Julia threw herself into the role, studying Italian and practicing arias. Perhaps, consciously or unconsciously, she modeled herself on Madame, for over the next few decades, terrified of abandonment in spite of her growing fame, she would often imitate Lisa Della Robbia's machinations in an attempt to dominate the men in her own life.

When Julia and Dan Reed had a play of their own on Broadway, in 1930, Reed told a group of reporters that real theater had arrived in Columbia on the night Julia first strode onstage as Lisa Della Robbia. In South Carolina, he said, *Enter, Madame* was often referred to as "You-should-have-seen-Julia." [11] The Town Theater was little more than a tumbledown cottage, and the dressing rooms were privies fronting the alley, but the risqué dialogue, the sumptuous costumes, and the elaborate stage sets delighted the audience. The two scheduled performances sold out, and six more were given before standing-room-only crowds. The Columbia papers billed *Enter, Madame* as the cultural event of the year and hailed Julia as a consummate actress. The play then traveled to Sumter and Charleston. The name "Julia Peterkin" adorned newspapers that Julia's family could not fail to see.[12]

Hoping to impress H. L. Mencken, Julia clipped the play's reviews and mailed them to her mentor.[13] Mencken, who loathed theater, was unimpressed. What would this amateur acting accomplish except to divert Julia from her writing? In truth, Julia was eager to be diverted. Inspired by her early successes, she had tried placing stories with a number of magazines, and now rejection letters were pouring in from all sides. A chastened Julia began to question her own judgment. "Tell me the honest-to-god truth," she begged Mencken. "Do [my stories] seem vulgar to you? Somehow there seems to be in me a lack of the modesty and reticence women normally have." The men in her family, she said, thought her sketches "rather indecent and coarse." [14]

Like his father, Bill Peterkin had everything he wanted on the farm. He had started college at The Citadel, a rigorous military school in Charleston, where he was a star on the football team. After breaking his nose and shattering his knee, he transferred to the University of Virginia. Never much of a student, he was mortally embarrassed when a professor ridiculed his compositions, pointing out that he was the son of a writer.[15] When Willie suffered an attack of appendicitis in the fall of 1923, Bill was grateful for an excuse to abandon his studies and move back home.[16] Once there, he played the country squire, elaborating the role in ways that his straitlaced father never had. Bill worked hard and played hard. He took up aristocratic pursuits like horse racing and joined exclusive social clubs, courting dozens of hopeful girls along the way. Julia actively encouraged this behavior, in part because "the young Cap'n"'s dashing image increased her own prestige. It thrilled her to have a handsome, rambunctious son who was always in demand.

At the same time, she belittled Bill and Willie to anyone who would listen. *She* was "the real farmer" at Lang Syne, she said, the one who made all the management decisions.[17] She harped on Willie's infirmities so convincingly that many of her friends assumed he was an invalid, confined to bed or a wheelchair. In letters to Mencken, Sandburg, and Clark, Julia implied that Willie and Bill were all but useless. There was a grain of truth in all this. Both men were occasionally laid up, and

Julia took an unusual amount of interest in such traditionally male subjects as fertilizers, crop rotation, plant varieties, and the fluctuations of the commodities market. By no stretch of the imagination, however, was she ever "the real farmer" at Lang Syne. Visitors to Lang Syne often found Willie roaming the fields or supervising the cotton gin with Bill at his right hand. It didn't matter. Somehow no one could believe that Julia would lie about such a thing; besides, her self-created legend made for a better story.

In December 1923, Julia finally felt confident enough to meet H. L. Mencken in the flesh. If he would not come to Lang Syne, she would go to him. Julia wrote to Mencken that she had seen all the sights New York had to offer, from the aquarium to the Statue of Liberty. "I'd really rather see you than anything there now," she taunted. "I know how you loathe women and Southerners and that you are annoyed now as you read this, but of course I am right to care more for what pleases me than for whom I please, and how could you know that I want to see you unless I tell you?" [18] She had planned to stay with her sister Laura but ended up at the Commodore Hotel. To her delight, Mencken called and agreed to meet her there one evening. He encountered a "tall, somewhat slim woman with a curiously exotic air." He noted that she was exactly his own age — forty-one — and that she looked it. Julia struck him as "distinguished," he later remembered, but also as "*seduisante*" — seductive.[19] The meeting itself was pleasant and uneventful. For Julia, the most exciting part by far was coming home, where she could shock her friends by telling about her encounter with the infamous H. L. Mencken.

Carl Sandburg was also in New York, touting Julia to his publishers. Ever prudent, Julia encouraged both men to do everything in their power, yet she put her trust in Mencken. "Give the manuscript to whomever you think. Cut out whatever seems not to fit. Have it retyped, or anything. I know nothing about making books," she protested.[20]

In the fall of 1922, Lavinia Berry appeared at Julia's kitchen door during a driving rainstorm, her clothes and hair "dry as a husk." She told Julia that Brother Bob, her long-dead husband, had held an umbrella over her all the way from the Quarters. He had come, she said, to take her with him to Heaven.[21] Lavinia Berry bought new shoes and a pair of white gloves, had a seamstress make her a white shroud and a head rag to match, and gave away her meager possessions. Then she crawled into her bed and waited, refusing to eat or drink. Slowly she wasted away, watched over by women from her church. Just before Christmas she died as she had lived, quietly and without self-pity.[22]

Vinner's death devastated Julia. Of all her friends, she felt that Carl Sandburg alone could understand what the flesh-and-blood Lavinia Berry had meant to her. In a poignant letter, Julia described the day she had told Vinner good-bye. She had glanced down, she said, just in time to see a "pale starved flat insect" crawling from the neck of the old woman's nightgown, a louse abandoning Vinner's cooling body. Julia confessed that she had laughed aloud when she saw the louse. She knew how it felt, she said, abandoned and homeless.[23]

Vinner's death triggered an attack of pleurisy and thoughts of suicide. Julia suddenly saw herself as a parasite, a leech. In stories like "Missy's Twins" and "The Right Thing" she had accused southern planters of oppression, but had either edited herself out of the story or portrayed the plantation mistress as a benevolent counterforce. The small audience who appreciated her work still believed what Julia wanted them to believe. To them she was a heroine, courageously and tirelessly doing her best to minister to the unfortunate and find solutions to the "Negro problem." No one outside her immediate family had accused her of duplicity or questioned the conflicting roles she had chosen to play. But people were pressing her to take sides, to get off the fence. If she went on exposing the evils of plantation life, would she be driven from her home? If she fled from Willie Peterkin, Lang Syne, and the South, could she make it as a writer? If she stopped writing, could she bear to live the rest of her life as Miss?

Julia did not want to choose. She wanted to add the power of the liberal press to the power of the plantation. The two institutions were antagonistic to one another, but Julia was used to living with contradictions, and in 1923 it seemed entirely possible that she would be forced to give up her pedestal whether or not she continued to write. Like Vinner, the former slaves who had befriended her and schooled her in the ways of paternalism were dying off. The cotton harvest did not produce enough money to pay the bills. Blacks continued to leave the state in such numbers that for the first time since 1820, South Carolina could claim a white majority.[24] Retreating from the threat that she might have to choose between privilege and principle, Julia again turned to fiction to explore her own sense of powerlessness.

"God's Children" (later published as "Whose Children") is an elaboration of Lavinia Berry's deathbed scene. Maum Hannah is dying. Missie, a "poor little motherless," comes to bid her good-bye. When a "pale flat insect" crawls from the neck of the dying woman's gown, Missie feels a sudden kinship with the louse and laughs out loud.

Once again, Julia had christened a fictional black girl with the diminutive of her own plantation name. Missie, of course, is not a parasite. She identifies with the louse because it is a fellow creature suddenly cut off from a familiar source of warmth and nourishment. Missie sees humor in the fact that she and the louse react alike, but there is no irony in her, and certainly no political metaphors. Instead of dissecting the complicated relationship between mistress and servant, Julia made herself black, young, poor, and unmarried. The pious old women who guard Hannah's deathbed mutter darkly about Missie's failings: she ran off with her foster father and had his baby. The women let Missie know that she is not welcome in the house, but Hannah receives her as a daughter. Missie—like the pious old women, Maum Hannah, and the louse—is God's child.

In real life, Julia was unwelcome at Lavinia Berry's deathbed because she was rich, white, and powerful. She saw herself as a frightened child, Vinner's rightful daughter. As Miss, it was her prerogative to visit Vinner whenever she pleased. A host of eager reporters would later marvel that Julia Peterkin was so beloved by the people of Lang Syne, so completely accepted. Yet she was never entirely welcome in their homes, never really an insider. No matter how many knife wounds she sewed up, no matter how many sickbeds she visited, no matter how many women confided their troubles with men, Julia felt excluded from the intense life of the Quarters. In writing "God's Children," she thrust herself into the center of Lavinia Berry's life by transforming herself into Missie, the poor little motherless.

Julia sent "God's Children" to the *Reviewer,* expecting Emily Clark to "take anything I send." [25] But there were some stories even Clark would not take, and the manuscript came back. "Maybe 'God's Children' was too bad for [Miss Clark]," she wrote to Mencken. "But it happened so. Just so it seemed to me." [26]

Julia had never really known her own mother. In deference to his second wife, Julius Mood seldom spoke of Alma Mood, and even Laura and Marian remembered very little about her. As a girl Julia had spent hours gazing at a little photograph in a blue velvet frame, trying to discover her mother in the faded sepia image.[27] The only person who could — or would — tell her anything about her mother was Alma's older sister, Florence Mulligan.

In April 1883, when Julia was less than two years old and her mother had just been buried, Florence began writing a memorial for Alma's three daughters. Florence had married and left home while Alma was still a girl. Unfortunately, the Alma she knew best was not a child or a vital young woman but a helpless invalid who had returned home to her family to die, tubercular, reduced to "a skeleton with skin on it." Her mouth was filled with bloody phlegm, but the membranes were too raw for her sisters to wipe the mess away. In copperplate handwriting on twenty-seven pages of notepaper, Florence recorded every nuance of Alma's last visit to church, her last words, her funeral, the flowers, and even the clothes she wore in her coffin.[28]

Florence Mulligan meant well; she poured her own grief into "Recollections of Sister Alma Kennedy Mood." Yet the three impressionable little girls were left with a vision of their mother as a living corpse, a tortured woman racked by pain and decay. This grotesque ghost haunted Julia for the rest of her life, superimposing itself on her treasured photographs of Alma the plump and fashionable beauty. Only once, in a story that remains unpublished, did she portray her mother in fiction — as a desiccated corpse visited daily in her glass-topped coffin by a daughter known only as "the girl who looked on death." Under the glass the daughter sees "a grinning skull . . . and skeleton fingers . . . intertwined on a breast covered with frayed, whit[e] cloth."[29]

Julia always said that her mother had been "disinherited" for marrying Julius Mood.[30] The truth, according to Florence, is less dramatic. The Archers, to be sure, were pious, humorless people; they were not amused by Julius's reputation for irreverent joking. When Alma and Julius eloped, Alma's parents were displeased, but there appears to have been no lasting breach. Soon Alma's father was bringing furniture, and when grandchildren began arriving, the family members put aside their differences.[31] And it was to her family that Alma turned when she fell ill. According to everyone but Julia, the Archers behaved generously. Julia preferred to pretend that her mother gave up everything for love.

Without ever telling an outright lie, Julia also led her friends to believe that her mother had died while giving birth to her. She claimed that her birthday was ignored by the family because her birth had "caused" her mother's death, adding that from earliest childhood she had felt doomed to destroy the people she loved most.[32] This tale never failed to move her friends and disarm her enemies; those who heard it made an extra effort to remember Julia's Halloween birthday with cards, candy, and flowers. But Julia had carefully rearranged the story of her mother's life and death in order to put herself at the center of the drama.

Laura and Marian were old enough to bid their dying mother good-bye, old enough to squat fearfully under the back steps while the coffin was carried out of the house. Laura and Marian — but not Julia — were considered old enough to live with their widowed father. After the funeral, Julius took his two older girls to spend the night at a hotel in Columbia. (Julia had been left in Manning with the Moods.) He put the children to bed and then left the room, perhaps to find a drink. Laura drifted off at once, but Marian was wakeful. Before long, one of the innkeeper's grown daughters slipped into the room and offered Marian a whole bag of peppermints if she would agree never to tell what she was about to see. Then she pulled out a pair of scissors and snipped off half of Laura's curls. Marian sucked her candy, Laura slumbered on, and the woman slipped away clutching a bundle of soft blonde hair to pin into her own coiffure.

In the morning, Laura and Marian put on their bonnets and accompanied their father to Manning. No one noticed anything amiss until Mrs. Mood removed the girls' bonnets to comb their hair. The sight, as Marian later recalled, made Mrs. Mood put down her head and cry. Who, she sobbed, would be mean enough to steal hair off the head of a poor little motherless child? [33]

When no one was around to contradict her, Julia sometimes told a different version of this tale, one in which she was the victim and the stolen curls were red. Even in her late seventies, she was revising the family history so that she could play a starring role in every scene.

If Alma Mood had lived, Julia imagined that she herself would have grown up "different, somehow." [34] For one thing, she might have been more feminine, in a conventional sense — better at mothering, less outspoken, less aggressive, with less need to seek the limelight. For another, she might have been more "white," and therefore less "black." Maum Patsy and Maum Vinner might have had less influence on her personality. Would having a mother therefore have made her a happier person? Sometimes, especially when she felt persecuted by white people who disapproved of her, Julia felt that it would have.

At Carl Sandburg's urging, Julia set to work revising the free-verse monologues in Vinner's voice that Harriet Monroe had pronounced "revolting" two years before. Most were in the form of advice from an older woman to a young one. In "Greed of the Ground," a dramatic monologue about an abortion, a girl has just died. "E been proud, E been foolish," says Vinner.

> E ain' wan' *own* wha'e do.
> E ain' hab husban'.
> E ain' wan' people fo know e gwine hab a chillen.
> E do someting nudder —
> E mek ese'f trow em way.
> E dig hole;
> E buried em.
> Da chile ain' been grow to be people —
> E been des a part o' e mammy.
> E mammy buried a part o' e own se'f da day.
> E le' de groun' tase em;
> E stir de groun' appetide.
> Ki! —
> De groun' wouldn' res' tell e swallow all.[35]

In Vinner's eyes, the problem is not that the girl aborted her baby; after all, the child was still just a part of its mother. What made the girl foolish — and caused her death — was the shame that made her try to hide the pregnancy. "Don' bury no part o' you own se'f," she cautions. The girl did just that, and it killed her. Another poem in Vinner's voice varies the theme:

> Don' shet up tings
> Too tight een you' heart
> Better open you' mout'
> An' talk 'em.

"Vinner's Sayings" recount the sexual attitudes Julia learned from the black women at Lang Syne. It is foolish and dangerous to deny strong feelings, says Vinner. Yet giving in to them can be equally hazardous. "Eye-love kin fool you," she warns. It can trick two people into getting married and then slip away, leaving "dem po creeter tie han' an' foot, all-two wishin' to Gawd dey ain' nebber see one anudder!" Yet eye-love's opposite, heart-love, "mos' always come wid sorrow. Seem lak heart-love an' sorrow be's one mudder chillen."

In the final section, "Prayer from Lang Syne Plantation," Vinner foresees her own death, when her teeth will "be shet gainst a silence" and her hands will be cold and empty. She compares human life to the sun's path across the sky, rising up bright in the east so that "ebyting look shine an' beautiful," then sinking at last in the west. Vinner calls out to God: "Be a light on da da'k crooked pat'," she pleads.

> Be a shade f'om da' hot bunnin' sun.
> Be a bridge fo' me ober deep water;
> Hol' my han' tell I git across,
> Tell I git across![36]

For almost two decades, Julia had counted on Lavinia Berry to serve as her own bridge over deep water. Now Vinner was dead, and she would have to look elsewhere for comfort. She had been orphaned for the second time.

CHAPTER 5

Green Thursday

hen Harriet Monroe wrote to ask for material suitable for publication in *Poetry,* Julia sent her a copy of "Vinner's Sayings," a revised version of a manuscript Monroe had declined two years before.[1] This time, Monroe not only bought the monologues but featured them prominently. Julia protested to friends that she didn't know whether the verses were good or bad. "They aren't poetry and pretty raw in spots too," she told Mencken. "But Life is weaving the patterns here, not I. So if I write raw things I'm not to blame. . . . I wonder if your approval in print didn't win me more friends than my own merit," she added.[2]

In 1923, the phrase "black culture" struck most white Americans as an oxymoron. In New York, Chicago, St. Louis, Philadelphia, Boston, and other big cities, however, there were signs that "Negroes" were about to be "in vogue," as Langston Hughes would later put it.[5] Audiences flocked to see all-black casts sing and dance their way through jazzy musicals like *Shuffle Along*. By 1925, tourists had begun to visit Harlem. A few influential editors, including H. L. Mencken and Frank Crowninshield of *Vanity Fair*, promoted black entertainers and writers as well as books about black life.

Jean Toomer, the light-skinned grandson of P. B. S. Pinchback of Louisiana, at that time the only black man to have served as governor of any state in the Union, had just published *Cane*, a lyrical, loose-jointed riff on the lives of southern blacks that Julia read with admiration.[4] Then she found out that Toomer was staying in Spartanburg, South Carolina, her mother's hometown, gathering evidence for a damning book about how southern whites treated blacks. Why would he take on such a project if he did not believe that, as Julia characterized his thinking, "to be white is to be odious"?[5] The blacks Julia knew did not dare to project such an attitude; she had never before encountered it.

Toomer was causing consternation among her contemporaries in the South Carolina Poetry Society, which published an annual *Yearbook of Verse* and sponsored monthly poetry readings. Toomer had petitioned for membership and sent a group of his poems by mail. He was duly accepted. According to the story Julia heard, DuBose Heyward, a charter member, thought that he had discovered a kindred spirit, a white poet who had taken his advice and turned to black folk life for inspiration. Heyward wrote a long essay praising his discovery. Then he received an anonymous telegram advising him that Jean Toomer was black and "threw all his carefully-written opinion into the wastebasket."[6]

Heyward's biographer, Frank Durham, recorded a tamer story, though without mentioning Toomer's name. John Bennett, a Charleston author and illustrator, was reading the *New York Times* one day when his eye was caught by an ad for a book by a "promising Negro writer." He recognized the name from the membership roll of the poetry society, which was about to be published along with an announcement of *Cane* in the annual *Yearbook of Verse*. Suspicious that Toomer had joined the society in order to make trouble, Bennett alerted Heyward.[7]

The leaders of the society realized that they had stepped into a minefield. Heyward, Josephine Pinckney, Bennett, and Hervey Allen craved national recognition, and they were just beginning to get it. Rejecting Jean Toomer would make them laughingstocks in literary New York. Accepting him would cause an uproar in Charleston. It was one thing to write verses about "the slum Negro of the South," as Heyward was beginning to do, and quite another to recognize and associate with a black poet.[8] Caught in the crossfire between Negrophiles and Negrophobes, they left Toomer's name on the roll but cut the book announcement, then prayed that the source of their discomfort would keep quiet and stay away.[9]

Ever since she met Carl Sandburg, Julia had been anxious to strike up an acquaintance with Joel Spingarn, president of the National Association for the Advancement of Colored People and the most influential Negro booster in America. Sandburg and Mencken agreed that Spingarn could make her literary career. Julia's earlier bid for Spingarn's attention had been thwarted by underlings at Harcourt. Now she avoided the tradesman's entrance and came knocking at his front door. Someone told her that Spingarn and his wife, Amy, were planning to vacation in South Carolina. She obtained their address and invited them to visit Lang Syne. Bill's saddle horse, guns, and dogs, she said, would be theirs to enjoy. Julia dropped Carl Sandburg's name and mentioned proudly that Mary Weeks, "my best friend here," had declared that "I myself am black all except my skin." [10]

When Joel Spingarn did not reply at once, Julia persisted. In April, when he turned up in nearby Camden, she wrote again, citing a longer list of her literary acquaintances and begging him to "please risk it" and come to Lang Syne. "There's no way to tell you who I am," she wrote. "I'm white, and have lived here all of my married life, twenty years, and these last two years, two I think, I'm trying to put people and things into words. It's very difficult for me." His curiosity piqued, Spingarn drove down to read her "raw material." [11]

Spingarn assumed that Julia was offering her writing for publication in *Crisis,* the official magazine of the NAACP. Julia, on the other hand, was hoping that he would urge her to submit another manuscript to Harcourt, and she seems to have convinced herself that that was what he meant when he invited her to send him something for publication. By the time she realized — or faced — the truth, she had agreed to appear in the pages of a black publication hated by white Southerners for its aggressive exposés of lynching. After all her snide comments about DuBose Heyward's two-faced treatment of Jean Toomer, Julia now found herself playing the same game. She could not bring herself to send Spingarn a manuscript, but neither could she bear to tell him why. A long silence fell between them, during which Spingarn assumed that Julia was working on a piece for *Crisis.*

Several months after his visit to Lang Syne, Joel Spingarn wrote to inquire about the promised manuscript. Julia failed to reply. He wrote again, asking why she was ignoring him. She answered that she had sent everything she had to H. L. Mencken, then hastened to do just that.[12] Finally she bowed to the inevitable and explained why she could not possibly allow her work to appear in *Crisis*.

At the funeral for her half-brother Ashleigh's wife, she said, the Mood family had taken her aside and declared that she must stop writing about blacks. To continue would be "selfish and inconsiderate." When Julia revealed that she had been invited to publish in *Crisis*, her relatives exploded, warning her that the move would bring her "scorn" from both blacks and whites. "I positively quailed before the eyes and words of my own aunt," Julia told Spingarn. Someday, when she felt secure as a writer, she might find courage "to face every aunt, uncle, cousin." Right now, she felt that she must hold back. "A cowardly man don' tote no broke bones," she reminded him.[13]

Julia also told Spingarn that her sister-in-law had been "perhaps my best friend here." Yet there is no other evidence that the two women were close, and it seems likely that Julia revised the facts to elicit Spingarn's sympathy. Margaret Ethel Mood had been sick for a long time before she died (on April 2, 1923) of Bright's disease. When she lost her sight, her sister Leah had come to nurse her. Ashleigh and Leah — a divorcée with several children — began an affair. Ethel evidently accepted the situation. "Rub my back and then you can go spend some time alone with Ashleigh," she was once heard telling her sister.[14]

Julia knew that Spingarn would be exasperated by her retreat and feared that he might complain to her admirers. Rather than let him spread the tale, Julia spread it herself. She had no interest in the race question, she told Mencken, and saw no point in risking ostracism.[15] Mencken shot back that if she wanted to write, she had better learn to ignore her enemies. "It is impossible to do decent work in America without being suspected and accused of crime," he said.[16] Chastised, Julia tried a more playful tack with Carl Sandburg. "There are lady Ku Kluxes now," she claimed.[17]

As her letter to Spingarn graphically reveals, however, Julia had been silenced by her own clan, not by white-robed night riders. Her Mood aunts spoke from experience when they warned her away from controversy. In the late 1870s, Julius's brother Preston Mood had been expelled from college and forced to resign from a teaching job for writing an essay about evolution. It was said that Henry Mood's rise through the ranks of the Methodist clergy stopped cold when the authorities discovered that one of his sons was a heretic; if Preston Mood had kept quiet, the family believed, Henry Mood would have been a bishop. After his expulsion, Preston moved in with his parents in Manning, where he taught at a private school and wrote for the local newspaper. Soon he was in hot water again. He discovered that several prominent citizens were operating a gambling and prostitution ring, and was about to break the story when someone shot him dead through the kitchen window, planting the gun so that it appeared to be suicide. Strangely enough, when telling Mencken the story, Julia said that Preston *had* committed suicide, in despair over his expulsion. She made no mention of his work as a reporter and neglected to say that everyone close to him believed that he had been murdered. Even when the truth made a good story, it seems, Julia preferred to write fiction. Either way, Preston had paid for his honesty with his life.[18]

Julius Mood had unpopular opinions, too. Rather than publishing them, however, he had found a safe outlet in the Fortnightly Club, a group of friends who met every two weeks to air their unorthodox notions. Julia described them to Mencken as "a group of Sephardic Jews . . . who are now being made uncomfortable by the Christians, . . . a few Catholics and a few Protestants and a few Nothings." In June 1923, the club invited Julia to speak, assuring her that it was all "grave-yard talk." She could say whatever she thought without fear of her words being repeated. Castigating the South in high Menckenian style, Julia drew loud applause from her father's cronies. Julius Mood, she proudly reported to Mencken, was "both pleased and disturbed" by the performance. Her father's friends made much of the fact that Julia was the only woman who had ever been asked to appear in front of the club. They patted her on the back and exclaimed that she was a fine speaker, just like one of the boys. Ashleigh, who was also a member, was "annoyed" that his sister would stand up in front of twenty-five men and pronounce her opinions, even the ones he agreed with. Willie escaped to Charleston, "to avoid hearing me," Julia suspected.[19]

It was thrilling to aggravate the men of the family, and Julia relished the moment. Echoing one of Mencken's pet theories, she proclaimed that simple boredom was the cause of most of the South's ills; it explained cockfighting, Bible thumping, dirty politics, and even the tendency to dwell on the glorious exploits of "some grandmother [who] was a famous belle."[20] Her own grandmothers had been nothing more glamorous than ministers' wives, and Julia longed to do something outrageous. "It is much better to be a wild reprobate and then suddenly escape grisly torture," she wrote to Mencken, "than not to be threatened at all." [21] Julia compared herself with the elderly Maum Ann, a former slave at Lang Syne who stole her own daughter's chickens and sold them. "I know how she felt," Julia told Mencken. "She had to do something." [22]

Before long, she had spun Maum Ann's chicken thieving into "Maum Lou," the story of an idle soul in a household where everyone else is busy smoking meat, quilting, sewing on buttons, half-soling shoes, mending harness, cooking supper, and hauling wood. For a time, Julia empathized so thoroughly with her aged heroine that she felt like a captive herself. Maum Lou "somehow would not be condensed," she later wrote. "I don't know what got wrong with her." [23]

Maum Lou's blindness has doomed her to an old age as barren as the life Julia foresaw in the depths of her postpartum depression: "Black, gloomy sameliness made every day like every other day. Never a new thing. Not a new thought." To stir up some excitement, Maum Lou figures out a way to sneak into the chicken coop each night and make off with a hen, which she secretly sells the next day. Her son-in-law, April, almost shoots her, mistaking her for a fox or a plat-eye when he catches her in the chicken house.

"Gawd done right when he made you blind," April laughs. "Ef you had-a had two good eyes, you'd be on de chain-gang befo' Sunday." Maum Lou explains that she only stole the chickens because she felt "so lonely. So lorn. So all-by-herself, day after day." The next morning, April tells his wife that they must not leave Maum Lou home alone anymore because she is too old to take care of herself. Fanny, unaware of her mother's midnight escapades, agrees. "Ma is ol' fo-true." she sighs. "Ol'! Ol'!" [24] Maum Lou's thieving, like Julia's writing, gets her just what she craves, company and attention.

Julia's newly discovered voice — and her courage — sometimes wavered. For several months she and Mencken had been passing back and forth drafts of "The Southern Imagination," her speech to the Fortnightly Club. Imitating Mencken, Julia suggested that when someone found a cure for hookworm, malaria, and boll weevils, the South would reject Billy Sunday, Coleman Blease, and the Ku Klux Klan. [25] The South as a region was still grieving over losing the Civil War, she said, still trying to reclaim pride and identity from the ruins of the Confederacy. The evangelists who shouted from southern pulpits traded in simple-minded escapism. "The idea of God has been for the South a more wonderful creation than Romantic love," she scoffed. "By means of it the people are entering again into fairyland."[26] After suggesting numerous revisions, Mencken offered to publish "The Southern Imagination" in *American Mercury,* a new magazine he and George Nathan were editing for Alfred A. Knopf; but Julia suddenly got cold feet. She wondered if she should choose a pseudonym, or, better yet, if the article could be printed anonymously. Mencken scolded her for backing down. "You are entirely right about pseudonyms," she conceded. "I have little respect for the fearful people who use them. One must either dare or keep quiet."[27] This time she decided to keep quiet. In 1934, when the southern renaissance was in full swing and such notions were no longer considered radical, Julia would take the essay out of a drawer and deliver it as a speech to a group of college girls.

Writing nonfiction required Julia to define her thoughts, an exercise she found exhausting. But writing stories was like setting off fireworks; she started with the traits that made up her personality, parceled them out to various characters, lit the fuse by throwing these people together, and observed the resulting explosions from a safe distance. The experience was purgative, almost orgasmic at times. "Things press in on me terribly . . . and my writing is a real relief," she wrote to Emily Clark. "I get rid of my own sorrows in repeating those of others."[28]

"Over the River," the story that arrived along with the letter to Clark, is a window on Julia's "sorrows." A man comes to work at a sawmill. He takes up with the girl who cooks for the camp. When the season's work is through, he gives her some money and leaves, not knowing that she is carrying his baby. Months later she goes after him, imagining how happy he will be when he sees her big with child. No doubt he will "laugh with surprise." She hopes the child will be like him, even down to his perfect teeth, "white as rice grains."[29]

The girl has been abandoned, of course, and the reader understands her situation long before she does. But the tale has a crueler twist. This girl is deaf and dumb. Before she got pregnant she was valued as a worker because "she couldn't hear and she couldn't talk and she didn't waste time." Now, too ungainly to cook, she somehow finds the strength to cross over to the other side of the river, balancing her swollen body on the splintery cross-ties of the railway trestle. Her only worry is how she will be able to describe to others the man she seeks.

The deaf-mute girl cannot make herself heard. She encounters a group of plowmen who turn "bold mean" eyes on her body, meaning to rape her. Just then the girl's former lover rides up, shouting. She watches enviously as "the muscles in his big throat quiver . . . with his voice." But the girl has no voice. Suddenly "her lips [are] twisted and wrung with trying to speak words," to tell him who she is. He turns away. Did he recognize her? He joins the others, laughing. The girl goes into labor and loses consciousness, hoping even as she falls for the touch of his hand. When she comes back to herself, she has a baby. An old woman hovers near her in a dingy cabin. She is crushed by humiliation. Her lover did not "own" her. He did not care. He laughed at her. The deaf-mute girl struggles to talk. "If she could only say words! They would help," she thinks. But she cannot say words. She stares at her naked, helpless baby, rousing herself to brush a mosquito from his tender skin. She cannot hear the baby's cries for food, but she can see its fluttering hands and feel its quivering. She turns her back, closes her eyes, and waits for it to stop moving. Though her breasts are swollen with milk, she does not offer them to the baby. At last he dies. The girl has done to her baby what the rest of the world has done to her. She has ignored its inarticulate pleading.

Still marveling at how much the child resembles his father, the girl uses a dull ax to hack out a shallow grave in the corner of the fenced collard patch, where the corpse will be "safe from the dogs and possums and cats." The girl weeps as she heaps dirt on the tiny grave. Then she takes up her bundle and turns toward the river, stopping to drink greedily from a little spring. "Soon," the story ends, "she'd be back. Back, over the river." The girl seems to draw courage from her baby's death. Her departure is strangely hopeful; having rejected the idea of suicide, she intends to go on with her life.

"Over the River" may be a literal account of a real incident. There was a deaf-mute girl at Lang Syne. Her name was Gussie, and Julia's first version of "Missy's Twins" was titled "Gussie's Twins."[30] But the story is also a "black" version of "The Confession," a tale Julia never published.[31] In "The Confession," Edna Clark, a white girl of good family, falls into a depression when she hears that her boyfriend, Keitt Williams, has gone up North to work. Both her mother and her mammy declare that it's a good thing; Keitt comes from "poor buckra," and they don't consider him good enough for Edna. Edna grows hysterical, raving that her mother cares about nothing but "family, family, and blood." Then she slips into a severe decline. The family doctor discovers that Edna is pregnant and recommends an abortion.

Edna's mother rejects this advice. Her minister suggests that the family make a public confession of sin and then send Edna north — over the river, so to speak — for a shotgun wedding. The groom dutifully meets them at the train station in Philadelphia, but the family then makes the mistake of letting him slip away to freshen up before the ceremony. He never returns; a phone call to his apartment reveals that he has taken the train for Chicago.

Edna and her family return home, humiliated. Mammy tries to console the girl. She's not the first woman who has been "fooled," Mammy says, and she will eventually live down her disgrace. But Edna dies in childbirth. Her little sister wistfully remarks, "Don't you wish they could have lived, Mammy? . . . I'd have loved it, wouldn't you? Twas so little, like a tiny doll." But Mammy wishes only that Edna's mother had listened to the doctor. "Deys some t'ings a preacher don' know nuttin' tall bout," she exclaims.

Chances are that "The Confession" would not have been accepted for publication in the early 1920s. White girls of good families did not get pregnant in print; neither did family doctors recommend abortion. But Julia knew that such things happened.

Illegitimacy, stillbirths, miscarriages, abortions, and infanticides occur in all of Julia's novels and in many of her short stories. "The Confession" may be nothing more than a story spun out of an incident from Julius Mood's practice or an anecdote Julia overheard. Perhaps Edna's dilemma dramatizes the philosophical conflict between Julia's two "fathers," one a doctor and the other a preacher. Still, viewed against the backdrop of Julia's other fiction, "The Confession" suggests that Julia herself made a journey "over the river," long before she began to write. Keitt was a family name from the Fort Motte area, and Clark was Julia's grandmother's maiden name. Even without knowing anything more about the facts in Julia's case, we can see a pattern emerging in her treatment of black and white women as fictional characters. She gives us the black girl's private thoughts, makes us feel her pain. But she shows us Edna only from a distance, reflected in the eyes of others. Because we have no access to the workings of her mind, Edna — silenter even than the mute — hardly seems human. Julia could let herself feel the humiliation of a black woman, but not that of a white woman like herself.

The crops were poor in 1923. The South Carolina economy was depressed. The Waccamaw Hunt Club took stock of its assets and decided that Brookgreen was not destined to fulfill Julius Mood's agricultural fantasies; no one had gotten around to planting rice, and the profits from such small-scale enterprises as lime burning and truck gardening did not come near to paying the $10,000 mortgage. None of the members had cash to spare. So Brookgreen was sold. Julia feared that Lang Syne would be next on the auction block.[32] In spite of the upheaval and adversity, or maybe because these threats freed her to speak, the words Julia had been straining to form began to take shape as a book. She was still unsure of her talent, still in search of instruction. Having completed her correspondence course, she enrolled in a summer class in short-story writing at Winthrop College in Rock Hill, South Carolina, where she told her roommate that she was just "gathering goose feathers."[33] Nothing could have been further from the truth. She was honing her tools, sweating behind the plow while her professor, James Eliot Walmsley, goaded her onward.[34] Unlike Walmsley's other students, Julia already had a manuscript under consideration by a major publisher.

Prodded by Mencken, Alfred A. Knopf and his wife, Blanche, invited Julia to come to New York for a conference. Julia begged Mencken to be there with her. "I've a certain kind of courage," she explained. "This very year I lifted a swarm of bees into a hive. I killed venomous snakes. I kept calm when a shark chased mullet through the breakers between me and the shore. I ride a half-broken colt every day. But the very thought of facing Mrs. Knopf makes me shiver with fear."[35]

Julia eventually *did* face Blanche Knopf, who had recently been appointed director and vice president of the company. Mrs. Knopf selected a dozen of Julia's stories, suggested strategies for tying them together, and offered Julia a contract, sighing all the while that such a book would never sell. Julia was more optimistic. "Maybe the book will sell better than she thinks," she told Mencken. "It would make me sorry if she loses money by doing it. I find that people often like my things."[36]

In its past decade of business, Knopf had earned a reputation for discovering talent and for producing beautifully designed and crafted books. Alfred Knopf had already published T. S. Eliot, Willa Cather, Wallace Stevens, Sigrid Undset, and Thomas Mann. Moreover, he owned Mencken's brand-new magazine, the *American Mercury*. Julia found both Knopfs condescending and unlikable, but if Mencken thought she should sign with them, she would do it, she said. Mencken was the "father" of her stories, and she was willing to put their fate into his hands.[37] Coming from the woman who had just written "A Baby's Mouth,"

"Missy's Twins," and "Over the River," this was a cloudy compliment at best. But Mencken was not looking for double meanings; he enjoyed claiming literary paternity.

Julia wrote to Joel Spingarn that she wished Mencken had sent her manuscript to Harcourt. "I dare say he thinks you are too busy with people who have arrived to give time to me," she explained. "Heaven only knows what [Mrs. Knopf] will do with Gullah!"[38]

Passing over the professional writers who had helped her get into print and the relatives who had tried to keep her out of it, Julia dedicated *Green Thursday* to the memory of Lavinia Berry, who had taught her not to "shet up t'ings too tight een [her] heart."[39] She knew, however, that Lavinia Berry had never trusted *printed* words. In Vinner's experience, reading lured people away from the plantation and infected them with dangerous notions. Writing was even worse because it created a permanent record of a person's thoughts that could later be used against him.

Green Thursday was slated for publication in the fall of 1924. How would it play in New York — and in South Carolina? The public loved plantation tales, but Julia had shunned gentlemen and belles in favor of farmhands; she had disdained parlor courtships and elevated near incest to romantic heights. Most shocking of all, she had written a book from the black point of view. Many white Americans had never imagined that black farming people *had* a point of view. Carl Sandburg counseled Julia to expect the worst. "Even if the South were culturally alive," he told her, "the book would have to make slow headway."[40]

America was not ready for a work that took blacks seriously, as evidenced by the public outcry when Eugene O'Neill's *All God's Chillen Got Wings* opened at New York's Provincetown Playhouse in May 1924 with Paul Robeson in the starring role. An urbane black football star from Rutgers, Robeson seemed perfectly suited to initiate white audiences into black culture. But the black actor was to appear with a white actress. When the mayor refused to license the play, the scene was read aloud by the director standing in front of the curtain. The reviews were good, but offended whites picketed the Greenwich Village theater and shouted protests.[41] If Eugene O'Neill could be censored in Greenwich Village, what would an unknown like Julia Peterkin face?

Green Thursday is a group of twelve short, spare, unsentimental stories about a couple named Killdee and Rose Pinesett, their children Jim, Rose, and Sis, and their adopted daughter, Missie. Julia was especially pleased with her portrait of Killdee, named in the African tradition for a long-legged American meadow bird, the killdeer. She boasted to Mencken that she had made a better job of Killdee than God himself could have done.[42] Killdee is a man hemmed in by poverty. His old dog is so hungry that it gets caught in a trap while trying to eat the bait. His mule is too rickety to draw the plow down the cotton rows, too weak to chew corn. Killdee doesn't have to worry about his hogs any more; they all died of cholera. The boll weevil has not yet arrived to thwart him, but weeds choke his cotton. His whole life is a battle between the grass and the plow. And yet, like Willie Peterkin, Killdee loves to farm. He dreams of getting ahead, of trading for a better mule, of buying nice things for Rose and Missie. Sundays are torture for him — he hates to sleep late and sit idle, and he won't go to church like his neighbors. He wants nothing more than to go about his work, "watching things grow and bear and ripen under his hand."[43]

Green Thursday is another name for Pentecost, the Christian holiday observed forty days after Easter.[44] As a character in another of Julia's novels explains, the angels flew Jesus to Heaven after the crucifixion. "Satan's lightning tried to strike him and scorched the angels' wings. That happened on a Thursday in May when the fields were green with grass. The angels named it Green Thursday."[45] At Lang Syne, plowing or even hoeing on Green Thursday was considered bad luck; it could cause lightning to "beat on de land" all summer, and, as Vinner put it, "de lightnin' won' stop tell e kill em. When e's dead no crop won' grow on em. De lil-es grass-seed won' trus' em. E haffer lay shame an' naked."[46]

Killdee is skeptical. Ignoring custom, he plows on Green Thursday, determined to keep the weeds in his cotton at bay. Rose, nine months pregnant, is quarrelsome. A thunderstorm blows up. The mule is frantic with colic. And then, somehow, the baby gets burned. No one was watching, so no one knows how it happened. Little Rose lives through the night, breathing softly as Mary West and Maum Hannah spread lard over her crisp ears and fingers. At daybreak she dies, leaving behind parents tortured by guilt. Who is to blame? Killdee, for plowing on Green Thursday? Rose, for neglecting her baby? God, for sending lightning and for making little Rose love to play with fire?

These questions shadow Rose and Killdee's marriage, hovering over every conversation. From story to story, as the years go by, Rose's chronic irritability intensifies, and Killdee's already strong urge to provide for his family becomes an obsession. Grief drives them apart. Hoping to avoid another accident, Killdee teaches Jim to stay away from fire by letting him burn his fingers. But poor farmers' lives are always perilous. As in Julia's earlier story "Nancy," a hungry chicken wanders into the house one day and pecks out little Sis's eye while she rests in her cradle. Rose's anguished cry is strangely defiant. "I can' wash no mo' today," she cries. "No. Not at mah baby eye done pick out."[47] Who would ask her to? Killdee, who holds her responsible for this second accident? Only, perhaps, an insensitive employer, who does not appear in the pages of *Green Thursday*. Nothing can be done for the baby, whose empty eye socket pours red tears. Killdee resolves to kill the rooster and cut down a chinaberry tree that may have brought bad luck when he glimpsed the new moon through its branches.

Though his marriage is deeply troubled, Killdee loves his wife. He likes the feel of her flesh and admires her character to the point of seeming foolish. Young Missie looks up to Rose and tries hard to please her. Yet, from the day Missie arrives, Rose resents the girl's hold on Killdee. Missie adores him, and he looks to her for the sympathy, kindness, and gentle encouragement that is not forthcoming from Rose.

For years, Missie meekly holds her tongue and submits to Rose's abuse. By the time Missie has grown into a young woman, the tension in the house has reached the breaking point. In a frenzy of jealousy, Rose tells Killdee that Missie doesn't care about him. Missie calls her a liar. Killdee takes his wife's part and gets a leather strap to beat Missie. But when the girl lays her wet cheek against his hand, Killdee drops the strap. The book ends with Killdee's yearning to "take one joy" while he can.[48]

The story "Plum Blossoms" shows Julia's mastery of Gullah as a nuanced, piquant literary language enlarged by interior monologues. Killdee thinks in a Standard English dignified in its simplicity. Plowing in the spring dusk, he imagines a future where things are better. "Easier. When his labor, his striving, would bear fruit. He'd give his folks a better house to live in. Give them pleasures. He himself would be different. Better. Happier. Freer. [But] the picture was never quite finished. Even the clearest, plainest dreams melted, faded — without ever telling the secret of what would make them come true." We are six pages into the story before there is any dialogue, long enough for us to get inside the heads of both Killdee and Rose. It is only then that Rose begins to reveal herself. "Do don' keep on a-singin'," she carps at the cheerful Missie. "Heah lately you all de time doin' like you's a-walkin' een you sleep. Wha' de matter ail you, gal?"

This is not pure Gullah, but Gullah-flavored English, the quaint, repetitive "do don'" fooling our ears into hearing a foreign language. The brilliance of the story springs from Julia's shifts between dialect and stream of consciousness. If she had chosen to give readers only what Rose and Missie and Killdee say aloud, they might seem almost as stereotypical as Gonzales's Sam Dickerson. Instead, we are led to identify with each of them in turn. "If Missie cared about things as she ought to do, she wouldn't be singing," thinks Rose. "Not with Mike dead and Killdee in debt for the new mule — and that new harness. Missie was old enough now to feel responsibility." By the time the dialect comes to dominate the story — when Rose and Missie fight — we are so eager to see what happens that irregular spellings like "yinner" and "'oman" hardly register as odd. The cadences of Gullah seem as natural and familiar as the twang of Mark Twain's Missouri river rats.

Julia drew on her own experience in writing about family rivalries. The war between Rose and Missie is a rendering of her lifelong resentment of her own stepmother, Janie Mood, a hard-shell Baptist from the backwoods. Julius Mood met Janie Brogdon when her brother lost an arm in a cotton gin accident and he was called to sew up the stump.[49] She later became his office manager and supervised the nursing staff at the Mood Infirmary, though Julia and her sisters always insisted that she was "practically illiterate."[50] According to Julia's sister Marian, Janie told Julius lies about his daughters in an attempt to turn him against them. Julia and her sisters tormented Janie, mocking her religion and rough country ways, yet all three girls went to their graves complaining that they were innocent victims of a wicked stepmother.[51]

In fictionalizing the relationship between herself and Janie Mood, Julia shifted all her anger at Julius Mood onto the woman who had stolen his affections. Though Killdee hurts his son for his own good in "Teaching Jim," there is no conflict, sadism, or bitterness in his relationship with Missie. Rose, on the other hand, is rude, mean, abusive, and deceitful. The sweet, passive girl does not deserve such ill treatment, and in the end she gets her reward, the love of her "father." The wicked stepmother is abandoned. Killdee's infatuation with the girl he brings home as a helper for his wife also recalled a more recent family scandal, her half-brother Ashleigh Mood's affair with his sister-in-law Leah.

If anyone had suggested that she was writing the family soap opera in blackface, Julia could respond that, with minor variations, *Green Thursday* was the true story of the plantation foreman and his wife. Nannie and Ellis Sanders lived almost in Julia's backyard, in a wing of the old farmhouse that had been moved down the hill when the new house was built. From her back porch Julia could observe their comings and goings. Not everything that ended up in *Green Thursday* really happened to Ellis and Nannie, but some of the most dramatic incidents did. In "A Sunday," for example, Rose spends the night with the preacher when they go off to a convention in the city. The congregation vows to turn Rose out of the church the next Sunday, and the news reaches Killdee's ears from Mary West.

Killdee has been slow to catch on to the fact that Rose is involved with another man. Until Mary West lays it out for him, he has carefully ignored his wife's newly acquired "stylishness" and her sudden interest in the church. He refuses to see what everyone else on the plantation knows. Mary herself is Killdee's sometime lover; he suspects that some of her children may be his. Yet he is angry with her for talking "this low-down talk" about Rose. Mary bristles. "Wha' I keer ef de deacons tu'n Rose out de chu'ch?" she snaps. "I ain' no member. No. I'd scorn to be one. You hanker fo' 'oman lak Rose, enty? A 'oman who kin set up een de choir. An' sing. An' pop chewin'-gum een 'e mout'. An' wear fine clo'es. An' shout 'bout Gawd an' Jedus. Dem is de kinder 'oman you crave, enty? Good Day! I gwine!" [52]

Hurt and angry, Killdee is not sure who is to blame. He talks over the problem with Daddy Cudjoe, the conjure doctor, who shrewdly suggests that Killdee must be afraid of something. Back home, Rose has taken to her bed. The preacher has not showed up for church. The congregation spends the week gossiping about how the deacons will surely turn Rose and Reverend Felder out of the church. The next Sunday, Killdee strides up the aisle, enters the pulpit, and faces the people. "I come heah fo' say des one t'ing. One!" he announces. "De fus' nigger eber call my wife name een dis chu'ch is got to deal wid me! Killdee Pinesett!" [53] After this outburst, nobody dares to mention Rose's name, so she remains a member in good standing. But Reverend Felder is not so lucky. He dies of lockjaw caused by a mysterious wound.

Julia loved to laugh about the time Nannie borrowed her silk nightgown from the laundry and wore it on an excursion with the preacher. Ellis followed them to town and blasted a load of buckshot through the locked door of their room. Nannie came home with pellets in her backside. Julia's nightgown came home with the rest of the wash, clean but full of holes.

Like Killdee, Ellis defied the congregation to call his wife's name.[54] He did run off with another woman, though not with his foster daughter.[55] A red rooster really pecked out the eye of Ellis's cousin, Maybell "Dode" Sanders. There was a man named Killdee at Lang Syne, and a woman named Rose, but they were not married to each other. Apparently Julia borrowed only their names.[56] The rest of *Green Thursday* was built of memory, gossip, observation, and invention.

If the book had opened with "Green Thursday," the title story, readers might have assumed that Killdee and Rose owned a small homestead. But the first story, "Ashes," sets the scene on a plantation, where the Big House is shielded from the Quarters by a thick wall of greenery. The plantation "sits always calm," unaltered in appearance by changes in the world outside.[57] Yet in "Ashes," the old traditions are breaking down. The original owners are "all gone." As Maum Hannah explains, "Times was tight. Dey had to sell de plantation an' go."[58] The blacks are left behind, squatters without a claim.

A white man builds a house next to Maum Hannah's cabin and tells her she must find another place to live. "We can't have you a-livin' here in our back yard," he says. "Of course, if you was young enough to work, it 'ud be different, but you ain't able to do nothing. I'll need your house anyway to put a cook in."[59] Hannah stays up all night waiting for a sign from God that will tell her what to do. The ashes in her pipe and the red glow of the sunrise make her think about fire. She gathers kindling and coals, and blows up a fire on the white man's new porch. Then she walks all the way to town to tell Sheriff Hill that she has burned down the buckra's house. "I reckon you haffer put me on de chain-gang — I done so ol', too — I wouldn't be much count at you put me on," she sobs.

Sheriff Hill knows that Maum Hannah is acting. He asks, "Did your house burn too?" "Oh, no, suh," she answers. "Jedus sen' a win' fo' blow de spark de udder way." The sheriff tells his cook to get Maum Hannah some breakfast. Then he drives her home, warning, "It's best not to talk much, Auntie." Sheriff Hill asks around and finds out that the white man has insurance on the house. To Maum Hannah's relief, he has no plans to rebuild, because "it's a bad-luck place."[60]

Like "Missy's Twins," "Ashes" is a realistic tale about the ritualized southern manners that keep social distinctions in place. Julia may have planted it at the beginning of *Green Thursday* to fend off criticism from both the left and the right. For conservative Southerners she offered a benevolent sheriff and an aristocratic family who had been forced off their land. For liberal Northerners she threw in social and racial conflict, with poor blacks pitted against an emerging white middle class with the money to buy property, build houses, and purchase insurance. None of this has much to do with Killdee and Missie and Rose, although Killdee is referred to in passing as Maum Hannah's "niece."

Peterkin was fascinated by the way Gullah speakers played with English conventions of gender, whether by blurring personal pronouns, by giving men "feminine" sounding names, or, as here, by reversing male and female nouns. Left to herself, she would have reproduced many examples of this reversal, but Mencken advised her that doing so would only confuse her audience.

Looking back over Julia's early stories after she won the Pulitzer Prize in 1929, Robert Adger Law singled out "Ashes" as marking a turning point in her attitude toward "the romantic past of Thomas Nelson Page." After writing this story, he said, Julia "turned away from her forebears and struck out for herself." [61] Once you get past "Ashes," to read *Green Thursday* is to live as Rose, Missie, and Killdee — to identify first with one, then another. The plantation as they know it is a small village that survives by farming, not a colonial enterprise designed and run by whites or the stage set for a costume drama. The villagers hope and worry and work, make love and mourn their dead. Many are full of pent-up rancor, which they spend on each other, and on themselves. Killdee blames fate, and God, for his troubles. "He could fight men," he thinks. "Settle with them. But God — Ha! — that was a different matter. God kept out of reach. Yes. He did his worst. He cut men at the very roots. Blighted them. He burned tender girl-children. And nobody could ever get even with Him!" [62] In reality, black men in Killdee's situation could *not* fight white men, or white women. For them, people like the Peterkins *were* fate. Eventually, Julia would be forced to confront this truth. In 1924, however, allowing Killdee his dignity was radical enough.

Two thousand copies of *Green Thursday,* bound in green-and-purple mottled covers, were published on September 12, 1924. Julia loved to tell the story of how she asked Hester Cheseboro to put a spell on the book in order to ensure its success. "Whoever read these here stories, they will be seal on his heart," Hester supposedly declared. [63]

Green Thursday reminded Julia of her newborn Bill, who, though "his poor head was a bit scrunched and his complexion was dreadful," had seemed precious and miraculous to her. [64] She had Knopf send advance copies of the book to Mencken, Bellamann, Sandburg, and Spingarn, and to her father, brother, and brother-in-law Robert Adams. Spingarn responded at once: "Nothing so stark, taut, and poignant has come out of the white South in the last fifty years," he wrote.[65] Sandburg called it "a real and fine book" and reported that novelist and critic Laurence Stallings had pronounced it "the best book ever written about the South." [66]

At home, the response to her book was stone-cold silence. Two long weeks passed. Nothing happened; no one said a word.[67] In the Robert Adams household, where Julia and Willie ate supper every Saturday, the book lay in plain sight, but it might as well have been invisible for all anyone said about it. Willie refused to read *Green Thursday;* the dialect was so obscure, he claimed, that he couldn't make sense of it. He may never have read far enough to discover that Killdee's heroic struggle to make a profitable crop had been inspired by his own.[68]

Julius Mood recovered his composure first, driving in from Sumter on the heels of a receding flood to tell Julia that he considered *Green Thursday* "the first real expression the negroes in the South have ever had." "I've won so little praise from him in my life that his evident emotion when he talks about this gives me a real tingle," Julia told Mencken. Willie's sullen annoyance was stifled by Julius's approval: "Now that Father has made his decision that the book is good, everything is settled. Concluded," said Julia.[69] The rest of the family would fall into line.

Meanwhile, book reviewers were hailing *Green Thursday* as a breakthrough in modern letters. The *New York Times Book Review* set the tone, describing the book as a novel of "negro peasant life in the South" utterly unlike "the darkey stories which infest our magazines." [70] Other voices chimed in. *Vogue* congratulated Julia for avoiding what it called "the hysterical Boston attitude — bastard of the abolition days — that, if anything, niggers are better than white people." The reviewer was pleased to find "none of the floridness that characterized Southern writing. It is simplicity itself," he said, "gruesome at times; keenly analytical at others." [71] Mencken announced that Julia's "poetic prose" almost brought "a lump to the throat." [72] Sandburg went so far as to suggest that *Green Thursday* deserved a Pulitzer.[73]

The *Columbia Record* reported that Gittman's bookstore sold more than sixty copies of *Green Thursday* in the first few days it was on the shelves.[74] It reprinted the *New York Times* review along with Henry Bellamann's opinion that *Green Thursday* was "by far the profoundest book that has been written about the negro." Bellamann expected it to shock South Carolinians. Some, he said, would find it "disagreeable and hideous." Others would argue that Negroes were incapable of introspection. "There are many people who live on Southern plantations who have little inklings of these tragic depths that stir so silently around them," he remarked.[75]

Bellamann was right. The *Columbia State*, a more important newspaper than the *Record*, kept Julia on tenterhooks. Julia sent the editor several reviews from other sources and waited weeks before a small excerpt was reprinted. When the *State* finally commissioned an original assessment of *Green Thursday*, the reviewer privately confided to Julia that his essay had been so drastically pruned that the piece as printed "looked like a dog with the tail cut off." "In the courts here when a criminal is too bad to be able to secure a lawyer for his defense the Judge appoints one," Julia told Mencken. "And so, the *State* agreed to print [this] opinion."[76] Julia had expected better. She suspected that Ambrose Gonzales and Charlton Wright, the editors of the *State* and the *Record*, respectively, were using her as a pawn in their own battle. Wright was a liberal who, as Gerald Johnson once remarked, "laid violent hands on taboos that no South Carolinian has dared touch for generations."[77] Gonzales was an unreconstructed Confederate.

Julia also assumed that because he too wrote dialect stories, Gonzales must be jealous of her success. No doubt the old man did crave praise, but not from the likes of H. L. Mencken and Laurence Stallings. Designated "the Dean of the dialect" by the South Carolina Poetry Society, Gonzales regarded the kind of tributes Julia was attracting as a sure sign that she had gone wrong.[78] Much later, Julia would come to feel a curious kinship with Gonzales. For now, however, he represented the breed of Southerner she most wanted to shock. According to her friends in Columbia, the whole staff of the *State* was "annoyed and mortified" by *Green Thursday* because she had "printed those fearful words 'S.O.B.'"[79] What really bothered Gonzales and his allies, of course, was the fact that Julia had portrayed blacks as fully human people and not as "supermonkeys" or "alligator bait."[80] The paternalistic white sheriff of "Ashes" did not soothe their feelings in the least. Too much the gentleman to attack Julia directly, Gonzales got back at her by editorializing that her friend Mencken simply did not understand the better class of Southerners, since he had "not yet met one of them." "I have made a social breach, and am being disciplined a bit," Julia told Mencken. "They're uncertain what I may write next time."[81]

The *State*'s icy treatment of *Green Thursday* amused Mencken; it was proof that Julia had hit a nerve. He expected South Carolina to come around eventually, just as Julius Mood had done. "Some day they will take visiting delegations of Elks and Rotarians to see her," he crowed.[82]

Sandburg took a longer view. "As sure as you do anything worthwhile, likely to stand the test of time, there will be murmurings. And old murmurs change and become friendly — while new murmurers arise." [85] Already, Julia reported, "the old lady who keeps the Relic Room of the United Daughters of the Confederacy" in Columbia had written to ask for a copy of *Green Thursday*, because "the children of tomorrow should know about the Negroes of today." "Queer relic it would be," quipped the author, wary that the UDC would find a way to embrace *Green Thursday* as a glorification of the Old South.[84]

When Julia retreated to Murrells Inlet to fish and swim in late September, she had to face the fact that Brookgreen was no longer part of her estate. Just a few miles up the coast, at Myrtle Beach, developers had begun to build hotels.[85] Home felt hostile. The more strangers praised her, the more her friends and relatives bristled. And Julia was not altogether gracious about her success. She boasted about her triumphs, taunting both her rivals and her detractors.

One great admirer of *Green Thursday* was Walter White, another of Alfred Knopf's literary discoveries. As assistant secretary of the NAACP, White's job was to investigate reports of lynchings. Knopf had just published White's first novel, *The Fire in the Flint*, the story of a young black doctor in rural south Georgia who antagonizes local whites by organizing sharecroppers to demand better treatment from their landlords, by accusing a white man of shooting a black, and by refusing to act less educated than he is. Kenneth Harper pays a terrible price for his self-assertion. His sister is raped; his brother kills her assailants and then shoots himself just as a mob closes in. Harper himself is shot dead by the Klan after he saves the life of a white girl.[86]

Walter White sent Julia a signed copy of *The Fire in the Flint* because, he said, he was so impressed with *Green Thursday*. Julia replied, "Your book moved me with such pity and such terror I could hardly go on to the end. What a stark picture you have made! . . . The county seat ten miles away staged a klan parade recently. . . . However, since the plantation is an almost complete world in itself and we are beholden to nothing but the earth for our living, it is unlikely that we shall be touched except lightly with all of this." [87]

Walter White provided influential black leaders with copies of *Green Thursday*, mailed out 250 copies of a favorable review to a nationwide network of black newspapers, and urged black-owned bookstores to stock the book.[88] These were generous deeds for a writer whose book was being compared with Julia Peterkin's and found wanting, but White hoped that *Green Thursday* might soften the hearts of people who taught their children that burning and dismembering black men was as much fun as "Christmas morning or the circus."[89] To him, *Green Thursday* seemed "a corking piece of work."[90] A reviewer for *Opportunity* magazine, a publication of the National Urban League, called the book "a quiet revolution" and marveled that "a refined South Carolina woman, isolated on a plantation," could write with such "penetrating sympathy."[91] In the *Atlanta Journal,* librarian Frances Newman put the matter into perspective: "Of course, I do not feel that I know whether or not Mrs. Peterkin has accomplished the almost impossible task of seeing into Killdee's heart and mind and soul, but whether it is his psychology or her own, the picture is always true to its own values."[92]

An anonymous reviewer for one of the country's foremost black newspapers, the *Chicago Defender,* was undecided. "For once we cannot say right off-hand whether we like [the book] or not," he wrote. "We usually have a pretty definite reaction to this race problem stuff." The reviewer was disconcerted by the fact that he did not know "Miss Peterkin's racial identity." He guessed she must be white, but "one can never be too sure these days."[93] The *Defender* was a militant paper with a huge national circulation; the question it raised would eventually become crucial to Julia's literary reputation. *Should* it matter whether the author of *Green Thursday* was white or black? Must we know the author's race in order to judge her stories? The one thing this reviewer *was* sure of, he said, was that the characters seemed overwhelmingly *real.*

In the *New York World,* Laurence Stallings marveled: "It is extraordinary that these sketches were done by a white writer." He predicted that *Green Thursday* would "stand alone as a contribution to American letters."[94] Two years before, James Weldon Johnson had decreed that "what the colored poet in the United States needs to do is something like what Synge did for the Irish. . . . He needs a form that is freer and larger than dialect, but which will still hold the racial flavor . . . which will also be capable of voicing the deepest and highest emotions and aspirations."[95] No one, not Laurence Stallings, James Weldon Johnson, W. E. B. Du Bois, or the staff of the *Chicago Defender,* had expected a privileged southern white woman to leap the fences and homestead in this uncharted territory. Yet Julia had done it, had staked her claim. As Carl Sandburg had predicted, the mistress of Lang Syne plantation had reinvented herself as "the Turgenev of the plantation niggers," the Synge of the American South. What would she do next?

CHAPTER 6

Cross Purposes

hen Willie Peterkin fell ill in the fall of 1924, Julia again bundled him off to Richmond for treatment.[1] Whether by accident or by design, his hospitalization coincided with a major book fair, and Julia, who had not been officially invited, checked into the hotel where it was being held. Writers and publishers bustled through the lobby, deep in conversation. Roaming the halls, Julia recognized Joseph Hergesheimer, the portly novelist and critic who had been warned away from her by Emily Clark. Hergesheimer's well-publicized tastes ran toward extravagant clothes, lush period interiors, and willowy women. "If I had been young and beautiful I'd have introduced my-self to him," she told H. L. Mencken. As it was, "I didn't dare." [2]

But Julia was not one to remain a wallflower for long. She made her presence known to Emily Clark, who hastily got up a "tea" in her honor.

It was a rollicking party, amply stocked with notables and bootleg gin, but Joe Hergesheimer never showed up, possibly because Emily had left him off the guest list. Julia consoled herself by taking charge of a "literary" young man who had knocked back too many drinks. Murmuring endearments, she fed him strong coffee until he sobered up enough to stagger to James Branch Cabell's house, where another party was in progress. There he passed out for the night.[3]

Despite a certain duplicity on the part of both women, a warm epistolary friendship had ripened between Julia and Emily, who had much in common. Both were southern women of good family who had launched themselves into the male world of letters without really understanding what membership in that society would entail. They compared scoldings from outraged friends and relatives, traded information about H. L. Mencken's state of mind, and looked to each other for professional reassurance. Emily was engaged to be married and was planning to resign from the *Reviewer*. The magazine would move to the University of North Carolina at Chapel Hill, where Professor of Philosophy Paul Green would assume the editorship. A white man who wrote plays drawn from black folk life, Green would nurture the "southern" character of the magazine, but the *Reviewer*'s quirky, eclectic spirit departed along with Emily. Her final issue included "Daddy Harry," a widower's lament in Julia's early style.

Back at Lang Syne, Julia celebrated the holidays as she had for the last twenty years, with rituals surviving from the slave era. On Christmas Eve, she attended Watch Night services at the plantation meetinghouse. "All night long," she later recalled, "singing voices float out into the darkness and join the blurred songs of the wind in the trees until the morning star rides high in the sky and the Christmas sun rises shouting in the east."[4] Shortly after dawn, the house servants began bursting into her kitchen, shouting, "Christmas gift!" Other, less favored residents of the Quarters arrived later, bearing new-laid eggs, live chickens tied at the ankles, bags of peanuts, ears of popcorn, or jars of sorghum. Julia returned these compliments with small gifts of her own — an apron, a box of candy, a bag of fruit. She poured each man a shot of whiskey, raising her own glass as they drank her health. Then everyone gathered around an enormous Christmas tree out on the lawn, where black children were presented with toys, fruit, and candy. (Visiting white children often received larger gifts.)[5] Afterward, the residents of Lang Syne sang Christmas spirituals. "The words of the beautiful songs are few," Julia would later write, "but their refrains repeated over and over in a thundering swirl unite us all in voice and faith and joy and help us to know that Christmas Day is the best day of our year."[6]

If these Christmas ceremonies paid tribute to racial harmony at Lang Syne, as Julia later chose to suggest, they were also a kind of command performance staged for the benefit of a white audience nostalgic for the trappings of slavery. Most inhabitants of the Quarters were cheerful enough about singing the old songs, for as soon as they did, it was officially "Christmas week," when no one was expected to do any work. Every night the big drums boomed out, announcing a party in somebody's cabin.

During the short Lang Syne winter of 1924–25, Julia puzzled over what to write next. Tired of doing dialect, and of fending off charges that she was a "negro propagandist," she yearned to write a book about herself, without the blacking. For some time she had been sketching in fragments of an autobiography, vignettes of her childhood and her marriage. Now she began piecing them together.

As the story of her life began to take shape, Julia returned again and again to memories of her "bastard lover," the man Julius Mood had prevented her from marrying.[7] She considered having her old boyfriend reappear, still mourning for the red-haired girl he had once loved. What would happen if he suddenly showed up, or if she met another man who stirred her in the same way? For Julia, as for most women of her day, where she lived and how she spent her days had been determined by her choice of a husband. Becoming a plantation mistress had been the side effect of an unhappy compromise: in marrying the staid, respectable Willie, she had sacrificed passion to social status. Or had she? Marriage to the son of a textile manufacturer would have made her the mistress of another realm — the factories and company towns of the upstate, with their poor white laborers. Could she have been happy as the wife of an industrialist who had no feeling for the land? How would she have been different in another situation? These were fascinating questions to Julia, of course, and she assumed they would interest other people, too. But the going got harder as she moved into the present and tried to explain who she had become.

By February, Julia had tired of wrestling with her image, and with her growing distrust of the Knopfs. In spite of the glowing reviews, *Green Thursday* was not selling well, and Julia blamed her publishers. Only the year before, she had felt flattered to sign a contract giving Alfred A. Knopf an option on her next two books. Now she felt trapped. The Knopfs, she complained in a letter to Mencken, seemed "determined that [*Green Thursday*] should fail." [8] Mencken couldn't believe his eyes. She should be grateful to have such a distinguished publisher!

It slowly began to dawn on Julia that Mencken and the Knopfs might be looking out for their own interests, not hers. She needed someone else to assess the situation, someone who understood their enormous power without being cowed by it. So in February 1925, when Maxwell Aley and his wife, Ruth, invited her to join them in Cos Cob, Connecticut, Julia jumped on the train. Max Aley, a literary wheeler-dealer with impressive-sounding connections, seemed heaven-sent for the role of assessor. He was an officer of PEN, the international writer's organization newly founded to combat censorship, and although he made his living mainly by editing a women's magazine, he was building up an impressive list of clients and contacts moonlighting as a "contact editor" for the publishing firm of Bobbs-Merrill. [9]

Aley hoped to divert Julia's next book to Bobbs-Merrill, so he was sympathetic to her problems. She wanted his help but hesitated to hire him as a go-between for fear of offending Mencken. Aley was willing to bide his time and provide some free advice. After sorting through the threads of Julia's dilemma, he coached her to force a showdown with the Knopfs. She made an appointment, went to New York, and presented a list of her grievances. The Knopfs remained cool. Yes, they expected first refusal on her next book. No, they could not devote more time and money to promoting *Green Thursday*. The book must stand or fall by itself.

Henry Bellamann, who had just accepted a job at the Juilliard School of Music, was also in New York, without his wife, and Julia arranged to meet him for lunch one day. Something about Bellamann had always brought out the devil in Julia. He was so circumspect, so dispassionate, so careful about everything he did; she couldn't help needling him to break loose. Bacheloring in the city, Henry was vulnerable, in the mood to take a dare, and he agreed to escort Julia to a party.

It was not just any old gathering; for Julia, it amounted to a coup. The hosts were Joel and Amy Spingarn, and the guest of honor was Walter White. Julia had a few drinks and got into the spirit of taboo breaking; soon she was the life of the party. Fascinated by Walter White's blond hair and blue eyes, she spent a heady afternoon discussing race, literature, and White's boundless admiration for *Green Thursday*. Henry watched from the sidelines. He had never expected their private lunch to lead to a scene like this. Afterward, Julia went back to South Carolina, and Henry stayed in the city. [10]

As always, Lang Syne seemed hushed and tranquil after New York. Julia looked forward to riding her horse, planting a garden, getting back to work on her new book. Yet before she even had time to unpack, a car careened into the driveway and her friend Isaac Weston leaped out. It was all over Columbia, he announced. Henry Bellamann had written about it to his wife, and everyone was talking. *Julia consorted with Negroes.*[11]

Julia was furious. Henry had betrayed her! To hear him tell it, she had set him up, tricked him into socializing with blacks. He knew who the Spingarns were, and he knew that any party they gave would include black guests.

It is easy to imagine what happened to Henry: the minute he sobered up, he started worrying that his wife would find out that he had gone on a date with Julia. It must have seemed safer to tell her himself, whipping up the race issue to divert her fury toward Julia. Katherine Bellamann took the bait and spread the damaging story.

Julia did not deny having deliberately attended a party with educated blacks. In South Carolina, that was the only fact that mattered.[12] Half expecting the Ku Klux Klan to appear on her front lawn, she begged H. L. Mencken to write her a "pleasant obituary" if they did.[13] "I only hope they didn't attempt to throw you in the river!" he jovially replied.[14] South Carolinians did not lynch prominent white women; they withheld invitations and whispered insinuations about their ancestry. "If it were not that I am blond," Julia wrote to Carl Sandburg, "I think an effort would be made to prove that I am half black. Maybe I am, spiritually."[15]

A few years earlier, Julia might have dodged Walter White, just as DuBose Heyward had avoided Jean Toomer. Now she peppered him with questions by letter. Why did White not pass himself off as a white man? Why did he risk persecution and rejection when, with his light skin and blond hair, he could so easily avoid them? White people could be just as nasty to other white people as to blacks. Why was he so bitter?

A consummate diplomat, White sidestepped the personal and asked Julia in turn how he could *avoid* feeling bitter when lynchings were epidemic and the white answer to the "Negro problem" was always "send them back to Africa" or "give them all a vocational education."[16] Feeling misused herself, and fishing for reassurance of the kind she had once received from Lavinia Berry, Julia complained that people in South Carolina (white people, that is) were attacking *Green Thursday* as "Negro propaganda." White is bound to have felt irritated by Julia's confidences. She seemed to share her neighbors' feeling that writing "Negro propaganda" was a sin and to think name-calling was as hurtful as lynching. But Julia was a potential ally, and rather than drive her away, White sought to convince her that they were soulmates in a great cause. Quoting Havelock Ellis, he pompously reminded her that "the greatest writers must spend the blood and sweat of their souls amid the execration and disdain of their contemporaries."[17]

However bruised she may have been from the critics' blows, Julia was certainly not suffering the kind of attacks leveled at black writers. White was an easy target for abuse and often put himself in danger, especially while traveling in the South. Julia, by contrast, was dealing with petty social slights. It hurt her to hear that Yates Snowden, the patriarch of the University of South Carolina's history department, turned on his heel, flourished his cape, and left the room whenever her name was mentioned in his hearing.[18] And when another professor at the university, Reed Smith, told his creative writing class that by publishing *Green Thursday* Julia Peterkin had proved herself unfit to associate with decent young people, she sent word by a mutual friend that she considered herself insulted. Caught in violation of the code of chivalry, Professor Smith hastily apologized. He had been maliciously misquoted, he said, and would be honored to have Julia come and speak to his class. Julia stayed home.[19]

As lonely as she felt, however, Julia was not the only South Carolinian drawing fire for writing about black folk. DuBose Heyward had just published *Porgy,* a story set on the wharves and backstreets of Charleston about a crippled beggar who falls in love with a prostitute. The book was a great hit in New York; in South Carolina, its reception was chilly. Yates Snowden fumed that *Porgy* was a "brilliant" book which ought to have been about "WHITE FOLKS."[20]

Writing for the *Bookman* later that same year, Heyward profiled a growing band of southern writers who offended the sensibilities of neo-Confederates like Smith and Snowden. Since well before the Civil War, the South had managed to stifle all discussion of the way poor people were treated there simply by declaring it to be in "bad taste." Literate whites knew what that meant: it was not polite to mention blacks, poor whites, mill workers, or sharecroppers except as comic relief.[21] Though Heyward stopped short of saying so, books sympathetic to the lower classes were resented by well-to-do Southerners as a threat to their status, to their comfortable way of life. He was no more capable than they of saying it, but such books raised ominous questions about who did the work, and who got the credit and the money. Ask the questions, and change was sure to follow, toppling the white elite.

For the moment, Julia was untroubled by dread of political upheaval; her contradictory life was bringing rewards. The critical success of *Green Thursday,* though it didn't sell many books, had created a demand for her poetry and short fiction. Mencken and Nathan accepted "The Sorcerer," a sustained psychological portrait of a man facing death, for *American Mercury.* E. J. O'Brien selected "Maum Lou" for his annual collection of *Best Short Stories,* and Harriet Monroe requested another installment of "Venner's Sayings" for *Poetry.* Even "Whose Children" finally found a home, in Knopf's *Borzoi 1925.* Julia was delighted to make it into the *Mercury,* yet when Mencken urged her to try her hand at nonfiction she begged off. "I'm so much alone that I have formed a habit of letting images take charge in my brain, and I cannot always get rid of them when I want to," she explained. "It seems rather dreadful not to have definite control over one's thinking, but I haven't, and there's no use to pretend about it." [22] One might think from this description that Julia had hit her stride; she sounds like a writer in the throes of inspiration, reaching into her subconscious for material. But something had gone awry.

The runaway images were part of her new novel, a fictionalized autobiography she called "On a Plantation." In January 1925, Julia asked Mencken to promise that as soon as the last page was complete, he would read it and advise her. "If it seems wrong to you, don't let me go further with it," she implored. "The world is already too full of trash." [23] On April 25, she mailed him a manuscript. He opened the package full of hope, but his excitement soon turned to dismay.

"On a Plantation" is a terrible novel. No one today would read it for pleasure, yet it is important for what it tells about Julia's evolution as a writer and how she saw her own life. Helen West, her middle-aged heroine, lives on a South Carolina plantation called Blue Brook. Her husband, Ellesley, spends most of his time in New England, where, like the "bastard lover," he owns several cotton mills.[24] Their son, Bill, is away at boarding school. The unnamed narrator, Helen's cousin, is a painter. Although he was born at Blue Brook, he was raised in the North.

When her attractive young cousin arrives for a visit, Helen takes him on a guided tour, pointing out people and filling him in on their history. The foreman has just died, she explains, after losing his toes and then his legs. Bully, the long-lost husband of Cely, the washerwoman, has returned to the plantation covered with smallpox. A black woman named Nettie approaches Helen and her cousin, clutching a tiny cream-colored infant. Helen whispers that Nettie is a thief who murdered her own husband. "You'd better be careful or before you know it, you'll be lying out in those rice-field mud-flats beside [your dead husband]," she hisses to Nettie. The startled narrator begins to fear that his cousin is "lawless and dangerous." [25]

How has Nettie come to live in a cabin so new that its boards are still yellow? Who is the father of the "pale, sickly tan" baby? How could this mother and child pose a threat to Helen's twelve-year-old son? The more the narrator presses for answers, the less information Helen volunteers. The baby probably belongs to the postmaster, she says, before quickly changing the subject.

Helen's cousin sees and hears other things that chill his blood. The servants mutter that the Wests have drawn bad luck to the place with their radios, electric pumps, and insecticides. Black women in scanty clothes gaze at the narrator "brazenly," flaunting their "candid breasts and lithe waist[s]." Someone lays a "death-sheet" at the foot of Helen's bed, and she and her "Da" (an intimate term for the black nursemaid-turned-bodyservant who raised her) discuss revenging this act by exposing the perpetrator (they assume it was Nettie) to smallpox.

There are no happy people in "On a Plantation." Everywhere he looks, the narrator sees open hostility simmering between whites and blacks. Speaking through him, Julia set out to contradict every sentimental stereotype of the plantation myth, even the ones she had earlier promoted. In a typical scene, Helen confesses to her cousin that as a small child visiting a black woman's cabin, she picked up a string of "birthing beads" and draped them around her neck. The owner angrily snatched them off, scolding that they were "not for little white girls to wear, but for grown black women." Though Helen offers no interpretation of this event, it is clear that the beads, brought over on a slave ship, symbolize to the black woman the one thing white women cannot borrow, buy, or steal — a spiritual link to Africa.

The inconsistencies in Helen's character infuriate the narrator. He wants her to be pure and simple, a damsel in distress. She is really a femme fatale playing him like a trout, leading him on, watching his reactions, making him fall for her, and then pulling back. Everything she says is calculated; everything she does is part of the game.

But Helen is not inhuman, and she sometimes drops her guard. Like Julia Peterkin, she envies her servants' expressiveness, narrative skills, and coherent system of beliefs. Also like Julia, she has spent the past several years transcribing their stories. "The negroes have no means of expressing what they think but with the pictures they put into words," she tells her cousin, and then proceeds to contradict herself. "I doubt very much that they believe [their myths] any more than I do, but they love to tell the wonderful tales and I love to hear them. They've made them tall enough and wide enough to fit the height and breadth of the sky — deep enough to hold all the mystery of the ocean." The narrator is irritated; to call black folk tales an "artistic achievement," he says, is going too far.

To her cousin, Helen West appears to be a desperate woman trapped in a remote and primitive hell, victimized by her cold-blooded husband and "tainted" by her long exposure to blacks. "I saw her standing alone in a world where there was no solitude but her own," he says. "She was being destroyed by that solitude." Casting himself as a knight in shining armor, the narrator decides to "save" Helen by taking her away to a place where people are "normal." That night he embraces his cousin and begs her to run away with him. She shrugs him off. "Little sins are not interesting," she explains, "and so I've waited for a big tempting sin to cross my path."

"Then what will you do?" he asks.

"I'll give up my hope of Heaven for it," she answers.

Sleeping with her handsome young cousin is not the big tempting sin Helen has been waiting for. Yet, "I'm wretched with you here," she moans, "for I know you cannot stay, and I cannot go with you." Suddenly a twig snaps outside the window, and the would-be lovers break apart. The scent of Hoyt's German cologne hangs in the air, a clue that they are being spied on by one of the servants. It is a hokey scene with a clumsy ending, typical of Julia's fantasies. But the narrator takes the episode very seriously and believes that Helen is in danger.

The next day, Ellesley West returns home and announces that he has decided to sell the plantation, which belonged to Helen's family. Cotton has become unprofitable, he says, and "no responsible parent unbound by sentiment would consent to have a son, an only son, too, grow up in a place like this. A death hole. Out of the world." Mr. West expects to sell Blue Brook as a hunting preserve, since "the place is worthless for anything else." Because the ancient boxwood bushes are "worth more than the rest of the place put together," he proposes a final indignity — he will dig up the formal garden and sell the plants separately.

Obviously this is a dreadful marriage, yet Helen has already announced that, like the state of South Carolina, she does not believe in divorce. If marriage is a sacrament, she reasons, then nothing but death can dissolve it. And if it is not, why *bother* with divorce? According to the modern psychology books she has been reading, people tend to repeat their mistakes. If a person chooses the wrong mate once, he or she will probably make an equally bad match if given a second chance. And Helen tends to fall in love with men who resemble her father. In Ellesley West, in fact, the narrator encounters a rival who is his double. Both men have extremely pale cheeks with a dark shadow of beard, "dangerous" eyes, and hair "black as a crow's wing." A servant remarks on the odd resemblance, adding that "the old Cap'n" looked that way too.

After a tense meal delayed by a thunderstorm, Helen points out a vase of deep blue monkshood flowers and dares her cousin to rub one against his lips. Monkshood is so poisonous, she purrs, that swallowing a single petal can kill a person instantly. Hours later, the butler discovers Helen's corpse, along with a suicide note addressed to her cousin. In it, she bequeaths him her unpublished writings and begs him to tell her story to the world.

All this may sound like promising material, but as Mencken soon discovered, "On a Plantation" is confusing, badly written, and unconvincing. In fact, despite the dramatic possibilities suggested by the mulatto baby, the death sheet, the smallpox epidemic, and Helen's flirtation with her cousin, "On a Plantation" is virtually unreadable. Mencken was expecting another *Green Thursday* — tight, spare, tragic, and black. What he got instead was a sprawling gothic romance about petty, self-absorbed white people.

Mencken advised Julia to stick with writing about blacks. When she did, her work was very, very good; when she wrote about whites it was terrible. Publishing "On a Plantation" would be professional suicide. The solution, to him, seemed obvious — Julia should scrap this draft and write another, removing all the white characters.

Distracted during most of 1925 by the spectacle of the Scopes "monkey trial" and by the death of his mother, Mencken never paused to ask what Julia was struggling to express. This book simply didn't work, and he knew what would fix it. History has proved him right. Stripped of its white characters and recast solely with blacks, "On a Plantation" would eventually become the critical and popular triumph *Black April.*

Yet something would also be lost in the translation: Julia's efforts to understand her own uneasy relationship with the plantation. Not so long ago, in *Green Thursday,* she had refused to shoulder the burden of southern history by removing the white landowners from the picture and assigning responsibility for black wretchedness to an amorphous force called "fate." Now, with the character Helen West, she was trying to move beyond this polite evasion.

Helen West sees herself as part of a long line of European colonizers who stole land from the Native Americans and then enslaved Africans to work it.[26] Though close contact with blacks has led her to distrust and even hate white supremacy, her fragile ego still depends on it. Helen West is a privileged prisoner of the dominant culture who does the bidding of white men. She revels in her power as the plantation's mistress. As a wife and lover of men, she is shrewd and manipulative. Yet as a writer she is tentative and apologetic, anxious to turn over her task to a man. Helen's overriding ambition is not to create art but to become the *subject* of art. Only in death is she successful.

Like most affluent white women of her day, and ours, Julia had been raised to see herself through male eyes. It is no accident that she created a male narrator to tell her own story. Helen's cousin is based in part on Isaac Weston, the friend who came to confront her about the Spingarns' party. Weston was distantly related to Julia's family through both the Moods and the Adamses. Like the narrator in several early drafts of the manuscript, Weston was born on a nearby plantation and had worked in a civil engineering firm. An amateur sculptor who exhibited works in a New York gallery and the All Southern Exposition in 1925, he had recently done a bust of Julia.[27] Perhaps a distillation of all the semi-sophisticated men who couldn't quite rise to Julia's challenge, the narrator may also be part Henry Bellamann and part Dan Reed, with a dash of Reed Smith thrown in.

Sounding like a contemporary romance novelist, Helen's cousin dutifully records the details of her dresses, shoes, furniture, draperies, voice, and gestures. It takes no great leap of the imagination to conclude that Helen is Julia as she wanted men to perceive her — "exotic, luxurious, colorful, yet curiously cool and self-controlled." She is worldly, predatory, and even — as she slinks around her country house wearing silk stockings and high heels — strangely androgynous. In the narrator's eyes, Helen seems "absolutely different" from all other women. But for all his verbiage, he never explains how. In the hands of a Henry James, this lapse would seem deliberate, a symptom of the narrator's half-baked romanticism. But in a novel this poorly written, it also reveals a failure of the writer's vision. Julia could not define herself.

Nor, in the context of this novel, could she reveal who she was from behind a black mask, for by giving Helen West "someone to talk to" she had thrown up a barrier between the white woman and the people of the Quarters. Helen talks to her cousin *about* the blacks, not to them, as Julia Peterkin did in real life, or through them, as she had in *Green Thursday.* Their experiences are reduced to little more than gossip, an acceptable way for genteel white people to bring up forbidden subjects.

Early in the novel, Helen tells Mary Weeks's story in order to open a discussion of adultery, confiding to her cousin that Cely's reconciliation with Bully has upset her. "For so many years," she says, "I thought her life was a sort of proof that a woman could love one man deeply and then forget him utterly in affairs with other men." She relates the story of Frank Hart's toes to show how brutal life can be on the plantation. Helen escorts her cousin to the foreman's funeral as though it were a tourist attraction and laughs aloud during the service. Frank Hart, whose name Julia changed to April, is important to the plot only because all the house servants attend his wake, leaving Helen alone in the Big House with her cousin, who seizes the opportunity to make a pass at her.

Only a few months earlier, Julia had published another version of Frank Hart's story that was as powerful as anything she would ever write. "The Foreman" was intended to be the final story in *Green Thursday* but ended up on the cutting-room floor. *Atlantic Monthly* rejected it as "too terrible," but Paul Green finally printed it in the *Reviewer* in July 1924. When "The Foreman" opens, Killdee is in his late fifties; if he ever did go off to live with young Missie, he has now returned to Rose, by whom he has ten children. One day Killdee's feet begin to grow numb; alarmed, he purchases a set of charms from the conjure doctor. Rose is sure that the charms will fail, and indeed, Killdee's health continues to deteriorate. Sitting by the fire, he rests his foot on a live coal and discovers that the flesh is "stone dead." "Gawd damn!" he snarls. "I blieb I'll bu'n dem off! Bu'n dem off!" Then he begins to cry. Resting his head on Rose's ample bosom, Killdee pines for the long-lost Missie.

Rose halfheartedly suggests calling the "buckra doctor," but in the end she treats Killdee's feet herself, with hot water and violet-leaf tea. The toes come loose and swim around the tub like evil little fish. "Rose git a stick, Gal! Git a stick! Knock da big one!" cries Killdee. At the end of the tale, some of the children are sent off to fetch a white doctor because, as Rose says, "You pa's done gone crazy. He done drap dead, too!"[28] Rose slips out the door to look for a charm she had buried in the woods.

"The Foreman" is a gripping tale, brutally real and surrealistic at the same time. By removing herself and her father from the story, Julia suggested that Frank Hart would have lost his toes whether or not she had tried to treat them. She avoided the appearance of self-justification by projecting her own horror and guilt onto Rose. The conflict is thus both simplified and universalized, refocused on mortality. It was this kind of imaginative transformation, and indeed this very scene, that would eventually turn the mishmash of "On a Plantation" into the hypnotic lucidity of *Black April.*

But in May 1925, despite H. L. Mencken's recommendations, Julia was still blissfully unaware that "On a Plantation" was a failure. She hoped to make final corrections and send the book to press before early July, when she planned to sail for Europe. "If you'll help me see what's worth keeping and what should be deleted, I'll send you a charm that will keep you young as long as your bones can hold meat on them," she wrote to Mencken on May 10. "Take out the white woman," he apparently replied.[29]

This time Julia got the message. "If the manuscript isn't worth bothering with, then it just isn't," she conceded.[30] A few days later, she reconsidered. "On a Plantation" was *her* story, and if Helen West was not worth writing about, then neither was she. Perhaps she could fix the problems without removing Helen. She would make the conflicts clearer, the plot more active.

Julia set out to rework "On a Plantation" as a murder mystery. She heated up the love scenes, deepened the gloom, and made Ellesley West even meaner. It was a futile and misguided effort. In version number two of "On a Plantation," Helen lives and her husband dies. Did Helen poison Ellesley? Was he struck by lightning? Did he succumb to chronic malaria? Did someone conjure him by laying the foreman's winding-sheet at the foot of his bed? Did one of the servants kill him? A chicken heart with a pin through it is found in Ellesley's room. A cup of brownish liquid, half full, sits by his bedside. The room smells of boxwood, which Helen had earlier identified as a poison. Julia succeeded in making Ellesley unlikable, but not in making him believable. Clearly the wife hates the husband. But why? Because he makes crude comments about blacks and women? Because he buys modern gadgets and threatens to sell the farm? The mystery remains unsolved.

In fact, if Julia *was* furious at Willie in the spring of 1925, the reason was probably Elizabeth Darby. A pretty flirt with a voice "like wind-chimes" who was married to the postman, Elizabeth was almost twenty years Willie's junior.[31] Like several other men in the neighborhood, he often visited her during the day while her husband, Buck, was at work.

No one is certain when their affair began, but it seems to have been common knowledge by 1927.[32] The two couples often played bridge together and shared Sunday suppers.

But Ellesley West has no lover in "On a Plantation," unless the mulatto baby is his. Nor has he conspired to sterilize Helen, though he does sell her birthright. As in all her attempts to write fiction about herself, Julia left out everything that made her angriest. The conflicts that remain seem superficial, insufficient to explain either murder or suicide.

No amount of tinkering could save the novel — it got worse instead of better. But in early summer, still hopeful that she had solved the problem, Julia mailed the manuscript to Mencken, requesting that he pass it on to Mrs. Knopf. Tired, perhaps, of arguing over a hopeless mess, he complied. The Knopfs turned it down.[33]

CHAPTER 7

Black April

eeling betrayed, Julia set sail for Europe with her old friend Blanche Kaminer and Blanche's teenaged daughter Binkie. Since joining the ranks of the literati, Julia had become painfully aware of her own provincialism. To people in Fort Motte, an annual trip to New York counted as foreign travel, but her new friends spoke blithely of drinking in Montmartre or running over to Biarritz. In her new role as a serious artist, going abroad seemed de rigueur. Once in France, she avoided the American artists and writers who crowded the sidewalk cafés of Paris and put out the word, a bit prematurely, that she preferred not to be treated as a celebrity.

She enrolled at the Alliance Française at Tours, immersing herself in French literature, music, and painting. After class she went sightseeing with Blanche and Binkie, drank in the cafés, shopped for souvenirs, and flirted with a Frenchman and an American professor. She spent some time in Paris, then made a side trip to Rome, where she bought a silver cross and "tree-of-life" chain said to have been blessed by the pope.

Julia and Blanche spent much of the trip looking for a boyfriend for Binkie, a pretty, vivacious young woman who suffered from deafness and a speech impediment. Men liked Binkie, who bravely tried to offset her handicaps by being extra charming and a little wild.[1] But no serious prospect appeared. Ocean liners were a fertile field for husband hunting, and as their ship sailed for home, Julia and Blanche stood conspiratorially on deck, scanning the faces of their fellow passengers.

As Julia surveyed the crowd, a sleek, graceful man in a striped jersey caught her eye. Lounging against the rail, looking faintly bored, he was making small talk with a pretty red-haired woman. Julia guessed that he was a foreigner, and married. For most of the journey he kept to himself, smoking a pipe and contemplating the horizon. Julia smoked cigarettes and studied his profile. On the last day at sea, she struck up a conversation.

Appearances to the contrary, Irving Fineman turned out to be single, Jewish, and American. He, too, had spent the summer in France, and he was melancholy at the prospect of returning to his job as an instructor of mechanical drawing at the University of Illinois. When Julia pressed, he admitted that he longed to make his living as an artist or writer. In fact, he had just sold an article to the *Menorah Journal,* a Jewish magazine. When the ship docked, Julia had his address.[2]

She mailed him a copy of *Green Thursday;* he reciprocated with a woodcut and a copy of his most recent publication. Though she misremembered his last name as Furness, Irving Fineman stayed on Julia's mind. Four and a half years later, he would become the object of her fiercest passion.

While Julia was jaunting around Europe, her short story "Manners" appeared in the *Reviewer.* Loosely based on the relationship between her former cook, Lucy Leacey, and the little girl Lucy adopted, "Manners" mirrors even more than the stories in *Green Thursday* Julia's childhood feud with her stepmother, Janie Mood.

"Manners" begins with a traumatic separation. Little Thomasina does not want to leave her mother to go and live with the fat, aggressive Lucy. Yet her own family barely has enough to eat, and like it or not, she finds herself "given away." "I'm gwine raise you to be nice," Lucy tells Thomasina on the way home. "I'm gwine learn you how to have manners."[3]

Lucy's cabin is "full of fine things," including a clock, a sewing machine, and an organ. Thomasina doesn't even own a nightgown. When she gets ready for bed the first night, she takes off her "lone garment" and stands before Lucy naked. "Jedus, gal!" Lucy laughs. "You ain't got no manners! An' no night gown! But you can't sleep naked in my bed!" Thomasina is put to bed wearing one of Lucy's gowns, which is big enough to "stretch across the room."

Lucy is not usually so gentle; she beats the child daily with thorny plum switches in order to teach her the rules and regulations she collectively calls "manners." "People with manners cry low and easy so the white folks at the Big House won't hear them and get disturbed," Lucy tells Thomasina. They do not eat green walnuts, handle toads, drink goat's milk, warm their bare feet on the sooty kettle, or suck their fingers for comfort. "Everything is bad manners," Thomasina thinks. "Everything." "Manners keep you from doing everything in the world you want to do." "Having manners" means denying your senses and repressing your emotions.

One day Lucy wakes Thomasina early. "You t'ink you got a Ma?" she asks. "Well, you ain't. . . . You' Ma died yesterday. . . . Gal, you' ma was a sinner. A turrible sinner. You chillen ain' got no daddy. . . . You' ma is hoppin' in Hell right now."

Thomasina is confused. She can't imagine her mother dead, much less hopping in Hell. After all, "when little chickens died, or mules, they lay still." Seeing her confusion, Lucy explains that "Hell's a fire. A awful fire. Seven times hotter dan we fire. Hell can't git you yet, you ain' twelve years old. But you better have manners or you might miss and go dere anyhow."

Lucy takes Thomasina home for the funeral. Her new shoes hurt her feet, but Lucy insists that she wear them anyway. The cabin smells queer. Several women huddle in the shed room over "a strange stiffness that [lies] covered with a sheet." Thomasina refuses to enter the room and confront "the thing on the bed." "Don' cut no crazy, gal," Lucy whispers. "You got to show respect for you' ma. You mus' come look at em."

When one of the women turns down the sheet, Thomasina peeps at her mother's feet and notes that they are not hopping. "Don't make me look at em," she pleads. "Shut you' mouth, gal," Lucy retorts. "You don' know you got to look at you' ma? Don' fo'git you' manners!"

Lucy and her friends hold Thomasina over the corpse and force her eyelids apart so that her eyes, "bare, uncovered," stare into the "two dead eyes" and "dark blue lips cracked open above a grin of cold white teeth." The body is carried out of the house, and Thomasina thinks the funeral party is about to leave her behind, alone with the horrible smell. Running after Lucy, the little girl begs, "Le' me go wid you, Cousin Lucy. I'm gwine try to hab manners."

Lucy's rules may seem strange, but they have a point: the little girl learns to avoid dirtying herself and her surroundings, and, even more important, to evade trouble by deferring to her betters. These lessons will serve Thomasina in good stead. But Lucy's insistence that the girl look at her mother's body is different. In essence it is sadism, hazing, an unequal contest of wills.

In the published version of "Manners," Lucy triumphs. Thomasina breaks down and plays by the rules. It is important to note, however, that in Julia's first draft the little girl revolts. "With wild shrieks she broke away, and ran and ran, until her shrieks were moans, then sobs, and then at last she fell, exhausted, lay still and went to sleep. They found her and took her back to the cabin, laid her on the other bed, still asleep. Sleep was as comforting as death." [4]

In the two endings of "Manners," as well as in multiple drafts of "On a Plantation," Julia Peterkin can be seen weighing the consequences of rebellion. For all women, black and white, having manners meant submitting to a woman's place. From early childhood, a southern woman was conditioned to keep her mouth shut, to suppress or hide her sexuality, and to accept abuse without complaint. Whoever refused risked abandonment; the only escape was through death.

Julia's revolt against the cult of southern womanhood extended to the words she chose to use. Compare the language of "Manners," for example, with that of her fellow South Carolinian Josephine Pinckney, whose poem "The Old Women" appeared in the same issue of the *Reviewer:* "Two negresses sit on the cabin steps / In the warm wind that carries the male reek of their cob pipes." Never would Julia have called Lucy a negress, though the term was considered a benign description by most of her contemporaries. In fact, the very title, "Manners," probably refers to an article by Laurence Stallings in which he gleefully pegged Julia as the ringleader of a new group of southern realists who were bent on "displaying bad manners." "It is bad breeding down South to do a book like . . . the Peterkin stories," he crowed. [5]

Julia's family was still angry about her writing, still determined to make her give it up. Resisting their demands was increasingly difficult, she told Mencken, especially now that the Knopfs had rejected "On a Plantation." Perhaps she would try taking out "the artist man," and Helen, too, if necessary. "Like the infant in the old Pear's soap advertisement," she joked, "I can't rest until I get it." [6]

Eventually, after several more halfhearted attempts at revision, Julia resigned herself to the idea that "getting it" would mean eliminating all the white people. Helen West and her Yankee cousin metamorphosed into an arrogant black man named April and his twelve-year-old "outside" son, Breeze. With that, the floodgates opened. Julia's authorial voice, choked off to a tentative trickle when she took on southern ladyhood, spilled its banks and ran upstream in a booming wave of exuberance.

The new novel opens on Sandy Island with a girl in labor.[7] It is April, a significant month to Julia — the month when her mother died and her son was born. The girl has stopped pushing, and the midwife doesn't know what to do. Old Breeze, the girl's grandfather, sets off across a flooded river to Blue Brook, to fetch Maum Hannah and her African "birthing beads."

Hannah discovers the trouble right away; the midwife has put a sharpened ax under the bed. But instead of cutting the pain, as intended, it has cut off the contractions. "Pain don' kill a 'oman, son," Maum Hannah reassures Old Breeze. "It takes pain to make em work steady till de task is done." [8] The beads do the trick, and before long a healthy baby boy arrives. But the weary girl loses consciousness before delivering the afterbirth. Then she begins to hemorrhage. "If she had been a nice decent girl, all this would never have been," thinks the midwife.[9] Maum Hannah stanches the blood with a mixture of spiderwebs and soot.

The girl won't tell who the baby's father is, but everyone suspects April, the foreman of Blue Brook plantation across the river. (Julia borrowed his feminine-sounding name from April Scott, a man who lived on Robert Adams's place and sometimes worked as a butcher in the Peterkins' store.) [10] April is the girl's half-brother, Old Breeze's son, so by conventional standards the baby is not only a bastard but the product of incest. On Sandy Island, however, he is just another fatherless child. Maum Hannah and the midwife urge the girl to name the baby April. Instead, she calls him Breeze.

Breeze's mother is nameless, always referred to simply as "the girl" or "the mother." April, on the other hand, is a living legend: "Everybody who came from Blue Brook had something to say about him, either of his kindness or of his meanness, his long patience or his quick temper, his open-handedness or his close-fistedness. On Blue Brook, April was a man among men." [11]

Eventually Breeze's mother marries someone else. When the boy is twelve years old, his stepfather murders Old Breeze, steals the family's savings, and disappears. Times are hard. The cow goes dry, the hens stop laying — even the collards won't grow. One day Cousin Big Sue arrives from the mainland and offers to adopt Breeze, promising his mother that at Blue Brook he will have a feather bed, new clothes, and a chance to make a little money and wear shoes. Exhausted and starving, Breeze's mother is no match for fat, sassy Big Sue; like Thomasina in "Manners," Breeze is "given away." The boy tries to protest, but his voice and his body are trained to obey. When Big Sue leaves, he follows: "He couldn't even stop his feet from stepping side by side with hers, one step after another." [12]

Conform, be good, do what people expect, no matter how you feel — Breeze is as much a prisoner of tradition as Helen and her overwrought cousin. And yet, being a child, he tugs at our heartstrings in a way that they cannot. Brought up on a remote island, the boy is viewed by the people of Blue Brook as an outsider in spite of his paternity, and Big Sue discovers that his education has been entirely neglected. Breeze does not even know that eels are he-catfish, she discovers, or that a cooked eel allowed to cool will turn raw again. He is ignorant of the fact that it is a sin to buy sugar on Sunday, and that if a coachwhip snake catches you, he will wrap his body around you, tie you to a tree, and whip you to death with his tail. It is news to him that tying up a child's "palate-lock" will cure sore throat, and that a guinea hen can't count higher than six.

Some of these practices and beliefs were authentic to Lang Syne and/or Brookgreen, but others apparently were not. Descendants of people who lived on Lang Syne in the 1920s claim never to have heard of many of them. "Miss Julia was a devil," declares Ella Weeks Walker. "She made all that up!" [13]

It is true that Julia did not always get her information about folk practices straight from the Quarters. Some of it came from Reed Smith, the University of South Carolina professor who once banned her works from his writing classes. Smith wrote a column for the *Columbia State*, an ethnic sampler called "Folklore Corner." Julia habitually clipped and saved it, noting in the margins such information as "frizzled chicken — bad luck to kill one," or "eel is a he-catfish." Many of the superstitions in *Black April* had appeared in Smith's column between 1925 and 1927, as well as in such sources as Newbell Niles Puckett's exhaustive catalog, *The Magic and Folk Beliefs of the Southern Negro.*[14]

In the first version of "On a Plantation" Julia had transplanted her plantation, Blue Brook, to the coast in order to disguise the autobiographical character of the novel. Now, rewriting the manuscript from the black point of view, she kept the fictitious Blue Brook but picked up the life of the seaside plantation several years after the Wests had sold it, effectively banishing the master and mistress and substituting an absentee landlord with no interest in agriculture. This imaginative change in ownership freed her to invent a southern black community where the residents, though tenants on a white man's land, are isolated from everyday racism.

"Let de white people go on. Dey is gwine to Hell anyhow!" huffs Big Sue, predicting that April will come to a bad end if he doesn't "quit tryin' to do all de crazy t'ings de white people says do. . . . Bad luck's been hangin' round ever since dat radio-machine at de Big House started hollerin' an' cryin' an' singin' year befo' last."[15]

Uncle Bill, older and less belligerent than Big Sue, protests that not all white people are bad. His former master, he fondly recalls, was "de Jedus of dis plantation."[16] Ol' Cap'n always warned his drunken guests against shooting the servants; "he'd always brag that he had the best stock of niggers and dogs and horses in the state, and he didn't want any of them hurt." Big Sue interjects that Ol' Cap'n is doubtless "hoppin' in Hell."[17] But Bill is sure that even if the old rascal couldn't quite make it into Heaven, God must have found him a "comfortable place in Hell, wid plenty o' people to wait on him."[18]

The racial conflicts that made "On a Plantation" so disturbing are removed from the foreground in *Black April*, subordinated to a more universal form of strife. Blacks never clash with whites; instead, the "saved" chafe against the "sinners," while those who "have manners" look down on those who do not. Women compete to attract men; men fight for the favors of women. Hunger is the result of drought, insects, and crop failures. Sickness and death are the ultimate enemy.

Whites, as pale and remote as the moon, exert only a distant pull. Their arrivals and departures mark the passing of seasons; no one cares what they do. A visiting Helen West could drop dead in the Big House and few would notice her passing. Race and class hold people in their places, set limits on ambition. But just as in a novel by Jane Austen, the social hierarchy is deep background. It is the byplay that hooks us, the games people play while competing among themselves for status.

Breeze is a silent spectator, rather like Julia herself. Born with a caul, as she was, he is thought to be gifted with second sight — the ability to see ghosts, predict events, and understand the ways of his fellow man. Far from being unnaturally prescient, however, Breeze often seems a little slow. Adult relationships baffle him. Every time he turns around, he stumbles across bewildering new evidence that his elders are linked to each other through undeclared sexual alliances as well as through the official ties of marriage and kinship. April, for example, is married to Leah but often has sex with Big Sue and several other women; Big Sue is also keeping company with Uncle Bill. Meanwhile, Big Sue and Leah are both plotting to seduce the new preacher.

Leah is operating under a handicap. Early in the book Breeze learns that she is "salivated" — her mouth is raw, she drools, and her teeth are loose. Eventually the teeth fall out, making her look like an old woman. The people speculate that Leah has been conjured, though "salivation" is an archaic English term for mercury poisoning. (Many patent medicines of the time contained mercury, and Leah had dosed herself with "white powder" to treat a stomachache.)[19] The women cluck and sigh, whispering among themselves that no one could blame April for losing interest in her now.[20] Later in the novel, Leah shows other symptoms of mercury poisoning. Her speech grows slurred; she has a hard time swallowing food. At first she seems depressed and withdrawn; later she grows so agitated that she splits Big Sue's cabin door with an ax.

The rivalry between Big Sue and Leah comes to a head when Leah steals Big Sue's newly butchered hog and throws it into the river. The two women fight, and Big Sue kills Leah. Then Sherry, April's son by Zeda, challenges April's authority. Father and son butt heads, and Sherry loses. April banishes him from the plantation. "I hope Gawd'll rot all two o' you feets off!" Sherry spits.[21]

Someone, presumably Zeda, lays Leah's death sheet across the foot of April's bed in an attempt to conjure him. Big Sue's daughter, Joy, comes home from college pregnant by Sherry, who has removed himself to New York. April marries Joy. Rather than acting jealous, Big Sue seems delighted that her daughter has caught such an important husband, but Zeda holds a grudge. When Joy miscarries — the unborn baby is Sherry's, and hence Zeda's grandson — Zeda throws another curse on April. "I hope a misery'll gnaw you' heart in two," she cries. "I hope you'll die of thirst an' hunger. I hope ev'y lawful yard-chile you had by Leah'll perish. I hope you' feet'll rot." [22]

They do. One day April's feet turn hard and numb, and from this point on, the plot of *Black April* follows that of "The Foreman," ending with the plaintive cry, "Bury me in a man-size box." [23]

Just as she had done in *Green Thursday*, Julia took care to provide both natural and supernatural explanations for every disaster. Leah, Zeda, Big Sue, and Sherry all try to curse or conjure April's feet and long legs, to prevent him from further "roaming." But we are also told that April put pesticide on the cotton when it was wet with dew, and that the arsenic dust stuck to his feet. A white doctor is quoted as saying that April developed blood clots that cut off his circulation and caused his feet to die.

The real April, Frank Hart, probably had diabetes, Buerger's disease, or Reynaud's syndrome, any of which can produce numbness and auto-amputation of the extremities.[24] Yet, as Julia was surely aware, leprosy causes similar symptoms, and it is tempting to read yet another level of symbolism into *Black April*. Lepers are legendary outcasts; their presence marks a place as unclean. Though we now know that leprosy is caused by a bacteria, the disease has been regarded since biblical times as a judgment, a curse.

Providing relief from the tragic undertone of *Black April* are two rambunctious episodes of low comedy typical of African American folk humor, both hinging on the overfastidiousness of the visiting preacher.[25] The night before the Reverend is to preach his first sermon at Blue Brook, Big Sue feeds him an "elegant" meal of frogs' legs. The next morning, she greets him with whoops of laughter. "Great Gawd!" she gasps. "You ought o' seen dem frogs dis mawnin'. Dat fool Breeze didn' kill em! He cut off dey hind legs an' turned dem loose in de back yard!" [26] The preacher gags. Still giggling, Big Sue assures him that the legless frogs have since been put out of their misery.

Breeze recognizes the minister as his former stepfather, the man who murdered his grandfather and stole the family's savings. The Reverend's impassioned sermon so inspires the congregation that they fail to notice he has left some crucial words out of the Ten Commandments. "Thou shalt kill!" he thunders. "Do, Lawd, help us to keep dis law," his hearers respond. "Thou shalt commit adultery!" "Do, Lawd, help us to keep dis law." "Thou shalt steal!" Finally Maum Hannah speaks up. "You got em wrong, son! Wrong!" [27] Nobody pays her the slightest attention.

At last the service is over, and everyone adjourns to the churchyard, where the lemonade committee debates whether or not to add more sugar to the brew. The preacher suggests that Leah taste the mixture and render an opinion. Leah bridles and daintily sniffs the barrel. "Before she had time even to turn her head, she gave one loud sneeze and all her white teeth flew out of her mouth" — smack into the lemonade.

Julia's gift for understatement makes the scene both realistic and hilarious. "It was a bad time. Leah said she'd have to have her teeth back right now. But they were mixed up with all those hundreds of lemon skins and that big block of ice. Every man on the committee took a hand at stirring for them, but the teeth rose up and grinned, then hid deep in the bottom of the lemonade before anybody could snatch them out."

The reader may instinctively recoil at the thought of dentures floating in lemonade, but to the people of Blue Brook, hygiene is not the issue. Leah wants her teeth back. The people want their lemonade. When the citified preacher suggests that they pour out the drink in order to retrieve the teeth, the congregation rebels. The people are thirsty. The lemonade will soon be low in the barrel. Leah will just have to wait.

Ever the peacemaker, Uncle Bill approaches the preacher with a brimming dipperful. "Have de first drink, Reverend," he says. "I know you' throat's dry after all de preachin' an' prayin' you done to-day!" [28] The preacher coughs and politely declines.

April is incensed. "Didn' Uncle Bill hand you a dipper o' lemonade? . . . How come you didn' drink em?" The preacher answers lamely, "Why — ah, I'm really not thirsty, Mr. Locust." April "leaped forward and seized the preacher's head with two powerful hands, held it like a vise, and bit a neat round mouthful" out of the preacher's cheek.[29] "Dat meat taste too sickenin'," he grumbles. April wins the argument and humiliates the preacher, but the legless frogs and disembodied teeth have foreshadowed his fate — and his wife's.

Black April is long, so long that the critics dubbed it an "epic." As Julia later explained to Carl Sandburg, "I thought I'd quit writing when I finished it, and so I jammed it too full." [30] While *Green Thursday* is a short book about troubled people who happen, almost incidentally, to have been born poor and black, *Black April* sets out to mythologize the agrarian folk culture unique to rural African Americans in the Deep

South. Teeming with life, Blue Brook as Breeze first encounters it is a Garden of Eden, southern style. The rich pastureland is

> unplowed, unsown, but covered with lush grass and sprinkled with flowers. Some of them bloomed so close to the ruts that their heads were caught in the cart wheels and shattered.
>
> The fields came next, ripe corn-fields, hay-fields ready to be harvested, brown cotton fields, dripping with white locks of cotton. Whirls of yellow butterflies played along the road. Flocks of bull-bats darted about overhead in the sky, twittering joyfully as they caught gnats and mosquitoes for their supper. White cranes flew toward sunset, field larks sang out, killdees rose and sailed off crying. The whole earth was full of sound.[31]

Unlike barren Sandy Island, Blue Brook is a bountiful place. In autumn, the road to the Quarters ran past

> sugar-cane patches where green blades rustled noisily over purple stalks. Sweet potatoes cracked the earth under vines shading the long rows. Pindars were blooming. Okra bushes were full of creamy red-hearted blossoms and pointed green pods. Butter-bean vines clambered over the hand-split clapboard garden fences that kept pigs and chickens out of small enclosures, where wide-leaved collards waited for frost to make them crisp, and scarlet tomatoes spotted straggly broken-down bushes.

Paradise does not last. When the boll weevil gains a foothold, spoiling the cash crop, the people of Blue Brook begin turning their backs on agriculture and leaving the land. Once, Julia wrote, the river marshes were vast agricultural factories, "canaled and ditched and banked" by April's and Breeze's ancestors, "African people fresh from the Guinea coast." Now the dikes are broken, the floodgates rotted. "The tide rolls over all as it did before the land was ever cleared. It has taken back its own."[32]

The plantation has reached a turning point; it appears to be withering under a curse. The church and the community are no longer able to enforce traditional morality. The midwife grumbles that "girls are mighty wild and careless these days," running around and pleasuring themselves too much to have healthy babies. Yet even she admits that "every child comes into the world by the same old road, [and] a thousand husbands couldn't make that journey one whit easier."[33]

The church is losing its hold; the riverboat and the general store supply more of what young people want, or think they want. They battle the boll weevil with store-bought poison and send April off to a hospital. The old folks warn of the jaws of Hell, stretched wide to swallow sinners just as the whale did Jonah. Yet by the end of the novel, most of the traditions people still believe in are nothing more than curses. They go through the motions of "seeking peace," but peace is nowhere to be found.

As Julia built up her portrait of April, she pondered Irving Fineman. "You and he are so far apart, so infinitely far. I'd like to have seen you together, once," she would later write to him.[34] Like her characters, Julia was turning away from the plantation, looking to the city for something to sustain her. Almost in spite of herself, she found it in Fineman's mannered, self-conscious style, his Jewish cosmopolitanism, his eagerness to discuss people's innermost feelings, his appreciation for books and pictures, his elegant taste in clothes. He was the opposite of everything she thought she should value, the embodiment of all she craved. "Which of these knows life?" she asked herself in verse: the laborer, a rough man who has smelled the earth, heard the cries of wild birds, and seen "how torn flesh appears and wounds lie open, exposing yellow fat?" Or the artist, with his smooth, slim fingers and "civilized" ways?

Work-roughened hands, rippling muscles, and sweaty clothes had long since lost their appeal. What Julia yearned for was Willie Peterkin's opposite, a man so suave and urbane that his very presence could make her feel refined. "I've never touched your hand, just piano keys where your white fingers wandered," she mused in a love poem. The print of the man's lips on a crystal wineglass, the scent of his hair on a silken pillow — these were enough to fire her imagination. "Since I looked into your eyes, I know I'm incomplete," the verse concludes. "The rest of me is you."

The love affair that followed makes it tempting to read "I've Never Touched Your Hand" as an early declaration of Julia's budding passion for Irving Fineman. Yet it is important to realize that before she settled on Fineman, Julia was infatuated with a series of other men, any one of whom might have inspired these lines. In fact, there is some evidence that she wrote the poem for one man and then changed the details when her interest shifted. The lover's hair, described as "sunny" in one version, is "dusky" in another.[35]

Whether or not Irving Fineman's were the only hands and lips and hair Julia yearned to touch, he loomed large in her imagination. Things were not going well for Julia. She had caught her heel on a rug and pitched forward, hurting her knee. Willie was ill. The family finances were precarious. Belle Taber, who had come to be a permanent fixture at Lang Syne, suddenly announced her engagement to a man whom Julia considered unsuitable. Hobbled by a plaster cast, confined to the house, and unsure that her new novel would ever be published, Julia begged Fineman to do her "a charity" and spend his spring vacation at Lang Syne.[36] He said no.

Unfazed, Julia took another tack and began to play Pygmalion. Fate, she said, had directed her to him. "It may be I am to help you form a contact, or a friendship," she speculated. First, however, Fineman must stop wasting his talent on third-rate magazines. "It seems obvious to me," she wrote, "that with your gifts, your very great gifts, you have something to do that's of importance."[37]

However dismal she felt during the frustrating spring of 1926, Julia pushed her pen across the pages with speed and conviction. By summer, the "black" version of "On a Plantation" was nearly finished. Knopf held the option on her next two books, yet Julia could not bear the thought of working with Alfred Knopf again. "He fairly reeks with antagonism when he sees me," she told Carl Sandburg.[38] Knowing that Mencken would side with Knopf no matter what he thought of the revised manuscript, Julia avoided him. Instead, she went to New York to confer with Max Aley, who pointed out that Knopf had rejected "On a Plantation." She was legally free, therefore, to take her new novel elsewhere. Aley was a contact editor for the firm of Bobbs-Merrill and would be glad to arrange a meeting with the editor.

Sorely tempted, Julia stalled. To change publishers and employ an agent would be to sacrifice the two alliances — with Knopf and with Mencken — that certified her as a serious writer. Could her work command respect without them?

While Julia struggled to make up her mind, Max and Ruth Aley were busy introducing her to their literary connections. They also encouraged her to entertain in their home. Shunning Mencken and his cronies, Julia invited a less controversial and less famous crowd of bookish young men who, she felt, might benefit by meeting the Aleys. Among them was Irving Fineman.

"Life is full of good things," Julia wrote to him afterward, "but to me the supreme pleasure is to talk with the people who interest me."[39] Another woodcut arrived in the mail, featuring a naked man. Julia's letters grew more flirtatious. "I wish it were customary to own slaves now and you belonged to me," she teased. "I like you a lot and should like you to keep me in mind." This confession led her to describe Mary Weeks. "She's a devil and a good woman too," Julia explained. "I want to write about her because she's had the courage to live fully, freely, wickedly, and still keep at peace with herself." [40]

But if Mary was much on Julia's mind in the summer of 1926, it was not only because of her sex life. Mary's son, twenty-four-year-old Cicero, had gone north to work and returned home with typhoid fever.[41] He died in Mary's arms. "Mute, self-controlled," Mary watched as the body was lowered into the grave. "It broke my heart," Julia wrote to Carl Sandburg, "and I . . . wished that I myself might in some way learn the secret of her courage. When I do I shall try to tell it to the world." [42]

These were prophetic words, yet before Julia could concentrate on telling the world about Mary, she needed to find a publisher for her book about April. Max Aley was both admiring and persistent, and in early October Julia gave him permission to show the manuscript to D. Laurance Chambers, the editor in chief at Bobbs-Merrill.

Chambers responded immediately: "We want to publish [the book] as it stands, without change," he declared, offering an immediate contract, a $250 advance, mass advertising, and the assurance that Alfred A. Knopf was a fool for having turned down such a distinguished book.[43] Julia signed, repressing the thought that she was leaving the publisher of Willa Cather, Joseph Conrad, T. S. Eliot, Ezra Pound, and Thomas Mann for one who boasted *The Wizard of Oz*, the mysteries of Mary Roberts Rinehart, and the Charlie Chan detective series.[44] Still, as she confided to Chambers, the proffered advance — "the price of ten bales of cotton" — was hefty enough to make "the men of the family begin to look respectful." [45]

An old hand at massaging authors' egos, D. L. Chambers had been with Bobbs-Merrill since 1903, climbing the corporate ladder from secretary to editor. Everyone in the office was crazy about the book, he told Julia; it was bound to be a huge success. Relieved to be free of the snooty Knopfs, Julia luxuriated in the warm bath of praise.

By mid-November she had received the first galleys, and suddenly Chambers's hands-off approach did not seem quite so reassuring. What should she cut? What should she keep? Hoping that Max Aley could fill Mencken's shoes, a desperate Julia rushed to New York, only to discover that Aley was more at home with sales figures than with the subtleties of plot and characterization. He suggested that she show the manuscript to another of his clients, Hudson Strode. A bright young scholar with soulful eyes, a childish face, and an ingratiating manner, Strode wrote short stories and taught fiction writing at the University of Alabama. Julia liked him at once and turned over the hefty stack of pages with relief.

Hudson Strode soon bogged down in the tangled swamp of blood relationships. April was Breeze's father, and also Sherry's. He was Old Breeze's illegitimate son. He was Big Sue's lover, but he married her daughter, who was pregnant by his own illegitimate son. How could anyone hope to keep track? Since paternity was obviously a central theme of the book, Strode suggested that Julia might supply descriptive chapter titles. She took his advice, instructing Bobbs-Merrill to divide chapter 1 into two parts called "April's Father" and "April's Son." [46]

Strode, his value as a copy editor established, took his place among Julia's growing stable of male admirers. Twelve years her junior, this quintessential southern gentleman was a master of sweet talk and prone to jealous sulking when Julia paid too much attention to other friends. In truth, Julia's affection for Strode seems to have been more maternal than romantic, perhaps because she knew his mental condition to be precarious. Chairman of his academic department, an aspiring novelist, and married for less than two years to a beautiful young woman named Thérèse, he had recently taken a leave of absence from both his job and his wife in order to undergo several months of intensive psychiatric treatment for "cyclothymia," now known as bipolar disorder or manic depression.[47]

The treatment proved successful—temporarily, at least—and Julia convinced Hudson that before returning home to Alabama he should "test his cure" by coming to Lang Syne. Exactly like Helen West, Julia trotted him around her domain, from the cypress swamps to the Quarters, telling stories about the people they met. Strode was intrigued. He later recalled an encounter with Hester Cheseboro as an almost mystical experience.

"Mr. Strode is troubled in his mind," Julia informed Hester.

The old woman narrowed her eyes. "Is you, honey?" she asked. "I see what's botherin' you. You is tryin' to move too fast."

Hudson Strode was thunderstruck by Hester's prescience; he believed that she had read his mind. The old woman did claim to have supernatural talents, but she was also unmatched as a shrewd observer of human nature. Hudson Strode *was* trying to move too fast. Resolving to slow down, he edited the rest of Julia's galleys and rushed off to Alabama.[48]

True to his word, Chambers suggested only one major change—in the title. Julia still preferred "On a Plantation" or "On Blue Brook." She also suggested "True Blue," "Cold Stream," "Black River" (all names of real South Carolina plantations), "The Foreman," and "Blood Kin." Chambers contended that the image of a powerful man with a name like April was more likely to sell books. Letters debating the possibilities flew between Indianapolis and Fort Motte. Chambers observed that another "color" title would be nice, to go along with *Green Thursday*. Eventually he had his way, naming the book *Black April*.[49]

Meanwhile, Julia struggled to redeem herself with H. L. Mencken, who had scolded her for deserting the Knopfs. "Knopf does the most beautiful books in America," Julia protested. "Do you think I'd go to a publisher none of whose books I'd ever read if I felt that Knopf really wanted me? Not on your life!"[50] Trying to win back his goodwill, Julia was uncharacteristically humble: "You are so generous, so utterly kind, your encouragement has meant such a lot to me," she wrote, "if you'd denounce everything I ever write from now on, I think I'd stay grateful for what you have done."[51] Julia believed that Mencken would melt in the end, but when Bobbs-Merrill shipped him a review copy in early December, she held her breath. "Of course he may damn me up and down!" she cautioned Chambers.[52] Mencken did no such thing. He ignored both her and the book. "Are you dead? Or am I?" Julia inquired.[53] There was no response.

Fortunately for Julia, Joel Spingarn and Carl Sandburg were bowled over by *Black April*. Sandburg received one of the first copies, along with Julia's warning to "take a few good drinks before you start reading it, please, or it may depress you, although you know pretty well everything in it already."[54] Spingarn provided plenty of quotable advance praise, declaring *Black April* "an extraordinary book, born of unusual insight into the hearts of black folk."[55] DuBose Heyward, the Charleston novelist, and Howard Odum, a respected sociologist who specialized in the problems of the black South, followed suit.[56]

Once again, black newspapers marveled that Peterkin's characters seemed like real human beings, with ancestors, family histories, and cultural traditions. Reviewing the book for both the *Chicago Defender* and the *Chicago Broad Axe*, Ernest Rice McKinney confessed that he had "raced rapidly through" its pages, "fearing that the dignified, almost reverent, tone would change." To his amazement, nothing broke the spell; words like "coon" and "darkey" never appeared. "If *Black April* is not the Great American novel, then Mrs. Peterkin is the one to write it," McKinney concluded.[57] Critics Laurence Stallings and Robert

Nathan hailed *Black April* as "one of the outstanding books of the year" and "one of the greatest novels ever written in this country." What was it about *Black April* that provoked such superlatives? The critics could not quite explain. The spell it cast defied analysis; you just had to read it for yourself.

"A more loathsome lot of niggers I never came across," exclaimed Gertrude Atherton, who in 1900 had published a popular novel about miscegenation. "And yet the book is so admirable in its atmosphere that it compels attention from first to last. It really is a perfect piece of work." [58] Chambers edited out Atherton's reference to "loathsome niggers" and used the rest as a blurb on the dust jacket. A few reviewers — surprisingly few — slammed the book for its realism.[59] "[*Black April*] is full of the superstition and dirt and squalor and degrading surroundings of the poor negro's life," groused a reviewer for the *Beaumont (Texas) Enterprise.*[60]

Stark Young, an expatriate Mississippian who wrote drama criticism for the *New Republic,* declared that anyone who failed to appreciate *Black April* was no friend of his. "I recommend it with a cold look in the eye," he told Julia, "as [if] to say, well, damn you if you don't like it." A novelist himself, Young was thrilled at Julia's warm appreciation of *The Torches Flare,* his story about an aristocratic southern family in reduced circumstances. "Bless you for your imagination and your heart," he exclaimed.[61] Over the years, Stark Young would become one of Julia's staunchest literary allies, and she his.

By the end of March it was clear that *Black April* was headed for success. Keith Preston of the *Chicago Daily News* declared that "with such books as *Black April* the South comes into its own in American literature." [62] Donald Davidson, a leading figure in the Nashville Fugitive movement who shared the prevailing view that "the white man has rendered the negro into artistic terms better than he has rendered himself," claimed that Julia had "forgotten more about negroes than Joel Chandler Harris . . . Thomas Nelson Page, and that prurient modern, Carl Van Vechten, ever knew." [63]

Yet Julia worried that South Carolina would "turn the book down completely" because, as she told Chambers, "Negroes are not people, here. And if they persist in pretending that they are, then they get lynched." [64] Bill Peterkin warned his mother that "nice South Carolina ladies" would "gnash their teeth violently" over the book. Sure enough, as soon as *Black April* appeared on the shelves, a "prominent" South Carolinian whom she declined to name denounced Julia for writing about "an illegitimate nigger baby." "There's no use trying to win praise from South Carolina as long as I write about Negroes," she wrote to Chambers. "People here cannot forgive me for it, no matter how much they love me." [65]

If some South Carolinians were offended by *Black April*, many others were beguiled by their state's latest celebrity. According to J. T. Gittman, the owner of a Columbia bookstore, crowds of people arrived every day asking for an autographed *Black April* to "put with their copy of *Green Thursday*." The American Association of University Women and the Orangeburg Lions Club invited Julia to speak. She declined, proudly reporting the invitations to Chambers. "Did it take the Lions Club and Association of University Women to prove to you that you're famous?" he teased.[66] As a matter of fact, it did.

The *Columbia State* held off reviewing *Black April*. Instead, the state's largest newspaper reprinted excerpts from reviews that had appeared elsewhere — but only those that compared the book unfavorably with the Gullah tales of its editor, Ambrose Gonzales. Friends in the newspaper business warned that the Gonzales clan was vindictive and could, if it chose, make life so "unpleasant" for her in South Carolina that she would be "forced to leave." [67]

Ambrose Gonzales was not the only southern newspaper editor with a grudge against *Black April*. W. T. Anderson, the editor and publisher of the *Macon Telegraph*, fulminated that although he hardly ever read books, he had been fool enough to make an exception for *Black April*. It was an outrage, he said, that perfectly good trees should have been cut down to make the paper to print such trash. Furthermore, he was certain that Julia Peterkin could not be southern, for if she were, she would know that blacks had a limited vocabulary. "Look in the dictionary for 'caul,'" he ranted, "and imagine that being a common word on the farm!" [68] In fact, had Anderson kept his own ears and mind open, he would have known that "caul" was a familiar word to most southern farmhands.

Up North, Julia's reputation was growing. "Other fiction of Negro life seems false in the light of Mrs. Peterkin's achievement," declared Charles Puckette of the *Saturday Review of Literature*.[69] *Nation* called *Black April* "the finest work produced thus far dealing with the American Negro" and predicted that it would "do more good than a dozen sociological tracts." [70] John Crawford, writing in the *New York Times Book Review*, praised Julia's deft handling of Gullah, which she had rendered as "a lucid, yet idiomatic, racy speech." Warning that some readers might be put off by all the incest in the book, he praised Julia's "ethical sternness." [71] Three months later, Edwin Clark, Crawford's colleague at the *Times*, again singled out *Black April*, noting that Julia had "reconciled the experimental with the traditional novel" through her use of "alien material" (the lives of black folk). [72]

"Ethical sternness," "alien material" — what did all this mean? Julia had found something new to say, and a new way of saying it. She took her readers to a place they had never been and made them believe that they lived there. Expressions and attitudes they found odd in the beginning took root in their minds. It was a rare thing for a novelist to accomplish, and no one was quite able to describe it.

The *Literary Review* praised Julia's "rugged, opulent talent." [73] The *Independent*, a black publication, declared that it would be a mistake to regard *Black April* as "simply another addition to 'negro literature,'" because it was "a book about the mysteries of human life, birth, death, battle, leadership, hatred, envy, love." Still, the reviewer declared, "it is the most sheer and absolute piece of race fiction that was ever written." [74] The influential black critic Alain Locke pronounced *Black April* "as carefully-studied a protrayal [*sic*] of peasant life as American literature has yet produced." [75] Even Rudyard Kipling praised it, though the Gullah baffled him. "I felt it would have been more comprehensible in some language that was outside English," he wrote to Hudson Strode. "It could translate in Basuto or Swahili." [76]

There were a few dissenters, among them Marie Brown Frazier, a black woman who hated *Black April* for harping on incestuous relationships and for what she considered its obnoxious characters and grotesque incidents. [77] Indeed, the issue of the year among black writers and social critics was whether progressive people should feel free to describe all aspects of black life or should concentrate on depicting black men and women as universally hardworking, wholesome, ambitious, and moderate.

Two years later, in an article for *American Mercury* titled "The Negro's Inhibitions," Eugene Gordon would make sport of the controversy, jeering that educated "Aframericans" had suddenly become "sensitive, secretive, and hypocritical" about their own culture. "Chicken, watermelon, spirituals, chitlings, pigs' feet, bright colors, black faces, kinky hair, friendly congregating, the old-fashioned razor, pork chops — all are now in the Index Expurgatorius of Aframerica," he ranted. "The

Caucasian may snigger at all this as a bad joke, but the 'better class' colored folk will not. 'Tis undignified to laugh, you know; the white man may think you boisterous!"[78]

In 1926, this debate was conducted with high seriousness; it affected the decisions of everyone who traded in images of African American culture. In March of that year, W. E. B. Du Bois and Jessie Fauset posted a challenge in *Crisis:* "The Negro in Art: How Shall He Be Portrayed?" The "artists of the world" were invited to respond. And for the next seven months, they did.

The central figure in this debate was a very white man named Carl Van Vechten, a gaudy devotee of all things black who looked like an albino rabbit. His own book about Harlem, *Nigger Heaven,* had enraged Du Bois, who condemned it as "a blow in the face" for the black race.[79] Other prominent black intellectuals, including Alain Locke, James Weldon Johnson, and Charles S. Johnson, defended it. According to his biographer, Bruce Kellner, it was Van Vechten himself who wrote the questions that were sent out to writers and printed in the magazine.[80] He was also among the first to respond. While most "wealthy or cultured" Negroes lived the same boring lives as their white counterparts, Van Vechten observed, there was still a lode of "exotic" material to be found among the black underclass.[81] The real question, then, was whether black writers were going to search out and use this material themselves or "make a free gift of it to white authors who will exploit it until not a drop of vitality remains."[82]

Langston Hughes, Countee Cullen, Charles W. Chesnutt, Walter White, Jessie Fauset, and Benjamin Brawley all contributed to the *Crisis* debate. Many white writers responded, too, among them DuBose Heyward, H. L. Mencken, Joel Spingarn, Sinclair Lewis, Sherwood Anderson, and Vachel Lindsay. Almost everybody took the position that art and propaganda do not mix, and that truth should always prevail. But black writers, living as they did in a racist society, understood better than whites that unsavory accounts of black life tended to reinforce disparaging stereotypes.

As the debate raged on, with writer after writer posting personal manifestos in the pages of *Crisis,* Julia Peterkin concluded that the time had come to defy her aunts. Julia's own statement appeared late in the game, in the September issue of the magazine. "The crying need" among blacks, said she, was to develop a strong sense of race pride. Educated Irishmen and Jews were not upset by jokes at their expense, she insisted, and Negroes should strive for the same impervious self-esteem.

"If America has produced a type more worthy of admiration and honor than the 'Black Negro Mammy,' I fail to have heard of it," she continued, referring to the NAACP's opposition to a proposed national monument. "It seems to me that a man who is not proud that he belongs to a race that produced the Negro Mammy of the South is not and can never be either an educated man or a gentleman."

No doubt Julia was defending the memory of Lavinia Berry against those "New Negroes" who might belittle her as a servile dupe. She was indignant at the modern tendency to devalue "women's work," tasks that included tending babies, nursing the sick, and managing the household. But above all, her sentimental ode to the Negro Mammy was a transparent attempt to turn criticism away from herself. Few blacks, educated or not, actually scorned women like Lavinia Berry or blamed them for their servitude. What they resented was the system that kept "mammies" in their place, and the very tactics Julia herself had dissected in stories such as "Missy's Twins."

Whether or not she understood the contradictions in her own racial attitudes, Julia must have felt uncomfortable trying to articulate them for *Crisis*. "I write about negroes because they represent human nature obscured by so little veneer; human nature groping among its instinctive impulses and in an environment which is tragically primitive and often unutterably pathetic," she asserted.[83]

As condescending as all this sounds today, Julia Peterkin was being touted by educated blacks as a sympathetic and objective authority on "the southern Negro." Whenever a collection or a symposium on black culture was being planned, someone was sure to mention Julia Peterkin. She was invited to the historic "Opportunity" dinners, where black writers gathered to honor their own. She was asked to write for the "Harlem" issue of *Survey Graphic,* which led to Alain Locke's classic anthology of the period, *The New Negro*. In the end, she participated in neither. She did contribute a short essay on Gullah to *Ebony and Topaz,* an anthology edited by Charles S. Johnson. Illustrated with Africanized woodcuts, *Ebony and Topaz* was intended to be an omnibus of contemporary black studies, and Julia's slight essay appears alongside more substantial works by Arna Bontemps, Phillis Wheatley, Paul Laurence Dunbar, Jessie Fauset, Langston Hughes, Alice Dunbar Nelson, Zora Neale Hurston, and Countee Cullen.[84] In an essay called "Our Little Renaissance," Alain Locke celebrated the recent outpouring of African American poetry, then went on to note the shortcomings of the literary movement. Too much black fiction, he said, was "anemic and rhetorical." So far, white writers like Peterkin and Heyward had dealt more effectively than black writers with "negro life and idiom." [85]

Even by today's Afrocentric standards, Alain Locke was right — the Harlem renaissance had yet to produce much fiction of enduring value. There were a few *significant* novels, to be sure, including Walter White's *The Fire in the Flint*, but none that stood out as fine and powerful writing. *Their Eyes Were Watching God, Native Son,* and *Invisible Man* were far in the future. In 1926, the field of serious "black" fiction did indeed belong to white writers such as Peterkin and Heyward.

A number of people, black and white, found this phenomenon disconcerting. Were white novelists inherently more talented than black ones? Had black novelists been held back from realizing their full potential by the bourgeois attitudes of those whom Wallace Thurman would later dub "Negrotarians"? Ever a keen observer of human behavior, the head "Negrotarian" himself, W. E. B. Du Bois, believed that the key to the mystery lay elsewhere. "White artists," he observed, "cry for freedom in dealing with Negroes because they have so little freedom in dealing with whites. DuBose Heywood [*sic*] writes 'Porgy' and writes beautifully of the black Charleston underworld. But why does he do this? Because he cannot do a similar thing for the white people of Charleston, or they would drum him out of town." [86] It was true: whites felt pressured to censor themselves when portraying whites, blacks when portraying blacks. For writers like Heyward and Peterkin, crossing the color line brought emancipation.

Julia dedicated *Black April* to Julius Mood to get his attention. She *wanted* her father to see through her disguise, to hear what she had to say about him. Because a cousin named Julius Mood had been killed in the Battle of the Somme, she asked D. L. Chambers to add the words "my father" to the dedication page. She later changed her mind, concluding that if the book *were* meant as a memorial, the dedication would read "in *memory* of Julius Mood." [87]

Julia sent her father many complicated messages through the pages of *Black April*, none of which she could ever have addressed to him directly. Even more than Killdee Pinesett, April Locust is Julius Mood, the powerful, arrogant, irresistible male force. The autobiographical elements include countless family names, private jokes, and jibes at absentee fathers. The most obvious appear in chapter 4, which is pointedly titled "Julia." In terms of the plot, very little happens in this chapter. Breeze and Big Sue ride to Blue Brook in a cart pulled by a decrepit mule named Julia. The driver, Uncle, rambles on about Julia's faults and wishes his old mule, Lula, were still alive. (Lula was the name of Julius's sister, one of the Mood aunts who had scolded Julia for writing.) Yet he defends Julia against the scorn of Big Sue.

Uncle then turns his attention to warning Big Sue that April's wife, Leah, is a jealous woman who might seek revenge if she thinks that Big Sue is getting too much attention from either April or the new preacher. (Leah, of course, was the name of Ashleigh Mood's second wife, who inherited him from her dying sister.) At the end of the chapter, the old man brings his stick down "with a whack on Julia's back," to punctuate his warnings.

Julia the mule crops up again and again in *Black April*. Why would Julia name a mule after herself and feature it so prominently? To kick her father in the pants. Julius Mood undoubtedly knew that the mule, a cross between a horse and a donkey, is sterile. In spite of ample evidence to the contrary, southern folklore held that mulattoes, too, were infertile, or at least "slow to breed." Indeed, the popular association between mules and mulattoes was so strong that historian Joel Williamson referred to it as "the 'muleology' of the South," noting that any reference to mules and mulattoes "instantly conjured up a rich and ready-built imagery in Southern white minds."[88] Julius Mood, a great connoisseur of off-color humor, could hardly have missed Julia's innuendo. His sterile daughter, culturally half black and half white, had learned a lesson from the plantation mules. She might be old and foolish, lazy, lame, and trifling. But she was also stubborn and liable to kick.[89]

Julia mailed an advance copy of *Black April* to her father, and once again he was painfully slow to respond. When a letter finally arrived from him, she sent it on to Chambers. "Read between the lines and you can see his utter lack of enthusiasm," she lamented. Her father, she felt, was behaving like a typical white Southerner, and therefore missing the point. "How can I get people to understand that to me these Negroes are not ugly?" she asked Chambers. "When I cry with them over Death and sorrow, I cry for myself along with them. And then, I ache inside, because they can at least laugh often and forget troubles, while I can't do that half so freely and gaily. I'm a d—— Nordic!"[90]

Avoiding any comment on mules, fatherless children, sex, religion, or mortality, Julius Mood wrote that he had discovered a number of factual errors in the text. Julia, who wanted to please her father even more than she wanted to hurt him, rushed anxiously to Sumter. The old man refused to say whether or not he liked the book, yet Julia was sure she saw tears in his eyes.[91] To her relief, the "errors" turned out to be minor, the kind of things that could be attributed to differences of perception. Wood ducks do not quack like other ducks, Julius told her; they "squeak and whistle." Trumpet-vine blossoms smell bitter, not fragrant. And "when an alligator settles in the water, he leaves not two bumps but three." [92]

At Julia's urging, Chambers agreed to change the plates to please her father before the book went into its second printing. He could well afford to be generous — *Black April* had shot into third place on Brentano's best-seller list.[93]

Alma Archer Mood, Julia's mother. She died of tuberculosis when Julia was eighteen months old.

The Archer family. Left to right: Florence Carroll Archer (later Mulligan), John Clifton Archer, Leonidas Archer, Alma Archer (mother of Julia Peterkin), Edgar Lycurgus Archer, Rachel Smith Archer, and Julia Archer (later Switzer).

Above.
Henry McFarlane
Mood and Laura Clark
Mood, the Methodist
grandparents who
raised Julia at her
mother's request.

Right.
Laura and Marian
Mood, Julia's sisters.
There are no known
photographs of Julia
as a baby or little girl.

Opposite.
Julius Mood, Julia's
"devilish and brilliant"
father, during the
Spanish-American War,
1898. "I didn't fight,
and I didn't bleed, but
I almost died — of
ptomaine poisoning,"
he recalled.

Janie Brogdon Mood, Julia's stepmother, center. (Photo courtesy of Jane Brogdon Pate and Edwin Moore Brogdon.)

Julia, second from the left, in costume for an unidentified pageant. The girl to the far left is dressed as a "Southern Belle."

Julia and
Laura Mood
on their
graduation from
Converse College,
1897. Julia was
barely sixteen.

Julia and Willie Peterkin on their wedding day, June 3, 1903.

Julia Peterkin in 1909, a red crayon drawing commissioned in New York, artist unknown.

Bill Peterkin dressed out for football.

The house at Lang Syne, built circa 1914. The servants complained that this new house could have fit into the ballroom of the old one.

The grand piano Julia bought to "cheat the stillness" of the country.

Henry Bellamann started giving Julia piano lessons and ended up teaching her to write. (Photo courtesy of South Carolina Historical Society.)

Carl Sandburg, American poet, circa 1930.

Julia in front of the cabin where she did her writing.

The cottage at Murrells Inlet, an early picture taken before
wide porches were built around the live-oak trunks.

Julia and photographer Doris Ulmann, her friend and collaborator on Roll, Jordan, Roll. *(Photo courtesy of South Carolina Historical Society.)*

Julia poses with two snapper fishermen on their boat in Mobile Bay. This photograph, probably taken by Doris Ulmann, inadvertently reveals the social gulf that lay between the two artists and their subjects.

*Four generations of the Sanders family in front
of Ellis Sanders's house, once an outbuilding for
the McCord mansion. Julia labeled this picture
"Ellis and Big Pa."*

Wallace Heyward, Julia's cook and the inspiration for Budda Ben.

A cabin in the Quarters.

Irving Fineman, by Doris Ulmann. (Photo courtesy of South Carolina Historical Society.)

Julia in a leopardskin coat, holding a Colt revolver.

"Julia Peterkin,"
by José Clemente Orozco, 1930.
Julia considered this painting
"too harsh."

"Drama,"
by José Clemente Orozco, 1930.
Julia is unattainable.

Julia Peterkin, by Carl Van Vechten, 1933. (Photo courtesy of Joseph
Solomon, executor of the estate of Carl Van Vechten.)

Asparagus packer at Lang Syne, by Doris Ulmann, from Roll, Jordan, Roll.
(Photo courtesy of South Carolina Historical Society.)

Julia near Maple Cottage at Bread Loaf Writers' Conference, Middlebury, Vermont, 1936. (Photo courtesy of The Bread Loaf Writers' Conference of Middlebury College.)

Julia Peterkin with the Hepburns at the horse races in Eutawville, South Carolina, 1941. At far left is Belle Stuckey. Far right, next to Julia, is Katharine Hepburn. The three women in the middle are Katharine's younger sisters, Peg and Marion, and her famous mother, Katharine Houghton Hepburn. The men are not identified, though the younger may be Marion's husband, Ellsworth Grant. This was Katharine Hepburn's second visit to Lang Syne.

Bill and Frida Peterkin.

Julia and Willie with
their grandson William,
shortly before Willie's
death.

Above left.
Julia Peterkin in 1942,
after Frida's suicide.

Above right.
Genevieve "Sister" Chandler
Peterkin, Bill's second wife.

Julia holding her grandson,
James Preston Peterkin, on the
porch at Lang Syne, 1957.

Dust jacket for Black April, *Triangle Books edition, 1941. "This is an extraordinary story about a part of our country which is as foreign to most of us as life in Timbuctoo," read the flap. (Photo courtesy of South Carolina Historical Society.)*

Cover for a Pocket Books paperback edition of Scarlet Sister Mary, *1949. "The sin of Scarlet Sister Mary was, in the eyes of the world, that she bore a heavy burden of passion with easy pleasure. Perhaps she loved her fellow man beyond conventional limits, but she lived a life which was warmly exciting and, in the end, happy." (Photo courtesy of South Carolina Historical Society.)*

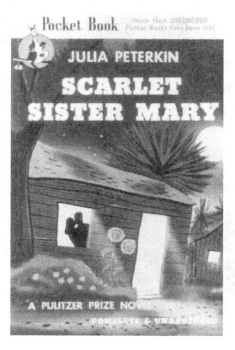

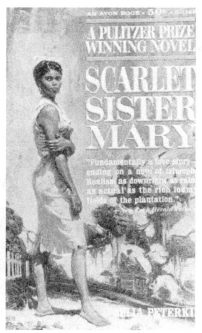

Cover for an Avon paperback edition of Scarlet Sister Mary. *(Photo courtesy of South Carolina Historical Society.)*

CHAPTER 8

Scarlet Sister Mary

ore than five months had passed since the official publication date, and the *Columbia State* had yet to print an original review of *Black April.* Julia took the silence as a personal insult, and no doubt that is how it was intended. By early July, forcing the *State* to take notice of the book had become a minor obsession. Ruth Aley, tired of listening to Julia's laments, impishly suggested that they should take a trip — dress to kill, drive up to Columbia, and pay a call on Stanhope Sams, the literary editor.

Rather than confront the old man at his newspaper office, where he could take refuge behind desks and secretaries, Julia and Ruth showed up at his house, thus laying claim to all the privileges of southern chivalry. Caught off guard, the courtly Mr. Sams "all but swallowed his tongue" explaining why the *State* had not reviewed *Black April,* leading

Julia to believe that his wife had pressured him to ignore it. "I cooed in her ear, then tried to look worshipfully at him," she wrote to D. L. Chambers. She followed up this performance with a note so saccharine that Ruth Aley expected it to backfire. But in less than a week, Sams had personally composed and printed a glowing review. "Not only is *B[lack] A[pril]* great, but poor 'Green Thursday' is also worth-while," Julia reported to Chambers. "I do feel like writing and inviting [Mr. Sams] and all his associates to step to Hell." [1]

Chambers, for whom courting publicity was simply business, pointed out that in the end Mr. Sams had done the right thing. But Julia was unforgiving: as she saw it, the man had "tried to humiliate me all he could, and then when he saw everything on my side, he hopped over too. Neither his praise nor his blame have any value, to me, except that he's a sort of bell cow who leads the S.C. herd to book shops. He's not even a worthwhile enemy." [2]

With or without the help of people like Stanhope Sams, Julia was becoming a celebrity. The public was suddenly fascinated with her life. Carl Sandburg recommended that she play up her role as plantation mistress, milk it for all it was worth. The public, he said, would never really understand the real Julia Peterkin anyway, just as it didn't understand the real Carl Sandburg. A few whiffs of magnolia wouldn't hurt, and would certainly help sell her books. [3]

Julia's public image began to jell during the spring of 1927, when the editor of *American Magazine* made a special trip to Lang Syne on Easter Sunday. Would she consider writing an inspirational article for his publication? Julia accepted the assignment, shrugging off a Bobbs-Merrill staffer who scorned the magazine as "that Horatio Alger monthly." [4] "Seeing Things" appeared in January 1928, alongside articles titled "Why I Do Go to Church" (by the popular poet Edgar Guest), "Turn Your Handicap to Your Advantage," "I am Proud that I Was an Orphan," "My Worst Fault and How I Overcame It," and "You've Got to Rub People the Right Way."

"Seeing Things" is Julia's only published attempt at straight autobiography. It reveals a self-conscious woman struggling to be charming while aching to "write what is, even if it is unpleasant." In some respects, the article is a remarkably frank treatment of Julia's long postpartum depression, her pervasive feelings of inadequacy, and the "sinister questions without answers" that had "crept into [her] mind and rankled" after her marriage. But in other ways, Julia, as usual, evaded and embroidered the truth. Writing about the day she came to Lang

Syne as a bride, she spun an antebellum fantasy in which an avenue of cedars and oaks sweeps up to a gleaming white mansion. Perhaps to increase the drama, she implied that she had never even seen the plantation before returning from her honeymoon, or met the servants, who spoke a mysterious language she did not comprehend.

After this inauspicious beginning, however, "Seeing Things" turns to a less hackneyed theme, Julia's initiation into African American culture. Living on the plantation had taught her "to pretend to have courage even when [she] lacked it most." And eventually she had adopted her servants' African belief that "all things are bound together into one common whole." [5]

In "Seeing Things," Julia admitted that anger, despair, and the urge to speak the truth had driven her to write fiction. Yet the article never mentions her own ambition, neatly sidestepping that greatest of feminine taboos. Indeed, to read any of Julia's interviews or autobiographical writing is to conclude that fame was somehow thrust upon her, an accident of fate. Only to H. L. Mencken had she ever been able to admit her craving for notoriety, but now Mencken had turned against her.

Early that spring a letter had arrived from Mrs. Edward MacDowell, inviting Julia to apply for a place at her artists' colony in Peterboro, New Hampshire. There was only one catch: Mrs. MacDowell wanted letters of recommendation from DuBose Heyward, a former colonist, and H. L. Mencken. Heyward was no problem — Julia sometimes referred to him as "my chief defender in S.C." [6] Mencken was another matter. Hoping for the best, Julia forwarded Mrs. MacDowell's letter and asked for a recommendation. Then she waited. A note addressed in Mencken's familiar handwriting arrived, and Julia tore it open. Mrs. MacDowell's letter had arrived safely, he said, but "unluckily I cannot decipher [it]." [7] Mencken was famous for holding grudges, and Mrs. MacDowell understood the situation. She assured Julia that the testimonials were simply a matter of form and asked her to join the colony anyway.

South Carolina had become unbearable, not because Julia had been ostracized but because she was too popular. At Lang Syne, the curious arrived night and day by way of the new highway, demanding to "see" the author of *Black April*. "If I as much as go to Columbia to visit the dentist," she complained, "my being in town is recorded as news." A new refrain crept into her correspondence: "I want to give one earth encircling howl, 'Please leave me alone.' " [8]

On July 4, 1927, Julia moved with her typewriter into a secluded orange and green studio on the grounds of the MacDowell Colony. Hudson Strode arrived two days later. DuBose Heyward was already there with his wife, Dorothy; so were Edwin Arlington Robinson, Frances Newman, Aaron Copland, more than a dozen other composers, a handful of painters, and one sculptor.[9]

To ensure that her colony was "no Bohemia," Mrs. MacDowell confined the single men to a communal dormitory and prohibited use of the private studios after dark. Colonists suspected of fornication were ejected, and dirty jokes were greeted by stony silence.[10] Yet even the redoubtable Mrs. MacDowell could not make instant Victorians out of her jazz-age guests. Julia liked to tell about the time she was seated at dinner next to a small, meek-looking man and his immense, solicitous wife. Suddenly she felt an insinuating pinch on her inner thigh. Incredulous, she shot her neighbor a hard look and kept on eating. He pinched her again. After supper, Julia announced that she would read palms. The pincher's wife pushed her husband forward. Furrowing her brow, Julia gazed raptly at the lines in his hand and predicted that he would go on a trip, meet a stranger, and have a run of good luck. Then she paused, gulped, and murmured, "Oh, I'm sorry — I see something very serious."

"What is it?" gasped the wife.

Fixing her victim with a baleful gaze, Julia whispered, "Shall I tell him?"

"Yes, tell him," urged the crowd.

"Someone . . . is . . . going . . . to knock your head off one of these days," she hissed.[11]

Despite the abundance of good minds there, only Hudson Strode, Frances Newman, and Elizabeth Shepley Sargeant seemed kindred spirits. The other men were absorbed in an eternal game of pool, and the other women seemed stodgy. The acid-tongued Newman, "brilliant and mean," a protégée of H. L. Mencken, was working on a novel called *The Hard-Boiled Virgin*.[12] Still trying to get a rise out of Mencken, Julia proposed that the three of them meet in New York for a mock wedding. Not hearing from him, she wrote again a few days later to say that the bride, Frances, had been stung by a hornet and the nuptials would have to be canceled. Mencken was not amused.

Elsie Sargeant, a plump, expansive staff writer for the *New Republic*, held the odd distinction of having been wounded on a battlefield during World War I, an experience she recorded in the book *Shadow-Shapes*. Best remembered today for her memoir of Willa Cather, who was one of

Julia's favorite writers, Elsie was a zealous social reformer well known in literary and political circles (she would later become an ardent New Dealer).[13] The two women exchanged many confidences at Peterboro; Elsie, in particular, seems to have confessed some things that she later wished she hadn't. Julia reassured her that their conversations would remain private. With Elsie, she indulged a sentimental streak that seldom showed itself in her relationships with other women. Elsie became "Precious," "Darling," "my dear," "dear child," one of the few people to whom Julia could say, simply, "I love you."

Julia and Hudson Strode often escaped the dorms and dining hall to take long walks through the surrounding woods and pastures, favorite haunts of romantic colonists in search of privacy. Inevitably, eyebrows were raised. Julia would later refuse to return to Peterboro because she and Strode had been the subject of so much gossip there; and Strode, who otherwise seems to have kept every scrap of paper he received through the mail, evidently destroyed all of Julia's letters from this period. Yet there is no evidence that their relationship went beyond friendship, and in writing about their walks in the woods, Strode described them less as trysts than as editorial conferences, during one of which he claimed to have invented the title "Scarlet Sister Mary" for Julia's new novel.[14]

If the MacDowell Colony insulated Julia against unwanted visitors and domestic distractions, it could not protect her from the United States mail. Every day her lunch basket arrived filled with letters, many of them requests for free books. "South Carolinians especially seem to think that now, since they see fit to read what I've written at last, I should at least furnish the books," she groused to Chambers. "Before long I shall insist on your printing me a number of slips, 'Please get to hell,' that I may send them instead of a letter in reply." [15]

Meanwhile, the push to sell *Black April* continued, bringing consequences Julia could never have anticipated. In January, Chambers's assistant Anne Johnston had asked her to send the firm some pictures of Lang Syne and its residents, "white and black." Julia shipped her Bill's photograph album, but Johnston returned it, explaining that the publicity department needed negatives. Julia bought a roll of film and strolled down to the Quarters carrying Bill's Kodak camera. She snapped an old woman smoking a pipe, a man tending some hogs. Then, in a move that would eventually cost her dearly, she casually suggested that Mary Weeks pick up a large wooden washtub and balance it on her head. Mary did as she was asked. Her two young grandsons, Willie

Henry and Keepsie, watched from the side yard, and Julia snapped them standing by the cabin next door.[16] When the pictures arrived in Indianapolis, Anne Johnston exulted over "the cunning little darkies." The photographs were exactly what she had been hoping for.[17]

On her way to Peterboro, Julia had stopped over in New York City, where she was interviewed by "the Boswell of New York," Harry Salpeter.[18] "I shall never write of white people. Their lives are not so colorful," she declared to him. Dale Warren, an editor at Houghton Mifflin, read Salpeter's admiring article and showed up in Peterboro using it as a bookmark in his copy of *Black April.* Julia was so taken with the handsome Warren that before the visit was over she had agreed to let him write a second feature story. Bobbs-Merrill, she said, would be glad to send him some snapshots of the plantation, including the one of Mary Weeks with the tub on her head.[19]

All this attention went to Julia's head; she started to wonder if Bobbs-Merrill might be taking her for granted. When Chambers congratulated her for successfully coaxing a review out of Stanhope Sams, she snapped back that publicity was Bobbs-Merrill's job, not hers. She and Ruth had merely been playing a game. Chambers, alarmed, tried to soothe her. He certainly hadn't meant that she should bear the burden of publicizing *Black April,* although he was always grateful for her suggestions. "Before you are through the South Carolina papers will be handing you the world on a gold platter," he predicted. Temporarily mollified, Julia passed on an obsequious note from the president of the South Carolina Federation of Women's Clubs. "I'm almost popular. Really, I am," she teased.[20]

By early September she had worked herself into a rage again, this time over what she saw as misguided advertising. "My audience read *American Mercury, New Masses, New Republic, Nation, Opportunity,*" she wired. "They are sophisticated and radical."[21] Chambers sent a placating reply — he would make sure that her advice was followed. But he could see clearly what she could not: Bobbs-Merrill's mass-market approach was working. References to *Black April* were popping up everywhere, and while some had been planted by his publicity people, many had sprouted by themselves. The *Dallas Times* ran a bizarre article that opened with a description of April's toes floating around in the washtub. Having grabbed its readers' attention, the piece went on to describe pyorrhea, a gum disease that can cause the teeth to drop out.[22] In Vacaville, California, an anonymous reporter ungrammatically described *Black April* as the saga of "a fearless, huge, negro, savage devoted negresses, sway intangible mysteries ruthlessly around a South Carolina Plantation."[23] This was the purple prose of bodice-rippers, a steamy language that would soon come to dominate Bobbs-Merrill's publicity campaigns.

Julia's new novel was "the story of a black girl who goes along as black girls do, until her husband leaves her." The heroine, of course, was Mary Weeks, thinly disguised as Mary Pinesett. Chambers was anxious to get the book out while he could capitalize on the popularity of *Black April.* He offered Julia a large advance as an incentive to write quickly, yet *Scarlet Sister Mary* failed to arrive at Bobbs-Merrill in time to make the spring list for 1928. In early May, Julia was still rewriting, hampered by the chronic drunkenness of her young male stenographer. At Chambers's urging she fired the stenographer and hired a female typist. Finally, in mid-June, the completed manuscript made its way to Indianapolis.[24] Chambers was delighted by what he saw.

Mary is an orphan, a "poor little motherless" who lives with old Maum Hannah and her crippled son, Budda Ben. The story opens on the day Mary is to marry July Pinesett, a guitar-playing rascal. In a scene that echoes Julia's own wedding day, Maum Hannah awakens to an omen that the marriage will not be happy: a rat has gnawed a hole in the wedding cake.

When the girl pulls off her nightgown to get dressed, Hannah observes that she is already pregnant. Mary has committed a "scarlet sin." After the wedding, July escorts Mary to a birth-night supper, where he abandons her on the sidelines while he dances with her second cousin Cinder, a tricky woman who "always knew some way to make the men take to her, although she was skinny and dry, and had a fox chin and squirrel teeth and a sly stepping walk like a cat."[25] Indeed, Cinder had tried hard to marry July herself. Mary is crazed with jealousy. Before the night is over she is dancing for July's twin brother, June, well aware that the deacons will turn her out of the church for it.

In spite of the rocky start, Mary and July are happy with each other for a time. Less than nine months after the wedding, Mary is on the way to the store, Grab-All, when a spasm of pain racks her body. She cries for help but no one hears; she delivers her baby in the middle of the road, then picks him up and walks home. The old women gossip, but Maum Hannah praises Mary for being so strong and forthright, when "so many women who are made in the image of God himself, lie down helpless, full of groans and bitter words, quickened by fear as much as by the pain itself." [26]

Little Unex (short for Unexpected) pleases Mary. He has "more teeth than he was due to have and his head [is] covered with crinky little wool. A blessed baby," Mary thinks. "A joy." Like all great joys, hers is short-lived; Cinder returns to the plantation, and soon July is staying out all night. Mary goes out herself, to the crossroads store, where June buys her a soda, a bag of candy, a can of salmon, and a string of beads. July finds out and beats her. Afterward, Mary lies very still, pretending to be blind and paralyzed. The ruse works — she rests comfortably for several days while July cooks, washes, and tends her like a baby. "A strong man's hand can fall heavy," Mary concludes, "and the best way to deal with strength is to be weak and helpless." [27]

Though it works for the moment, this strategy is not the one that will serve Mary best in the long run. Daddy Cudjoe, the conjure doctor, warns her to buck up. "You must stop frettin an' bein scared," he says. "Keep you belly full o victuals, make you mouth smile, laugh an' be merry if you can. Don' never let people see you down-hearted, or a-hanging you head, an' lookin sorrowful. Dat ain' de way. No. Mens don' crave a sorrowful, sad-lookin 'oman." [28] He gives her a love charm to lure July back.

For a little while, the charm seems to work. July stays close to home. Even so, Mary's jealousy "gnaw[s] a hole deep down in her heart." Before long, July and Cinder go off together on an excursion to town and fail to return.[29] Mary slips into a deep depression.

In a scene typical of Julia's most evocative writing, Mary sees her state of mind reflected in the landscape. The "hot fields, spread out before her eyes, looked silent and cruel. They offered her no hope for better things, no way of escaping sorrow. . . . Misery dimmed the sunshine, blackened the shade, blighted her pleasure in the flowers and trees and in all the things she loved best." No one can rouse her — not Maum Hannah, not Budda Ben, not even the threat that her breast milk may poison the baby if she continues to fret. Her jealousy is "a sickness, a weakening ailment." At first, people are sympathetic, but eventually they become impatient with "her silence, her tottering walk, her haggard body." [30]

Time passes, and Mary's grief wanes. July's twin brother, June, reawakens her interest in life and fathers her daughter, Seraphine. Mary discovers that by wearing her love charm she can catch and hold any man who takes her fancy, though she seldom wants the same one for long. "Men are too much alike," she thinks, "with ways too much the same. None is worth keeping, none worth a tear; and still each one is a little different from the rest; just different enough to make him worth finding out."[31] Mary takes many lovers, including a man from "Poughkeepsie" who gets off the riverboat for just long enough to beget a baby that Mary names "Keepsie." Unex, Mary's "heart-child," leaves home; Seraphine goes off to town to get a "depluma" and comes home pregnant instead.[32] More babies arrive as the older children disperse, until Mary has offspring by nine different fathers.

One day while Mary is frying corn cakes, a strange man appears at her door. It is July, holding out his hands. "Paralyzed with joy and with misery," Mary hesitates. When she finally speaks, her voice sounds "hollow and strange." "No, you ain' my July," she says. "I ain' had no July in twenty years." Shivering with desire, she sends him away.[33]

Mary has learned to fight strength with strength, to deny the man who abandoned her. We yearn along with her for a passionate scene that will reunite the lovers, wipe the slate clean. But Mary has long since stopped needing a husband to feel whole. For the reader as well as for Mary, the scene is as painful as it is invigorating.

Unex returns home with his newborn baby, whose mother has died of a fever. He soon takes sick himself, and dies in Mary's arms. Mary is heartbroken. "Oh, Gawd," she cries out as the pine coffin is covered, "why couldn' you le me keep my child a lil bit longer?"[34] Nearly despairing, Mary decides that "God ha[s] plagued her long enough." Hoping that he will "cast out" her misery, she retreats to the pine woods to seek peace. A specter of the dead Unex shows her a white cloth with ten scarlet stripes, nine for her nine children "born in sin," and the tenth for Seraphine's "sin child," for as Unex explains, Mary "set de pattern" and Seraphine simply followed it. Mary rolls on the ground and begs Jesus to wash away the stripes. Nothing happens. At last she decides to pray for her sins one at a time, and when morning breaks, the cloth is washed "whiter than snow, and so shining her eyes could not face it."[35]

The deacons schedule a meeting to decide whether Mary's vision means that her sins are forgiven or that "Satan had sent a dream to deceive her." Dressing for the examination, Mary deliberates whether or not to wear her charm. One part of her says, "Take it off," while another part reminds her that the deacons are men who need "to be ruled in her favor to-night."[36] She wears the charm.

The deacons are spellbound as Mary relates her vision. Brer Dee announces that Mary must be rebaptized. Andrew has never heard of baptizing somebody more than once, but Brer Dee is adamant. After all, he points out, "Si May-e has been a turrible sinner. E has sent many mens to Hell." At the end of the meeting, everyone comes up to welcome Mary back to the fold. Daddy Cudjoe comes last and whispers to Mary, "If you gwine to quit wid mens now, Si May-e, do gi me you conjure rag. E's de best charm I ever made." Mary looks him in the eye and smiles. "I'll lend em to you when you need em, Daddy, but I couldn' gi way my love-charm," she says. "E's all I got now to keep me young." [37]

Julia often led people to believe that *Scarlet Sister Mary* was the biography of Mary Weeks. To Stark Young, an expatriate Southerner, she wrote that the heroine was her "best black friend, the woman who has taught me to remember I am of no more importance in the great pattern of things than a flower or a worm or a wisp of smoke." [38] Mary Weeks's living relatives confirm that much of the plot of *Scarlet Sister Mary* was borrowed from Mary's experience. But they are mortified by several details that Julia added, and infuriated by the omission of Bessie and Essie, Mary's half-Peterkin daughters. What gave Julia the right to air their dirty laundry, they ask, without revealing where the first stains came from?

In fact, Julia *did* want to tell the whole truth; from the time she first began to write, Mary Weeks's affairs with her brothers-in-law cropped up in early drafts of story after story. Yet she always backed away, always deleted all such references before the manuscript reached publication. Describing Mary's life in the first draft of "On a Plantation," for example, Julia wrote the truth; two of Cely's children are white. She later revised this passage to read "one was white." By the time she completed *Scarlet Sister Mary,* even that one mixed-race child had disappeared, although echoes of Mary's liaisons with the Peterkin brothers are detectible in the published version of the novel.

Mary first appears "fetching water up the hill from the spring." As we have seen, carrying water was Mary Weeks's special job, the one that got her into trouble. "As soon as she had grown big enough to toddle back and forth holding to Maum Hannah's apron, she had helped fetch water, first a tin can full, then a small bucket full, until at last she could come up the hill with three full-sized buckets, all filled to the brim, one balanced on her head and one in each hand." [39] But the silver pitcher and the boys in the Big House are nowhere in sight.

While Julia suppressed the parts of Mary's life that reflected poorly on her own family, she added several other episodes for dramatic effect. To this day, Mary's family is dismayed by a scene near the end of the novel in which Si May-e has twins and a third newborn — her daughter's — mysteriously appears in the bed while she sleeps. That never happened to Mary Weeks, they say — Julia Peterkin made it up. They also point out that the real Mary never gave birth to a baby in the middle of the road.[40]

To the novelist, of course, events are raw material waiting to be shaped. The illusion of reality is all that matters; facts themselves are irrelevant. Perhaps the trouble with Mary's family could have been averted had Julia chosen a different name for her heroine — Bina or Harpa, maybe, anything but Mary. Henry Bellamann suggested *Scarlet Zeda*.[41] Yet, to Julia, the name was essential to the story. "Mary" reminds us, as it reminded Julia, of the Virgin Mary, but also of Mary Magdalene, that ancient symbol of sexual appetite who is used to represent the Bad Woman, the sensual woman, the inveterate sinner who seeks redemption late in life.[42] For obvious reasons, however, Mary Weeks's daughter Minnie Logan was offended by the comparison.

There is a certain poetic justice in the fact that the friendship between Julia Peterkin and Mary Weeks broke up over hauling water. Dale Warren's admiring article appeared as a full-page spread in the *Boston Evening Transcript*, accompanied by the snapshots of Mary with the washtub on her head and her two little grandsons.[43] On January 8, 1929, the *Columbia Record* reprinted the story in its entirety. Minnie Logan, who was living in Columbia, opened the paper that day and exploded. The photographs were demeaning. Her mother no longer carried water that way, for white people or anyone else. Minnie drove to Lang Syne and ordered Mary to pack up. She was moving to Columbia, out of Julia Peterkin's domain.[44]

Mary liked the attention she was getting and did not want to leave Lang Syne, but her aggrieved children were adamant.[45] Her youngest daughter, Rudy Mae, wanted her to sue. (Such a lawsuit, of course, would have been doomed to failure in Jim Crow South Carolina.) Rudy Mae, known to her family as "Kutch," had other reasons to resent the Peterkins. Six years earlier, Julia had published a story called "Cootch's Premium," in which the "premium" was an illegitimate baby conceived while the girl was away at school. Some family members say that this story is true; others say that Kutch never had a baby out of wedlock.[46]

But Rudy Mae *had* gone off to the city to school and had come back to Lang Syne with a high school diploma. Because she was educated, older people often asked her to check over their accounts. Convinced by Rudy Mae that she had been shorted, one old woman confronted Willie Peterkin with a discrepancy in her bill. "How would you know?" he is said to have asked. "You can't figger."

"No, but I mark it down here every time, and Kutch adds 'em up for me," she replied.

Shortly afterward, Rudy Mae ran into Willie in Fort Motte. "Come on, Kutch, and I'll give you a ride home," he said. She got into the car, expecting him to drive straight down the road to Lang Syne. Instead, he made a detour, winding slowly through the woods and past the cemetery. Rudy Mae was terrified. But all Willie wanted to do was talk.

"You going to school up in Columbia?" Willie asked.

"Yassuh," Rudy Mae answered.

"What you studying? Arithmetic?"

"Yassuh."

"Now, Kutch, don't you go a' figgerin' for any of these people, you hear?" Willie warned.

"Yassuh," Rudy Mae answered. He drove her on home.[47]

Julia told none of her literary friends that Mary had left the plantation. "I love [the real Mary]," she had written to Chambers when *Scarlet Sister Mary* was finished. "If the nice Southern ladies fail to roll their eyes and hold up their hands to heaven over her, I'll be sad. . . . She has helped me over some rough spots, and when I die I hope she will be here to close my eyes and shroud me."[48] It was not to be; prodded by her daughter, Mary had declared her independence. But move where she would, the real Si May-e would always be overshadowed by a fictitious version of herself created by the woman she was fleeing.

Mary's grandson William Seabrook, one of the little boys who watched in wonder as Julia posed Mary with a tub on her head, remembers his grandmother as meek, exploited, and terrified of white people. But Mary Heyward, Mary's granddaughter and namesake, describes a far more complicated personality. "You've got to remember that long before my grandmother was 'Scarlet Sister Mary' she was 'Raped Sister Mary,'" Mrs. Heyward says. But she adds that "rape" may not be the right word for what happened between Mary Weeks and the Peterkin boys. A black woman in Mary's position could not easily have refused the sons of her employer. But Mary may also have complied because she "liked the money," as Mrs. Heyward puts it, or because consenting to have sex won her better food, nicer clothes, more freedom within the household. Jackie Whitmore, Mary Weeks's great-great-nephew, speculates that Mary may have had yet another motive. Maybe she was just a normal teenager, curious about sex and thrown daily into close contact with two attractive young men.

Julia dedicated the book to Willie Peterkin because, she told Chambers, he had been "patient for so long." [49] In fact, the novel sent Willie a different message: Julia knew about his dalliance with Elizabeth Darby. Julia was no stranger to fits of jealousy, of course, and her account of Mary's breakdown could have been inspired by any number of experiences that had nothing to do with Willie. Yet his affair with Elizabeth was at its height in 1928, and Cinder's flirtation with July at the dance mirrors Julia's description of Elizabeth working a Fort Motte social, dancing suggestively with both Willie and Bill. As Julia later told it, she walked up to Elizabeth and loudly announced, "You've got my husband, but you leave my son alone!" [50] Julia may have hoped that Willie would recognize his own behavior in the pages of *Scarlet Sister Mary*, though in most ways he bore little resemblance to the hot-blooded spendthrift July. Evidently he never read the book.

Her father, who also had lovers, did read *Scarlet Sister Mary*. More sophisticated by far than his son-in-law, he must have understood that Julia was attacking the sexual double standard that tacitly gave men the right to stray but declared promiscuous women abominations.

As usual, Julia also turned her attention outside the immediate family. For Budda Ben, she looked for inspiration to a more remote past. There had been a slave named Ben living on Lang Syne during the early 1800s. A Canadian surgeon who visited Louisa McCord was distressed by the sight of the twelve-year-old Ben, so paralyzed by "contraction of the flexor tendons" that "he could only lie down in the sand and crawl in the sun." At his suggestion, Mrs. McCord "sent to Charleston for a tenotomy knife." The two severed the rigid tendons and "straightened him out in no time," or so the story goes. [51]

Louisa McCord's daughter, Louisa McCord Smythe, also mentioned Ben in her memoirs of Lang Syne, but the tales Julia heard about him probably came from Anaky Bryant, Lavinia Berry, and the other elderly black women who nursed her. [52] One of Julia's earliest stories, sent to Carl Sandburg for criticism, tells how Ben came to be crippled. In this version, the plantation mistress is obviously the villain.

The story begins when "Old Miss" orders Charity to marry Champagne, a young boy from Lang Syne. [53] Charity already has a baby by a man on another plantation, yet she has no choice but to obey her mistress. Miserably unhappy, she picks up little Ben one night and struggles through the dark woods to see her lover. While trying to cross a stream on a fallen log, she falls and crushes the baby's spine. Charity blames herself and her sin, but Julia was blaming Old Miss and the arrogance of white slaveholders.

In describing Budda Ben, Julia also drew on the personality of her handicapped cook, Wallace Heyward, who endured his own trials with good humor. The antebellum Ben shouted gibberish, pretending to preach the gospel, but it was Wallace who supplied the philosophy for Julia's portrait of Budda Ben.

Just as they do in *Green Thursday* and *Black April*, many of the characters in *Scarlet Sister Mary* have Africanized names or nicknames. June and July were based on James "Bully" Bryant and one of his brothers.[54] (Bully was not a twin, but Mary Weeks did have children by a pair of twins, Josh and Caleb Jackson.) Latin slave names such as Caesar and Cicero were fairly common at Lang Syne, but Julia avoided using them.[55] She toyed with the idea of calling Doll "Bina," an African name that means "Tuesday," then changed her mind before the book went to press. The nickname "Keepsie" came from one of Mary's sister's children, who did indeed have a father who came to Lang Syne from Poughkeepsie.[56]

Traditional names cannot obscure the fact that the old ways are fading in *Scarlet Sister Mary*. On her wedding day, Mary contemplates Maum Hannah's cabin, which has not altered in her lifetime, and not even, she thinks, in Maum Hannah's: "The cupboard where her clothes stayed and the leaning shelf by the window with the four sad-irons resting on it after their hard week's work had never been out of their places since they were put there by women who lived here before Maum Hannah was born."[57] By the time Mary reaches middle age, however, the government is sending workers to teach the midwives a "new" way of catching babies. People go to church to watch movies. Unex shows up with a mysterious "fireless bottle" for his baby; Doll nags her husband to buy a used car. Up-to-date corpses are buried in ready-made shrouds and store-bought coffins, "varnished up and painted like a bureau with a glass window in it to show their wicked faces."[58] The young are heading for the cities.

Strange mail continued to arrive at Lang Syne. A man from Chicago demanded to know "what substantive authority you have for your position as regards Ethiopian toes, i.e., that they float." An eighty-four-year-old vegetarian astrologer from California claimed he had known Julia in another life and proposed marrying her to formalize the bond. Her next good year would be 1929, he said, and her lucky colors were scarlet, black, and golden brown.[59]

Whatever his eccentricities, the astrologer's predictions turned out to be right. Julia submitted her new novel under Hudson Strode's title, *Scarlet Sister Mary.* Chambers liked the name, partly because the color in the title linked the book to *Black April* and *Green Thursday.* But after trying the name out on friends in Fort Motte and Columbia, Julia developed second thoughts about it. The word *scarlet* was almost a profanity in South Carolina, she wrote to Chambers, and the title might insult Mary Weeks. She thought "Pure Scarlet" might be less offensive, less like a "cheap movie title." Chambers disagreed. In the end, Julia gave in. "I hope [Mary] will forgive me for this," she added.[60]

There was talk of putting Mary's portrait on the cover (presumably an artist's rendering), but Julia opposed the idea. Who knew, she thought, what a New York artist might conceive? A photograph would be better. But there was Minnie Logan's reaction to consider, and that idea was soon dropped.[61] By August, Julia was reading page proofs, and on September 27, 1928, she received the first copy along with a check for $760. This time, the *Columbia State* did not dally — an enthusiastic review appeared *before* the official publication date.[62]

With *Mary* safely between boards, Chambers pressed Julia to move quickly on the Harlem book. Again she explained that she was feeling "wrung out" and was not ready to begin another project. "Quit counting on a novel a year," she warned. "That would be merely doing potboilers. I won't begin that yet. We've a good cotton crop." She spoke too soon. Lang Syne was hit by a hurricane that "whipped [the cotton] to shreds" and smashed acres of valuable timber. Downed trees blocked the road to Fort Motte, and the swollen Congaree River ripped out the new highway bridge, a loss that also entailed a gain, since it temporarily stemmed the hateful flow of tourists.[63]

Julia asked for, and promptly got, a large advance against her royalties. In a flush of gratitude, she wrote to Chambers, "I expect to give Bobbs-Merrill not only my next three novels but *all* I ever write, provided you are managing the affairs of the firm."[64] Then she retired to bed with tonsillitis.

Scarlet Sister Mary was passed over by the Book of the Month Club and the Literary Guild.[65] In early October, when ads were already placed and books on their way to the bookstores, Walter White approached Julia with an offer from the Book League of America. Never having heard of the Book League, Julia inquired of Mr. Gittman in Columbia and D. L. Chambers in Indianapolis whether "The National Book League" was really a legitimate outfit. All of them were wary of a brand-new enterprise whose business was being conducted by a black man. Bobbs-Merrill settled the matter by going ahead with publication.[66] Assuming a fatherly tone, Chambers explained to Julia that he would "hate to see *Sister Mary* in a cheap setting and under doubtful auspices."[67]

Walter White was perplexed. The arrangement would have brought Julia at least $1,500 in cash. Bobbs-Merrill's stubborn refusal to negotiate struck him as unreasonable. Privately, Julia wondered what White stood to gain if the deal went through. She had heard that two of her fellow South Carolinians had recently fared much better with the older book clubs. The word was that E. C. L. Adams's *Nigger to Nigger* had been bought by Book of the Month, and DuBose Heyward's *Mamba's Daughters* by the Literary Guild.[68] Julia's friends in South Carolina gave her to understand that it was "no feat to have your picture sitting up in a store window with the books around it looking like a red-light district."[69] Chambers patiently replied that *Nigger to Nigger* was not a Book of the Month Club offering, nor, as far as he knew, had *Mamba's Daughters* been bought by the Literary Guild (actually, it had been). "Everybody in Columbia" he concluded, must be "absolutely insane."[70]

With *Scarlet Sister Mary* nearing release, Julia again went after H. L. Mencken, pelting him with note after note. He did not reply. At her wits' end, she told Mencken that she felt old and useless, and said she had begged her doctor for some "pleasant" capsules strong enough to kill her.[71] Mencken took the bait. "You will never be old. You will always be charming. All your best work is still ahead of you," he immediately wrote back — or so Julia told Chambers.[72]

Julia knew that the threat of suicide would unsettle Mencken. Less than two years ago, a male friend of his had taken cyanide just after seeing him. There were rumors that the two had quarreled and that Mencken had driven the man to kill himself.[73] The last thing he needed was for a desperate former protégée to kill herself. But Mencken was not willing to go very far with his assurances. He still would not say anything that could be used to promote Julia's books. On receiving an advance copy of *Scarlet Sister Mary*, he adroitly avoided comment by thanking her before reading it.[74]

Other old friends were kinder. Henry Bellamann, writing for the *State*, praised the book's lack of "clutter"; and Hudson Strode waxed effusive in the *New York Herald Tribune*. "Mrs. Peterkin is unsurpassed by any writer in America," he declared. "Certainly as an interpreter of the Southern negro she is pre-eminent." [75]

In the *New York Evening Post*, reviewer Herschell Brickell pronounced himself "astounded" at the way Julia's narrative control had developed over the past year. Other critics, he said, were wrong to treat her work as a kind of "super-reporting"; Julia Peterkin was an artist, probably an unconscious artist, spinning her instincts into fiction. [76]

Much of what was written was flattering nonsense. "Sometimes her story sags with too much beauty, but to err in that manner is super-human and quite easily forgiven," wrote Robert Chamberlain in the *New York Times*. [77] Commenting on the state of southern literature, novelist Ellen Glasgow pointed out that "Julia Peterkin is interpreting an alien race with beauty and truth and that something more which pierces deeper than even beauty or truth." [78] *Survey*, a magazine of African American culture, declared that "no other author of white blood seems able to do what Julia Peterkin can do: write of the primitive negro with an almost pure-black comprehension." [79] In fact, Julia's genius had nothing to do with "alien races" or "primitive negroes." The critics were blinded by their own prejudices. The inevitable discussions about blackness and whiteness served only to muddy the waters, obscuring what really mattered. Julia could make the strange seem familiar and the familiar, strange. She could make her readers laugh and cry, could make them stay up all night turning pages. She was, in short, a great storyteller.

By the end of the year, Bobbs-Merrill had printed seventy-six thousand copies of *Scarlet Sister Mary*, and contracts had been negotiated to issue British, Spanish, Italian, Danish, and Hebrew editions. [80] The day before Christmas, a huge bouquet of yellow roses arrived from Laurance Chambers. "Perhaps I'm growing weak-minded but I dripped tears over the roses, and then over your letter," she wrote to him. Changing the subject, she launched into a confession. "I've been unhappy over this, think I'll feel better to tell you, so here goes." What she disclosed was professional infidelity: earlier in the year, over Chambers's vehement objections, she had discussed writing a children's book for another publisher. Chambers believed he had talked her out of it, but "because . . . things were rather bad here financially at Lang Syne," she had accepted a $1,000 advance. The roses, along with the check Chambers had thoughtfully included, had caused her to reconsider. She sent the other publisher's money back, effectively terminating the contract. "How could you, how could you fail to call on us for money when you wanted it?" Chambers asked. "I'll get a check up of royalties on *Scarlet Sister Mary* . . . and let you know what they amount to." [81]

Julia was riding the crest of a wave, savoring the fruits of her fame. Both she and her publishers foresaw many books to come—more prizes, more praise, and more money. Sooner than they thought, the tide would turn; there would be no more checks or flowers. But for the moment, Julia was on top; when she talked, people listened.

CHAPTER 9

Gabriel's Harp

ulia liked to tell her literary friends that the people of Lang Syne and the surrounding countryside were insulated against racial violence. It was true that Willie and most of his neighbors tended to call the sheriff instead of pulling a gun when they felt that their interests were threatened. Troublemakers were jailed or banished from the area — or, in extreme cases, legally executed. While the system was anything but color-blind, and was, as Julia had shown in "The Merry-Go-Round," an instrument of white control, it did preserve a semblance of due process and discourage vigilante justice. Through the early 1920s, while lynchings swept the country, Julia had believed that her little corner of South Carolina was different. In 1925, two bloody incidents shook her awake.

On April 25, in Aiken, fifty miles west of Fort Motte, a white sheriff and three deputies, all dressed in plain clothes, arrived at the home of a black man, Samuel Lowman, ostensibly to search for moonshine. Lowman was away at the local mill, having cornmeal ground. His wife and eighteen-year-old daughter, Bertha, were making soap in the backyard. Bertha panicked; only two weeks before, her twenty-two-year-old brother, Demon, had been beaten by white men who arrived in the yard unannounced. She whispered to her mother that they should try to sneak back inside the house.

When the white men saw the women head for the door, they drew their guns and started running. Bertha and Sheriff Howard reached the back steps simultaneously, and when Bertha screamed, the sheriff hit her in the mouth with the butt of his pistol. Mrs. Lowman grabbed an ax, and one of the deputies shot her to death.

Demon and a fifteen-year-old cousin, Clarence, came running from a nearby field and got some guns out of a shed. Bullets began to fly. When the dust cleared, Bertha, Clarence, and Demon were wounded. The sheriff was dead.

Five members of the Lowman family were arrested and jailed: Bertha, Clarence, Demon, and two of Sam Lowman's other children. Three days later, a bottle of liquor was discovered in the Lowmans' backyard, and Sam Lowman was arrested for selling moonshine. He was later sentenced to two years on a chain gang. Bertha got a life sentence; Demon and Clarence were condemned to die. Their lawyer, a black man, appealed the case to the South Carolina Supreme Court. This time Demon was acquitted, on the grounds that because the white men had failed to identify themselves as officers of the law, the Lowmans had been justified in regarding them as intruders. It seemed fairly certain that Bertha and Clarence would also be freed.[1]

But on October 8, 1926, a white mob "overpowered" the jailer and took the doomed souls to a tourist court near town where "some two thousand [white] men and women were gathered." The prisoners were untied and told to run for their lives. When they did they were shot in the back. The boys died immediately, but Bertha continued to struggle. The lynchers pumped more than fifty bullets into her body before she finally expired.[2]

The NAACP sent Walter White to investigate. Posing as a sympathetic white man, he coaxed the story out of the killers themselves. Then he mailed Governor Thomas G. McLeod of South Carolina a six-page letter listing the names of the executioners; the names, addresses, and occupations of twenty-two members of the lynch mob; and the names of eleven other people who had watched. According to White, the mob had included not only the new sheriff and his deputies, a number of prominent businessmen, and three men related to the governor, but also "at least one member of the Grand Jury investigating the lynching."[3]

White saw to it that the Aiken killings made the news across the nation. The *New York World* ran the story on its front page, and other major papers gave the incident prominent billing. Even the *Columbia State* and the *Charleston News and Courier* published editorials condemning the killers. When he got out of prison, in February 1927, Sam Lowman, stooped and frail, took his story on the road. Speaking to the National Negro Development Union in New York, he claimed that one of the deputies had shot the sheriff in order to get his job. This man, he said, had led the lynch mob.

For many Americans in the mid-1920s, Aiken became synonymous with lynching. But it was the death of V. H. "Pink" Whaley that brought the problem home to Julia. Whaley, a black entrepreneur who lived in St. Matthews, had accumulated a small fortune dealing in cotton and real estate.[4] He "held mortgages on the homes of many whites," owned "the main building [in downtown] St. Matthews," and controlled the votes of a black Republican majority.[5] For years he carried on his business without incident, until suddenly, around 1924, he started receiving death threats, apparently because his political influence had kept a white woman from being elected postmistress.

Whaley was not the sort to cave in to terrorism. He demanded an appointment with Governor McLeod to ask for protection. It was not a reassuring interview. The governor had summoned the Calhoun County sheriff, who warned Whaley that he should leave St. Matthews if he wanted to stay alive.[6] Whaley left and stayed away for almost a year. But then he came back to see to his business. Following a cotton auction, Whaley was lured into an abandoned warehouse and shot in the head. An NAACP informant reported that his wrists were "slit to the bone to make sure [of] death." At the coroner's inquest, Whaley's wife wept. A white man turned to her and hissed, "You shut up your d—— mouth ere you get your d—— brains blown out."[7]

Though he apparently did not visit St. Matthews to investigate, Walter White collected testimony from Whaley's friends and relatives and accused Governor McLeod of conspiring with Sheriff Hill to drive Whaley out of St. Matthews. Dancing around the subject, the governor went on the offensive and denied having *written* anything to V. H. Whaley, avoiding all mention of the meeting in his office. Any investigator who claimed to have seen a letter warning Whaley to leave town, he said, "should be dismissed from [the NAACP's] employ and [told to] seek membership in the 'Association for the Promotion of Liars.'"[8]

Rightly suspecting that people she knew had helped to engineer the murder, Julia initially shied away from involving herself in the case. Though she deplored Whaley's murder to Joel Spingarn in 1925 and wrote to H. L. Mencken in 1926 that she was thinking of writing about Whaley, it was three years later, in the fall of 1928, that she begged Walter White to tell her everything he knew about the Lowman and Whaley killings. By way of replying he mailed her his files, including all the original letters. It was an amazing gesture of trust, but the main thing Julia had hoped to learn was missing. Who had fired the bullet that ended Pink Whaley's life? White didn't know. He encouraged her to contact Whaley's sister, Blondell Whaley, and another man connected with the case, Miller Whitaker, who lived in Orangeburg.[9] Obsessed with bringing lynchers to justice, White hoped Julia would ferret out additional evidence or take a public stand. He didn't know her well enough to understand that she was fascinated by the violence itself.

For White, it must have seemed worth the risk to have Julia owe him a favor. The NAACP had very few allies among white South Carolinians, who tended to defend lynching as a necessary deterrent to black criminality. A few liberal journalists, such as Charlton Wright of the *Columbia Record*, condemned the practice as murder, but theirs was a minority opinion. Even the federal government was divided over the issue. An antilynching bill had finally passed the House in 1922, only to be waylaid by a Senate filibuster. "Whenever the Constitution comes between me and the virtue of the white women of the South, I say to hell with the Constitution!" bellowed South Carolina senator Coleman Blease, who offered to "personally defend" any man indicted for the Lowman lynchings.[10]

For several months in 1927 it seemed that Julia might speak out on the subject. In mid-November, she met with Walter White in New York to pump him for more information. "The Negroes themselves," she told Chambers evasively, had asked her to write about Whaley's life. But she then dropped the subject cold, never to revive it. When Julia met with her editor to discuss her next book, she talked not about Pink Whaley but about Essie Geiger, the daughter of Mary Weeks and one of Willie's brothers. Essie had grown up at Lang Syne and then emigrated to Harlem. None of Essie's living relatives can remember exactly when she left Lang Syne. She was probably one of several young women who went to New York around 1918, attracted by manufacturing jobs spawned by the Great War. An accomplished seamstress, Essie quickly found work in a garment factory, where she advanced to the rank of supervisor.[11] Eventually she married Robert Geiger, a wealthy fellow South Carolinian who had made his fortune selling Harlem real estate.

Alone among Mary's daughters, Essie seems to have liked Julia and approved of her books. In fact, Essie was so eager for Julia to write a novel set in Harlem that she offered to arrange guided tours of night-clubs, hospitals, and private homes. Carl Van Vechten's *Nigger Heaven* was insulting, she said, and Julia should set him straight.[12] Julia went along for the ride. Her crash course in Harlem atmosphere started out at Smalls Paradise, one of the most popular nightclubs in the city. Essie picked her up at her hotel in an armored limousine, escorted her into the bar, and presented her with a bottle of fine champagne. Observing the customs of South Carolina even while in Harlem, however, Essie would not sit at Julia's table.[13] Smalls Paradise held a special interest for Essie — her husband owned the building, and the proprietor, Ed Smalls, had been born near Lang Syne. At Essie's urging, Mr. Smalls proudly showed Julia the "enormous" check he paid Mr. Geiger for the weekly rent.[14]

Julia and Essie also visited a Harlem hospital where the head surgeon turned out to be from the midlands of South Carolina. "How he does hate me!" Julia marveled, startled to encounter an educated black man who openly resented her as one of the planter class who had bought and sold his forbears. She did not mind the doctor's attitude, she claimed; in fact, she was glad to see "how much and why" he despised her.[15] Essie was apparently willing to continue serving as Julia's guide to Harlem, and there are hints that Julia may sometimes have stayed in her home. There is also speculation that Essie sometimes passed for white; it is possible that she crossed the color line while in Julia's company, taking in the sights of white Manhattan just as Julia was touring black Harlem. By southern standards, such behavior was outrageous, but Julia always took care to cover her tracks. When in the city, she behaved like a liberal New Yorker. When in the country, she displayed "good manners" by acting like a proper southern lady.

D. L. Chambers was enthusiastic about the Harlem project. *Nigger Heaven* had made a small fortune for its publisher, and Claude McKay's sensual, cynical account of the black underworld, *Home to Harlem*, was climbing the best-seller lists.[16] Chambers exhorted Julia to work quickly, but she refused to commit herself, protesting that she felt "too weary for Harlem." It was risky and exhausting to deal with mixed-race people, in life as well as in literature. Before tackling a novel set in Harlem, she experimented on a smaller canvas in a setting closer to home. "A Proudful Fellow," published in the May 1928 issue of *Century* magazine, is the story of a half-white man with the Africanized name "Earth Wine."[17] Earth, or Ut, as the people call him, longs for "a bit of land and a home, and a chance to make something of himself." If Ut had wanted to run a still and sell whiskey, his mother would have understood, and if he had committed a crime she would have hidden him. But Ut's mother believes that ambition is a perversion. "White blood has a strange way of poisoning men so that they cannot rest unless they own things," she thinks. Ut believes that black people are out to "tear down all he had worked and striven to build up." Both are convinced that "blood" determines personality, and that whiteness and blackness are opposites.

Ut's racism dominates "A Proudful Fellow." Though his father was white, Ut's skin is very dark. He is in love not with his wife, Harpa, but with the lightness of her skin. Ut hires Mocky, tough and black, to serve as Harpa's maid. After working around the house for a few days, Mocky tells Ut that he "mus' be blind as a bat" not to see that Harpa and his brother Joe are having an affair. Instead of confronting Harpa, Ut dismisses Mocky as being "mean, jealous, vain[, and] unhappy," because "her ways and her heart were black."

At the end of the story, Ut catches Harpa and Joe in bed together. He shoots them both, then sets his own house on fire. "Do, Jesus — master — look down on dis poor meeked man — I'm done ruint — ruint," he cries. Undone by simple jealousy, not by white blood or black, Ut has nothing left "but a rope — a shroud, and a new cold grave." Julia started out to write a story about race and ended with a tale about blind egotism. Ut Wine's problems are those of any ambitious man saddled with a pretty, lazy wife.

While staying at the MacDowell Colony in Peterboro, New Hampshire, during the summer of 1927, Julia had tried to contact Irving Fineman, the handsome young engineer who had caught her eye on her return voyage from Europe, only to discover that his mail was being forwarded to Paris and Palestine. Now Fineman was in New York, seeking a publisher for his first novel, *This Pure Young Man*. Julia read the manuscript, praised it extravagantly, and drew up a list of editors he should take it to. "Something has happened to you that has made you more lovable," observed the grateful Fineman after a visit, thanking Julia for her "essential sanity and simplicity." [18]

Aroused, perhaps, by Fineman's sudden warmth, the nudes in his woodcuts, and the semiautobiographical disclosures in *This Pure Young Man*, Julia began dropping none-too-subtle hints that she was a discontented wife. "Marriage is hideous as an institution," she declared. "To be a fallen woman is far better — in most cases. Fallen women are really enviable." [19]

At her direction, Irving Fineman submitted his manuscript to publishers where she had contacts, including Knopf, Houghton Mifflin, and Bobbs-Merrill. His name was already familiar to Chambers, for Julia had earlier asked that this "talented young Jew" be commissioned to do some illustrations for her next book.[20] Nothing had come of it. Anticipating another rejection, she warned Irving that Chambers was capable of showing an appalling lack of taste. "Publishers are discouraging, truly," she complained. "Sometimes I loathe them all." [21] Normally ungenerous where other writers were concerned, Julia was determined to help Fineman. "You're one of the very few men I've known who is worth a tear, maybe two of them," she wrote.[22]

Returning the compliment, Fineman sent her a pastel drawing of a naked lady with long red hair using a tiny bouquet as a fig leaf. Julia merrily reported that she had hung it "in full view of two nude and wretched gentlemen already on" her cabin wall. "I'll watch to see if she eases or increases their anguish," she teased. "Corsages should be used so always." Fineman asked for a photograph and she sent it, protesting that the one he liked was "silly" because it omitted all her freckles and lines. She regaled him with the story of her recent visit to the local bootlegger, who lived in a hovel in the sandhills. The large family had almost nothing, yet the wife struck her as "rosy, happy, care-free," casually nursing a baby in front of several men. "Intellectual barren women ought to be stamped out," Julia concluded, with barely a trace of irony. "They're a curse to the race." [23]

But if poverty sometimes looked like a form of freedom, Julia could see no advantage in a sudden loss of wealth. And she was having money troubles of a new and sinister sort. Both she and Willie, on the advice of Willie's brother-in-law James Crouch, had invested heavily in real estate in the booming textile town of Greenville. Crouch was married to Willie's brother Eddie Peterkin's widow, Charlotte, who was also Robert

Adams's sister. When the local economy crashed a few months later, the Peterkins lost thousands of dollars.[24]

For all her swagger about making the men in her family show respect, Julia was uncomfortable in the role of breadwinner. She liked the prestige that earning money brought, but she dreaded the thought that her family might come to depend on her income. Reviewing a book called *Prima Donna* for the *Book League Monthly* (Walter White had persuaded her to serve on the editorial board), she extolled women's new freedom to have it all — love, home, and career — then worried about the consequences. "Many men who used to be tall and strong because they bore the heavier burdens are becoming fat and flabby from soft living; their women are developing muscles and shrewdness, and independence. Where will all this end?" she asked.

Julia, of course, was a prime example of the "new" woman, just as she was one of those "intellectual barren women" whom she called a blight on the world. What did she hope to accomplish by reviling her own kind? Why was she using her hard-won status to argue that women should be subservient? In the review, titled "An Ideal Woman for a Man-Made World," Julia seemed to be imploding, ricocheting from one extreme to another as she tried to say what she thought. "Medea [is] my patron saint," she declared, claiming sisterhood with the ruthless Greek magician who eloped with Jason, dismembered her brother, scattered his bloody limbs along the road to distract her pursuing father, and eventually killed her two children in order to take revenge on her unfaithful husband. Yet only a few paragraphs later she urged women to "lean and be helpless, or we'll have no worthwhile men left and women cannot submit to being loved by inferior men." Julia's lame conclusion, which has nothing to do with *Prima Donna,* is that women should be "grateful to all men for all things, good or bad." [25]

That philosophy, such as it was, would soon be put to the test. On February 2, 1929, James Crouch was discovered dead in his bathtub. Crouch had carried a $90,000 life insurance policy with double indemnity in case of accidental death. If he had slipped, knocked himself unconscious, and drowned, as he appeared to have done, the insurance company would owe his widow $180,000 in benefits. If he had died of natural causes, the widow would get $90,000. If he had committed suicide, she would receive nothing. Two days after the funeral, the insurance company ordered Crouch's body to be exhumed and autopsied. The widow consented. No evidence of suicide or murder was discovered, and Crouch was reinterred. A few days later the insurance company had him dug up again. Again, nothing was found. The Metropolitan Life Insurance Company mailed the widow a check for $180,000.[26]

As much as the insurers, though for very different reasons, Julia wanted to know for certain whether the brother-in-law who had lost her money had taken his own life. A good-looking charmer who for many years had been one of the few well-educated men in her orbit, Crouch seems to have meant more to her than his tenuous connection to the family would explain.[27] Julius Mood had never liked Crouch and had warned Julia against having dealings with him; Willie trusted him implicitly, but Willie was notoriously gullible. For years to come, the mental image of Crouch's handsome body rotting in the grave would return to haunt Julia whenever she was sick or distressed.

Fortunately, pleasanter events were already on the horizon. The financial crisis was not dire enough to stop Julia and Willie from taking a vacation, a group tour organized by the South Carolina Press Association to Havana, Cuba.[28] With its anything-goes atmosphere and free-flowing liquor, Havana seemed like "Nirvana." [29]

Before they left there was talk that *Scarlet Sister Mary* had been nominated for the Pulitzer Prize, along with a pedantic socialist tract about the Sacco-Vanzetti case, Upton Sinclair's *Boston,* and John Oliver's turgid tale about a deposed Episcopal priest, *Victim and Victor.* By mid-March, rumor had it that *Victim and Victor* would win the award. Ever the optimist, D. L. Chambers believed that *Scarlet Sister Mary* would triumph.

"I begin to suspect that I am a better judge of human beings than you are," Julia wrote to her editor. "I have had no more idea of winning the Pulitzer Prize than of winning the harp of the angel Gabriel." One of the judges, Dr. Richard Burton, had once been a guest in her home when "something occurred which made him seem ridiculous. I was not to blame but he has always felt I was." (She did not reveal the details of the incident.) Since then, she said, Burton had insulted her repeatedly. "Now," she declared, "he and his auburn wig may go to hell and burn for all I care." [30]

In late April, Burton damaged his own integrity by declaring to an audience in Minneapolis that *Victim and Victor* was "a book not just for a year but for many years." *Publishers Weekly* took this statement as a premature announcement of the Pulitzer winner and printed the story as fact, causing a scandal. The advisory committee at Columbia University denied that a winner had been named and demanded the names of other books the jury had considered. Burton replied that *Scarlet Sister*

Mary was "practically" the judges' second choice.[31] The prize committee reconvened.

The Pulitzer Prize had been under attack since 1926, when Sinclair Lewis, egged on by H. L. Mencken, had refused to accept it for *Arrowsmith*. According to the original terms, the winner was supposed to represent "the wholesome atmosphere of American life, and the highest standard of American manners and manhood," a prescription that, as Lewis put it, encouraged writers to "become safe, polite, obedient, and sterile."[32] In reality, the judging committee had been blithely ignoring Joseph Pulitzer's old-fashioned directions for years. The 1928 winner, Thornton Wilder's *Bridge over San Luis Rey*, was not even set in America, and the 1927 winner, Louis Bromfield's *Early Autumn*, glorified an adulterous affair. Trying to recover its stature, the committee decided to revise the terms. Henceforth the winner would be an "American novel published during the year . . . preferably one which shall best present the whole atmosphere of American life."[33]

Scarlet Sister Mary won the prize. The May 13, 1929, announcement catapulted *Scarlet Sister Mary* into the top ten on the best-seller lists, along with Sinclair Lewis's *Dodsworth*, DuBose Heyward's *Mamba's Daughters*, and Erich Maria's Remarque's *All Quiet on the Western Front*. Julia received hundreds of congratulatory letters and telegrams, but nothing from Mencken. Still hoping for a reconciliation, she went on the offensive and sent *him* a wire. "Have you noted how wisely Pulitzer Price [*sic*] has been awarded?" she inquired.[34] Mencken replied that he hoped Julia would do like Sinclair Lewis and reject the prize.

"I thought when I wired you about the Pulitzer Prize going to my Mary, the out-standing harlot of this plantation, you'd laugh," Julia reproached him. "How could you be serious over it? . . . Maybe you have not read Mary and do not realize that she preferred to have all her children fathered by different men." In bringing up Mary's many lovers, Julia was not just appealing to Mencken's love of putting one over on the "boobouisie," she was claiming the right to have different men father her own literary "children." Mencken had deserted her, and she had, of necessity, taken up with someone new. Now he was acting as though she had committed a crime by accepting an honor she had not sought in the first place. "It is all so silly, so futile, whether I take the prize or refuse it could not possibly matter; and to refuse a gift seems to be in such bad taste," she goaded him. "I've not the heart to."[35]

Mencken, too, could wield a mean double entendre: "Dear Mrs. Peterkin," he wrote. "Probably you are right. It was my first impression to wire you at once, imploring you to refuse the prize. But in view of the amusing effects of receiving it, I begin to believe you are wise to keep it. Human existence in the United States grows increasingly ridiculous. I begin to fear seriously that some day I'll laugh myself to death." [36]

Five presses were put to work turning out copies of *Scarlet Sister Mary*. The Bobbs-Merrill publicity department sprang into action — and so did the censors. Like almost every other book worth reading, the novel was banned in Boston. In Gaffney, South Carolina, the town librarian refused to circulate *Scarlet Sister Mary*. In protest, George Lay, the editor of the *Cherokee Times*, a semiweekly newspaper in Gaffney, contacted Bobbs-Merrill and arranged to serialize the novel. Bobbs-Merrill sent press releases praising this brave gesture to all the major newspapers; even *Time* picked up the story. [37]

Julia found the "Gaffney affair" amusing. "I'm tired having ugly things whispered around. Let them be said out loud in the papers." [38] She cackled when she heard on the grapevine that she was Mencken's mistress. But other stories made her "long to commit murder." Julia wrote to Mencken that winning the Pulitzer had served only to bring to the surface "rotten things which some of the sweet and vicious S.C. ladies have been saying." In a final bid for his sympathy, she confessed, "I am sore as the deuce, down in the heart, hurt. You know how to keep your poise. Could you tell me any way to get cheerful again?" [39] Apparently Mencken felt that she deserved to suffer. He offered no encouragement.

The prize itself was $1,000. Julia put $100 in a savings account for Bill, and another $100 in an account for her nephew Ashleigh Mood, who was staying at Lang Syne. [40] At the end of May, she asked Chambers outright for an advance on her royalties, blaming "hail, sand storms, swollen rivers" for her need. "I'm going to try my hand now at a bit of business," she noted cryptically. [41]

Julia's financial troubles were small potatoes compared with the turmoil inside Bobbs-Merrill. Old Mr. Bobbs had recently died, and his son Julian coveted Chambers's job as editor in chief. Eventually the company would be reorganized, and Julian Bobbs would withdraw his claim in return for a substantial settlement, but in the meantime the power struggle distracted the staff's attention from the task of selling *Scarlet Sister Mary*. [42] Bobbs-Merrill did manage to produce something called a "featherweight airplane edition" of *Scarlet Sister Mary*, a tiny, limp-backed forerunner of today's trade paperbacks. Julia told Chambers that her family would be thrilled, since her father had recently bought a second airplane and her twenty-one-year-old twin nephews had just received their pilots' licenses.[43]

For the moment, Julia seemed to have cornered an exploding market. As Albert Halper observed in *Dial*, America's appetite for African American fiction was still being fed not by black writers but by "whites writing up the blacks." "So far," observed Halper, discounting Jean Toomer, Walter White, Jessie Fauset, and James Weldon Johnson, "this country has not produced one negro capable of presenting a sincere picture of himself or his people."[44] But 1928 would mark a turning point for African American fiction, and for southern American fiction as well. In 1928 and 1929, Fauset's *Plum Bun*, Claude McKay's *Home to Harlem*, Rudolph Fisher's *The Walls of Jericho*, Wallace Thurman's *The Blacker the Berry*, and Nella Larsen's *Quicksand* appeared, one right after the other. Though none is a great book by any standard, all portray a type of black American — urban, self-conscious, angry, and depressed — who would later find fuller expression in Ralph Ellison's masterpiece, *Invisible Man*. Nineteen twenty-nine, sometimes pegged as the zenith of the southern renaissance, also brought William Faulkner's *Sartoris* and *The Sound and the Fury* and Thomas Wolfe's *Look Homeward, Angel*.

Though this creative and cultural ferment would soon unseat her, Julia was now regarded by average Americans as the top southern writer and "Negro novelist." In less than a year, *Good Housekeeping, Country Gentleman*, the *Ladies' Home Journal*, and the *Saturday Evening Post* all carried stories by "the Pulitzer Prize–winning author." The money was welcome and the exposure helped to sell books, but deep inside the apple of success, the worm of commercialism was working. When tucked between the covers of the women's magazines, Julia's stories took on a cautionary, moralistic note. "The Diamond Ring," which recounts the unsupervised, morally confusing, and disorganized family life of a small black boy, was in strange company on the pages of *Good Housekeeping*, where the American fixation on sanitation was promoted with breathless prose. A flurry of ads reminded women that they stood between their families and contagion: Johnson's furniture wax fights disease by sealing off germ pockets; copper water tubing will reduce a hostess's anxieties about whether the water in her bathroom really *looks* clean, and choosing Northern toilet paper can mean the difference between life and death: "You alone, mothers, must save them . . . from infection by harsh, impure paper."

It was not just the ads and the other articles that trivialized Julia's most commercially successful stories. Nor was it the illustrations of wistful pickaninnies and eye-rolling mammies. It was Julia's headlong rush to a happy ending. While "The Greasy Spoon," "Santy Claw," "The Diamond Ring," and "Heart Leaves" all show flashes of Julia's power to draw readers into the minds of troubled people, they also lack the uncompromising edge, the "bad manners" that had driven her to "write what is, even if it is unpleasant." [45]

"The Diamond Ring" gets off to a promising start by revealing the stingy self-righteousness of Bubba's foster mother, Nancy, a vice she tries to pass off as a virtue. Nancy is saving her money to go to a Sunday school convention. When Bubba asks her for a dime to ride the merry-go-round, she insists that riding merry-go-rounds is sinful and wasteful. "Besides it would kill him sure as the world, and he would be no good to her dead. To bury him would cost money. She wanted him to stay alive. She had worked hard to raise him." [46]

Getting ready for the convention, Nancy borrows a diamond ring and a pair of shoes from friends, and snitches a pink satin chemise from the white folks' washing. While ironing the pink "shimmy," she lectures Bubba about stealing: "I wouldn' steal nothing, not for de whole world. Stealing is a sin, Bubba. People what steals goes to hell, straight to hell. Don't you never steal, son. It's a sin. A awful sin."

Still yearning to ride the merry-go-round, Bubba gets into a series of scrapes, the worst of which is selling Nancy's borrowed diamond ring to a man who wins him over with cash and kind words. While Nancy is gone he rides the merry-go-round eleven times, dreading her return all the while. Just when it seems that all his sins will be revealed and Nancy will skin him alive, a Dickensian coincidence intervenes to get him off the hook. Nancy, it turns out, has married the man who bought the borrowed ring and is wearing it on her finger. Not only that, but the man knows Big Sue, who owns the ring, and has already paid her more than it is worth. When Bubba tries to confess to his aunt, she brushes off his apologies: "Don' fret bout de ring, son. If it wasn' for you a-droppin' 'em, I might not a got me dis fine husband." [47] It's all a little too neat.

The same can be said of "Heart Leaves" and "Santy Claw," both stories about powerless people — old folks and children — who chafe under the yoke of authority. "Heart Leaves" starts off as a sour diatribe delivered by a dried-up old woman named Anaky. Fussing about modern young people who bleach their skin and iron their hair, she complains about a rival midwife, rants that "even the dogs have lost their manners," and plots to seduce Daddy Cudjoe, the conjure man, in the hope that he will "wither up" the Bury League, the worst offender on a long list of newfangled inventions. But Daddy Cudjoe nods off over his rice and buttermilk, and she sends him home. Anaky is tired, too. She crawls into bed to smoke her pipe and soon falls sound asleep.

The old woman awakens with the pipe still clenched in her jaws and her mattress engulfed in flames. Her spirit leaps free of her body, hovering while the neighbors call her name and try to break down the cabin door. Freed from worry, Anaky lingers until the flames die down, watching Daddy Cudjoe pick sadly through the ashes for "some bit of her to lay away in the graveyard." Up to this point, the story is convincing; Anaky's out-of-body experience is handled matter-of-factly, as a description of her final moments. Because there is nothing for the Bury League to bury, Anaky will be spared their "store-bought shrouds and store-bought boxes."

The story should have ended with Daddy Cudjoe's sobbing. But catering to the taste of her public, Julia tacked on a grotesque and sentimental anticlimax. The old man discovers Anaky's heart among the ashes, "a strange knot of flesh," still beating. Anaky goes on to heaven, "to be forever with the angels and her little baby girl." [48] A heart-shaped lump in the ashes, maybe — but a *beating* heart-shaped lump? The crotchety Maum Anaky has been transmuted into a twelfth-century saint.

Always before, Julia had left such moments ambiguous, evading direct description. Her *characters* might believe that April's feet were conjured; Julia clearly did not. But in "Heart Leaves" she crossed the boundary into mysticism, and Daddy Cudjoe's discovery rings false.

Maybe Julia heard a tale like this one around Lang Syne, though the real Maum Anaky, according to her descendants, "died good" — died in her bed, that is, repenting and praising God. She would never have fooled with a conjure man or set her bed on fire.[49] More likely, Julia's inspiration in this case came from a literary source. The unburned heart is a common theme in nineteenth-century romances, from the poet Shelley's seaside cremation to Nathaniel Hawthorne's short stories.

More plausible than "Heart Leaves," "The Greasy Spoon" and "Santy Claw" are classic Julia Peterkin sprinkled with sugar. Seraphine, a blues singer in "The Greasy Spoon," is happily reunited with her abusive husband. A beloved grandson plays "Santy Claw," pleasing his grandparents by proposing to the old-fashioned local girl they love instead of a short-skirted floozy who hates oysters. Both stories have their moments; both fall short of genius.

Her stories in the *Ladies' Home Journal*, the *Saturday Evening Post*, and *Good Housekeeping* did more than any Pulitzer Prize to convince ordinary people in South Carolina that Julia was a real writer. Droves of ladies tried to scrape her acquaintance, purring that her work was improving. Julia complained that she spent all her money just telegraphing would-be visitors that she was not at home. "I'll soon be queer. I see that," she wailed to Chambers. "I like to be courteous, but I find I can't be, now." [50]

All through the fall of 1929 she complained of "throat trouble," her code for too much mail and too many guests. [51] In late October she booked passage to Bermuda, where Hudson Strode was recovering from another mental breakdown. With his beautiful young wife, Thérèse, who was working for a member of Parliament, Strode was staying in a spacious house near the beach. The atmosphere was soothing, the climate mild. Automobiles were prohibited, liquor was legal, and the walled gardens were fragrant with drifts of yellow freesias. Julia walked, wrote, and drank dark rum with the Strodes' literary friends. [52]

She left on a steamer out of Charleston and returned by way of New York. And while she was gone, the world turned upside down. On Tuesday, October 29, two days before her forty-ninth birthday, the stock market crashed. It was the dusk of the Roaring Twenties, the dawn of the Great Depression. It was also the beginning of a tempestuous love affair.

On November 23, while Julia was still in New York, photographer Doris Ulmann threw a birthday party for the Mexican muralist José Clemente Orozco. A fragile, sensuous-looking woman with a huge personal fortune, Ulmann often invited celebrities to pose for their portraits in her New York apartment. She also took pictures of rural folk and had recently exhibited a series of Deep South, Appalachian, and New York photographs at the Delphic Studios, a gallery just across the street from the newly opened Museum of Modern Art.

Delphic Studios was owned and operated by two wealthy and eccentric widows, Alma Reed and Mme Sikelianos, who lived together in an apartment they called the "Ashram." Until Alma Reed took him under her wing, Orozco had been virtually unknown in New York, although he was famous in Mexico for his monumental renderings of revolutionary soldiers and peasants. Reed became his self-appointed guardian, publicist, and broker, introducing him to collectors with money.

At the party, Orozco zeroed in on Julia, drawn to her flaming hair and "topaz" eyes. He shadowed her for the rest of the evening, telling stories, laughing at her jokes, asking questions about Lang Syne. When the party ended, Ulmann suggested that Orozco might like to paint Julia's portrait. According to Alma Reed, he "instantly accepted." [53]

José Clemente Orozco produced an arresting likeness of Julia Peterkin, as stark and psychologically revealing as her early stories, none of which he had ever read. "Eternally young, eternally old," as Alma Reed put it, the face is muscular, androgynous, and framed by kinky, almost African hair.[54] The skin is mottled with freckles. The eyes seem to embrace the world, to understand and accept its complexities. The portrait is magnetic, to be sure, but as Alma Reed later remarked, "It [is] not pretty." [55]

Much to Reed's distress, Julia refused to purchase the finished painting, which she considered ugly and "harsh." Orozco also produced another image of Peterkin, one she apparently never saw, although it was exhibited in New York in 1930. Erotic, surreal, and physically flattering — everything that the portrait is not — *Drama* shows a red-haired woman in translucent white draperies vanishing through the wall of a room. An artist kneels at her feet, clutching the hem of her robe. The painting tells the story of their encounter. Orozco was smitten; Julia played the tease and kept his interest high by staying out of his bed.

Under different circumstances she might have given in and become the mistress of a famous artist, but her mind was on another man. On November 30, 1929, Julia went to dinner with Irving Fineman. He walked her up to her hotel room afterward and pressed her to let him stay. As she had with Orozco, she said no, but his touch dissolved her scruples. A fire that had been banked for the past four years suddenly blazed into flame.

The next day, Fineman sent a bunch of talisman roses; Julia wrote that she had "kissed them warm" before boarding the train for Lang Syne.[56] "Love is the source of Life itself," she reminded him, and "heart-love is strong as death." [57]

CHAPTER 10

One Lovely, Tempting Place

"Heart-love is strong as death." With those words, Julia Peterkin embarked on what would become a great literary correspondence. To read her letters to Irving Fineman is to read the novel she never achieved: the story of a narcissistic white woman jockeying for power in several worlds; seducing a handsome, theatrical young man; and struggling to keep her balance when their affair turns serious.

"When a woman gets in love she loses what sense she has, whether she is old or young, well raised or ignorant," Julia would later write.[1] Her moods, always volatile, grew wildly erratic. At first, she rejoiced to Fineman that "a miracle is." But soon she felt "a terrible blackness" closing in.[2] Petulant and sarcastic, she blasted D. L. Chambers for neglecting *Scarlet Sister Mary*. At home, she was jittery and impatient. Coming upon two black men butting heads along a railway siding, she muscled her way through a crowd of spectators and exhorted them to act like "men, not beasts." The combatants "fell apart, shivering." The local white men, she told Fineman, were offended by her brashness. Ladies were not supposed to even see such brawls, much less to intervene. "Perhaps I'm not at all the plantation mistress, not at all the nice white lady," she suggested. "God only knows what I am, or what will become of me."[3]

Julia believed that she was in love with Irving Fineman. Capable now of earning her own way, she knew that she could choose to live without Willie. Yet "there's no way out for me. No way," she told her lover. "I must, must accept what is, even if it kills me." While Irving groaned that his days were gray, Julia bubbled with excitement. "I'm mad," she confessed, "utterly, happily, thank God."[4]

Irving wanted her full attention. Julia fended him off with one of "Venner's Sayings." "If I could give you everything you want, that would be a joy," Julia wrote. "But I cannot. I cannot give a leaf to a tree, not a single spark of color to the roses which the frosts have paled here." She promised to find an excuse to come north soon; after all, she claimed, "Fate owes me something." She even hinted that she might like to go further, if only the law allowed it. But as Julia was fond of pointing out, the South Carolina constitution prohibited divorce. Once a couple was legally married, nothing but death could disjoin them in the eyes of the state — not adultery, not desertion, not mental cruelty, not even physical assault. And the South Carolina courts refused to recognize divorces granted elsewhere. The laws were written in such a way that men could manuever through legal loopholes, but women had no recourse. Even as late as the 1920s, if a wife left her husband and moved to another state, she was still considered to live in South Carolina, because it was her "wifely duty" to be there. And if a husband deserted his wife and moved to another state, *her* legal domicile was still South Carolina, which did not allow divorce. (The husband's legal residence, on the other hand, automatically changed when he moved, so he was free to file for divorce in another state.)[5] "Sometimes I think marriage should be stopped," Julia wrote. "No two people should be allowed to live together unless they cannot possibly be happy apart. Then as soon as their love wanes even a little, they should feel it indecent to be together for an hour longer."[6]

"Indecent" it might have been, yet Julia made no move to leave Willie. "I must not get a yellow streak down my back," she wrote, begging Fineman to put up with her. Wait, she said, and maybe something would happen.[7] In the meantime, Julia urged him to get a copy of the December issue of *Country Gentleman* and look at the photographs of her garden, her piano, and her cabin. Fineman must have found it a painful assignment, for "A Plantation Christmas," the essay that accompanied the pictures, is a hymn to the Old South in which Julia thanked "the kind fate that has placed me in a home which is removed from the beaten track." She wrote fervently of defending the old ways (including, presumably, monogamy and white supremacy) "against anything which tends to destroy them or to lessen their brightness."[8]

The Lang Syne she described is luxurious, a striking contrast to Irving's sparsely furnished rooms, the frugal meals he took in inexpensive restaurants, the solitary precision of his drafting table and slide rule. Servants polish the silver, sing while they pick cotton, and show up at the Big House at dawn on Christmas Day bearing gifts of pullets and new-laid eggs. They gather the walnuts, preserve the figs, press scuppernong wine, grind the sorghum, and stuff the white folks' turkey. The people who live in the Quarters are also seen pursuing separate holiday rituals — they whitewash their houses, go out for barbecue, and celebrate Christmas Eve in a joyous all-night marathon of prayer, "shouting," and singing. But through it all runs Julia's mantralike insistence on "we," "our," and "us." And as in her early letters to Sandburg, their meaning is often blurry.

"Individuals are few," Julia wrote near the beginning of the piece, "so each one counts for much. Hours are long and quiet and time is abundant. Since loneliness is one of the evils which threaten us, our holidays are important occasions. . . . When nothing is left of the merrymaking but withered holly and faded mistletoe and the few red embers that still shine among the hickory ashes of the Christmas backlog, we rejoice that we are spared to pause and wonder over that strange miracle we call life."[9] Who is this "us"? Who is "we"? Are these the sentiments of everyone on the plantation, of just the white people, or are they Julia's alone? The latter, one suspects.

"A Plantation Christmas" is a paternalist's feel-good fantasy about family values in the plantation South. But its power springs from a hidden source: the illicit passion for Irving Fineman that beckoned Julia to leave Lang Syne. Even her description of a crossroads store is charged with veiled sexual energy: "Paper bags threaten to burst and spill the loads of fruit and candy and cakes they are given to hold. . . . [B]unches of bananas . . . swing from the ceiling [amid] the rank scent of the dried herrings in their stained slatted boxes." In the garden, "cape jasmines linger to help the tea olives keep the air perfumed, and vagrant butterflies hover over the frost-tinged zinnias and marigolds." Even the sweetgum trees seem "drunk on the warmth of the mild winter sunshine."

Whether or not she realized what she was doing, Julia had discovered an effective strategy for managing Irving Fineman. Her letters to him over the next few years would follow the same basic formula: an insistence on loyalty to her marriage coupled with steamy, suggestive prose.

Still reeling from the loss of his life savings in the stock market crash, Julius Mood stumbled into the path of a speeding car while leaving church on the Sunday before Christmas 1929. Julia rushed to Sumter, where her father lay injured, "a hurt child," hardly able to look after himself, never mind his daughter.[10]

Julius had mellowed as he aged and Julia grew famous. Now that he was dependent on her, the old man seems to have considered it prudent to give his youngest daughter some of the praise and affection she had craved from him for so long. Welcome though her father's overtures were, Julia felt deflated. She was addicted to the battle; now that the war against her menfolks seemed won, she hardly knew what to do. Though Irving Fineman was no Julius Mood, he was headstrong and self-centered enough to serve as a stand-in. Julia let him know from the beginning of their affair that she expected him to fill her father's shoes. "Love me much, not a little," she directed. "I need floods and floods. Don't forget." [11]

Before the New Year began, Julia and Irving had settled uneasily into a long-distance relationship. Yet by the middle of January, his side of the correspondence had begun to flag. A crisis had been reached and passed; he was still alone. Julia shipped him tokens of her love: in winter, boxes filled with red turkey berries, followed by bunches of sweet violets, wild flags, and daffodils. "I like you very much, Irving," she gushed. "It does seem to me that nobody else is quite so fine, so altogether right as you are." [12] Furthermore, she said, if she ever saw a chance to help his career, she would.

As luck would have it, the Longmans-Green publishing company provided a perfect opportunity by inviting her to judge a contest for the best unpublished novel of the year. First prize would be publication and $7,500, "the largest literary [award] ever offered," according to the company.[13] Irving Fineman entered *This Pure Young Man*, and the manuscript appeared in Julia's mailbox. She read the novel three times, debating what to do.[14] If she spoke up and disqualified herself, people would wonder why. Besides, the novel seemed brilliant to her, far better than any of the other entries. Not voting for Irving would have seemed wrong, and so, in the end, she did. The other two judges, Ernest Boyd and Lewis Mumford, favored other books, and for the moment there was no decision.

At the end of January Julia was back in New York, feeling "defenseless . . . against the telephone, the noise, the people." [15] Her old friend from the Town Theater, Dan Reed, had just completed a stage adaptation of *Black April*, and Julia had hopes that Paul Robeson might play the lead. Reed came to the project with good credentials; he had connections, he knew Lang Syne, and for the past several years he had directed the Provincetown Players, the highly acclaimed Greenwich Village troupe associated with Eugene O'Neill. But a promising résumé does not make a play, and from the beginning it was evident to Julia that Reed's *Black April* was sluggish and overearnest, less a dramatization than a humorless parody.

She should have pulled the plug before the project went so far, but Julia loved Isadora Reed and dreaded insulting Dan. Moreover, the Reeds had seen her with Irving, and Dan was a notorious gossip. "He always watches and suspects me," Julia worried. "He loves and hates me." [16] Fearful that an angry Dan might spread rumors about her attachment, she chose not to burn her bridges. That decision would prove catastrophic.

The wisest course for Julia as an artist would have been to have it out with Dan and face the consequences, whether they came in the form of a lawsuit, malicious gossip, or a damaged friendship. Even if it had been broadcast from the rooftops, the news that Julia Peterkin was involved with a younger man would not have caused a ripple in literary New York, and in the long run a lawsuit defending the integrity of her work could only have done her good. But Julia was a southern lady trained to avoid confrontation, and however much she admired forthrightness in others, she was often incapable of it herself.

There was, of course, a darker reason for her appeasement of Dan Reed: she feared he might accuse her of trying to throw the Longmans-Green novel contest. It would not have been the first time the judge of a competition, literary or otherwise, had slept with one of the contestants; nor would it be the last. But it was highly unusual for a woman to be the judge — and to bestow favors on a much younger lover. One night in New York Julia awakened in a panic, sure that her fellow judge Ernest Boyd had noticed her "indiscreet" enthusiasm for *This Pure*

Young Man. Filled with foreboding, she fired off a midnight telegram to Fineman. For the sake of his career and her reputation, she said, Irving *must* conceal their friendship.[17]

Fineman accused Julia of trying to control him. She denied it. "I'm here, you're there, but since that cannot be changed, let's not torture ourselves, or each other," she begged. "It's too cruel." "I trust you completely. I respect you whole-heartedly. . . . I'm sure you'd guard me more carefully than you'd guard yourself. I was not thinking of you or me, but of the book." [18]

They made up, spent several nights together, and caught "glimpses of complete happiness." But while Julia was out with Irving one evening, someone broke into her hotel room and rifled through her papers. Irving reported the incident to hotel security. Though nothing was stolen, Julia went to pieces and sobbed through the night. Fineman had his hands full. Julia was moaning like a madwoman, and she could not, or would not, say why. The next morning, she seemed herself again, but she cut short her visit and left at once for Lang Syne. Several days later she wrote to confess "why my orchestra failed me."

Though calculated to tug at Irving's heartstrings, it was not a very convincing explanation. According to Julia, the hotel detectives had called up memories of the "merciless" insurance adjusters who had dug up Jim Crouch to examine his body and caused her to go "insane." [19] She implied that Crouch had lost her money, died, and been exhumed during the past month or so. In truth, his remains had been resting peacefully for better than a year. The cause of Julia's present delirium had nothing to do with Jim Crouch. She wanted to be with Irving, wanted to help his career and be known as his friend, but she dreaded getting caught. The break-in convinced her that someone was spying on her. Worse yet, the report filed by the house detectives would link her name with Fineman's.

Julia arrived in South Carolina to find her father racked with pain. He had rebounded after his auto accident only to be stricken with angina. "His strength is forever gone," Julia realized, "his good days are over." [20] Sure that her father was dying, Julia phoned Doris Ulmann and asked her to search New York for her older sister, Laura Schneider. Once found, Laura hurried south to her father's bedside, attempted to heal him by "thinking right," and hastily returned to New York when Julius showed signs of improvement.[21]

Even in old age, Julius Mood inspired violent rivalries among the women in his life. His daughter Marian, his wife, Janie, his cousin

Emma Mood (who was rumored to be his longtime lover), and various sisters, admirers, and grateful former patients all hovered around his sickbed. Julia told Irving that she was her father's only comfort. The other women seemed to her like "an evil chorus" glorying in Julius's pain.[22]

Having supervised the slow decline of countless elderly heart patients, Julius Mood knew what lay ahead of him. He talked of suicide, and Julia sympathized: "I'd rather kill him myself than see him degraded by the bare hope that his days may be prolonged a little," she wrote to Fineman.[23]

The idea of committing suicide to avoid the horrors of aging was not new to Julia; in fact, it bordered on an obsession. At least since the spring of 1928, she had been trying to wheedle her doctors into prescribing a "pleasant capsule," probably cyanide, that could "put [her] to sleep forever." Albert Bigelow Paine, an old friend of Doris Ulmann's, claimed to have access to some such drug, and Julia had cultivated him in hopes of obtaining it.[24]

Was Julia herself suicidal, like her heroine Helen West? Apparently not, for she lived to a ripe old age. Yet her letters to Fineman describe crushing despondency, black moods she blamed on her mysterious "ductless glands." Scientists had recently discovered that endocrine imbalances could bring on depression. Synthetic estrogen was being promoted as a fountain of youth for middle-aged women, a magic pill that could cure neurosis and make sex more satisfying. Ironically, given her medical history, Julia cherished an abiding faith in the superior wisdom of doctors. She took a keen interest in hormone research, and around this time began alluding to another sort of "tiny tablet," a drug that might change her personality.[25] The events that followed strongly suggest that she had begun using estrogen.

She continued to ship armloads of flowers to Irving's New York apartment, where he toiled over a novel based on the Talmud. "I think your soul is purple," she wrote, "not like the violets so much as like the darker purple flags which stand so proudly on their stalks now. Velvet hearted and spotted with flecks of gold."[26] It was the seductive language of "A Plantation Christmas" cranked up a notch or two. The silky, half-veiled eroticism of the passage was designed to excite Irving, to divert him from Julia's inconsistencies and fasten his hopes on their next meeting. While she carefully steered clear of overt sexual references, her prose was as insinuating as a touch. Every blossom, every bee, every slender blade of grass reminded her of Irving. As romantic as all this sounds, it was calculated to convince a skeptical Irving that Julia's love for Lang Syne was not what kept them apart. The plantation landscape, she would have him believe, was just a reflection of him. "The crab-apple thickets are so pink and tender and fragrant it's just heart-aching," she wrote, "like your eyes and your mouth and your hands."[27]

Spring brought swarms of mosquitoes along with the crab apple blossoms, and for the first time in years, both Julia and Willie came down with malaria. Julia bounced back; Willie lay near death. "This is no decent place for white people to live," Julia told her lover, eerily echoing Ellesley West. "If I could, I'd leave here cheerfully this minute and never even wish to come back. But I must face what is and make as decent a gesture as I can." Her account of Willie's "pitiful, distressing" condition was carefully calibrated to encourage Irving's hopes while painting herself as a tragic figure.[28]

It worked. Irving sent her a tiny portrait of himself tucked inside an antique silver locket. "When the face on my eyelids grows dim or seems far away, all I have to do is open the case and there it is, with your dear hands too," Julia wrote. She hung it on her tree-of-life chain from Rome, in place of the "Pope-blessed cross."[29] For years, it was the only piece of jewelry she wore.

Restless and uneasy, Julia stayed away from Lang Syne for most of the spring, though she was seldom in Irving's company. She had written him many passionate letters in the past three months, but always she stopped short of making promises. When he fished for reassurance, she parried: "Can't you easily guess that when you see me again I'll be the famous Mrs. Peterkin, dignified, austere, cold. Of course I shall. The mere mention of a sandwich will make me lift an eyebrow and to speak of a quiet island will touch no memory at all. Indeed, I shall probably stifle a yawn or a great sigh of boredom. Why ask when you are already sure of all this Mr. Fineman?"[30] Though offered in jest, these comments emphasized that he was the courtier, she the queen.

There was still much finagling over the fate of *Black April*; Dan Reed refused to give it up, and so did his producer, Arthur Hopkins, who offered to come to Lang Syne in person for a conference. The time he proposed was inconvenient; Julia had scheduled a speaking engagement at the University of Illinois. Anything else she might have canceled, but Urbana was Irving's old stomping grounds, and so the place aroused her curiosity. She arranged to meet Hopkins in New York on her way home, a clever compromise that gave her an excuse to visit Irving. Stopping off in Chicago, she played bridge for high stakes, won money enough to pay her hotel bill, and was feted from morning till night. She spoke twice in Urbana, each time to packed houses, and felt, as she told Fineman, that "Urbana was full of you."[31] Then came New York, and Irving.

It seems reasonable to assume that Julia and Irving had a satisfactory sexual relationship. After all, they wrote dozens of love letters to each other in which they schemed to spend time alone. Julia often spoke of holding hands and made coy allusions to kisses. She was infatuated with Fineman's body, from his chiseled lips to his hard, flat stomach. But even in the most fervent of her many love letters, she never described what happened during their "islands" of time alone. Perhaps she was embarrassed to talk about sex, or afraid of getting caught. Perhaps she considered it vulgar to reduce physical intimacy to words. Or perhaps she saw no reason to rehearse experiences they had shared. Yet there are hints in both her writing and Irving's that when it came to intercourse, she was tolerant but not terribly interested. Irving seems to have considered this provocative, a challenge to overcome. Whether or not he succeeded is a matter for speculation.

And even when Julia was in New York, Irving often felt shunted aside. People recognized her on the street and begged her to sign their books. She was invited to all the best parties, often several in one night. The infamous nightclub hostess Texas Guinan sent an armored limousine to ferry her around town. New Yorkers seemed to regard her as a kind of guru, a reputation that was catnip to the media.

In the early spring of 1929, *Forum* magazine invited Julia to describe her philosophy of life. "I'm more than ever uncertain what my beliefs are," Julia wrote to Fineman from her father's bedside. "Life looks awry."[32] Yet she soon warmed to the task. In language shaped by African traditions of attributing personality to objects and abstractions, she explained that her beliefs seemed "bent on hiding their starkness behind . . . gentler and more comforting things." She saw herself straining to "seize" these beasts "and drag them into the open."[33] The ambivalence of the imagery is striking. Julia was still trying to cut herself a mouth, to shake off her cultural blinders. Yet she was sorely tempted to give up the struggle and settle for a sheltered life.

Doris Ulmann had visited Lang Syne in the spring of 1929 to take photographs of people at work, as she had in Appalachia, and Julia had given her the grand tour, escorting her to the fields and cabins and churches, persuading people to pose for Ulmann's camera. The pictures were a success, and Doris returned in a chauffeured limousine. She coaxed Julia to shelve her new novel and ride along on a working trip through the Deep South. The expedition sounded irresistible, a perfect excuse to go roving with a friend and blow off some of the restless steam built up by her confusion over Irving.

"All my worries seem to have peeled off like a snake's skin," she marveled to Irving from Alabama. "[Doris] says she's never been foolish before. . . . Husbands call on us but wives are uncertain about us. No other woman here smokes." After a few days, though, the novelty of the road wore off. Heat, dust, and bad food made Julia irritable, as did Doris's weakness for "slick, sweet-talking southern males." Not to be outdone, Julia flirted with a trio of tattooed snapper fishermen in Mobile Bay who tried to get her drunk. "I need life, life in the raw, under the naked sky," she grandly proclaimed. Yet evening found her perched in Doris's hotel room, "manicured and hair-waved, high-heeled and rouged."[34]

Julia could have kicked off her pumps, mussed up her hair, and walked out of that room. Instead, she followed Doris, complaining every step of the way. The real reason for her discontent was not that Doris was idle, but that she was too busy. Despite a personal fortune that was large even by New York standards, Doris led a hard, disciplined life, working with her eyes and hands at a craft that demanded intense concentration. A frivolous woman Doris Ulmann was not, though she insisted on dressing the part. Perfectly coiffed, gowned, and shod, she would trek miles over impassable dirt roads to find a subject in a mossy cabin. In the evening she would closet herself in a darkened hotel room and bring out her developing trays. "Poor little . . . Doris" seemed "consumed by ambition," never at rest, never content, never happy, Julia lamented.[35] Hobbled by stylish clothes, afraid of her own servants, clinging and aloof by turns, she reminded Julia of herself.

In other ways, they were poles apart. Doris was frank about her interest in certain men and childishly eager to compare notes. Julia was secretive, especially when it came to Irving Fineman. In an expansive moment the year before, Julia had suggested that he get to know Doris, who was an attractive woman and a kindred spirit but "not young enough to fall in love with you to the degree of peskiness."[36] Eager to make connections, Fineman wrote a note to Doris and was invited to tea. He enjoyed the visit, he later reported, but was mystified by Doris's melancholy air. She obviously had plenty of money and friends and was dedicated to her work. He speculated that she must have the blues because she was single.[37]

Doris *was* attracted to Fineman — not to the point of peskiness, perhaps, but enough to pursue him a bit. She invited him over for a photo session, and as was her custom with artists and writers, she asked him to pose wearing whatever he usually wore to work. Tilting a sleek eyebrow, Fineman offered to pose nude.[38]

In his letters to Julia, Irving pretended to be put off by Doris, but his behavior suggested otherwise. One spring evening, he telephoned Doris and invited her out to dinner. She begged off, explaining that she had another appointment but promising to call him back later that night, when she was free. By the time she finished work, she was tired and dirty, and instead of calling back, she went to bed. Fineman felt slighted and ran to Julia for an explanation.

"Doris undoubtedly is looking for a mate," she replied. "You were a potential one but she suspects you may not be forth-coming. [Another man] is now being looked over instead. Forgive her and don't bother one way or the other."[39] Instead, Irving confronted Doris, who was surprised to hear that he cared. She explained herself and they made up. "[I] wonder whether I do these things frequently and am utterly unconscious of them!" she exclaimed to Julia. Innocent of Julia's double-dealing, Doris thanked her for playing matchmaker.[40]

Both Julia and Doris wrote to Irving from Alabama, urging him to join them on their wanderings. Unaware that her friends were lovers, Doris joked that if Irving were to arrive unexpectedly, he would have to choose between sleeping with her or with Julia.[41]

At the end of their southern adventure, Julia rode to New York with Doris and spent several days holed up in Irving's apartment. They drank coffee and ate sandwiches, watched the lights of the city from his window, read aloud, compared notes about Doris, and listened to Beethoven on Irving's phonograph. It was harder than ever for Julia to leave. "I miss you. Bitterly," she wrote from Lang Syne. "I cannot bear not to have what I want, not to do what I choose to do."

In fact, Julia had chosen to go home, arriving just in time to help grade the asparagus, a new crop Willie was trying in place of cotton. At her direction, the hands cut logs and built a one-room cabin in her side yard where she could work undisturbed. "A room of my own completely," she crowed, echoing Virginia Woolf's essay on female creativity.[42] Sprawled on the grass, she tried to work on *Bright Skin* and was sidetracked by thoughts of Irving. In hours like these Julia was at her happiest, suspended in a sensuous daydream of yearning as the steamy Lang Syne summer rolled in.

Reinventing herself for Irving Fineman — callow, second-rate, and self-centered as he was — spurred Julia to do her finest work. The thought of leaving the plantation for good made her see it with new eyes. The fresh-turned furrows, the moss-bearded oaks, a gold hoop in an old man's ear. The red brand on a flour-sack petticoat edged with tiny, even stitches. A sharp turn of phrase, a curious saying. All became fodder for her letters and *Bright Skin*, the first a blow-by-blow account of how it felt to be a white woman writer presiding over a plantation, the second a novel about growing up black in the same time and place. The two fit together like the halves of a walnut, their rich, dark sweetness the same meat, yet absolutely distinct.

It was Julia's correspondence with Irving Fineman that gave her the courage to write *Bright Skin*. Irving was the perfect audience for her act, a prop for her fragile ego. The world might sneer at her white woman's problems and demand to read more of Killdee's, Mary's, and April's. Irving was different. He read her letters and commented at length, sometimes sensibly, sometimes not. And while the real Irving was a muddled New Yorker who resented his lack of status, the Irving of Julia's imagination possessed a cool, detached worldliness that transcended personality, time, and place. In fact, this sophistication was a quality that Julia had discovered within herself and projected onto her lover. Irving's books and letters are pedestrian and self-indulgent. But he brought out the best in Julia Peterkin.

In early June 1930, Laura Mood Schneider arrived at Lang Syne carrying a book-length manuscript — her autobiography. Laura had once been the person Julia loved most in the world, even though the two had lived in the same house for only a few years, while they were in their teens. When Laura graduated from high school, Julia was so distraught at the prospect of another separation that she studied frantically and passed her college entrance exam two years early. The sisters were packed off to Columbia Female College, the starchy Methodist girls' school over which Henry Mood had once presided. They hated it. According to one account, they got themselves expelled; according to another, they prevailed on their father to free them. At any rate, they left after a few weeks. From there they went to Converse, a brand-new women's college in Spartanburg, where their Archer relatives could keep an eye on them. It was a much better match; Converse, though serious-minded, was less repressive, and the curriculum extolled music, their great love, above all else. Julia was awkward and chubby; Laura a natural star. "I took a strange pride in her superiority," Julia later recalled, "not only over my-self but it seemed to me, over every other girl." [43]

This worshipful intimacy came to an end in 1897, when Laura graduated, packed her bags, and headed north. Her father refused to give her any money. Undeterred, Laura spent all her money on a steamship ticket to New York. On the boat she met a disciple of evangelist Mary Baker Eddy and was healed of the seizures she had periodically suffered since childhood. Laura converted to Christian Science. Arriving in New York with empty pockets, she made friends with Louisine Havemeyer, also a Christian Scientist and the wife of wealthy sugar importer H. O. Havemeyer. For two years Laura studied voice in New York, then moved to North Carolina to teach music at a girls' school. In 1900 she was living in New Jersey, teaching etiquette at a military academy. Then she made her way to Paris, where she earned her living by singing in the choir at Saint Luke's Episcopal Church.[44]

Laura had many admirers during those years, but they were all eclipsed by Andreas Schneider, a gaunt Bavarian musician who introduced himself as the great-grandson of Franz Joseph Haydn. Orphaned at an early age, Andreas and his brother were raised by Jesuit monks, who groomed them for the priesthood. On the eve of taking final orders, Andreas sneaked out of the monastery and fled west across Europe on foot, sure that angry Jesuits were in pursuit. He made his way to America and worked for a time as a lumberjack in the Georgia forests, but he became convinced that the Catholic church had sent emissaries to persecute him even there. When a European circus crossed his path, Andreas joined up, doing odd jobs in return for passage back to the Old World. Laura met him in Paris, where he was working as a clerk in a tiny bookstore. They married in June 1905, sealing Andreas's decision to renounce the priesthood.

Though Laura had always been eccentric, her marriage tipped the balance toward craziness. Andreas spent so much time dodging nuns and priests that he could not hold a job, though he was, according to the dean of the Columbia University Law School, a cultivated and well-educated man.[45] Soon Laura and her husband had a baby boy, and no money. One day, Laura left the baby on the street in his pram while she slipped inside a shop to make a purchase. Two nuns appeared and leaned over the carriage as if admiring the baby. Laura tore out of the shop, but the nuns were gone and her precious baby was dead.

That, at any rate, was the story Laura told, and no one, including Julia, seems to have checked with the Paris police or tried to confirm it. A distant relative speculates that Laura's baby really died of malnutrition.[46] But if Laura had anything in common with Julia, it was the ability to put over an outlandish story. No one seems to have asked her the most obvious questions, either at the time of her baby's death or later.

The fate of Laura's high-strung husband seems prosaic by comparison. In 1907, Andreas Schneider developed tuberculosis. Not knowing what else to do, Laura took him home to her father. Julius scandalized the neighbors by installing his foreign son-in-law in a tent in the backyard, where he would be exposed to curative fresh air. Laura drifted around Sumter, babbling about homicidal nuns. When Andreas died, she caused even more talk by wearing a white dress to his funeral.[47]

If Julius expected his daughter to stay home like a good southern widow, he was sorely disappointed. She made tracks for New York, where she located her old friend Louisine Havemeyer and soon was named First Reader in the First Church of Christian Science. From that day, Laura never drew a salary. She believed that whatever she needed would come to her, and for the most part it did — not only necessities but luxuries like Oriental rugs and antique furniture. She accumulated many fine things and often gave Julia the surplus.[48]

Julia did not do for Laura what she had done for Irving Fineman. There is no evidence that Laura's manuscript was ever submitted to a publisher. Yet Laura's efforts to write resulted in one small miracle; after decades of estrangement caused by Laura's beliefs, the sisters found common ground. "Now the wound seems healed," Julia wrote to Irving.[49]

Julia still dreamed that she and Irving would someday be together. "If I were your good friend, I'd be advising you to find a nice girl for your-self, marry her, settle down, raise children," she admitted. "Instead of that, I'm wondering how, where I'll see you again." Irving quipped that perhaps he should propose to a country girl who lived near his sister's upstate farm. "If you marry the squire's daughter," Julia blustered, "I shall go straight there and shoot her!"[50]

But it would not be another woman that came between them. On June 6, 1930, *This Pure Young Man* was awarded the Longmans-Green Prize, with its staggering cash award. Disavowing credit, Julia claimed to be only an instrument of fate. "It was to be," she wired him. "I am very happy."[51] Fineman quit his teaching job and purchased a ticket to France. Before sailing, he sent "Dear Mrs. Peterkin" a formal note of thanks for her assistance.

Back at Lang Syne, Julia complained of an "overdose of energy." She longed to do something wild, an urge that was only partly appeased by going deer hunting, at night and out of season. She promised, not for the first time, to "come to some sort of conclusion" about leaving Willie. "For weeks I have been merely an empty tube through which life passed mysteriously," she wrote to Fineman. "I know nothing to do but quit wanting to see you." Perhaps she really meant to try. Before leaving for her summer house she burned all his letters.[52]

But there would soon be plenty more. En route to France, Irving wrote to Julia every evening, declaring that there was no one on board, male or female, who could possibly interest him. He went on to describe his encounters with pretty women, including a tipsy girl who sat next to him at dinner, a young brunette studying architecture at Boston Tech, and a red-haired adventurer named Mrs. Bradley, who not only resembled Julia but turned out to have met her.[53]

Irving's thick packet of shipboard letters arrived near the end of July, throwing Julia into a frenzy of indecision. "What shall I do next? Which way shall I turn? Where is my chance to escape defeat?" she wailed. "Oh, Irving, I'm in a really sad plight so closely do I find myself cleaving to you." Yet she would not leave her home or her husband, not even for a month. "If I were less well known I could so easily plan many things for us, but I suspect you hardly realize how many people recognize me," she wrote. As for Irving's wish to "enrich my life and make me happier," she brushed it aside: "That wish has been fulfilled long ago, didn't you know it? Only yesterday I said to the group here discussing happiness, 'I've no idea what's ahead of me, but I can say honestly that nobody in my whole acquaintance is as happy as I am.'"[54]

Yet she recognized herself in a "gorgeous red bird" pecking compulsively at her windowpane. "I see how easily I could spend my strength working my own destruction trying to get into one lovely tempting place which I see so clearly and covet so keenly," she wrote.[55] This relationship might be a mirage, a reflection of her own image.

One day she would resolve to keep herself free, since "the wish to possess people, things, causes much sorrow." The next day she'd take it back: "Today, I laugh at [myself] for I know there's no such thing as freedom. Love that is free is not love at all, for love lays bonds upon us."[56] Doris Ulmann, she reported, had acquired a new boyfriend, a doctor named Arnold Koffler. They asked to visit her at Murrells Inlet, but Julia scotched that plan, afraid that her summer crowd would be shocked by an unmarried couple traveling together. Instead, she arranged to meet Doris and Koffler in Myrtle Beach, where they would blend in with other vacationing Yankees. Forgetting her earlier pique,

Julia looked forward to the visit. But Doris's idea of fun had not changed, and Koffler proved to be just like her. "Neither of them fish, swim, play golf, ride a horse, shoot, enjoy lying on the sand," Julia scoffed. "My God, how can people become adults and remain inanimate?" [57] Less than a week later, she drove them to Charleston and left them. "I could not stay another minute with them," she told Irving. "Unhappiness does not agree with me." [58]

When Fineman made it plain that he was surrounded by attractive women, Julia countered with a list of handsome men. Henry Bellamann arrived, without Katherine, to spend "many a happy afternoon together in the water." Her "Atlanta cousin," a Harvard graduate, was also at Sunnyside, looking like "an advertisement for Abercrombie and Fitch." "Three very charming bachelors" had the house next door, one of them "good looking, with a good mind, a fine swimmer, an excellent dancer, and stone deaf." [59] Julia described his muscular physique as well as his enigmatic smile.

She was careful to imply that these men were mere playthings to divert her until Irving's return. "Already my heart speeds like the motor throbbing on the boat passing by when I think, 'yes, I'll see him again,'" she wrote in July.[60] Two months later, the moment arrived. "The radio plays 'Happy days' *every* night. I sing with it for they *are* almost here." [61]

Yet when Irving's ship docked in New York, Julia was not there to meet it. With *This Pure Young Man* already in the bookstores, she feared being caught in the spotlight. Irving retreated to his sister's farm in Wappingers Falls, New York, where he angrily took stock. Apparently Julia was too prudent to play Juliet, too spineless to risk a flap.

"How wrong you are about me," she protested. "Nobody was ever so torn by conflict, so oppressed with loneliness, fear — Do you know that marvelous verse from Micah, 'Therefore I will wail and howl; I will go stripped and naked; I will make a wailing like the dragons and mourning as the owls.' Something deep in my heart is doing just that." It was all true, in a way, and at the same time obviously a lie. She had, after all, been bubbling about how happy she was just the other day. "I'm trying to protect you by keeping away, for the present," she continued. "Maybe you do not understand my own lack of privacy. People on the train walk up and speak to me, even the Negro porters know who I am." [62]

Still operating under the illusion that *This Pure Young Man* was about to become a best-seller, Julia coached her lover from the sidelines. "Why not have a movie made from it? . . . Do think this over," she urged. "'Twill be good publicity for you." Meanwhile, she advised him to go along with anything his publishers might suggest to court publicity. "There's nothing to do but to use your wits and succeed financially as well as otherwise," she recommended. "You must go before your public with a *sharp* bang." [63]

A dull thud was more like it. "Prig's Progress," *Time* magazine dubbed *This Pure Young Man*. "Empty of interest and almost void of merit," sniffed the *Bookman*.[64] Reviewers were put off by Fineman's incessant moralizing. He "bludgeons his point home with a sledgehammer," complained *Christian Century*.[65] Faced with a flood of negative reviews, some of which wondered why such a mediocre effort had been awarded a literary prize, Julia dismissed the critics as moronic. "Next time you write a book resolve to read *no* reviews of it," she advised. "They're annoying. Most of them are utterly stupid." [66] She could never admit that the man she had slept with — and sponsored for the prize — was regarded as a hack.

Julia no longer depended on reviews to measure her own success, or to inflate her opinions about herself. Wooed by agents, movie directors, and other publishers, she hardly knew whom to encourage. "Life is like that," she drily observed. "Nothing or too much." The most tempting deal, offered to her anonymously, promised large cash bonuses, mass-market advertising, and huge royalties for her next novel. Julia wavered, wiring the agent, "Changing publishers is like changing husbands so tell me this gentleman's name, reputation, character, all about him, stop. He must prove to me he excels my present one in all respects before he asks me for any answer." [67] Her suitor turned out to be the Cosmopolitan Publishing Company, an ambitious Hearst affiliate with no track record to speak of.

Julia passed the offer along to D. L. Chambers, who reminded her that she'd promised not to leave Bobbs-Merrill while he was with the house. He scoffed at the marketing tactics contemplated by Hearst, vowed to top any offer, and reminded Julia that Bobbs-Merrill held an option on her next two novels. "You are not the sort of person who tries to jump a contract," he added, conveniently forgetting that she had done just that in leaving Knopf for Bobbs-Merrill only four years ago. "We are all absolutely convinced you are the greatest writer in the world and the most wonderful person. Every one of us is your rabid and devoted partisan." [68]

Irritated by such transparent flattery, Julia retaliated with a hard-luck story. "You've no idea what problems we farmers have," she reproached him. "It has become impossible to break even any longer." [69] A year and a half after the fact, she returned to the subject of Jim Crouch. "The lawyer who had charge of all we had has suddenly and mysteriously died. The insurance company says ugly things; declines to pay full insurance. We are the losers. My husband is broken in health and spirit. I find my sense of humor failing. Worry hinders my writing anything decent. . . . Loyalty to those in my care must come ahead of every other loyalty." [70]

Bested, Chambers turned conciliatory. "Times are hard for a lot of people, but I want them always to be easy for you," he said.[71] Times were indeed hard at Bobbs-Merrill. Salaries had been slashed and employees laid off; benefits had been cut. The work week was reduced to four days. Bobbs-Merrill could not afford to offer bonuses or to commit itself to expensive advertising. But news like this might send Julia scurrying to another house, so Chambers kept quiet. Instead, he dispatched a check for her accumulated royalties.[72]

Julia returned the money. "What is there that we might do now that would help you most?" pleaded Chambers.[73] He even suggested that she contact his banker, who could reassure her that the firm was solvent.[74] George Shively, his counterpart in the New York office, packed his bags and got on a train bound for Fort Motte. Touched by their efforts, and leery of making a change, Julia decided to stay put.

One balmy summer night in 1930, in the house next door to Julia's cabin at Murrells Inlet, a man named Jim Sprunt "put his pistol in his mouth and pulled the trigger." Julia saw an ominous pattern emerging. "When I first came here many years ago," she told Fineman, "the few cottages next door were owned by friends whom I really loved because they had such amazing qualities. One by one each of those men has killed himself. This house stands next in line for a suicide." [75] Not hers, she hastened to add, not yet.

But suicide was much on her mind, particularly the suicide of an ambitious white woman. In the wake of her flirtation with José Orozco and her affair with Irving Fineman, Julia wrote a spectacularly bad play about a red-headed woman named Alma Ingraham who longs to be immortalized in art.[76] *The Mona Lisa* opens at a cocktail party, where a famous painter named Andreas Schneider begs Alma to sit for her portrait. (The play, in classic Freudian form, is filled with names drawn from Julia's life. Andreas Schneider was her priest-fearing brother-in-law, Alma was both her mother's first name and that of Orozco's patron, and one of Julius Mood's sisters was married to an Ingraham.)

Flattered by Andreas's interest, Alma agrees to let him paint her wearing a "soft white draped garment" like the one in Orozco's *Drama*. The love scene that follows is unintentionally hilarious. While sketching in the painting, Andreas coaxes Alma to talk about her life. She says that she likes to drive fast and has never feared the "speed cops." When they break for lunch, she continues to flirt, still wearing the flimsy toga. She even coaxes the artist onto a daybed, but then, instead of crawling in with him, she offers to fix his lunch. Exhorting Alma to live for the moment, Andreas grabs for her hand. "Your face is on my eyelids," she cries, repeating a phrase Julia had used to great effect on Irving Fineman and Carl Sandburg. "I must be mad!" This overwrought scene is mercifully terminated when Andreas's jealous wife crashes through the door.

Alma leaves. The wife takes a brushful of bright red paint and defaces Alma's image. Alma skips her next scheduled sitting but shows up shortly afterward. "Love is a madness," she wails to Andreas. "It's a disease! It's a terrible thing!"

"I become a God when I'm with you," the artist intones. "Together — we'll show the world what greatness is."

Alma bridles. Knowing him, she claims, has had a "terrible influence" on her, an effect that is "almost immoral" because it takes away her freedom. Though Andreas and Alma agonize, their dilemma seems just plain silly. As usual when Julia was writing about white people, she reduced them to brittle shells. And also as usual, she injected random acts of violence, hoping to make the characters' lives seem tragic.

The climax of *The Mona Lisa* is straight out of Italian opera. Andreas shows Alma the damaged painting and lets her believe that he destroyed it. They arrange for him to repaint the face, but Alma abruptly grabs an antique dagger and plunges it into her breast. Andreas kneels to cradle her as her life oozes away. His wife bursts into the room, assumes she has interrupted a tryst, snatches the bloody knife, and stabs Alma's dead body again and again.

Comical as they seem when handled so ineptly, the elements of *The Mona Lisa* are straight from classic English and European models. There are numerous allusions to Browning's dramatic monologue "Andrea del Sarto," in which an artist is doomed to mediocrity because he dotes on his wife. The overwrought lovers are modeled on Romeo and Juliet, Tristan and Iseult, Lancelot and Guinevere, Manon Lescaut and Monsieur des Grieux, and the dozens of lesser-known doomed couples who dominate Western literature. Why did such an evergreen plot wither in Julia's hands? She had already written about a crime of passion in the story "A Proudful Fellow." Why could she build a tragic story around Ut Wine but not around Alma Ingraham? It all comes down to Julia's two fatal flaws, narcissism and self-deception. She could portray Jim, Harpa, and Ut Wine as vain, petty, and needlessly destructive in their pursuit of adultery and murder, but to attribute such faults to Andreas or Alma would be to admit her own triviality. When it came to herself, she had no sense of irony.

Clumsy and silly to boot, *The Mona Lisa* has no saving graces. Yet it deserves attention not just for its awfulness but because Alma's lines betray a significant change in Julia's outlook. Alma refuses to become involved with Andreas because she suspects that he will paint a masterpiece in her image, and she doesn't want to go down in history as "a mirror for the artist's mind." Julia had spent most of her adult life trying to be the heroine of some man's story, the muse who inspired creation. Now she seems to have vanquished that obsession and come to terms with her talent. Julia Peterkin was not destined to be a mirror for any man's mind. In spite of failures like *The Mona Lisa*, she was a great artist herself.

A Stiff Masquerade

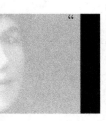

"If I were bent on suicide, interest in what the next mail held would make me post-pone it, I'm sure," Julia once joked.[1] In the summer of 1929, her mailbox was fuller than ever, jam-packed with fan letters, offers, and inquiries. Among them was a telegram from Elisabeth Marbury, a theatrical agent, saying that a famous American actress wanted to bring Mary to the stage.

From the time *Scarlet Sister Mary* first appeared in print, there had been speculation about who might play the title role in a stage production; Julia herself favored Ethel Waters, a nightclub singer who would later become a stage and movie star.[2] Then, as now, there were few big roles for African American actresses. Rose McClendon, who had appeared in DuBose Heyward's *Porgy* and in Paul Green's folk drama, *In*

Abraham's Bosom, dreamed of playing Mary, and so did several other black actresses.[3]

Knowing that the role was a plum, Julia was unimpressed by Miss Marbury's cryptic urgency. "First tell me who Elisabeth Marbury is," she calmly wired back. Marbury, who represented Eugene O'Neill and George Bernard Shaw, among other famous playwrights, introduced herself and disclosed her secret: the actress she represented was Ethel Barrymore, the "Queen of the American Theater."

Barrymore had discovered *Scarlet Sister Mary* for herself, devouring the novel on a voyage across the Atlantic.[4] As soon as her ship docked, she called her producer, Lee Shubert, and told him to buy the dramatic rights and commission someone to write a script. Shubert made a few inquiries and discovered that Dan Reed was already working on a dramatization of *Black April*. Reed signed a contract with Shubert and Barrymore on June 10, 1929, and delivered a script shortly afterward.[5]

Julia met Ethel Barrymore in March 1930 in a luxurious Philadelphia hotel room. "Ethel and I are somehow strangely akin," she observed. "Yet thank God, I've not her bitter weariness. . . . She made me all but drop tears in my coffee." Julia, who seldom embraced even her closest friends, was taken aback by Ethel's exuberance. "Her joy in seeing me, holding my hands, kissing my cheeks, my mouth, wrung me, for I recognized her loneliness," she told Irving Fineman. He ventured to wonder how an actress like Ethel Barrymore could possibly play Mary.[6]

Miss Barrymore had made her fortune impersonating proper British society matrons, yet she did not doubt that she could bewitch American playgoers into seeing her as a Gullah Mae West. She prepared for the challenge by listening to recordings of African American folk tales as rendered by Samuel Gaillard Stoney, a white Charlestonian (and a distant cousin of Julia's). Julia, hearing her read her lines, was won over completely. "Lord, how [Ethel] knows Mary, *knows* her," she marveled.[7] Near the end of the visit, Ethel's telephone rang. The actress listened for a moment, frowned, then grandly informed her caller, "I'm going to do *Scarlet Sister Mary* next. Nothing but death can hinder me."[8] "Death, or [the lack of] a good supporting cast," Julia quipped later to her editor.[9]

Barrymore's *Mary* was a publicist's dream, the kind of happening that spawns headlines for months in advance. The sheer number of Barrymores involved in the production enthralled the press for weeks. Ethel was directing the play under the transparent pseudonym E. M. Blythe, and the company swarmed with her relatives, in roles that mirrored their real-life relationships. Georgie Drew Mendum, Ethel's sister-in-law, was cast as Mary's sister-in-law Doll. Ethel Barrymore Colt, Ethel's teenaged daughter, was slated to make her stage debut as Mary's daughter Seraphine, thus launching a fifth generation of theatrical Drew-Barrymores. "Unless Ethel has reduced that daughter of hers, I fear she is too heavy for Seraphine," Julia remarked.[10]

Dan Reed was named assistant director, a post that carried little clout. The play was financed by the famous Shubert brothers, Lee and Jacob, and produced by Arthur Hopkins, a "quiet, round-faced, unassuming little man" who was a powerful figure on Broadway.[11] In the beginning, a serious attempt was made at authenticity. Composer Maurice Nitke, hired to create an original score based on authentic plantation melodies, was dispatched to the lower South to collect folk songs and absorb the atmosphere. Accompanied by Dan Reed, Nitke spent two weeks at Lang Syne, then moved on to the Penn School at St. Helena Island, where he conferred with the all-white Society for the Preservation of Spirituals before visiting a black church to hear "genuine" singing and shouting.[12]

Even so, by late summer it was clear that *Scarlet Sister Mary* would not be distinguished for its fidelity to Gullah culture. The devil, as the saying goes, is always in the details. Though Ethel taught herself to smoke a pipe, she did not learn to sing or "shout" with any kind of conviction. She and her all-white cast delivered their lines in imaginary dialects that made Julia cringe. Hudson Strode unkindly commented that Mary's wedding was played as a conventional Episcopal service, and that the scene in which Cinder and Mary clash "would have fitted perfectly into a drawing room comedy of manners by Somerset Maugham."[13]

Ethel Barrymore had set out to prove that Mary's race mattered less than her character. This was, for its time, a radical notion — and a risky career move besides; many whites thought Ethel was lowering herself by impersonating a black woman. It is hard to imagine the patrician Barrymore delivering lines like "I ain' gwine drap dis cake. Whoo!" But the problem went beyond misguided casting, as the original script of the play reveals. The instructions to the actors are unbelievably condescending. Budda Ben is described as "deformed," "a gnome"; Cinder as "a wiry and flashy type of negress"; and Daddy Cudjoe as a "grotesque little man." Baby Unex is listed as a prop — "one black large life sized year old baby dressed by the costumer."[14] Though the dialogue lifted directly from the novel retains much of its power, Dan Reed's added flourishes intrude and destroy the effect.

The play was scheduled to go on the road for several weeks, to work out the kinks before opening on Broadway. "I'm not even sure I want to see [it]," Julia wrote to Irving in mid-August; a month later she joked that she had invited her father to accompany her to the opening in case it was so upsetting that she needed a doctor to revive her.[15] She skipped the first performance — in Columbus, Ohio — only to find her fears confirmed by the reviews. Something would have to be done. When the play moved on to Cleveland, she attended in disguise, posing as "Mary Wallace."[16]

In Cleveland, excitement ran high. The line for the gallery began forming at the unheard-of hour of 4:30 P.M., and the box office quickly sold out.[17] But changing cities had done nothing to improve the play. The first act was even worse than Julia had feared. Rushing backstage between acts, Julia discovered Ethel sprawled drunk in her dressing room. The rest of the cast scurried around aimlessly. Desperate to avert a catastrophe, Julia telephoned Ethel's brother Lionel and begged him to do something.[18] Apparently he could not or would not intervene, and the show lurched grimly on. Julia was mortified. When the curtain finally dropped, she could hardly believe her eyes. The audience rose to its feet and gave Ethel a standing ovation.

The press, however, was not swept away by sentiment. The *Cleveland Plain Dealer* lived up to its name by calling a spade a spade: "A white actor blacked up looks like a white actor blacked up," declared William McDermott.[19] The *Cleveland News* called *Scarlet Sister Mary* a "stiff masquerade" — too long, too slow, and too white.[20]

"Can I legally stop this thing?" Julia wired George Shively.[21] She couldn't. Someone leaked her telegram to Walter Winchell, who gleefully printed a paraphrase in his gossip column, "Walter Winchell on Broadway." Winchell had been feuding with the show's producers on and off for years. "I made the terrible mistake," he quipped in 1926, "of panning fifty-four of [the Shuberts'] shows, when it appears they produced only fifty-two."[22] To make matters worse, he was still seething at Ethel Barrymore for remarks she had recently made about him to the *New York World:* "It is a sad comment on American manhood that Walter Winchell is allowed to exist."[23] Now she was not only disgusted with Winchell but livid at Julia for playing right into his hands. Trying to make amends, Julia asked Bobbs-Merrill to issue a press release praising Miss Barrymore and denying that Julia had sent the ill-fated telegram.

The next day, Ethel summoned Julia to another performance. "I shiver when I think of seeing her again, for each time has been painful," Julia wrote to Fineman. "I wouldn't except that she's put it up to me as a loyalty to her effort." [24] Before the performance, Julia had two dozen long-stemmed pink roses delivered to Ethel's dressing room by a messenger. The second night was worse than the first. When the final curtain came down, Julia mustered all her self-control and headed backstage. Ethel was holding a bundle of bare stems; the floor was littered with pink petals. She had wrung the neck of every rose.[25]

A few days later she told a pushy reporter that in her opinion, journalists were worse than whores. Though aimed at Walter Winchell, her comments angered the critics, whose good opinion she urgently needed. Claiming that she had been misquoted, Barrymore beat a hasty retreat. But to no avail. The press was out for blood.

As the early reviews stacked up on their desks, D. L. Chambers and George Shively began to sweat. Bad publicity could damage book sales. With Ethel drawing fire for impersonating a black woman, Julia's white skin was changing from an asset into a liability. *Scarlet Sister Mary* was set to open in Washington, D.C., on October 13, 1930. George Shively sent a telegram to Julia in Fort Motte, proposing to escort her. But the postmistress misplaced it, or so Julia claimed, and it was not delivered until after she returned home.

Doris Ulmann called long-distance, offering to come to Washington and bring Irving with her. "I *must* form a matrimonial bureau, and try Doris for my first client," Julia teased Fineman. "Will you give me a commission if I make you this successful marriage? Or a better commission if I keep you free?" [26] Irving prudently steered clear. Julia and Doris met in Washington, whose shabby, littered streets bore witness to the deepening of the Depression. Attending the play unannounced, they shared a box with a contingent of southern clubwomen, who, according to the *Washington Times,* "gave [them] some frank opinion on the Gullah characters." [27]

The offstage drama in Washington interested reporters more than the play. Ethel's ex-husband, millionaire Russell Colt, showed up in the audience, fueling speculation that the couple might be on the verge of a reconciliation. They weren't — Colt had come to see his daughter act. But as the play rolled on from city to city, it was not Julia's displeasure, Ethel Colt's debut, Russell Colt's intentions, or Ethel's gibes at the press that caused the most talk — it was the "fudge-colored greasepaint."

"The smell of burnt-cork hovers over the evening," sneered a reporter from the *New York Times*.[28] The *Washington Star* praised Ethel for using black (as opposed to "copper or amber") makeup. But as the play stumbled and the comments grew crueler, she would gradually lighten the skin tone and refuse to be photographed in blackface. An enterprising photographer from *Time* magazine was ejected from the theater three times before finally managing to snap a blurry picture.[29] Everybody made much of Albert Ridge, the "real colored pickaninny" who played baby Unex and whose natural dark skin drew extra attention to the fakery.

It was so easy to make jokes about fudge that most critics soft-pedaled the fact that the play was badly written, badly produced, badly directed, and badly acted. By rights it should have closed after the first dismal week. But the circus atmosphere, the hilarious reviews, and even Julia's covert protests made people curious. Every performance sold out, and the weekly gross receipts exceeded $25,000. As Julia unhappily observed, "Ethel sees money in this road business."[30]

It was a distressing autumn in other ways, too. Arthur Hopkins announced that Paul Robeson had agreed to play the lead in *Black April*. But in the wake of the early reviews of *Scarlet Sister Mary*, Robeson pulled out, explaining through his agent that pending concert engagements would "interfere."[31] Once again, Julia begged George Shively to have a team of Bobbs-Merrill lawyers comb her contract with Dan Reed for loopholes. "I may go both gray and crazy if I have to go through another dramatization," she pleaded.[32]

Yet she liked the idea of having her name in lights and wouldn't have skipped *Mary*'s New York debut for love or money. When Dale Warren warned that New York audiences could be merciless, Julia made fun of his concern. "[Dale] seems to think mercy is to be found outside of NY, in SC for instance," she told Fineman. "I find it rarely, here or anywhere."[33]

She did hope to find it in Irving's apartment. "Will you give me sandwiches and coffee as soon as I come?" she asked. "And read to me? And let me put on the strange brown robe to keep warm?"[34] She warned him not to let other girlfriends, especially book critic Isabel Paterson, walk in on her. "I'm too big to hide under a couch well," she teased, "and I can't stand closets since the days I used to get shut up in one for my badness."[35]

The strain was taking a toll on everyone. "The play has wasted my time and exhausted my soul," Julia complained to Irving.[36] Both she and Ethel fell ill in early November; Ethel missed two performances in Detroit, and Julia underwent "a minor operation in an Orangeburg hospital." [37] Bill, Willie, and a visiting nephew were sick for several weeks, and so was Julia's favorite maid. A friend, probably Elizabeth Darby, stepped in to help and saw the family through the crisis. But Julia suspected that the neighborhood ladies were "not altogether sorry I've had this down-fall." [38]

Both Julia and Ethel recovered in time for the New York opening on November 25. Outside the theater, the sidewalks swarmed with rubberneckers. Inside, photographers cruised the aisles popping flashbulbs at celebrities. As one of the newspapers put it, "everybody — well, everybody on Broadway" was there, "dressed in finest bib and tucker." [39] The play was a sad anticlimax. "A Very Bad Evening" and "A Very Bad Play," sniffed the *New York Post.* "Though *Scarlet Sister Mary* may be news, it is very bad news." [40] Other reviewers used words like "baffling" and "incomprehensible." [41] John Anderson of the *New York Evening Journal* echoed the *Cleveland Plain Dealer:* "a cast of blacked-up white people . . . looks like a cast of blacked-up white people." Robert Garland of the *New York Telegram* could not resist remarking, "All evening you have had the suspicion that a Barrymore is lurking in the woodpile." [42]

Playing across the street from *Scarlet Sister Mary* was another drama about rural blacks, *The Green Pastures.* Adapted by a white playwright (Marc Connelly) from the short stories of a white writer (Roark Bradford), the play itself was no more "authentic" than *Scarlet Sister Mary,* yet there was an important difference in the production. The cast was entirely black. Sentimental and full of stereotypes as it now seems, *The Green Pastures* caught on with whites and blacks alike, and is still hailed as a milestone in African American drama. [43] *Scarlet Sister Mary* could not escape comparison.

Most hurtful of all, even Julia's old friends Stark Young and Henry Bellamann joined in the chorus of abuse. Writing for the *Columbia Record,* Bellamann pronounced *Scarlet Sister Mary* "drab, uninteresting, and peculiarly annoying." Had he put the blame on Dan Reed and Ethel Barrymore, Julia might have forgiven him. But "at the end of the third act," he noted scornfully, "Mrs. Peterkin, Mr. Reed and Miss Barrymore have conspired to permit [Cinder] to say, 'Well, olive oil [*au revoir*], as they say in the city.' I heard it myself, or I should have been skeptical." [44]

If the play had been good, Ethel Barrymore might have gone down in history as a heroine who challenged the color line. Instead, she and

Julia were vilified, their reputations tainted. The production would become a national laughingstock, a latter-day minstrel show. For black artists and writers, the hype was infuriating. *Of course* Ethel Barrymore looked and sounded ridiculous — who with any sense would have expected otherwise? Rose McClendon collected hostile reviews and pasted them into her scrapbook.[45] Ten years later, describing the wreck of the Harlem renaissance in his autobiography, *The Big Sea*, Langston Hughes would immortalize 1930 as the year Ethel Barrymore ("God help us!") played *Scarlet Sister Mary* in blackface.[46]

Mercifully, the play closed on Broadway after only thirty-four performances.

To Julia, it seemed as though evil spirits had been set loose in the land. Nothing she cared about was safe; everything she touched turned sour. Late in the fall of 1930, Irving Fineman complained of feeling ill and depressed. Preoccupied by her own troubles, Julia was impatient with his whining. "Please, Irving, be happy," she urged. "Try hard." Other people had worse problems, she told him. "Two days ago a cunning little black girl sat on a wood-pile playing. A tiny cousin lifted the axe and let it fall on her fingers. One fell away, the others hang — Through it all she has not whimpered. . . . I'd be raving, but in that cabin nobody raves. They're too good mannered," she wrote.[47]

Though Julia did not know it, Irving was suffering from heart disease, the result of a childhood bout with rheumatic fever.[48] His brother, a doctor, had prescribed digitalis and advised him to avoid all strain. Embarrassed and angry at his body's betrayal, Irving tried to keep his illness a secret. Aware only that her lover seemed run-down, Julia suggested that he come south to a health resort, perhaps in Asheville, Charleston, or Savannah. "Do this for me," she ordered. "Go to a drug store and get a bottle of Squibbs mint-flavored codliver oil and take a tea-spoon full three times a day. . . . If I could only have the care of you for a little while, I'd have you fine and fit in no time. I'd do it painlessly too." [49]

Willie was also having health problems — an unspecified operation was scheduled for the following week — and Julia herself came down with an attack of pleurisy. It was a chastened Julia Peterkin who rang in the new year. "I hope," she wrote to Irving, "that this year Fate [will] lead my feet over naked earth and not toward paved streets." [50] In late November she had toyed with the idea of taking an apartment near his. Now she spoke of retreating, alone, to the Yaddo Writers' Colony in Saratoga Springs, New York.

Their relationship seemed as false and hollow as Ethel's rendition of Mary. "How pathetic we humans are in our efforts to bridge the space between ourselves and those dearest to us. How we strive to send our souls out on a bridge of words yet are doomed to be known only as flesh and a voice," she reflected. Determined to "start the new year fresh" — to clear her desk of embarrassing evidence — she burned the bulk of Fineman's letters. But she was still far from ready to make a clean sweep. Ten letters were spared from the flames to be locked in a box with her other "treasures." [51]

Everywhere she turned, perils appeared. Shortly after the first of the year, one of the bird dogs developed a strange sickness, staggering and refusing to eat or drink. Julia nursed the dog herself until he started foaming at the mouth, snapping, and rolling his eyes. Then everyone realized he had rabies. Fortunately Julia had not been bitten, but then neither had a man she had seen die in agony many years before. He had picked up the disease through saliva that dripped onto a cut on his hand. Rabies serum was available, but the treatment was long and excruciating. Julia waited and worried. Another dog took sick. The infected animals were shot, and the rest locked up for observation. Meanwhile, Ellis Sanders had a run-in with a horse, which kicked in his cheek and jawbone. A doctor advised against taking him to the hospital, saying he was too old and too badly injured to move.

Julia took it all in stride, nursing dogs and men, but by late January 1931 she was planning an escape to Bermuda to visit Hudson and Thérèse Strode. Irving offered to follow her there, politely inquiring whether his presence on the island would disturb her in any way. She assured him that it would not. "I here with promise to be henceforth a sister to you, and a most discreet sister at that," she teased.[52] He suggested inviting Doris; Julia jokingly objected, then invited Doris herself. Doris declined.

Julia and Irving plotted to sail on the same boat, thus assuring themselves a few days alone before Julia joined the Strodes. At the last minute, however, Irving sent word that his plans had changed — he would meet Julia later, on the island. Hiding her disappointment, she dined with Doris and planned to meet Irving's ship when it docked in Bermuda "unless something absolutely prohibits. Something like rain or a hurricane (or Hudson)." [53]

"Something like a hurricane" turned out to be an apt description of the whole trip. The captain of the ship made a pass at Julia, who gave him to understand that "to me the captain of a ship is no more than the conductor of a train." [54] Irving eventually arrived, but he lodged at the Elbow Beach Hotel while Julia stayed with the Strodes.

Unbeknownst to Julia, Irving had been delayed in New York by more heart trouble. Convinced now that he was facing death, he was morose, demanding, and irritable. Julia was already hurt that he had canceled their shipboard rendezvous; his churlish behavior made her angry. Partly in order to punish him, she let herself be monopolized by Hudson, who pointedly excluded Irving from parties and outings. Torn between the demands of a jealous host and a jealous lover, Julia was miserable. The month, so eagerly anticipated, slipped away in a dreary string of misunderstandings and disappointments. Just as Julia was about to sail for home, Irving's frustration erupted. Striding angrily along the beach, he accused her of being cruel and vain.

Julia boarded the ship in tears and then collapsed in a faint while walking in to dinner. She spent the rest of the trip in bed, berating herself for hurting Irving. But as soon as she stepped off the boat in New York, a friend greeted her with the unwelcome news that Irving had a girlfriend. He had lived with her in Paris the summer before and continued to see her in New York.

Julia felt she had been played for a fool. "You are a gold-fish too," she told Irving. "No more privacy, no more secret pleasures." She hoped he was well and happy, and that the sun still shone in Bermuda. But human beings were disgusting "worms, hell bent on crushing each other." [55]

Stung by Julia's sarcasm, Fineman did not deny that he had other lovers, yet he scoffed at the story of the disappointed girlfriend, joking that Doris must have started the rumor to get back at them for leaving her behind. [56] He went on to explain why he had not left for Bermuda with Julia as planned — he had been in the hospital, on the verge of heart failure. The trip should have been healing. Instead, it was so upsetting that it could easily have triggered a fatal attack. Fineman worked himself into a frenzy just thinking about it. He was an innocent victim. Everything was Julia's fault. She was his queen, he loved her still, and he was prepared to bow to her whims, even if what she wanted was for him to leave her alone. In a crescendo of self-pity, he assured her that he would never subject her to his tears, and that he would gladly take whatever crumbs of affection she chose to offer. [57]

Julia was shocked. She had had no idea that Irving was ill, or that she had injured his pride. "Please let's start over," she entreated. "I need what you give me. I can't go on without it." "For heaven's sake, forget Bermuda. To remember disappointments or spoiled hopes is sheer foolishness." His point made, Irving relented and the storm blew over. "I *want* your approval. . . . I miss you horribly," Julia reassured him.[58]

What seems to have frustrated Irving most was Julia's lack of physicality. To him, a love affair without frequent sex was like a picnic without food. But the more Julia talked about needing and wanting, the less time she actually spent in his company. The more she described the violence of her passions, the less she seemed inclined to act on them. She even seemed willing for him to have sex with other women as long as his emotions weren't involved. The trouble was, when he slept with a woman, he tended to fall in love.

Realizing this, Julia humorously suggested that he should have himself castrated. Irving had happened to mention that some biblical scholars believed Daniel to have been a eunuch. "As for Daniel," Julia gibed, "it may be that Jehovah wished him spared temptations that would take time from his prayers. I can't see why all you men who have set your hearts on goals hard to reach, do not at once set about freeing yourselves likewise."[59] She urged him to schedule the operation at once, for the good of his career.

It was evident to Irving (if not to Julia) that she preferred to make love by letter. He was an avid correspondent, the best she had ever found, and yet she realized that her words alone would not be enough to hold him. Late in the spring of 1931, she agreed to come north, partly because she wanted to see him and partly because she knew that he was slipping away. "Please, when I do come, be glad to see me," she commanded, "for if you're not I may stick you through and through with an icepick or a hair-pin — or maybe only with a flower stem. A cyclone can send wheat straw through an oak."[60]

CHAPTER 12

Bright Skin

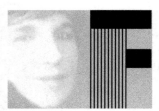

or better and for worse, *Scarlet Sister Mary* had become a household name. When *Denver Post* columnist Caroline Bancroft asked her readers to write an essay explaining which characters from literature they would choose as companions on a desert island, the winner, a white man, picked Si May-e, because he assumed she would be a good cook.[1] The novel occupied a place of honor at the Chicago World's Fair in an exhibit of the one hundred best books by women.[2] An activity recommended by the *Wilson Library Bulletin* to occupy "Children of the Depression" during their unwanted leisure was to start a reading group and discuss *Scarlet Sister Mary*.[3]

Newspapers and magazines solicited Julia's opinion on "the Negro problem." The rigidly conservative *Charleston News and Courier* declared that she had a "better understanding of public questions than our politicians have." [4] Simon and Schuster reprinted "What I Believe" in a book called *I Believe: The Personal Philosophies of Certain Eminent Men and Women of Our Time.* The twenty "eminent men" included Albert Einstein, John Dewey, Theodore Dreiser, H. L. Mencken, Bertrand Russell, and Lewis Mumford. (There was only one other "eminent woman," the British social economist Beatrice Webb.)

A movie studio offered a screenwriting job. Alfred A. Knopf reissued *Green Thursday* and asked Julia to consider returning to the fold. "[Knopf is] a good publisher but a disagreeable person," Julia told Fineman. "And life's too short to be bothered with people who annoy me." [5]

Her head swelled by celebrity, Julia was more prone than ever to contradict herself. "My roots lie around people, not places," she declared to Fineman after a long, lyric description of her attachment to Lang Syne. "You're wrong in thinking I've a place where I belong. I haven't. I've never had." One day she fretted that she was superfluous on the farm; the next she complained that she was overworked. "You've no idea how many things I do, how full my time is of trivial matters that must be done or upset the whole machinery here," she fussed.[6]

Julia had perfected the art of deflecting criticism by playing one part of her life against the other. If D. L. Chambers suggested that she hurry up and write, she said she was busy farming. If the family pressured her to stay home and act the lady, she remembered an urgent business meeting that could not be put off. Boring visitors were solemnly informed that an important deadline loomed. When the *New York Herald Tribune* invited her to write an article about younger black people who had left the plantation during the 1920s and were now returning to beg for sustenance, Julia disingenuously replied that she had too much housekeeping to do. Nobody dared to argue with her priorities.

Perhaps because *Scarlet Sister Mary* extolled female self-reliance, perhaps because Julia liked to suggest that her husband was an invalid, perhaps because so many struggling women were hungry for reassurance, Julia was reinvented by her fans as an abandoned woman who had pulled herself up by her bootstraps. Ladies from Calhoun County visiting friends in other states were infuriated by the blatant falsehoods they encountered at book club meetings. Where did these women get the idea that Julia was born poor, married young, and widowed without a penny? Julia was supposed to have run the farm alone, saving it from foreclosure. Her son, it was said, was a frivolous ingrate who ran off and got married, leaving his poor mother to "paddle her own canoe." [7]

Those acquainted with Julia and her son knew that the opposite was true: Bill was unusually — some might have said unnaturally — devoted to his mother. Not that he was a mama's boy in any traditional sense. As Julia liked to say, he was "no mild man."[8] Strong and handsome, he loved pretty women, good liquor, and horse racing, and was the life of many a party. He liked to farm, to make things grow, and he liked even more to play lord of the manor. He was funny and opinionated, a good storyteller like his mother. Julia encouraged all these dashing traits as appropriate to his position, even boasted about them to friends. Yet she also put him down constantly for being more athletic than intellectual. "My grandfather was the most intelligent man I have ever known, and my father the second most intelligent, but the brains have run out in this generation," she sometimes berated him.[9]

And far from having married against his mother's wishes, twenty-six-year-old Bill had just announced his engagement to Elfrida DeRenne Barrow of Savannah. Her mother, also named Elfrida, was an old friend of Julia's, and a number of people suspected that the two matriarchs had engineered the match. A philanthropist and a writer herself, Mrs. Barrow had established several annual literary prizes, was a pillar of the Georgia Poetry Society, and had published in the *Reviewer* and *Poetry.* After *Black April,* when so many Southerners had snubbed Julia, Mrs. Barrow had written her a fan letter.[10] Frida's father, a physician, worried about Bill's finances but was prepared to take up the slack. "How much money did you clear last year?" he asked before giving his blessing. "Five hundred dollars," Bill admitted. "Then I hope you will not be offended if I send my daughter a monthly allowance," his future father-in-law replied.[11]

It was not immaterial to Julia that Bill's fiancée came from a family well endowed with land and money. Like her father before her, she would have moved heaven and earth to stop her offspring from marrying down. Among the upper class, the consequences of marriage stretched far into the future; families consolidated or diffused their wealth and property through inheritance. Julia often played the piano for the weddings of friends and relatives; she treated the ceremony with respect.[12] Yet she had also soaked up some contradictory ideas from her left-wing friends up North. "Marriage," she groused to Irving, was "the deadliest convention of them all. It never would have been except for economic reasons. It will become obsolete as soon as civilization is more general."[13]

Even as she insisted to her lover that marriage had nothing to do with romance, Julia worried that Frida might be more "in love with love" than with Bill. Worse yet, she suspected that the girl saw Lang Syne as a kind of country club. "I've tried to tell her that underneath all this strange beauty of earth, sky, fields, forests, a fearful brutality lies hidden," she wrote to Fineman. "Her very blue jewel-like eyes widen." [14] Frida seems to have shrugged off Julia's warnings, and preparations were soon under way to bring her into the family. Bill began building a small house a few hundred yards from his parents'. Willie deeded part of the farm to him, and Julia gave him her engagement ring, a spectacular three-carat diamond, to give to Frida.

Probably, as Julia later told Bill's second wife, the family could not afford a suitable ring in those cashless days of the Depression, and she didn't want Bill to be embarrassed.[15] Her gift was a sign that she had come around and now approved of Bill's choice. But Julia's giving Elfrida her ring through her son also marked a turning point in her relationship to Willie and Bill, a shift in the balance of power at Lang Syne. Julia felt that her own marriage was over, even as the anger that had shackled her to Willie for so many years relaxed into a mellow tolerance. But the more Bill filled his father's shoes, the more she would come to resent him. And the more Frida seemed to be taking over as "Miss," the more Julia would dislike her. With the gift of her ring she was staking a claim: Bill and Frida were wedded to her and subject to her whims.

So, in a way, was Irving. Julia gave his fledgling career another boost in the spring of 1931, recommending him to Marian MacDowell for her artists' colony. Declining to join him in Peterboro, Julia explained that she had caused too much talk when she was a colonist by taking long walks with Hudson. She did promise to visit, with Doris in tow, sometime near the end of the session.

To hear Irving tell it, his stint at the colony was tranquil and monotonous. The other male guests seemed "dull or affected," and the women "anti-aphrodisiac." Julia knew better. "Surely there's *one* attractive woman who has fallen for you," she taunted. "If not, I suspect something ails you. I think, however, you're being modest and not boasting of your conquests." [16] She was right. Within three weeks, Irving had acquired a new girlfriend, the poet Frances Frost. Young — only twenty-two years old — slight in build, and the mother of two small children, Frost drank and cursed like a sailor and preferred wearing trousers to skirts. At heart, however, she was a clinging vine with a flair for romantic verse. "One of the most gifted of America's young lyrists [*sic*]," the *New York Times* had called her.[17] The year before, Julia had clipped one of Frost's poems from the *New Yorker* and sent it to Irving Fineman. Titled "Warning," the poem cautions:

> If you would be invulnerable
> Let nothing enter in
> The intimately empty breast,
> The delicately thin
> Walls of brain. Walk lightly,
> Hands upon your eyes,
> For he who looks on wild earth once,
> Looks until he dies.
> Who roots a face within his heart
> Has no safe road to go,
> And love is such a thing as lays,
> The proudest laughter low.[18]

It was a prophetic introduction. By July 21, Frances and Irving Fineman were sneaking off to the sheep pasture every night to make love beneath the stars. Julia, vacationing at Murrells Inlet, complained that she was surrounded by affectionate drunken women who gave her "the creeps." "I can't bear for a woman to touch me, anyhow. Can you?" she unknowingly teased her lover.[19]

Soon Fineman wrote that he was leaving the colony early to visit the Maine coast. "Perhaps you'll be better off," Julia decided. "Unless you are lucky enough to find at least one congenial person [at the colony], you'll hate it. . . . Still, you are one of the lucky, aren't you?"[20]

While Frances "went down beneath [Irving's] steady mouth, cleanly as grass beneath a long-swung blade," Julia embarked on the "last lap" of *Bright Skin*. "I fear it's disorganized, wavering, confused," she lamented.[21] In mid-August she promised to send the manuscript to Bobbs-Merrill within the next few weeks; by mid-October she still had not come through.[22] Hoping that one of the better magazines might buy the serial rights, she shipped the text to the Carl Brandt agency. No one made an offer, and the delay antagonized Chambers.[23]

Irving, meanwhile, was finally successful in encouraging a woman to get out of her marriage. After three idyllic weeks in Maine, Frances returned to her parents' home in Burlington, Vermont, where she visited with her children and filed for a divorce. By September 30 she was a free woman, though forbidden to remarry for six months. Out of money, she sold her car to pay the court costs.[24] She wrote to Irving at least twice a day, inundating him with a torrent of plaintive confessions that blunted his interest in Julia's letters. "You've a short memory," Julia chided him. "I wrote you last week same as ever. You forgot." Irving prudently kept her in the dark about the reason for his forgetfulness; he never mentioned Frances. "Your life sounds too exemplary," Julia declared. "It makes me uneasy."[25]

In October, Frances moved to New York, anticipating a happy reunion with Irving. Meanwhile, Julia blithely sent word that she was coming north the first week of November, as soon as she could get there after Bill's wedding. The thought of juggling the two of them was more than Irving could handle, especially with a bad heart. To Frances's bewilderment, he suddenly turned cold, refusing to speak to her. When she begged him to tell her what was wrong, he retreated into a black mood.

Gloom and raw nerves were not unusual symptoms that fall, for the nation was in economic collapse. There were frantic bank runs, even in Columbia, and speculation that the schools might have to close. Unemployed white men trudged down the highway near Fort Motte, looking for a handout. Julia considered locking her doors, something she had never before had to do. But the keys were lost, and nobody ever got around to changing the locks. Life at Lang Syne went on as usual.[26]

Bill Peterkin got married on Halloween night, his mother's fifty-first birthday. Declaring that she would be "glad to turn [Bill] over to another woman," Julia paused before the ceremony to wonder what sort of grandmother she would make.[27] The wedding was performed at the Barrows' house on Chippewa Square in Savannah, the elegant candlelit rooms filled with pink, yellow, and orange roses and pots of bronze chrysanthemums. As he was kneeling in front of the beautifully dressed wedding guests, Bill realized that the soles of his dress shoes were almost worn through.[28]

Elegant in a straight, simple chartreuse satin gown, Julia played mother of the groom. Greeting guests, exchanging compliments, she shook her head over the mounting bank failures. As soon as the reception was over, she headed for New York.

Irving had just finished his new novel, the one he had started on the boat to France, about his affair with Julia. He asked permission to dedicate it to her, and although the book was far from flattering, Julia consented. *Lovers Must Learn* is the story of a man torn between two women: Susan, a sweet, innocent girl, and Lyda, a manipulative older artist. Don is obsessed with Lyda, "the world's most self-possessed woman," who has reduced him to "a ridiculous pleading figure." One moment he suspects she is frigid, the next he is sure she is a "tired and indifferent whore." He finally talks her into bed, where she grimly submits to his embraces. Nothing he does seems to move her. When the passionate, good-natured Susan happens along, Don finds her a huge relief. They make love, Susan gets pregnant, and, after weeks of transatlantic brooding, Don decides to marry her.

Julia recognized herself in the poisonous Lyda and jokingly threatened to sue Irving for plagiarism because he had borrowed so many lines from her letters.[29] But she didn't act hurt or insulted by the portrayal, and she seemed genuinely pleased by the dedication. Encouraged, no doubt, by Irving, she chose to imagine that she was also the model for Don's true love, Susan. Had she known about Frances Frost, who naturally thought that *she* was Susan, she might not have been so forebearing.

On her way home, Julia rode with Doris Ulmann, who had been ill for some time. George Uebler, Doris's imperious German chauffeur, kept the accelerator flat on the floor. "We slid over . . . miles of road like bats out of hell, fleeing Satan," Julia wrote to Fineman. "'Twas a mad journey, no time for any enjoyment but a swift leaping around cars, dodging, lurching, holding onto our souls for fear they'd be left naked in the road whenever we sped around a curve." Doris was installed in Miss Eastway's Sanitarium in Columbia, where Julia was sure she would rebound if only she would "eat, sleep, rest" instead of working. "She clings to frailty," Julia observed. "Maybe her longing for sympathy, love is the hidden reason."[30]

Books about Harlem were selling briskly, and *Scarlet Sister Mary* was a very hot property — Bobbs-Merrill had just sold the rights for a Norwegian translation, and other sales were in the works. Julia felt that Chambers owed her a good contract and a hefty, nonreturnable advance. But Chambers was nervous and wanted to see a completed manuscript of *Bright Skin* before he made a commitment. Squeezed between the precarious finances of the firm and the continuing challenge to his authority, he could not afford to take a chance. Julia did not help her own case by claiming that she had tossed off the book "at odd times when it was neither too hot nor too cold and nothing more amusing offered."[31]

Her casual pose was a smokescreen. Far from being a pleasant diversion, the writing of *Bright Skin* had been a four-year battle waged against herself. The resulting book was far ahead of its time. A withering dissection of the plantation in decline, *Bright Skin* is a tale of rejection, dispossession, and exile. One morning, young Blue is "roused from sound sleep" and removed from his home by his angry father because his mother had committed adultery.[32] He is sent to live with his grandparents, Cun Alfred and Aun Fan, on Blue Brook plantation, where he meets his cousin Cricket, a "poor little motherless" with skin "the color of a ripe gourd."[33] "How could this bright-skin child be his cousin, his own blood-kin cousin?" wonders Blue.[34]

Only a child would ask such a question, for the answer, so simple in a biological sense, poses a threat to the social order. Blue falls in love with Cricket, only to discover that the "bright skin" he finds so beautiful makes her an outcast in the Quarters. "A bright skin ain' got no place in dis world," huffs one of the field hands. "Black people don' want em an' white people won' own em. Dey ain' nothin but no-nation bastards."[35]

Julia had begun *Bright Skin* intending to focus on her heroine's adult life in Harlem, but Cricket's childhood came to dominate the book. Cricket lives with her Uncle Wes and Aun Missie, a childless couple who think themselves better than the common field hands because Wes is the plantation foreman. Repeating one of Julia's classic situations, Wes adores his foster daughter, and Missie abuses her. Just as she had in *Green Thursday,* Julia made it clear that the father-daughter bond (technically, in this case, the uncle-niece bond) verges on the incestuous. "I'd take de shirt off my back for Cricket any day in de year," Wes taunts his wife. "E would too," Cricket innocently puts in. "An' I'd take my-own off for him."[36]

For a long time Wes refuses to send his niece to school, declaring that the other children "ain' in his class."[37] (Julia made witty use throughout *Bright Skin* of the Gullah disregard for gender.) When she does finally enroll, Cricket is shunned and humiliated. The teacher demands to know who her daddy is, and Cricket declares that she doesn't have a daddy. "Everybody has a father," the teacher insists. "Tell your Uncle to write your father's name on a piece of paper, Cricket. Bring it to-morrow."[38] Everybody knows that Cricket's father is the son of the plantation owner, but that truth cannot be spoken. "If dat fool teacher asks who you Daddy is, Cricket, you tell em it ain' nobody in particular," Aun Missie angrily declares, echoing the real Mary Weeks.[39]

Cun Hester helps Cricket write a letter to her father, asking him for money so she can go away to school. The letter goes unanswered. As one of the field hands observes, "Cricket's white kin wouldn' spit on em, much less give em money."[40] The owners of the Big House have abandoned the girl in more ways than one — Man Jay finds out from the "store-man" that soon there will be no more farming at Blue Brook because "some rich white people up-North wanted to buy it to hunt on in de winter."[41] The aristocracy has sold out — cut its losses and run.

Unlike the innocent rustics who populate Julia's earlier books, Cricket, Man Jay, Bina, and Missie realize that they are poor. They look at the fancy goods pouring in by steamer and compare them with their own shabby possessions. They listen to visitors from Harlem talk about having so much cash that they have to hire bodyguards for protection. Most of all, they dream about living in town, where the future holds something besides "pinching, saving . . . praying . . . [and] backbreaking work."[42] A few, like Blue, are content to buy new horses and buggies and build new cabins on the plantation. The rest covet the cars and rolls of green money that can take them far away from the cotton fields. As Cricket puts it, "I ruther . . . sell liquor dan to weary my life out pullin fodder an' pickin peas, sewin frocks for other gals to dance in. . . . If I stay on here . . . nothin ain' ahead for me but to dry up an' get sour."[43]

Poverty is not the only source of discontent. Early in the book we learn that Old Blue, Cricket's grandfather, lost his religion and tried to commit murder when his daughter was raped by a white man. He left the plantation and visited Africa, and now he has reappeared as Reverend Africa, who so inspires his followers that "dey had to wrap quilts around de posts in de church to keep em from brokin dey arms and legs."[44]

Reverend Africa's message is hatred of the white race, a strain of angry black separatism that owes much to the earlier Back to Africa movement of Marcus Garvey and the Harlem ministry of Father Divine. Though he grew up on the plantation, Reverend Africa represents what sociologist Edgar T. Thompson aptly termed "the counter plantation culture," a set of attitudes that developed in the urban black ghetto.[45] But radical and modern as it seems to the people of Blue Brook, the Reverend's Afrocentric religion has its roots in traditional beliefs. The old people at Blue Brook practice an Africanized version of Christianity, in which, as Hester tells it, "sweet little Jesus looked down from Heaven and saw Hell's burning lake piled up with white people." Tormented by the thought of so many lost souls, Jesus, "black as a crow's wing," came down to tell the living that the way to get to Heaven was to sell all they had and use the money to feed the poor. The people in Africa heeded him, but "the white people got vexed and hung him on a cross alongside thieves and robbers."[46]

Hester is not the only source of such stories. Old Blue's father, Big Pa, prays to God and Jesus in an African dialect. Brought to America long after the ban on slave importation, he still sports the filed teeth and gold hoop earring of his tribe. This son of a king was captured in a tribal war, sold into slavery, and smuggled to America, a place where "the black people were as strange as white ones. Nobody talked his language." [47] Big Pa became a fisherman for the plantation, hid out in the swamps around Blue Brook, and met a girl who persuaded her master to buy him. He had a son, but then his wife died. Conditions were so terrible on the plantation that he decided to leave. So "he took the boy and tried to find the Unity States. Nobody knew where it was." [48]

"The Unity States" is a mythical place where blacks can get a fair shake. Failing to find it North or South, Big Pa and his son return to Blue Brook and resign themselves to slavery. The Civil War erupts, bringing freedom but not equality. And then the whites invent Jim Crow, the humiliating set of laws that mandate segregation.

Far more than any of Julia's earlier stories, *Bright Skin* presents racial prejudice as the force keeping black people down. Visiting town for the first time, a little boy named David is arrested for entering the "white" restroom at the train station. David explains to a policeman that he needed to go to the bushes but there were no bushes in sight. "A lady told him to run inside the depot and he would see the place. He ran in. He saw a door. He opened the door and the policeman came in." Denied the use of a toilet, a refinement he has never heard of, David insists that he still needs to go to the bushes. Uncle Ben says, "I don' see none, but yonder's a tree. Go git behind em. It can' be against de law to stand side a tree. Even a dog ought to could do dat widout gittin arrested." [49]

Unconnected as it is to the rest of the plot, this poignant scene is the moral center of *Bright Skin*. Little David's first encounter with white supremacy exposes the absurdity of segregation. More typical of black fiction from the Civil Rights movement than of anything written in the South in the 1930s, it forces us to see Cricket's flight from the plantation as an escape from indignity and injustice.

Still, the book is not about politics or social justice, and Cricket and her friends are more concerned with church, school, and birth-night dances than with the fixations of white folks. Time passes; the children grow up. Blue tries unsuccessfully to court Cricket. Man Jay and Cooch go off to town, Man Jay to get a job, Cooch to get a diploma. Cooch comes home pregnant with Man Jay's baby. Left behind, Cricket is "unrestless."

Blue takes her to a dance, only to be cut out by Caesar Weeks, a slick-talking "yellow man" who has come from the city to set up a still. Soon Cricket is engaged to Mr. Weeks. Blue expects her aunt to object, but Missie can't see past Weeks's fine car and stylish clothes. Neglecting her garden, leaving the pigs to go hungry, Missie brags that after Cricket is married she will move to town and let someone else wait on her.

Missie's vain insistence that her child marry someone rich echoes Julia's reaction to Bill's engagement. Once again, Julia was playing with a variant of Miss, pointing up the autobiographical. There is also a "Jule" in *Bright Skin*, a vulgar, no-nonsense hussy who makes sport of Missie's snobbery. Missie is no more the Missie of *Green Thursday* than Jule is the mule of *Black April*. Both characters are slashing self-parodies — Missie representing the Julia who was a stiff-necked social climber, and Jule the Julia who drank at dives and told dirty jokes.

In *Bright Skin*, both women are left behind as the young people race toward the cities. After all her insufferable boasting, Missie's ambition is thwarted. On the night before the wedding, Caesar Weeks disappears. Cricket waits at the altar for a groom who never shows, then collapses; Blue offers to marry her. She accepts. Days later, a pack of dogs turns up Weeks's remains in a cornfield. There is an inquest, during which suspicion for the murder briefly falls on Blue. Cooch's father, the owner of a rival still, is known to be the real killer. But since nobody will admit to knowing anything about anything, the white sheriff soon "got cross, cursed everybody for a pack of liars, threatened to put them all on the chain gang, looked at his fine gold watch," and stomped off to catch the steamboat.[50]

Cricket grows sick and listless, and her belly begins to swell. In a scene reminiscent of Julia's early story "The Confession," her premature baby is born dead. Blue, who has never made love to her, is shocked. He had no idea that she was pregnant.

Eventually Cricket recovers and begins having sex with Blue, but then a letter arrives from Man Jay, who now runs a gambling racket in Harlem. More letters come, and a box of expensive presents. Cricket grows fastidious, recoiling from Blue's sweaty, dirty clothes. More than ever she longs to get away, to go someplace, anyplace, where she can make money, buy nice things, and move into the middle class.

Blue harbors no such thoughts, but he is devoted to his wife. To make Cricket happy he takes a job ferrying rafts of lumber downriver to a sawmill, thus leaving subsistence agriculture for a place in the money economy. The mill is in a big city, where dangerous vices abound, and as soon as he collects his wages, the luckless Blue falls prey to a pick-pocket. He borrows a little cash, gets drunk, and picks up a prostitute. When he finally reaches home, his pockets are empty and Cricket has run away.

Feeling abandoned, he takes up with Cooch, who already has a baby by Man Jay. When Cricket writes to say that she is out of money, he asks Cooch to mail a reply, handing her five dollars to put in the envelope and assuming that Cricket will soon appear. But Cricket never shows. Aun Missie suggests that Blue go to town and find her, but he doubts he would succeed among "those miles of streets and houses."[51] Eventually a letter arrives to say that Cricket is in Harlem with Man Jay. Blue seems paralyzed by indecision. When Cooch gets pregnant, he moves in with her, never dreaming that the arrangement will become permanent. Lovers come and lovers go, but a man's wife is his wife forever. Things run differently up North, however, and Cricket sends word that she wants a divorce. Cooch and Blue have never heard the word, and neither has anyone else on the place. Soon Cricket and Man Jay appear in person to explain that a divorce is "a paper what unmarries people." Blue is scandalized. "Dat is pure heathenish doins," he cries. "Decent people don' act so."[52]

Cricket no longer believes in decency and indecency; her values have changed. Living in the city, under the influence of Reverend Africa, she has become self-consciously "heathenish," reclaiming her African roots. Not that the path she chooses is profound, or even very dignified — dancing in nightclubs as "The Princess Kazoola," she wears nothing besides "small circles over her breasts and a narrow band around her thighs."[53] At heart an exhibitionist, like Julia, Cricket has discovered a world where her mixed heritage is an asset, and she means to take full advantage.

Like the finale of a comic opera, the end of *Bright Skin* is manic. Cooch goes into labor. Man Jay picks a fight with Blue and tries to choke him to death. Cricket defends Blue by bashing Man Jay over the head with a poker, but when Blue revives she tells him she plans to leave with Man Jay in the morning. Cooch delivers a fine pair of twins, both boys. The book ends on a melancholy note: Blue will stay on Blue Brook; Cricket will live "up-North." Like Julia herself, Blue cannot leave the plantation, even for the love of his life.

The characters in *Bright Skin* are based on real people, many of whom remain recognizable even after more than half a century. Big Pa is modeled on Frank Bryant, Maum Anaky's husband, who was born in

Angola and spoke English with a heavy accent. Celebrated to this day among his descendants for resisting slavery, Frank made a career of stealing from whites. He is said to have maintained two families, one at Lang Syne and one on Daufuskie Island, many miles away. After the Civil War, he seems to have settled permanently at Lang Syne.[54]

Uncle Ben is much like Willie Powell, Julia's longtime gardener. Missie and Wes resemble Nannie and Ellis Sanders, and Hester is Hester Cheseboro. The scene in which Caesar Weeks's body is devoured by dogs was inspired by the mysterious demise, in the early 1920s, of a man named Sammy Glover.[55] Cooch is modeled not on Rudy Mae Bryant but on another of Mary Weeks's daughters, Virginia. The real Brudge was Mary's son.[56]

Cricket, of course, was inspired by Essie Geiger, who, according to Julia, was delighted with the idea of being immortalized in a book. But Julia dreaded the reaction of Essie's half-sisters, Minnie and Rudy Mae, who had been enraged when they saw Julia's pictures of their mother balancing a washtub on her head. Wrongly anticipating that Minnie and Rudy Mae would read *Bright Skin*, Julia planted angry gibes of the sort she had once aimed at her father and husband. "I wonder what Cricket's Mammy would say if e saw em totin water on his head for you pot, Missie," smirks Bina. "Everybody knows how Cricket's Mammy was. E toted hot water in a silver pitcher for white gentlemen to shave in but e wouldn' tote water on his head from de spring for nobody."[57] Few besides the Weekses and the Peterkins (and Carl Sandburg) knew that Mary had been carrying water in a silver pitcher when she was seduced by the Peterkin brothers.

It is unclear how well Cricket's life in Harlem matches Essie's; family members insist that Essie was a seamstress, never a stripper. Like Cricket, she was originally married to a man from near the plantation, whom she divorced in order to wed Mr. Geiger, a South Carolina–born Harlem entrepreneur. By the time *Bright Skin* was published, Essie had moved to a mansion on Long Island, where she mothered a large brood of mixed-race foster children.[58]

Julia also aimed a few barbs at her sister Laura, and some of them found their mark. When Cricket "seeks peace," she has a vision in which a man warns her never to take any kind of medicine. As a devout Christian Scientist, Laura was forbidden to use drugs. "Julia stole my story, and she made me black!" Laura later complained to Bill's second wife.[59] Indeed, Julia may have been thinking about Laura when she wrote about Cricket's yearning for the city. After all, she had just read her sister's autobiography.[60]

Julia finished *Bright Skin* in December 1931. Chambers broke down and offered a $15,000 advance plus 17 percent royalties, reminding Julia that the bottom had fallen out of the book market in the year since her offer from Cosmopolitan. Hearst and his competitors had long since backed off, but Julia still hedged, telling Chambers that she was suffering from an infected throat and would be unable to decide what to do about *Bright Skin* until she recovered.

In truth, her trouble was located elsewhere. More than a quarter century after the operation that stopped her menses, Julia's "tiny tablets" had unleashed a scarlet flood, a final desperate surge of youth and sexuality. Hemorrhaging was a common side effect of early estrogen therapy, the result of too-large doses.[61] The bleeding was soon brought under control, yet Julia remained frail and irritable. Just before Christmas 1931, she and Doris, who had injured her knee and had to walk with a cane, took off for New Orleans.[62] For the first time in her married life, Julia skipped the rituals of a plantation Christmas — the toasts, the Christmas tree, the family gatherings. The trip got off to a rocky start. As if to punish Julia for neglecting duty, the headlights on Doris's car went bad. George Uebler drove like a madman, as usual, and nodded off at the wheel; they slept in fleabag hotels and ate at greasy spoons. Doris and her chauffeur were peeved by Julia's habit of sleeping late in the morning, which slowed their usual pace. Once in New Orleans, matters improved; the women established themselves at the Hotel Monteleone and erected a small pine tree in Julia's room, complete with tinsel and candles.[63]

They were joined by the handsome, enigmatic Lyle Saxon, a forty-year-old Louisianan whom both had met while he was living in Greenwich Village a few years before.[64] Men and women alike found Saxon irresistible, and Doris, according to Julia, had repeatedly thrown herself at his feet. Saxon stayed aloof, except when drunk, but Doris persisted even in the face of behavior that Julia saw as downright rude. Earlier in the summer, he had given in and taken her to Melrose plantation, on the Cane River some thirty miles southeast of Nachitoches, Louisiana, where he stayed for extended periods as the guest of Cammie Henry, a patron of the arts who had made him one of her special projects. Saxon himself had recently been ill, and Doris wore out her welcome quickly by pestering him for assistance.

If Doris's crush on Lyle Saxon seems masochistic, Julia's regard for him as a writer is disconcerting but understandable. The author of mawkish popular books about life in the Old South, Saxon pretended to be a son of the aristocracy who had fallen on hard times. In reality, his experience with plantations came secondhand, from wealthy friends. He was an old drinking buddy of William Faulkner and Sherwood Anderson, who despised himself for selling out but lacked the willpower to aim higher. Six years later, Saxon would publish *Children of Strangers,* a stark novel about a mixed-race woman who is shunned by her community. But in 1931 he was still caught up in the troubles of upper-class white women, especially plantation mistresses.

Julia needed sympathy and reassurance, perhaps more than ever before. *Bright Skin* had taken all her reserves, drained her of self-importance. She wanted to feel that her life at Lang Syne had not been mean and hollow. Irving Fineman's love had bolstered her through the painful process of creation, but he still wanted her to leave South Carolina and complete her metamorphosis. Lyle Saxon admired her for staying put; he indulged her melodramatic flights of self-pity. "Oh, Lyle, I cry over myself, the poor thing that I am," she had written him two Christmases before, "and I wanted to be a fine lady, a grand lady, so much. *So* much." [65] Lyle always stood ready to reassure her that she actually *was* a grand lady.

Depressed, ailing, fighting with her editor, and in retreat from both her husband and her lover that Christmas of 1931, Julia hoped that Doris and Lyle would divert her from worrying about the future. They all tried hard to be happy. Saxon concocted flaming drinks and squired Julia and Doris around the city. The three ate, drank, told funny stories, and laughed until dawn every night. On Christmas Eve, Julia accepted Chambers's offer for *Bright Skin* and began going over the dog-eared manuscript, "trying to delete every unnecessary word." [66] Then she started to bleed again. Doris and Lyle found her a doctor, and by January 6 she was back at Lang Syne, resting up after another "wild journey" in Doris's car. She apparently had a dilation and curettage of the uterus to "finish up what should have been done" a month before.

"The doctor here says the long auto-mobile trip was bad for me and put me to bed stuffed with gauze," she wrote to Irving. "Poor Doris. Her eyes are as big as saucers. She feared I'd die on her hands." [67] Julia told Fineman that she had been lucky — her New Orleans doctor knew "the anatomy of women as well as I know the alphabet." [68] Comparing herself with Susan in *Lovers Must Learn,* she added that there was "nothing mysterious about all this, just consequences that seem forever to follow to me, I guess. The gods resent happiness." [69]

Plaintively, she wrote to Irving that she had made her will, leaving him her silver locket and chain "to give to your sweet-heart some day." [70] On January 18, she shipped the manuscript of *Bright Skin* to George Shively. She used the advance to finish paying her debts, including those left over from the Jim Crouch debacle.[71] This book would be her last, she claimed; there was nothing left to say. Yet empty days stretched out in front of her. "What can I do with these hours of spare time?" she asked. "What? Nothing else so exciting as writing offers me temptation." [72]

CHAPTER 13

Roll, Jordan, Roll

riting, once such sweet release, had become "heart-breaking drudgery."[1] At the same time, however, Julia's books and magazine stories had become one of Lang Syne's more important cash crops. A surplus in the fields had brought disaster at the bank. The boll weevil infestation was finally subsiding, and the 1931 cotton harvest was huge, the third largest ever recorded. Because the supply was larger than the demand, cotton was selling for 4.6 cents a pound, the lowest price since 1864.[2] Of course, literature was unpredictable, too, but as long as Willie was planting cotton and Julia was pushing a pen, there was some possibility of a bonanza.

Like a bird pecking at its own reflection, Julia turned back to the thing she did worst: writing about a privileged southern white woman. In the spring of 1932, she decided to write a biography of Theodosia

Burr Alston, the legendary plantation mistress who had once lived near Brookgreen. Julia regaled D. L. Chambers with tales about Theodosia's ghost haunting a creaky old house in Murrells Inlet, where "human blood stains mark every room floor."[3] Chambers cheered her on, even delegating his staff to check libraries and bookstores for sources. He enlisted his nephew, a staffer at the Library of Congress, to compile a list of primary sources.[4]

Theodosia's troubles reminded Julia of her own. A "poor little motherless" after age twelve, she was ruled by her tyrannical and often absent father, Senator Aaron Burr of New York. It was Burr, a future vice president of the United States, who decided that Theodosia should marry Joseph Alston, a millionaire planter from South Carolina who was, as his descendant Julia put it, one of "a hard-drinking, cock-fighting, horse-racing, mean lot who made life hell" for their women — and their slaves.[5] Thrust into this southern gothic world, Theodosia foundered. After the birth of her only child, a son, she slipped into a depression so severe that at age nineteen she expected to "vegetate forty years in a sort of middle state between life and death."[6]

Theodosia eventually recovered, only to face a traumatic adulthood. Her son died when he was eleven. Her father killed Alexander Hamilton in a duel and was later arrested for treason. Theodosia spent several years traveling around the country, trying to raise money for his defense. Her husband was elected governor of South Carolina in 1812. Only a few months later, Theodosia took her pet dog and boarded a ship for New York. Somewhere off Cape Hatteras, they ran into trouble. It might have been pirates, it might have been a storm; nobody knows for sure. The ship, its cargo, and everyone on board disappeared without a trace. But some people in the Carolinas still believed that Theodosia faked her death. Along with her dog, the story went, she had swum safely to shore. Sick of scandal and unwanted celebrity, she assumed a new name and lived out her life on the Carolina Outer Banks.[7]

Whatever her end, Theodosia's story was the stuff of which historical romances are made, and Chambers dreamed of a swashbuckling love story full of duels, stallions, silks, and famous names. Julia's Alston ancestry would be a great hook when it was time to put out press releases. But Chambers's hopes were soon dashed. Julia sat at her desk, pored over old books, and visited the coast for inspiration. Nothing happened. In June, she broke the news to Chambers: "Theodosia . . . seems far away, dim, uncertain."[8] If Julia ever produced a sentence of the biography, the manuscript did not survive.

Still unable to write about a tortured white woman, Julia again turned to playing one. The director of the Columbia Town Theater, an expatriate Englishman named Belford Forrest, invited her to act the title role in Ibsen's *Hedda Gabler*. For the entire month of February 1932, Julia lived in the Columbia Hotel, retreating to her room between rehearsals to correct the proofs of *Bright Skin*. She loved playing the scheming, cold-hearted Hedda, who sets out to seduce her husband's academic rival, Eilert Lövberg, an old lover now engaged to a friend of hers. Bored, pregnant, and irritated by his success, Hedda starts Lövberg down the road to despair by hiding a brilliant unpublished manuscript on which he has staked his career. The loss drives him back to drink, a habit he thought he had overcome. Hedda offers Lövberg a gun, suggesting that he "die beautifully." Much to her satisfaction, he takes it and shoots himself. But someone has been watching. Judge Brack threatens to tell on Hedda unless she becomes his mistress. Scornfully she takes the gun and puts a bullet through her own head.

"In her place I'd probably do just what [Hedda] did. Maybe worse," Julia wrote to Fineman. To illustrate her point, she sketched a "happy ending" for the play in which Hedda shoots the other characters and lives to tell the tale. "I'm much like 'Hedda,' too much, really," she boasted.[9]

Doris Ulmann, who was wintering in Columbia, played Aunt Julia Tesman, a prudish, wizened old woman. "She suits her part amazingly," Julia sniped to Irving.[10] Wrapped up in his on-again, off-again affair with Frances Frost, Irving seldom found time to compose long letters to Julia. "I warn you, if you marry, I'll poison her," Julia wrote, admitting to herself that he must have a steady girlfriend. "You'll be sorry to see me go to the electric chair. Won't you?" These Heddaesque threats were softened by the reasonable tone of her postscript: "Please don't bother to answer this flood of letters. I know you're busy."[11]

For the moment, Julia could afford to be without Irving's attention. She was exactly where she liked most to be: holding court in the glare of a spotlight. Her name was given top billing, listed on the program above Ibsen's and Hedda Gabler's. Flourishing a pair of antique duelling pistols, she told reporters on opening night that she had not bothered about makeup since no one expected her to be beautiful. In the first act she sported an amethyst velvet gown, in the second a sea green taffeta by Worth. Dancer Martha Graham, who was performing in Columbia during the rehearsals, had arranged for the cast to borrow a collection of nineteenth-century clothes once owned by the Vanderbilt family.[12]

Julia was glad to be "alive, well, strong, zestful, happy." [13] "[I] wish I'd gone on the stage thirty years ago," she told Chambers. "I quite adore it." [14] Though Irving seldom wrote, Julia took his silence philosophically. "I'd begun to think you had kid-naped [*sic*] the Lindbergh baby, and had disappeared altogether with it and its milk-bottles," she joked, referring to the famous aviator's search for his son, which had dominated the headlines for months.[15] By the end of March, *Bright Skin* was in print and she had other things on her mind.

Realizing that *Bright Skin* was ahead of its time, Julia feared that the critics might "pounce on" the book and "tear it to pieces." [16] She was wrong. Far from arousing anger or outrage, *Bright Skin*'s Afrocentrism left most reviewers cold. John Chamberlain, writing for the *New York Times*, dismissed Julia as a "second-hand writer" striving to re-create "a drama which she cannot wholly feel." [17] ("Drat Mr. Chamberlain of the N.Y. Times. May he wither," Julia groused to Chambers.) [18] *Nation*'s Gerald Bullett echoed Chamberlain's reservations: "One suspects that Mrs. Peterkin, for all her sympathetic familiarity with the externals of these strange people can never get at their insides. She has made them gay or drooping or disappointed puppets." [19] In the *Bookman*, Archer Winsten proclaimed that "we have learned little which was not said in the earlier volumes." [20] Julia tried to keep her perspective, rationalizing that "too much praise might turn my head. All sunshine makes a desert." [21]

No reviewer commented on the poignant, cynical dialogue, which is far more incisive and true to life than that in *Scarlet Sister Mary*. No one identified with the fierceness of Cricket's yearnings, or the futility of Blue's. People were familiar with plantation stories and wild tales about black Harlem. But they saw *Bright Skin* as a kind of half-breed, or hermaphrodite, disturbing because it blurred the usual categories. Like *Green Thursday, Black April*, and *Scarlet Sister Mary*, it shows the plantation as an African American construct where whites are all but irrelevant. Unlike them, however, *Bright Skin* portrays the grandchildren of slavery uneasily evolving from dirt-poor field hands into urban bootleggers, slumlords, bail bondsmen, and chorus girls. The readers who looked to Julia for nostalgic diversion were put off by what they saw as the intrusion of ugly modern tensions into the primeval world they had come to love. Yet Cricket and Blue were not aggressive enough to suit the Marxist critics, who were beginning to demand that serious literature show the masses engaged in class struggle. In short, *Bright Skin* did not deliver a message that anybody wanted to hear.

There were a few good reviews, but none of the sort that make people flock to the bookstores. Henry Bellamann pronounced *Bright Skin* a great novel, richer and more nuanced than *Scarlet Sister Mary.* Herschell Brickell, although he found the portrait of Cricket "annoyingly sentimentalized," predicted that the novel would certainly survive, "regardless of shifts in the fickle winds of public taste." [22] But gone were the days when adoring critics compared Peterkin with Chekhov and Turgenev. One of the most harmful attacks came from Laurence Stallings, who had once been a great fan. Julia had seen it coming; the previous December she had visited Stallings while he was ill, "full of pain, liquor, misery." All he could talk about was William Faulkner, who had published five books in the last three years, including *Sartoris, As I Lay Dying,* and *The Sound and the Fury.* Faulkner, said Stallings, was "greater than Dostoevski"; he defied Julia to disagree. [23]

Julia did disagree, and loudly. He might be a genius, but Faulkner gave her "the creeps." He and his novels seemed to her "degenerate." [24] Stallings took offense, lectured her about her lack of taste, and prophesied that her own reputation was about to be eclipsed. As it turned out, he was right. Faulkner's *Light in August* would appear in October 1932, just six months after *Bright Skin.* Faulkner was hailed as an innovator while Julia was brushed aside as a has-been. In reality, Faulkner's vengeful mixed-race character, Joe Christmas, is a direct descendant of the evil male mulattoes in countless plantation novels, while Peterkin's Cricket transcends the stereotype of the tragic octoroon. [25]

Julia reacted to the critical chill by withdrawing into her shell, refusing to lecture or talk over the radio. She hated the idea of stumping for a book, of attempting by the force of her personality to reverse its failing fortunes. Half-seriously, she suggested a new tactic in the perennial quest for notice — "Tell the public I'm queer, refuse to be seen or heard, that nobody can discover why. For nobody has ever seen me except [a] few times," she wrote to Chambers. [26] Unmoved, he urged her to visit colleges and bookstores.

Julia was not an obscure figure. She was a best-selling author and a Pulitzer Prize winner. She still had market value, and there were people who held contracts on her future, especially on the theatrical front. Ethel Barrymore gave her fits by threatening to revive *Scarlet Sister*

Mary. Meanwhile, *Black April* was still on hold. Paul Robeson refused to star in a play coauthored by Dan Reed, whose name, he said, would be a "fatal handicap" after the burlesque of *Scarlet Sister Mary.*[27] Working through various intermediaries — Max Aley, George Shively, Elisabeth Marbury — Julia encouraged Reed to pull out so that Stark Young and Maxwell Anderson could write a new script. Reed stood his ground, threatening to file a lawsuit.[28]

Julia had lost faith in the aging Elisabeth Marbury but hesitated to choose another agent. Even her old friend Maxwell Aley seemed to have turned traitor. And as mad as she was at the bumbling Dan, she did love his wife, Isadora. It was all a hopeless tangle of hidden agendas, hurt feelings, and pointless legal nit-picking. Exhausted by all the cutthroat politeness, Julia sought out one of her favorite illegal activities, a cockfight. Willie worried that she would be arrested and, far worse, get her name in the papers. His uneasiness added to her pleasure. Julia stayed at the fights all day, mesmerized by the high-stakes betting.[29] Some policemen did arrive, but they, too, had come to gamble. Julia was energized by the struggle in the pit — gimlet-eyed gamecocks armed with steel spurs slashed each other to death. Here was competition at its rawest — no apologies, no dissembling, and no hard feelings.

There was soon to be a new source of tension in Julia's life, one that she had so far avoided confronting. In March, she finally found out that Irving was involved with Frances Frost. It happened in New York, at a party. The bombshell was dropped by Dorothy Day, a former editor of the socialist journal *New Masses* and now a driving force behind the *Catholic Worker* movement, which promoted, among other things, voluntary poverty, communal farming, and settlement houses for the poor. A former bohemian herself and the veteran of a common-law marriage, Day insinuated that Julia, as one of Irving's senior girlfriends, ought to know what he was up to.

Julia exploded. Mustering all her majesty, she warned Irving against "shaking peach trees whether they're full of fruit or only blossoming." She even suggested that perhaps he should get married and "free [himself] from woman problems."[30]

Irving had no intention of marrying Frances, though she forced him to consider it nearly every month when her period was late. Frances's taste in clothes offended him, and he had no use for her children. Dorothy Day's disclosure helped bring matters to a head. Furious at Frances for talking about their affair, Irving made plans to travel south and see Julia. Hardly believing her good luck, Julia indulged in happy reveries about showing him her world. But Irving had also applied for some screenwriting jobs, and just as he was about to leave for South Carolina he was offered a position in Hollywood. Julia's congratulations were tipped with poison. "I knew you'd get the work. God knows if William Faulkner could, surely you could. He's crazy, I'm convinced."[31]

She let herself speculate about how Irving would have reacted to the peculiarities of Lang Syne. "Would you like the cotton fields, the weird swamp, the high hills overlooking the river . . . ? Would the negroes amuse you with their happy-go-lucky manner or would their pitiful dependence make you sad? Would you like my new slip covers, my new frocks, a game of tennis? Would you rather ride a horse with three gaits or five? Would you like dinner at two and supper at eight or nine? Mint juleps better than 'old fashions'?" she wondered.[32]

As he crossed the country by train, Irving replied with doleful letters that kept her fretting about his health. "Please, darling, guard yourself, don't fail to rest long enough," Julia begged. "I need the assurance constantly that all is well with you, or I get utterly wretched."[33] To Frances Frost, lonely and broke, Fineman sent a similar litany of complaints. She begged him to get cold injections and cover up well at night.

With Fineman off to Hollywood, Julia regretted refusing last year's movie offers. She had accepted an invitation to spend most of the summer at the Yaddo Writers' Colony in Saratoga Springs, New York. But when the University of Colorado asked her to lecture in Boulder, she jumped at the chance. "If it were not so far I'd pay you a visit," she wrote to Irving. "If only I had wings."[34] Once past the Continental Divide, she soon found an excuse to push westward. Yaddo was running short of funds and had asked that she delay her arrival. "I refuse to admit to my-self that you . . . are the reason for my taking this long journey, but if the mountain will not ever come to Mohammed, what's poor M. to do?" she teased Irving. "Don't dare to be too involved with some wife or duty to spare me part of your time."[35]

She stayed at the Beverly Hills Hotel, "the most prestigious address on the Pacific Coast," and lunched with Laurence Stallings (who, she thought, looked "a trifle embarrassed" to see her), had tea with the actress Alison Skipworth, and wondered why Faulkner was working for such a small salary "when money pours all over the place." Laying aside old grudges, she visited the set of *Rasputin*, a "glittering pageant" starring all three Barrymores — John, Lionel, and Ethel.[36] In between, of course, she spent time with Irving, the real reason for her trip. They took long drives in the country and walked by the moonlit ocean. As usual, whatever they did in private went unrecorded.

On the return trip, Julia ventured into Mexico, where she reported attending the funeral of an unfaithful wife who had been stabbed to death by her husband. In El Paso, Texas, she saw a "cow-boy camp meeting," and in New Orleans she drank with Lyle Saxon. Continuing on to New York, she addressed a meeting of the Southern Women's National Democratic Organization, where she sentimentally claimed that the West had made her sad because there were no frontiers left to conquer.[37]

In truth, Julia was sad not because the West was won but because *her* horizons had shrunk. Panned by the critics and without a book in progress to occupy her mind, she sank into a stupor. Money was scarce, and while her desk was piled high with lucrative offers, she couldn't make herself write. Nothing lasted; nothing mattered; everything she had ever achieved seemed to be going up in smoke. The crowning blow came when the Internal Revenue Service demanded $260 in back taxes on her royalties from *Scarlet Sister Mary*. Royalties, the auditor explained, counted as "unearned" income. Julia appealed to Chambers for help. "If writers do not work for what they make, in God's name, who does?" she wailed. "I've 1001 faults but am not guilty of the ones of which I'm accused."[38] Chambers referred her to a certified public accountant.

In late September, Julia inquired how much she was due for *Bright Skin* and discovered the awful truth: she owed Bobbs-Merrill more than $6,000 for the unliquidated advance and other expenses. Not only was *Bright Skin* not selling, but the company had charged her for services like copying the manuscript and altering the proofs that in happier times had been borne by the firm.[39] Ironically enough, by most standards the book would have been considered a commercial success. *Black April* had been declared a best-seller when it reached 23,000 copies. The first printing of *Bright Skin* was 15,000 copies; seventeen days later, Bobbs-Merrill ordered another 10,000 copies; three months later, 5,000 extra books were printed. Things were no better at home. Around Lang Syne, she told Chambers, "lands held for several centuries are being sold for debt. Negroes come home from the North where they found work several years ago seem glad to be put on chain gangs where they at least have food and shelter."[40]

Conditions at Brookgreen and Lang Syne were changing so rapidly that the events described in *Bright Skin* seemed almost like ancient history. Lang Syne's venerable blacksmith shop was now being used as a machine shed. The smokehouse held not hams and bacon but a gas-driven water pump.[41] Looking for profitable ways to diversify, Willie and Bill had opened a veneer mill, where logs could be shaved into paper-thin sheets for manufacturing plywood and furniture. In the fields, a new machine called a combine harvested a new crop, soybeans. To Julia's amazement, the operator was a white man, "cultivated" and "civilized" enough to stay in her guest bedroom. "When he comes down stairs dressed for dinner, you'd think he was ready for a party at Doris'," she marveled. "And when he takes a hand at bridge, his white fingers are better manicured than mine." [42]

The plantation landscape was being reshaped by engines, outsiders, and money. Nowhere was the shift more dramatic than at Brookgreen, now owned by millionaire industrialist Archer Milton Huntington, who was transforming the place into an open-air museum for his wife's sculptures. Julia was disgusted. The Huntingtons had torn down the quirky old farmhouse and built themselves a Spanish-style mansion on the beach, within sight of her cottage ("200 feet square, and it looks like a penitentiary," she tartly observed). Deriding the raw "mustard-colored" walls in the sculpture garden, she repeated an aged black man's scornful comment on one of the statues: "De lady *call* em *man*, but e look like 'oman widout bosom to me." [43] Yankees with their ready money were desecrating what remained of the Alstons' antebellum empire.

Julia dug in and tried to protect her privileges. She grew terrified of her diminishing status, nostalgic for a time when blacks, by knowing their places, had defined hers, and desperate to preserve a social code that could protect her in old age. In the long run, she would have done herself a favor by following her first instincts and going into hiding while Bobbs-Merrill pushed *Bright Skin*. Had she died in 1932, without writing another word, her work would surely have been rediscovered before now. Instead, she grew garrulous and furnished strident opinions to everyone who crossed her path.

On June 5, 1933, she gave a lecture at Winthrop College in Rock Hill, South Carolina, that seemed to contradict everything she stood for. "The whole world now agrees with warm admiration that South Carolina along with the other colonies lying south of the Potomac created the one real civilization America has ever achieved," she announced with characteristic finality. It was an ordinary thing to say in South Carolina, and her audience took it calmly. But it was an extraordinary thing for *Julia Peterkin* to say, especially just after having written a book as Afrocentric as *Bright Skin*. Where was the revolutionary black consciousness of her novels? Had Julia not listened to the words her characters were saying? Had she not understood their point of view?

To anyone who knew the real Julia, the Winthrop lecture would have sounded like a joke. She declared to the all-female student body that "a poor marriage is better than none at all," "education is the ability to tell a good man when you see one," marriage "is a woman's most important career and the one in which she will find the most happiness," and "the love that comes with motherhood is perhaps life's richest experience."[44] And it was not only at Winthrop College that she pontificated in this vein. Approached at a fund-raiser for the Town Theater, she lambasted a startled reporter: "Divorce is not a good thing." "Woman's suffrage has proved a failure." "Congenial companionship is the basis of a happy marriage."[45] One might think that she was buttering up southern audiences by telling them what they wanted to hear. But in June, she told a reporter for the *New York Herald Tribune* that young women should dedicate their lives to preserving "the art of life as we have known it and they have known and loved it."[46]

These pronouncements were widely published, irritating feminists and progressives who had regarded her as one of them. "Julia Peterkin feels that the public is forgetting her and that she must have some free publicity," jeered a former fan in Atlanta.[47] In fact, Julia seems to have meant what she said and to have felt that she had a duty to say it. She was trying to talk herself into believing the things she had been taught in childhood.

It was as if another personality had invaded her body and was struggling for control. Several years later, Stark Young would tell Margaret Mitchell that Julia began seeing his psychotherapist around this time, "a Viennese, with a huge practice among millionaires, artists from every profession and people otherwise of all kinds."[48] Julia, he wrote, had "grown despairing" and developed a dread of death.[49] Fearing that she would be branded as crazy if her neighbors found out she was seeing a psychiatrist, Julia never spoke or wrote directly about her treatment. She did, however, record many of her new insights in letters to Irving Fineman, who had become a sort of sounding board for her flights of self-analysis. She had long realized that her stories were a means of venting anger, jealousy, and lust. She had been pleased several years earlier when Elsie Sargeant reported that her own analyst, Carl Jung, considered Julia's stories a perfect illustration of his famous theory of the collective unconscious.[50] Now, however, she began to regard her writing as a symptom of mental illness.

When Julia ruefully confessed to Irving that she had "slipped entirely out of [her] role" in order to become a writer, she meant that she had finally understood what old Yates Snowden and her crusty Mood aunts had been trying to tell her. Books like *Green Thursday* and *Bright Skin* were dangerous to her family's status and wealth, and thus to her own security. The very changes she had chronicled and advanced were threatening Lang Syne.

Ideas that were just ideas in the 1920s were turning into movements. In 1928, the American Communist party had called for "self-determination of the black belt" and the formation of an independent "Negro nation" in the South. Now they had organized black farm laborers in Alabama to form the Share Cropper's Union and demand higher wages and better living and working conditions.[51] It was not, so far, a very widespread campaign, but it was making headlines. Like most of her fellow planters, Julia reacted to the implied threat by treating it as a joke. In September 1933, she told a group of reporters that any communist labor organizers who tried to cause trouble at Lang Syne would be sadly disappointed. She was sure the farmhands would listen politely, but "back home there will be a lot of thigh-slapping."[52]

At the other end of the spectrum from the Communists were the Nashville Agrarians, who in 1930 had published a nostalgic manifesto called *I'll Take My Stand*. The book argues that the South committed "moral and spiritual suicide" by embracing such modern abominations as gasoline engines, cost accounting, and chemical fertilizers.[53] Led by Andrew Lytle, Donald Davidson, Robert Penn Warren, Allen Tate, Stark Young, and John Crowe Ransom, the Agrarians discussed asking Julia to contribute an essay but never extended the invitation.[54] If they had, she would have been the only woman represented, and the only person directly dependent on agriculture for a living.

I'll Take My Stand is the wounded cry of twelve frightened southern white men who, like Julia, were stunned by the sight of their inherited power base rapidly melting away. They might "wish the Negro well," as Warren put it, but not at the expense of their own comfort. Somebody had to chop cotton, dig ditches, clean houses, and wash clothes so that intellectuals had time to read, talk, and think. In the old days, in the Old South, there had been no question about who would do these things, and in that sense Heaven was located in the past.

Both Julia and the Agrarians stopped short of saying that southern culture rested on a black servant class, but they all knew it was so. "If anything is clear, it is that we can never go back," Stark Young began his "defense" of the Old South in *I'll Take My Stand*. "Dead days are gone, and if by some chance they should return, we should find them intolerable."[55] Yet he was unabashedly nostalgic for the "fine flower" of antebellum civilization, a life "founded on land and the ownership of slaves."[56] Even while Julia was writing *Bright Skin*, a reproach to the white man's arrogance, what she wanted for herself was a return to those dead days and the possession of absolute power. Like the Agrarians, she felt that the modern South was losing its soul along with its traditions. She rejected the idea that people were created equal and regretted the passing of the aristocracy.

It would be fascinating to know what sort of "stand" she might have taken in 1930, torn as she was by such contradictory sympathies. Certainly she agreed with Andrew Lytle that since 1865 the southern farmer had been "turned into the runt pig in the sow's litter, [sucking] the little hind tit." But she could never have gone along with his prescription for a cure: refuse technology, avoid participating in a money economy, and reject the products of industry. "A farm is not a place to grow wealthy," Lytle argued. "It is a place to grow corn."[57] Because she was married to a farmer, Julia grasped the flippancy of this sentiment. Money mattered. You needed it to buy things like insecticides, irrigation equipment, and the services of a good veterinarian. A lifetime of effort could slip away in a few ruined crops, an outbreak of hog cholera, a plague of insects, a drought, a flood, a fire. Julia distrusted all ideology — Communist, Agrarian, and otherwise. Competition, she felt, was a law of nature, and the race would always go to the swift.

His prize money dwindling and the screenwriting job winding down, Irving Fineman applied for a job at Bennington College, a newly founded experimental girl's school in Vermont. He asked Julia, the most powerful person he knew, to write a letter of recommendation. "I longed to tell [the president] you're a sweet-talker, an expert in emotions, a counter who will inevitably become a squeezer when age overtakes you," she replied. Instead, she "resisted the impulse and wrote sweetly," keeping him in her debt.[58]

Fineman got the job. "Irving Fineman, Novelist, to Teach Prose Writing and Study of Literature," the school announced.[59] Still living from hand to mouth (and several hundred dollars in debt to Fineman), Frances

Frost also applied to teach at Bennington, a mere seventy miles from Burlington, where her parents were raising her two children.

Frost did not get the job, and she suspected that her status as a divorcée had something to do with it. Jobless, moneyless, but determined to stay near Irving, she rented a tiny cabin without plumbing and dug in to endure the bitter Vermont winter.[60]

Julia, too, pronounced herself "broke," though unlikely to go hungry, what with "the figs and grapes ripe and the place running over with chickens."[61] *Bright Skin* was still not selling, and she blamed Bobbs-Merrill. "Perhaps it would have been better for us both if you'd have encouraged me to accept Viking's offer of the $20,000. Jews are, after all, God's chosen people," she gibed, angry not only at Chambers and at fate, but at Irving Fineman, whose star seemed to be rising as hers sank.[62]

"I'm in the depths," she confessed in September when her favorite horse, Marigold, was attacked by a wild boar. The pig's sharp tusks slashed the horse's tendons, and Marigold had to be destroyed. Julia drove out into the country on a muddy road to avoid hearing the fatal shots. The boar was caught, killed, and castrated by Ben, one of Julia's most trusted employees. "But why?" she asked, with uncharacteristic gentleness. "That does not make Marigold alive." Ben, who knew her well, had expected to please her by "cutting" the boar and was "puzzled" by her lack of enthusiasm.[63] The old Julia, he knew, would have grinned.

Willie fell ill, and Julia cringed at dealing with his new secretary, "a tiny hunch-back with small bristly black moustache and shrewd blue eyes." "I hear things inside him yapping at me," she complained to Irving.[64]

The fact that Irving seldom answered her letters did not discourage her from writing. "I always feel that talking to you is like pouring water into a deep well," she explained. "The well doesn't care and I'm rid of the water." Still, given a choice, she preferred that the well answer. "Tell me . . . anything," she begged, "and arrange to have the letter arrive on the evening mail when it's black night and darkness comes in through the windows and sits in corners, behind chairs, tables, piano."[65] This order went out by air mail, and Fineman did as she asked.

Julia's troubles multiplied. In late October, Julius Mood was hurt in yet another car wreck. Again he spoke of suicide, confessing that twice he had "started toward the bathroom to lock the door, turn on the gas and get relief." Hurrying to the post office one bright fall day in hopes of finding a letter from Irving, Julia herself had an accident. A little black girl darted in front of her car and disappeared under the wheels. Julia scooped up the child, a "poor little motherless," and rushed her to a hospital in Orangeburg, twenty-five miles away. "She's still alive," she wrote to Irving that night, "no bones are broken but her head is *hurt*." [66]

For the first time since she had latched onto Fineman, Julia's talk of suicide sounded serious. "I'm alive," she wrote in early November 1932, "but I thought yesterday, why? Even so today. . . . Horrors have swirled around me until my mind wavers." [67]

The injured child recovered, and so did Julius Mood. And so, at last, did Julia's spirits. She joked about visiting Bennington in the spring to speak to Irving's students about "civilization's three great menaces" — liquor, automobiles, and men.[68] The college was closed from Christmas through March. Irving took off for Winter Park, Florida, and raised Julia's hopes by telling her that he might stop off at Lang Syne. But at the last minute he called to cancel. Though he didn't say so to Julia, Frances was with him.

Still longing for a reunion in early February 1933, Julia urged Irving to meet her in New York. He asked her to come to Bennington instead when classes reconvened. After some hedging, she agreed, warning that "at Bennington I might place you in a position so compromising, your resignation would not be suggested but insisted upon!" [69]

Irving was already in a compromising position. In addition to Julia and Frances, he had been seeing a third woman, Elizabeth Hawes, the twenty-nine-year-old estranged wife of sculptor Ralph Jester, who was also on the faculty at Bennington. Not that the cosmopolitan Hawes actually lived in Vermont. The self-described "Panther Woman of the Needle Trades," she owned Hawes, Incorporated, a haute couture fashion salon in New York that catered to glamorous theatrical clients like Lynne Fontanne, Dorothy Gish, Claire Trevor, and Katharine Hepburn. Gutsy and dashing, Hawes had been the first American designer to show her work in Paris and the first to put her name on a line of ready-to-wear dresses for American department stores. She contributed sardonic antifashion bulletins to the *New Yorker* under the pen name "Parisite," and socialized with avant-garde artists and writers from Alexander Calder to Nathaniel West to Edmund Wilson, who saw her as a "little swart mouse-beady-eyed Jewess" (in fact, her parents were Episcopalian).[70]

"Only a quadruple exposed negative could give the faintest idea of my life [in 1933]," Hawes later wrote.[71] In love with a married French tapestry designer, Jean Lurçat, she saw Irving Fineman as a fling — good sex and no commitment. But Irving was seriously hunting for a wife and had convinced himself that Hawes needed a husband. Relegated as it was to the shadows of Hawes's life, their affair might have run its course without either Julia or Frances ever being any the wiser. But in the midst of a bitter quarrel with Frances, Irving spilled the beans. Frances got drunk and told Doris Ulmann, and Doris told Julia, just before her trip to Bennington.

Already in a state of near collapse over a damaging story spread by columnist Walter Winchell, Julia was in no shape to cope with the news. It started when Langston Hughes, the noted African American poet whose *Fine Clothes to the Jew* she had reviewed favorably for *Poetry* in 1927, came to call at Lang Syne after lecturing in Columbia and visiting at the nearby plantation home of Dr. E. C. L. Adams, author of *Congaree Tales.* Hughes had met Julia in New York at the Spingarns', where, he believed, she had invited him to come and see her if he were ever near Lang Syne.[72] Arriving unannounced, Hughes knocked at the door. It was opened by a white man — probably Willie — who informed him that Miss Julia was not at home. Hughes felt sure that Julia *was* home and was refusing to receive him.[73]

Julia was certainly capable of such a dodge; Hughes did not misjudge her personality. But it is also possible that she was really *not* at home, or that someone in her household took it upon himself to turn Hughes away without telling her. The name Langston Hughes meant nothing to Willie, who would have been astonished to discover a black man — any black man — knocking at his front door. But Langston Hughes was lionized by Julia's literary friends, and everybody read Walter Winchell. Soon the facts hardly mattered. Even Carl Sandburg, who had never before said a harsh word to Julia, let her know that he was angry.

Julia arrived at Bennington as planned, expecting the entire faculty to rise up and ask, "Were you at home when L[angston] H[ughes] called?" She managed to address the assembled students, feeling all the while like a "red-haired monkey" as they stared at her "features, head, arms, hands, body." No one was rude or accusing, but the lights seemed so hot that her freckles "rose up into big copper coins." [74]

Afterward Julia and Irving tramped the snowy mountain roads, sat by the fire in his cozy house, and listened to Beethoven sonatas on the gramophone. It would have been an idyllic interlude had Julia not grilled him about Elizabeth Hawes. Irving confessed, then lay grimly on the couch while she lectured him about integrity. At the end of that tense weekend, Irving seems to have delivered an ultimatum. He would not give up his affairs with other women, though he would stop concealing them from Julia. He reserved the right to marry when the right woman came along and made it clear that he hoped to have children. If Julia was able to accept these terms, their romantic friendship could continue. If not, it would have to end.

For weeks after this unhappy visit, Julia's letters were filled with flattery, recriminations, and apologies — vain attempts to win back the old terms. She eventually talked herself into believing that their discussion had "killed only what needed to die and left what is stronger than life itself, than even death, to me." [75] But "how I laughed at your resolution to be henceforth indifferent to your reputation," she taunted. "When in God's name have you cherished it? The most I've ever hoped of you was that you might, perchance, be moved to protect somebody else's. Even that hope was due merely to my own wish that you would." [76]

Brash and cavalier as he appeared to Julia and Frances, Irving was out of his depth with Lisa Hawes. Nothing, it seemed, could throw her off-balance, not even an unwanted pregnancy. When she discovered in early summer that she was carrying Irving's baby, she took her problem to an abortionist. [77] Railing against the heartlessness of modern women, Irving turned to Julia for sympathy. She lit into him, defending Hawes's decision. "Here you, who ought to know better, say 'she would bear him no child' as casually as you'd say 'she would cook him no breakfast,'" she angrily chastised him. "In the years prior to contraceptives, women were helpless and priests and wise men comforted them by saying 'It is God's will.' We know better now." [78]

No one was talking about abortion rights in 1933. People were worried about feeding their children, keeping their jobs, protecting their farms and businesses. Banks were failing, strikes were erupting, and homeless people lined the highways. Bringing a message of hope to "a stricken nation in a stricken world," Franklin Delano Roosevelt was sworn in as president on March 4, 1933. On March 6 he closed all the banks, declaring a four-day "holiday" during which Congress was to draft emergency legislation reorganizing the banking system.

Several guests were stranded at Lang Syne, unable to travel without cash. Julia took comfort in knowing that the vegetables she could grow, and the chickens, sheep, cattle, and pigs, stood between her and starvation. "It's good to . . . know that out of the earth can come food, fuel, cotton for clothing, in this mad seizure of fear that has paralyzed the country," she told Fineman. "If you become penniless I'll employ you to survey and install a water power I've always hoped to have developed . . . I'll pay you with food, shelter."[79] Julia would have her dam soon enough, though not with Fineman's help. Operating on the same principle, Roosevelt's Reconstruction Finance Corporation would employ needy young men to build it.[80]

Like most other Americans, Julia feared being immobilized by the monetary crisis, but for her it soon passed. By mid-March she was off for Chicago, where she cheered at a boxing match, attended a play and a party for a "Chicago mogul," and shared the spotlight at the Chicago Theater with an old friend, the speakeasy queen Texas Guinan.[81] Texas threw a party in Julia's honor. Another Pulitzer Prize winner, Thornton Wilder, was also among the guests, but Julia stole the show.[82]

Knowing how he felt about the Langston Hughes scandal, Julia wondered if Carl Sandburg would even consent to see her. He proved friendly and willing, and introduced her to a group of writers as "the Queen of Sheba, Pharaoh's Daughter, Cleopatra."[83] The attention, the social whirl, and the reassurance that Sandburg had forgiven her all helped Julia to "get a grip." "Chicago's ice, snow, biting wind, cleared my heart completely, left it clean as a pebble in a swift stream," she wrote to Irving.[84] She rode back home in a brand-new Pullman car, christened, in her honor, the *Fort Motte*.

D. L. Chambers was furious to discover that Julia had visited Chicago without letting his publicists know. Julia was not contrite. "Publishers are a dumb lot, worse than politicians," she groused to Fineman. Sounding more like her old self, she added that with Adolph Hitler dominating the world news and the South Carolina legislature voting to exempt Ku Klux Klan property from taxation, she was "all for blowing up the whole inhabited world and letting reptiles, bugs, worms try their hand at making something decent" out of it. She was sure that "not one in ten thousand [people] is worth his breath," and that she had too few friends to provide her with a full set of pall-bearers.[85]

After the long, unprofitable struggle to write and sell *Bright Skin*, Julia was open to low-effort projects that promised a quick payoff. At the urging of her friend Dale Warren, she authorized Houghton Mifflin to publish "A Plantation Christmas" as a gift book, complete with line drawings of capering darkies serenading the Big House. The little volume was promoted as "a charming essay on the customs and rituals that Southerners zealously preserve." Unfortunately for Julia's literary reputation, it was an immediate and enduring commercial hit.[86]

In April, she agreed to write the text for a book of Doris Ulmann's Deep South photographs, to be published by the new firm of Robert Ballou.[87] Disclosing the deal to Chambers, who held an option on her next two novels, Julia was careful to stress that her job was just to write captions. Chambers resented the project anyway and tried to dissuade her. "My chief talent seems to be annoying my publishers," Julia wrote to Irving.[88]

It was an awkward time to begin a collaboration, for she and Doris had drifted apart. Julia carped that her friend was in North Carolina, "working," and hadn't even bothered to get in touch. "I can't make out her urges at all," she told Irving.[89] In fact, Doris's urges were a lot like her own. With the help of John Jacob Niles, a handsome man ten years her junior, she was taking photographs in the highlands of Kentucky, Tennessee, and North Carolina to illustrate Allen Eaton's forthcoming *Handicrafts of the Southern Highlands*. Niles was building a reputation as a singer, collector, and arranger of folk music, yet people whispered that he must be Doris's gigolo because she bought him expensive clothes, took him to plays and parties, and stayed with him in hotels, where they sometimes covered the windows with black drapes. Meanwhile, she was helping to support Lyle Saxon, too, sending him frequent checks.[90]

A kept man Niles may have been, but as Doris grew progressively weaker, Niles became her arms and legs.[91] Julia considered him a pompous fool and made no secret of her feelings. "Women in love are such utter idiots," she wrote to Irving in disgust. "I often wonder why the Creator made them so they cannot tell gentlemen from other men. None of us can where our emotions are involved. It's pathetic."[92] It was the same sort of thing she had said to the college girls in South Carolina when she advised them to marry sensibly. Now she was saying it to her lover. But Irving was too full of himself to realize that she classed herself among the "idiots."

Without Doris at hand to encourage her, Julia's enthusiasm for their joint project rapidly ebbed. She cobbled together some of her early *Reviewer* stories and some newer pieces she had sold to various newspapers, adding an introduction, some general descriptive essays, and a few original stories. She fell ill in midsummer and had to rush to meet the deadline. By August she had begun to hate the whole enterprise. "When I look over what I've done, a slight sense of nausea seizes me," she told Fineman. The sketches, she thought, were "mixed together in dangerous confusion."[93] Still, the project gave her an excuse to go to

New York. She spent a weekend with Fineman, retreated to dictate to a typist for two weeks in a house on Staten Island, and returned to the city to spend another night with Fineman.

Noting that the book needed some kind of foreword, Robert Ballou suggested that Julia write an "appreciation" of Ulmann and her photographs.[94] Still angry at Doris, she refused, made the few adjustments requested by the publisher, and washed her hands of the whole matter. Before leaving New York she entertained friends and reporters in her "tower apartment" at the Duane Hotel, casually leafing through a pile of photographs "taken by one of her friends," as an article in the *New York Herald Tribune* put it.[95] "I feel that it has become my book and is only illustrated by [Doris's] pictures," she commented to Fineman.[96]

In fact, *Roll, Jordan, Roll* was a hybrid, one of the first of many photo-documentaries that have shaped our collective memory of the Great Depression, including Erskine Caldwell and Margaret Bourke-White's *You Have Seen Their Faces* and James Agee and Walker Evans's *Let Us Now Praise Famous Men.* It had the potential to be both a best-seller and a critical tour de force. But too many things went wrong.

Robert Ballou submitted *Roll, Jordan, Roll* to the Book of the Month Club, hoping it would be chosen as a main selection. On a tip from one of the judges, he cut corners to rush the book into print. Then Walter Winchell struck again, announcing in his column that "Julia Peterkin's new opus" would be the next Book of the Month. If the judges had really intended to select *Roll, Jordan, Roll,* Winchell's leak deterred them. Another book was chosen.

Ballou was a novice at overseeing production, and his lack of experience showed. There are two different versions of *Roll, Jordan, Roll:* a sleek, large-format volume and a nondescript trade edition printed on spongy paper. Aesthetically, the big book is a polished diamond, the small one a lump of coal. Sadly, few people would see the diamond, which was limited to 350 signed copies. The trade edition was issued first, just in time for Christmas. The masterpiece followed in January and was not sent out for review. Beautifully bound and exquisitely printed using an expensive process, hand-pulled copperplate photogravure, the big book sold for $25 and included eighteen additional plates.[97]

The photographs show black people at work, at worship, and at play. People cut and sort asparagus, drive mules, plow with oxen, haul cotton, iron, sort figs, ring church bells, pray, get baptized in the river, and fish with cast nets. A chain gang in striped uniforms digs a ditch. Some of the most affecting images are still lifes and landscapes that depict the simple possessions of modest people: a clapboard cabin dappled with sunlight, a child-size chair squatting by a hearth, a gravestone jutting from a drift of fallen leaves, trailing a wake of stopped clocks and broken crockery.

Some of the pictures were taken around Lang Syne, but others came from Doris and Julia's trips to Murrells Inlet and Beaufort, South Carolina, Mobile, New Orleans, and points in between. At least six were taken at Melrose plantation, which Julia apparently never visited.[98] A few of the faces would have been familiar to Julia's readers if she had provided identifying captions. There are portraits of Ellis and Nannie Sanders, who inspired parts of *Green Thursday* and *Bright Skin*, and one of Ellis's mother, Maum Martha. There is a picture of Katie Jones, the original speaker of "Roots Work," who died the year before *Roll, Jordan, Roll* was published. Lavinia Berry is missing — she died before Julia met Doris. Near the front of the book there is a picture of a woman balancing tubs on her head. But she is not Mary Weeks.

Julia worried from the beginning that Doris's soft-focus platinum-print photographs might not reproduce well. Sadly, her fears were justified.[99] In the trade edition, many of the faces are crude "black blobs," as critic Dorothy Van Doren observed.[100] Detail is swallowed up in an inky sludge that reduces many images to cloudy abstractions; even in closeups, it isn't always possible to make out what people are doing or what they are wearing.

While the original photographs (and the reproductions in the limited edition) distinctly reveal such things as patched burlap trousers and ragged shirts, the trade edition might lead one to presume that Ulmann intended to obscure or romanticize the poverty of her subjects. Julia's opening sentences reinforce that impression. "Some of the charm that made the life of the old South glamorous still lingers on a few plantations," she wrote. "Wistfully holding to the past when they were part of a civilization never excelled in America, they keep their backs turned to the future and persistently ignore that strange thing called progress which so often means change without betterment."[101]

Julia laid a curse on the book with this nostalgic opening so out of tune with the times. In *Bright Skin* she had judged Lang Syne through the eyes of her employees, who paid "a day's work every week God sends for rent of a broke-down house."[102] Now she seemed to be pulling back, disowning that point of view. This may have made it easier for her to go home again, but it sank her literary reputation.

To be politically correct in the 1930s meant condemning the exploitation of laborers. Instead, in *Roll, Jordan, Roll* Julia chastised her field hands for their improvidence. Writing in the *New York Times,* John Chamberlain (who had not obliged by "withering" after his damaging attack on *Bright Skin*) slammed Julia for showing "a happy land of kindly masters and contented slaves." [103] African American historian Sterling Brown, a great admirer of *Green Thursday,* charged that *Roll, Jordan, Roll* was filled with racial stereotypes "that go back to *Swallow Barn*" (antebellum romanticist John Pendleton Kennedy's prototype of the plantation novel). [104] Yet *Roll, Jordan, Roll* won the "enthusiastic endorsement of the National Association for the Advancement of Colored People," and Walter White ordered several copies to give as Christmas gifts. [105]

How could a single book be both racist and socially uplifting? Like most of the people who read and judged *Roll, Jordan, Roll,* Julia and Doris were responding to a whole spectrum of contradictory, confused, and uninformed attitudes toward poverty and race. Consider, for example, the section on children. The photographs show remarkably pensive and attractive little people going about their business. "Black children are more dependable and capable than white children of the same age are ever expected to be," Julia wrote. "Most of them are eager and alert, in many cases brighter than white children of the same age." [106]

Yet when black children reach puberty, she went on, "even those with promising minds seem to develop physically rather than mentally." Unlike most of her contemporaries, Julia attributed this difference largely to culture, not heredity, and saw it as a result of the permissive sexuality she herself envied. Yet she accepted no responsibility for perpetuating the cycle, blandly declaring that "life has sentenced" black plantation children to a host of "disadvantages." [107]

The most offensive section is chapter 5, which describes the mutual dependence of "Cap'n" (Bill) and his "boy." The black man, Julia wrote, was proud of his employer and "delighted in watching him take part in the old-fashioned tilting tournaments which are held in the neighborhood several times each year." [108] These contests, though a venerable plantation tradition, were a modern excuse to dress up, ride horses, and deliver flowery speeches about the nobility of southern womanhood. Julia presented them as endearing relics of a lost civilization. What she portrayed as comic was the behavior of Bill's "boy," a notorious womanizer who finally got married, only to end up shooting his wife's lover. During his murder trial, he drifted off to sleep, secure in the knowledge that his "Cap'n" would get him off. The chapter is illustrated by photographs of a black youth kneeling before a white man's stylish boots, taken at Melrose, not Lang Syne.[109]

Julia's greatest strength as a writer had come from her ability to create characters in conflict with one another, to spin anecdotes about human behavior into highly charged psychological dramas. Now she seemed to present these anecdotes as evidence that rural blacks were primitive. In an essay about religion, she related Wallace Heyward's reaction at a revival when a woman beside him got the Spirit. Wallace

> just eased the scarf pin out of his necktie and jabbed it into her fat backside as deep as he could send it. She gave one long yell, rolled back her eyes, and went off in a trance. The people thought she had got more religion than she could stand, but he secretly jabbed her again until she leaped up and cavorted about, then ran bawling outside in the churchyard so fast the sisters and brothers who had crowded up around her thought a bee or a wasp had crawled up her leg.[110]

No doubt this tale was hilarious when Heyward related it, but Julia used the incident to "prove" a dubious point: "While there is often a real and earnest concern over religion [in the black churches], hysterical emotions that have little to do with salvation are sometimes displayed."[111]

Julia herself was far more interested in sex and violence than in piety and virtue, and *Roll, Jordan, Roll* is liberally salted with tales about shameless women. A woman named Jinny stabs her lover as he walks into church with his arm around another woman. At her trial for assault, several people swear on the Bible that Jinny spent the evening on her own front porch peacefully cutting her toenails with a butcher knife. Even the injured man tries to protect her, claiming that he has "no dreaming idea" who might have cut him. But just as the case is about to be dismissed for lack of evidence, Jinny takes the stand and insists on telling her story. "I cut dat low-lived scoundrel, Judge," she says, "an e knows good as me I cut em. . . . An what's more, if I ever catch em walkin out wid dat black, slew-foot hussy to church or anywheres else again, I'll sure cut his coward-heart out of em."[112] The witnesses howl with laughter. The Judge gives Jinny a suspended sentence, and she walks out of court arm in arm with her victim.

In another story, a tall, ungainly girl gets pregnant by the head asparagus grader, who is engaged to another woman. The "tree-tall gal," like Julia, is "'a motherless' with only a father to tell her what is what." The other graders charitably agree that while she was foolish to get pregnant, "no woman is to blame if her love happens to alight on somebody who does not love her." [113] But before long the head grader begins to sicken, and rumor has it that the girl must have thrown a "hand" on her former lover.

The boy's mother buys a countercharm, then goes to the girl's father, once her own boyfriend and now a church deacon. The man takes his daughter's part, suggesting that the boy deserves "a sound thrashing"; merely being turned out of the church is far too mild a punishment for someone who "spoiled-up a church deacon's house." Vowing to stand by his daughter and help her raise the baby, he informs the other packers that "he would never consent, while he lived, for any daughter of his to have a husband who did not want her." [114]

The "tree tall gal" has her baby but kills him with an overdose of aspirin. Rather than "fretting or grieving . . . like she was due to do," she gobbles rice and greens. By the next Saturday she is playing ball in the Quarters, and in the end she gets her man. When last we glimpse them, the head grader has "put his arm so tight around her she could not get away from him even if she tried." [115]

These new stories were almost as electrifying as "Maum Lou," "A Crutch," "A Wife," "The Flies," "Roots Work," and "Over the River" — all stories that had appeared in the *Reviewer* almost a decade earlier. (Some of them had already been reworked as episodes in *Green Thursday, Black April,* and *Scarlet Sister Mary.*) Good as the stories are, and limited as their audience had been when they were first published, their use in *Roll, Jordan, Roll* reinforced the impression that Julia had run out of new things to say and had begun to repeat herself.

In a way, of course, she had. Yet in reworking the narratives to suit a new purpose, Julia saw herself as imitating the "elasticity" of African American spirituals, which are perpetually "re-created by the singers to express the immediate emotion. It is not unusual," she wrote, "for a new song to be mixed with an old one to make both take on a different meaning." [116] Thus "Roll, Jordan, Roll," the spiritual from which she took her title, could be sung one way at a funeral, another at Christmas Watch Night meetings, another to celebrate Easter Day, and yet another by weary field hands on hot afternoons.

Most of the *Reviewer* sketches are reproduced verbatim, patched into the text as episodes in a frame story about the foreman and his family. Even in this clumsy arrangement they seem vivid and contemporary —

by far the most forceful part of the book. Only one, "Over the River," the story of the voiceless pregnant deaf girl whose lover refuses to "own" her, was radically altered.

In the 1923 version of "Over the River," the girl delivers a baby boy and seems too depressed to suckle him. At the end of the story, still unable to speak, she buries her dead infant and sets off in search of a new life. The tale as Julia shaped it then reflected her yearning to form words. The girl remains mute, yet she finds the will to keep walking.

The story as it appears in *Roll, Jordan, Roll* is Julia's renunciation of literature. The first ten pages follow the original almost word for word, until Julia reveals that this baby is a girl, and deaf like her mother. Moreover, the woman in *Roll, Jordan, Roll* deliberately starves her baby. "Better to starve than to live on, deaf and disowned," she thinks, wishing that she had never crossed the river to discover "the naked truth." [117] This second version can be read as an angry parable of Julia's life as an author. The women who tend the feverish girl treat her like a "rattlesnake." Flies swarm over her flimsy dress to gorge on the milk that leaks from her breasts. Maggots — "death's servants" — breed in her feet. People arrive to gawk at her misery. The maddened girl longs for death, reaching out with eager arms. As it clutches her throat, she finds her voice, crying, "Breast milk been too hot — I feed de baby wid cool spring water." [118]

Finding a voice does not save the girl or bring back her baby. Self-expression accomplishes nothing. Julia had begun to wish, like the girl, that she had never journeyed away from her home in search of "the naked truth." For the remaining twenty-eight years of her life, she would write nothing but letters and book reviews.

CHAPTER 14

Smash-up

gents offered Julia fabulous sums if she would lecture, talk over the radio, write for the movies. She refused, convinced that by writing she had "poured out [her life] like water on the ground." She intended to give up Irving, too, but that was harder to do. "Of course I love you and I'm furious with myself about it because it keeps you on my mind and I don't want to have you there," she lied. "I'll find a way to cure myself some of these days soon, and then we can be good friends just like we used to be, and we'll both feel better too. So have long patience with me until I find a remedy, or a substitute or something which will relieve you of the responsibility you've had to bear now for some time." [1]

Fineman bought a small farm, hired a black servant, and set up housekeeping in earnest. He had just finished a book called *Hear, Ye Sons,* the

Jewish novel he had abandoned to write *Lovers Must Learn*. Feeling secure, productive, and responsible, he grew serious about finding a wife and renewed his overtures toward Elizabeth Hawes. On stationery emblazoned with a giant pair of shears, Hawes informed him that his needs failed to interest her.

Frances Frost picked the same moment to bolt. Penniless and frightened, she married the eccentric Charlestonian Samuel Gaillard Stoney, an alumnus of the MacDowell Colony and the great-grandson of Louisa McCord, Julia's predecessor as mistress of Lang Syne.[2]

Irving was overcome with self-pity. Women were fickle, he complained. Julia was unimpressed. "If we play with fire, we must not whimper when we get burned, must we," she scolded. "You are a very grown-up, intelligent person except for this business of forever falling in love, forever being faithless, yet forever expecting unswerving loyalty and devotion."[3] Abandoned by his other lovers, Irving suddenly realized that Julia, too, might really "find a substitute." When she canceled a trip to New York, he accused her of hurting his feelings. Julia apologized. "I shall stand by you to the end of my days," she promised.[4]

In need of a boost, Irving once again made plans to visit Lang Syne during his long winter break. This time he actually appeared, accompanied by his servant, John Broaddus. Julia set out to show him "the real South," as she put it, "decadent, proud, ignorant, poor."[5] They walked beside the little stream where turkey berries grew, visited the Quarters, and talked for hours. After so many years of resenting Willie from afar, Irving discovered that Julia's husband was human, and even rather likable. Everyone behaved with such perfect propriety that the visit seemed anticlimactic.

On New Year's Day 1934, Irving and John Broaddus left for Savannah, where Julia had arranged for Irving to meet the Barrows. That afternoon, the phone rang at Lang Syne and a doctor from Ridgeland, South Carolina, came on the line. Irving's car had skidded on a rain-slick road and crashed into another vehicle. John Broaddus, who was driving, had escaped with a bruised shoulder. Irving appeared to have broken his back.

Willie and Julia sprang into action as though Irving were their own son. They arranged to have him taken by ambulance to the Central of Georgia Hospital in Savannah and put under Dr. Barrow's care. "Don't let him die and don't let his back be broken," Julia sobbed to herself all the way to Savannah.[6]

As it turned out, Irving did have a broken vertebra, though Julia was forbidden to tell him so. Dr. Barrow insisted that he would get well sooner if he didn't know the extent of his injury.[7] Willie had Irving's car towed to a garage and arranged to have it fixed, and he wrote a check to the driver of the other car to cover his repairs. He and Julia discreetly made certain that Irving had money "for little things."[8] She took John Broaddus back to Lang Syne and put him to work planting grapevines.

Dr. Barrow assured her that Irving would be fine in a week or two. Julia joyfully planned to welcome him back to Lang Syne with a dinner of aged English pheasant. "I'm not a bad nurse . . . and John's here to bathe any islands that must be hidden from modest woman eyes," she teased. Then Mrs. Barrow called to say that Irving was scheduled for surgery.[9]

Julia fought down panic by listening to the radio, digging in the garden, riding her horse, and playing the piano. She promised fate, "or whatever runs this show," to ask no more favors if only Irving recovered. "You say that now," she admitted to herself, "but when he's well you'll still go trailing him from one end of the world to another."[10]

Upsetting as it was, Irving's accident infused drama into a relationship on the verge of fizzling out. All of Irving's telegrams and phone calls were directed to Julia, who in turn reassured his sister, his father, his publisher, and even Frances Frost Stoney. Julia entertained many visitors that month, including photographer Walker Evans.[11] But her heart was in Savannah. When one group of guests began talking about love, she blurted out, in Willie's presence, "Irving is one of the few people I love dearly." Without missing a beat, Willie chimed in, "I can easily understand that, for I like him so much my-self."[12]

In early February, Julia's vigil was interrupted by an invitation from Frances Perkins, the United States secretary of agriculture, to lunch in Washington with Eleanor Roosevelt. She went, of course. Even Irving's desperate state couldn't outweigh that summons. The Capitol swarmed with eager petitioners clamoring to get their hands on some of the new federal subsidies Roosevelt was creating to jump-start the economy. Julia drank moonshine with the governor of South Carolina and sixty-four other state officials. " 'Twas fun, rather, to hear all the sweet-talk they handed me, in true S.C. style," she bragged. Next to her in the hotel was a delegation from Louisiana, led by the boisterous Huey Long. Though she claimed to dislike both snow and politicians, Julia was in her element.[13]

For the rest of her life she would entertain friends with an account of her lunch with Eleanor Roosevelt. Two haughty maids and two starchy butlers presented the humble waffles, which were served along with a "*tomato juice* cocktail on a bitter cold, snowy day!" An "assortment of [Mrs. Roosevelt's] daughters-in-law" was also in attendance. Julia was given the place of honor at Eleanor's right hand.[14]

When the other women withdrew after lunch, Mrs. Roosevelt got right to the point. She wanted Julia to serve as chairman of the South Carolina Democratic party. Roosevelt had won a majority of the state's votes in 1932, but he had alienated a lot of well-to-do people by raising taxes to help the poor.[15] Julia, as it happened, was one of them. "Mrs. Roosevelt is a fanatic," she wrote to Fineman, "more so now than ever."[16]

Although distrusting the Roosevelts' social reforms, she was alert to the fact that New Deal spending could be used to further her own goals. "My family has never gone in for politics," she politely told the First Lady. But if President Roosevelt wanted to spend some money, he should put one of his new agencies to work building a schoolhouse for the blacks of Lang Syne. Mrs. Roosevelt solemnly promised to see what she could do. "I would love to visit your plantation if I might come *incognito*," she added.[17]

Julia scoffed at the thought of Eleanor Roosevelt escaping recognition at Lang Syne, where her portrait hung beside a picture of Jesus in almost every cabin. But she had to admit that Mrs. Roosevelt was quick on the draw. When she reached home a few days later, a crew was breaking ground for the new school.[18]

Irving fretted about his medical bills and worried about getting to Baltimore in time to deliver a lecture. Julia pressed him to accept a small loan, forget about the speech, and relax at Lang Syne for several weeks. Even Willie, she claimed, was "bitterly opposed" to his driving north so soon.[19] John Broaddus made himself useful at Lang Syne, managing Julia's kitchen while Wallace Heyward was ill. He had even found a girlfriend, Lucinda Jackson, also known as "Sing." Julia refrained from telling Sing that her beau had a wife in Vermont, but she supplied Irving with all the details of John's new conquest.[20]

Her personal interest in Lucinda Jackson was a holdover from earlier days. For the most part, Julia had cut herself off from the black men and women who served her. Many of her favorites had died in the past few years or, like Mary, had moved away. There were as many domestics around her house as ever, but she did not try to turn them into friends. She seldom mentioned individuals by name; when she referred to her servants, it was "the cook," "the foreman," or "the maid." She still got upset when the maid's boyfriend beat her, and she took the battered woman to Columbia for treatment. But the unfortunate woman was not a person with a name; she was merely "the broken-armed maid."[21] Sing seems to have caught her interest only because of her link to Irving through John Broaddus.

Dr. Barrow pronounced his patient fit to travel in mid-February. Irving collected his car, drove to Lang Syne, and let Julia fuss over him for a few days. Then he rode the train back to Bennington, leaving John, who was suffering from tonsillitis, to drive the car when he recovered. As Julia understood it, John was to take his time and wait until his health and the weather improved. But she didn't know about the letter Irving had sent to John directing him to come ahead. Broaddus dawdled, nursing his infected tonsils and courting Sing, and then disappeared en route, apparently with Sing in tow. Irving complained about it to Julia, who took John's side, pointing out that "in his place you'd probably have done as he did."[22]

Eventually John showed up to face Irving's wrath. "Dear Miss," he wrote to Julia, for whom he had developed an apparently genuine attachment, "I am sorroy I give you lots of truble this winter. I hope this will not hoppy again. . . . please dont felling like you dont want to see me enymore Love to Wallice."[23] Sing somehow found her way back to Lang Syne.

Though he made it safely home, Irving Fineman's troubles in the South had just begun. The driver of the other car involved in the accident, a Mr. Mears, sued for further damages, encouraged, Julia thought, by mention in the South Carolina papers of Fineman's $7,500 prize. Julia and Willie consulted with their own lawyer and then, on his advice, enlisted the aid of another lawyer and a state senator. "I hope . . . you've nothing tangible and that your farm is not yet paid for but under mortgage or something," Julia ominously remarked. When Irving protested that Willie had done enough already (the lawyers feared he had compromised the case by paying the other driver), Julia assured him that "what we do for you is done with as much pleasure as if it were for ourselves." The best tactic in South Carolina, she said, was to "post-pone, delay, delay," until the plaintiff either gave up or grew too old to continue.[24] Fineman was impatient with all this finagling; he wanted the lawsuit settled.

Sustaining Irving's spirits and straightening out his affairs consumed Julia for most of January, February, and March. She planned a trip to New York in April. "Please save the last dressing for me to take off," she joshed.[25] But her mood was far from light. Julius Mood had just had exploratory surgery that revealed cancer of the colon.

Julia wrote Irving the bad news, expecting a return of the attention and sympathy she had lavished on him when he was hurt. But Irving failed to deliver. He came to see her only once when she was in New York, near the end of her visit. When he did, Julia let herself give way to what she called a "break-down."[26]

Afterward, she referred sheepishly to her "inexcusable" loss of control. "I am a very lonely woman," she explained. "You see me gay, among people who flatter me, shower me with attention . . . but . . . these things leave me lonelier, emphasize to me the fact that . . . I'm defeated. . . . My deep disappointment with what I have become distorts my judgment." She spoke of suicide, then ruled it out: "Even though I wail, I know I love life so much that I'll hold on even though I realize I'm seeking what I shall not find."[27]

What *had* Julia become that was causing her pain? A neo-Confederate, a "Negro propagandist," or some uncomfortable mixture of both? A dominatrix or a pitiful wretch in thrall to an indifferent man? She worried the subject endlessly, reaching the same conclusion: she regretted having exposed herself, both by writing and by sleeping with Irving.

Irving tried to comfort her, but he only made matters worse. Nothing could disguise the fact that he was trying to pull away. It became painfully obvious when he hired a lawyer of his own, taking the management of the liability suit out of Julia's hands. The attorney took one look at the evidence and advised him to settle out of court. The victim agreed to drop the charges in exchange for $200. Julia protested that Willie said Mears shouldn't get "one cent."[28] But Irving heaved a sigh of relief and paid the man.

Meanwhile, back in Sumter, Julius Mood was sinking. He caught pneumonia in the spring and was rushed to the hospital, where he lay gasping for breath. But then, against all odds, he rallied, and by the middle of May he was back at home, installed in an adjustable bed. Julia tried to joke about her fear and anxiety. In language that betrayed her fury at the men who were letting her down, she wished that she could take control and prevent horrible things from happening. "If I were president of the U.S.," she wrote, "I'd have all males nailed up in stout boxes with only cracks for food and water to be put through, until whatever malign stars now shine have moved on."[29] By late spring, she was almost sure that "some evil force must be upon [the whole world], maybe a chemical sent out from the sun's rays or from some magnetic influence springing from the earth's bowels."[30] Malign stars and evil forces — all aligned against her. There seemed no point in jousting with fate; she must simply accept what came.

She liked to think about Irving's little farm and to advise him how to manage it. He didn't know one plant from another, a deficiency she was eager to correct. Now that he had a place to put them, she began sending rooted slips instead of cut flowers. It was illegal to ship uninspected plants across state lines, but Julia had connections. She finagled a box of tags from an agriculture official that certified her specimens as pest-free. "The top layer is sweet potato plants," she wrote to Irving, "then come rose vines, wisteria, honey-suckle, periwinkle, violets, and the stiff bunch is ligustrum. The rose vines are Dorothy Perkins and American Pillar, small, pink." It pleased her to think of "Lang Syne blossoms brightening [Irving's] home and its sweet potatoes filling [his] dishes."[31]

By midsummer she had decided to "fling . . . convention to the winds" and follow the plants to Bennington. "God knows I deserve some care-free days, and I hate the thing in me that warns me to be careful not to do anything that may cause malicious tongues to wag," she wrote. "Give John [Broaddus] my greetings and tell him I appreciate his wanting me to come. And please don't tell Walter Winchell that I am."[32]

Julia had a convenient explanation for her trip to Vermont, one that even Winchell might have swallowed. She had accepted an appointment to the faculty of the Bread Loaf Writers' Conference in Middlebury, where her duties included giving talks, reading manuscripts, and dispensing wise advice to "authors who have 'Problems.'"[33]

People like Bernard DeVoto gloried in the "frenziedly, maniacally literary" atmosphere at Bread Loaf.[34] Julia, who was no longer writing, found it "wearisome," even when she was drunk. "To be soft here is to be a fool," she complained. Still, she thought the experience might be good for her: "I needed to sharpen teeth and claws and I already see with pride that I can draw blood when I want to!"[35] For all her reservations, she put on a terrific show. "Five minutes after she began to talk at the first lecture, the whole audience was in the palm of her hand and for two weeks her progress down the white marble paths was that of a queen with her court, or of a surgeon and his gallery," reported Fanny Butcher in the *Chicago Tribune*.[36]

Julia's stay at Bread Loaf ended abruptly on August 28, 1934, with the arrival of a telegram. Doris Ulmann was dead. Julia took the night train to New York.[37] The news, she told Fineman, was a "terrible wrench" but "rather exciting, too," for Doris's death made her feel "like somebody I've never been before." [38]

The old Julia might have felt thrilled over the death of a close friend, but she would have found a more evasive way of expressing herself. The new Julia prided herself on her shockingly blunt revelations. But her exhilaration soon gave way to "storm, horror, terror." [39] Doris had made a will in 1927 that left most of her money to her sister, Edna Necarsulmer, to Edna's daughter Evelyn, and to another niece and a nephew. Shortly before her death, she had changed her mind and created a new will. In it, she left most of her assets to the John C. Campbell Folk School in Brasstown, North Carolina, where she had photographed in 1933 and 1934. The new will assigned her photographs to John Jacob Niles and provided him with an annual stipend.[40] There was no mention of the Necarsulmers, except that Edna's husband, Henry, was designated a member of the Doris Ulmann Foundation, formed to administer her estate.[41]

Julia was faced with the awkward task of explaining to Henry and Edna Necarsulmer who Jack Niles was. Henry was a lawyer, and the family decided to contest Doris's will. They wanted Julia to testify in court that Niles was a con artist who had taken advantage of Doris when she was too weak to resist. Meanwhile, George Uebler, Doris's chauffeur, sought Julia out, determined to tell her what had really happened. He seemed to Julia "hysterical, almost like a madman." She whisked him away to a hotel room and listened to his hair-raising tale.[42]

Niles, he said, had been Doris's gigolo for the past two and a half years. She had paid for his car and rent and utilities, bought his clothes, and given him a charge account, and in return he treated her "like a dog." Doris had fallen ill on August 3 and started home to New York. On the way, in Scranton, Pennsylvania, Niles had convinced her to make a new will leaving all her pictures and equipment to him, along with $10,000. He asked a man from the hotel to witness her signature. The man refused, saying she seemed "dopey" to him, and tore up the paper. Uebler had saved the pieces as evidence. Back in New York, Niles summarily dismissed all the servants, but Uebler refused to leave. For eleven days, from August 17 until her death on August 28, Niles tried to keep Doris secluded, allowing no one into her room. Uebler suggested that Niles had poisoned Doris, since he allowed no one else to feed her or administer medicine. Julia decided that the best she could do for Doris was to hush the whole thing up, even if it meant that Jack Niles got away with murder.

Meanwhile, George Uebler sent Lyle Saxon an urgent letter decrying the treachery of Doris's "lousy giglio" and enclosed a photostat of the shredded will from the hotel in Pennsylvania.[43] The letter was written in such fractured English that Saxon asked Uebler to tell his story to a friend and have the results typewritten. Did he think Doris had been murdered? How had he gotten hold of the pieces of the will? Saxon was especially disturbed by Uebler's use of the term "gigolo," which cut a little too close to home; Doris had been sending *him* money, too. He also asked Uebler if he had told Julia the distressing story, and wrote to ask her himself.[44] Uebler was telling the truth, Julia replied, but "justice matters far less to me than protecting [Doris] from scandal."[45]

Unsettling things began to happen. An unsavory character Julia had met through Doris, a man she always referred to only as "the Racketeer," called her repeatedly at the hotel. When she went out to make funeral arrangements, someone got into her room and rifled through her papers. She suspected Doris's family of hiring someone to harass her. "Well, if a letter from Doris to me was wanted, none was here," she wrote to Irving, "and heaven knows [they are] welcome to read the requests of aspiring authors on my desk." "It's none of my business," she added, "and I shall keep out of it entirely."

Furious at "poor Doris" for leaving a mess that threatened her own reputation, she advocated treating female lovesickness as a punishable offense: "Women in love should be jailed, fed on bread and water until they recover from their insanity." Male lovesickness, on the other hand, was a condition she wanted to encourage — at gunpoint, if necessary. "Men not in love," she grandly decreed, should simply "be shot."[46]

Doris's sister followed Julia to Lang Syne, still begging her to intervene. Julia stonewalled. "Doris is dead," she kept pointing out. "No word of mine can bring her back or change her last will."[47]

Julia's role in the Jack Niles flap emboldened some of her closest men friends to confront her about Irving Fineman. Hudson Strode did it face-to-face, right after Doris's funeral. Julia admitted nothing. Dale Warren wrote a nasty letter to Irving and sent it to Julia for forwarding. She tore it up. Warren then went all the way to Bennington and broached the subject of wealthy women who fall for younger men. "He did not go to discuss Doris. Of that I'm sure," Julia scoffed to Irving. "For some obscure reason he resents my friendship for you. Maybe he fears you'll break my heart! He has a deep-rooted conviction that you've broken many nice ladies' hearts, that it's a habit of yours."[48] Dan Reed talked behind her back, which made her even madder. And in the rumor mill that processed gossip from New York to South Carolina, Julia and Irving's liaison got mixed up with Jack and Doris's. Almost a year later, in Columbia, Julia would still be hearing rumors that the "scoundrel" Irving Fineman had seduced Doris Ulmann, married her, and killed her "for her money." [49]

Irving, though he was innocent of killing Doris, did have reason to feel guilty. Frances Frost Stoney had decided that her marriage was a mistake and had begun meeting him again. He pestered her to get a divorce, but Frances dragged her feet. Irving dated other women and swore each time he saw Frances that it would be the last. Yet he continued to come whenever she called. He had always found married women irresistible.

"Go on and get yourself a wife, have your children," Julia advised. Irving wanted to know why she was suddenly so determined to get him "hitched." She retaliated by sending clippings of newspaper ads that promised "love, wealth, happiness through marriage" with "book of photos and description free, many wealthy." [50] But once again she reminded him that if he married, she would poison the bride.

Julia arrived in New York on April 10 with a sense of foreboding. "If I could see you just one time, hold your hand and talk to you, it would give me relief, although . . . please bring along an extra shirt and collar in case I soak the one you have on with tears," she wrote to him just before leaving. "Even if you must lie and deceive somebody in order to come see me . . . go ahead and do it." [51]

There was a "somebody," she soon discovered, a beautiful twenty-seven-year-old divorcée named Helene Hughes. Julia warned Irving that if he got married, she would no longer be able to see him. "One of my articles of faith and conduct is to leave men belonging to other women absolutely alone," she claimed. [52]

They had been through this before, and Julia expected to find the same sexy Irving eagerly awaiting her. But never in the long history of their relationship had he seemed so aloof. He took her to see a play, Lillian Hellman's *The Children's Hour*, but he refused to spend the night. Julia cried — "bleat[ed]," she later admitted. [53] He promised to come again the next weekend, but only to take her to lunch.

The days in between were misery. Julia drank vodka and soaked her pillow with tears. "Greedy soul that I am, I wish I could induce that bit of mid-day to stretch on and on until another day comes at least," she wrote to Irving. "I wish . . . you might spare me a bit more of your time."[54] But Irving was busy breaking up with Frances — she, too, was in the city — and making love to Helene.

The lunch date finally arrived, and Irving showed up as promised. He could talk of nothing but Helene and the endearing way she had of trembling when frightened or upset. When the meal was over, he left.

Julia wrote him a catty letter implying that Helene was a fake. "Trembling's grand fun, and how men adore it! If only I could work the eye part." If Irving was that easily taken in, she said, he might as well "go on and take up with a trembler and try to tremble with her."[55]

Julia returned to South Carolina convinced that all was lost, and checked into Miss Eastway's Sanitarium. "I *must* learn to stand alone," she wrote. "To let my-self smash-up because emotion has over-come my reason is absurd."[56] Not wanting word of her condition to leak out, she dragged herself back to Lang Syne for a scheduled visit from columnist Fanny Butcher, then returned to the hospital when the coast was clear.

Trying, perhaps, to soften the blow, Irving wrote that he felt torn between marrying Helene and staying single. "Why in God's name are you so irresolute?" Julia shot back. "You know what you want, what you intend to do. Why blame it on desperation?" Weary of waiting for the blow to fall, she goaded him to go ahead and "dive off the spring board into deep water." Probably he should marry *three* women, she said, since "no one woman alive could possibly fill all [his] needs."[57]

Julia had reason to feel abandoned: in one way or another, it seemed, everybody she cared about was deserting her. At the beginning of June, May Darby, her closest friend in Fort Motte, was committed to the state insane asylum, raving about dead fish.[58] Compared with May's hallucinations, Julia's breakdown seemed mild. Yet her outlook on life was veering toward paranoia. "Stealthy roots creep maliciously around my plantings," she wrote to Irving, and "choke them before I know it." Ginkgo seedlings tried to "annihilate all the larkspurs and tulips." A hawk hovered near the chicken coop, trying to get at the chicks. Julia stood guard with a gun, but she felt that in the end there was "no escape" from the predator's will.[59]

Julia lost weight and complained of fatigue. Life seemed "meager." She attributed her despondency to a chemical imbalance caused by her old foes, the "ductless glands."[60] Medical tests revealed nothing. When people expressed an interest in her life, she took it as a threat. Henry Bellamann sent her into a tailspin by proposing to write her biography.

"It's painful to be talked about," she said, "to be written about is worse." When an admirer suggested to D. L. Chambers that he would like to organize a "rally" in her honor and place a marker at her birthplace, she hit the ceiling: "I'll run away and never be heard of again if they persist in this foolishness."[61]

The rest of the world was slow to grasp that Julia had quit writing for good. Henry B. Alsberg, director of President Roosevelt's newly created Federal Writers' Project, a division of the Works Progress Administration, invited her to serve as the head of the South Carolina division, at a salary of $2,300 a year. She would oversee the preparation of a state guidebook including "history folklore art geology archaeology etcetera." Julia declined. "The government's crazy," she wrote to Irving.[62] (The job went to a woman named Mabel Montgomery.) Like many of Roosevelt's schemes for economic recovery, this one struck her as a disgraceful waste of taxpayers' money. Good writers, she insisted, did not need such jobs, and poor writers should not be encouraged.

On the other hand, the completion of the four-room school building she had wheedled from Eleanor Roosevelt gave her "a real thrill." In addition to regular classes for children, she set up a night school for adults, many of whom could not write their own names. Willie dismissed it all as "foolishness," she told Irving, "but I'll have worse sins to answer for I suspect."[63]

In May 1935, on the 150th anniversary of its founding, the College of Charleston presented her with an honorary doctorate, along with millionaire Bernard Baruch, journalist Gerald Johnson, a former United States ambassador, and the chief justice of the Supreme Court. But bad luck followed her to the coast. Leaving Folly Beach, just south of the city, Julia pulled out on the highway into the path of another car. She and her two passengers, both men, were unhurt, but the car was badly damaged.[64]

For the first time since 1929, Julia was without her touchstone. Since her last tear-stained visit to New York, Irving's letters had all but ceased. "Did you marry the girl?" she finally asked.[65] He lied and said that he had. In fact, as he confessed to Frances, he and Helene had moved in together but hadn't bothered with a license. Frances pointed out that Irving would lose his job if anyone found out. She told him to take Helene out of the country and marry her as quickly as possible.

Irving didn't trust Julia with his secret. But Helene was a part of his life, and he wanted Julia to meet her. Would Julia stop by on her way to Bread Loaf and spend a week at Three Mountains? Julia was astounded that he could contemplate such a scene. "What right have I to go to [Helene's] home, . . . a total stranger, in the midst of her happy honeymoon, and without her invitation?" she asked.[66] Prompted, no doubt, by Irving, Helene sent an invitation of her own.

Julia gave up and arrived at Irving's farm the first week in August. In spite of herself, she liked Helene, who was modest and unassuming. Irving looked "fit" and "buoyant." But it was not a pleasant visit. Julia felt like a third wheel, and it brought out the worst in her. "If I were a *wicked* woman, certainly I'd be well-nigh consumed with envy of your blessings, but being *good* I rejoice in your gifts and your good fortune," she joked in a bread-and-butter note meant to be shared with Helene. In a letter to Irving alone, however, she apologized for the Julia who *was* jealous, "bad-tempered, bad-mannered, [and] mean-spoken." Somehow she had goaded John Broaddus into quitting, leaving the couple without a cook. It was an old form of southern revenge — tampering with the other woman's servants. But Irving, who was in a forgiving mood, invited Julia to come again on the way home from Bread Loaf. "Why, I'd be scared to," she rudely replied.[67]

After the strain of meeting Helene, Bread Loaf was a relief. Poet John Crowe Ransom was on the faculty, and Robert Frost gave a guest lecture. Julia went out of her way to be helpful and charming.[68] One girl called her "a perfect dear" and gushed to a reporter, "she smiled at me!"[69] But Julia was less an eager practitioner teaching in one of the country's foremost literary workshops than a traveler who had been to the wilderness and returned to warn people away. "Why Write?" she asked in one of her lectures, without providing much of an answer. For her, the "Penalties of Being a Novelist" had outweighed the rewards.[70]

"Peace is far better than the drudgery of writing or the ferment that forces us to try to create," she wrote to Irving that fall. "You and I both know that few books have value except to the people who write them."[71]

Letters, too, disappointed her. "Written words," she told Irving in December, "are a poor way to communicate. We need to hear a voice, see a facial expression, gestures, to really enjoy what is being said."[72] Yet her letters to him continued to pile up, more robust and outrageous than ever. Language was her bait and hook, the line that reeled him in. And far from ending their correspondence, Irving turned prolific now that he was settled. As soon as domestic life lost its novelty and Helene began to act like a wife, Irving found that he needed a confidante just as much as Julia did.

Both of them dropped the lacquered sentimentality of the early years of their affair. Now when Julia got irritated with Irving, she told him a mean dirty joke. Most of them involved circumcision, castration, or mutilation of the male organ. "The train ran over a Jackass and cut him to pieces," she wrote a few months after Irving's "marriage" to Helene. "The mangled carcass was removed from the track, all except one very particular portion of his anatomy which fell between the cross ties. Two black sisters came walking beside the track on their [way] to church. One of them spied the black length left from the poor dead beast, and gave a long mournful howl. 'My God,' she shrieked, 'De Ku Klux is come an killed our pastor!'"[73]

Having held on to her youth longer than most people, Julia lost it in record time. Pictures taken in the summer of 1935 show a handsome, smooth-faced woman, strong and full of juice. A year later, she was ravaged and wrinkled, her face a mask of pain.

Life dealt her some crushing blows in the course of those twelve months. Her father died on February 7, 1936. That night, Bill and Elfrida were awakened by the frantic yelps of a mother cocker spaniel. Their house was in flames. They got out, but the house burned down. (It had been rewired that very day to accept current from the water-powered generator.) The young couple lost everything, and Bill missed his grandfather's funeral.

In March, Willie developed serious lung trouble and was hospitalized in Columbia, coughing up blood. A boiler at the veneer mill exploded, scalding four workers and wrecking the machinery. Julia was "dazed, bewildered" by so much misfortune. When she looked back over that year, she could remember only "shocks . . . like firecrackers tied to a poor dog's tail."[74]

As always, her first instinct when in trouble was to plead with Fineman for sympathy. An affectionate letter arrived from him promptly, and Julia gratefully replied that reading it helped her "sleep the night through for the first time in weeks."[75] He was the only person besides her father, she said, who had ever really understood her. Unsure how to respond to this heartfelt declaration, Irving sent her, at her request, some state-of-the-art fire extinguishers.

In the summer of 1935, bound galleys of Margaret Mitchell's *Gone with the Wind* arrived in her mailbox. "I've just finished a book you must read," she wrote to Irving, "a faithful account of people in these parts during 1860–64. It revived my childhood hatred of Yankees."[76] When she reviewed the book for the *Washington Post*, she pulled out all the stops. "*Gone With the Wind* . . . is the best novel that has ever come out of the South. In fact, I believe it is unsurpassed in the whole of American writing." [77]

The kind of Southerner Julia was becoming is revealed in these few sentences. After fifteen years of reaching eagerly for everything the North had to offer, her "childhood fear of Yankees" was indeed returning to claim her. She felt used, defeated, plundered, even raped by her former allies; and the Lost Cause, as imagined by Mitchell, gave her a country to come home to. Repelled by William Faulkner's "degenerate" characters, contemptuous of Thomas Wolfe's self-pitying grandiloquence, Julia found no fault with Margaret Mitchell's apelike "darkeys" eager to "dig ditches fer de wite gempmums to hide in we'en de Yankees comes." [78] She saw herself as the "embittered" victim of a ruthless "swarm of scavengers." [79]

In actions as well as words, she endorsed segregation. That fall, she wriggled out of appearing at a book fair alongside several black writers. "I hardly think it's a smart idea to have whites and blacks on the same program," she wrote to D. L. Chambers, "since they'd put us entirely to shame with their ease and eloquence," [80] Chambers took the hint and had the speakers rearranged.

Julia would produce one final book review before falling silent forever. Lyle Saxon's *Children of Strangers* appeared in 1937. Like Julia's Cricket, Saxon's Famie is neither white nor black. Julia noted that ten years ago, such a book "would have been roundly denounced and the author punished as a traitor to his social group." [81] Now the subject of interracial sex was almost tame. This shift, though she had helped to bring it about, made Julia uncomfortable.

"Time for writing has been lacking," she wrote to Saxon, "but I'm steaming up to get at it in 1938." [82] Sadly, the pressure never rose. She still had some business in the literary world, but it was leftover business, loose ends. Robert O. Ballou dissolved his publishing firm. Bobbs-Merrill bought out the remaining stock of *Roll, Jordan, Roll* and reissued it in a new dust jacket. Dan Reed was still pushing for a production of *Black April*, with or without Paul Robeson. "Trouble has been hounding me persistently for some weeks now," Julia told Fineman. "God knows why it got on my trail, but until it leaves off, I'd hesitate to undertake anything that mattered to me as much as what might happen to 'Black April' would matter." [83] Nothing public seemed worth the risk; to Carl Sandburg, she confessed "turn[ing] coward." [84]

Fed up with the demands of college teaching, Irving Fineman asked Bennington for a semester's leave to pursue his other interests. Julia was invited to replace him. She was sure that Fineman must have suggested her, yet he denied it. "If you'll get me a job at Williams, I might consider [teaching]," she joked. "Boys are more to my taste than girls." [85] Henry Bellamann would be a better choice for the job, she felt, since "he's really erudite, and civilized, and the ladies never fail to adore him." Growing generous in her old age, she gave Bellamann credit for her success. "Except that he insisted I could write, I'd never have dreamed of trying," she admitted. " 'Twas all a sort of 'Trilby' business, something like super-hypnotism." [86]

In the end, Julia accepted the job at Bennington and invited Willie to go along. To her surprise, he agreed. His doctors had recommended that he get away from the farm, where bad weather and crop failures kept him on edge. It had been many years since they had taken a trip together, and Julia bought a new green Ford roadster for the occasion. [87]

At the last minute, Willie changed his mind and decided to stay home. Julia worried about her new car; how would she get it to Vermont? For all that she loved to drive, such a long trip alone seemed beyond her. A friend volunteered to accompany her to Vermont, solving the problem of the car. Julia spent her usual two weeks at Bread Loaf, then moved on to Bennington.

She had often wondered how she would cope with a regular job. Now, huddled miserably in her drafty furnished rooms, she admitted to "stage fright," made few friends, and spent most of her free time complaining about the silliness of her students and the nastiness of her apartment. [88] The faculty, with few exceptions, were just as Irving had described them — pompous, standoffish, and paranoid. She did make friends with Thomas Foster, a young man who found her "entrancing." [89] Irving was still in town, and he tried to make her feel at home. But Julia could never be really happy with Helene in the picture.

Many of her students came from wealthy families, and some had a disagreeable tendency to treat their teachers like the help. During registration, one young woman slouched into Julia's office and draped herself across the desk, smacking a piece of chewing gum. "Well, what have you got to offer?" she demanded. Julia drew herself up and retorted, "Not a damn thing to you, my dear." [90]

Julia led tutorials on the work of her white male contemporaries: Theodore Dreiser, Sinclair Lewis, Sherwood Anderson, John Dos Passos, Ernest Hemingway, William Faulkner, and Thomas Mann. No women writers were included in the syllabus, although her pupils were all female. Writing, she told them, was "a waste of time" because "everything has already been said."[91]

The new green Ford provided some relief, but Julia was terrified of driving in the snow. Late one night her car jumped an embankment and sputtered out in an icy field. Julia managed to restart it and find a path back to the road, but the incident shook her up so badly that she stopped driving alone.[92]

Among her pupils was Marion Hepburn, sister to the famous Katharine. Julia and Marion hit it off, and Julia invited the younger woman to spend her Christmas holidays at Lang Syne. Marion accepted. Willie, who had come up to drive them home, found Julia in bed with the flu.

The semester ended on a sour note when Irving and Helene left for the Bahamas without saying good-bye. Julia was fit to be tied. She claimed that Irving had been rude to Willie, which was all but inexcusable after Willie had been so kind to him the summer before. But that was not really why she was upset. Irving had told her that he and Helene were trying to have a baby.

The islands worked their magic. Helene got pregnant, and Irving belatedly took Frances's advice and managed to marry her secretly. Julia found it hard to act gracious when Irving told her the news. "With a baby to fill . . . your already full days, you'll never be going anywhere again except for health's sake, or work's sake," she warned.[93] She berated him for sounding like a whiner when he complained about his domestic burdens. "What a paradox you are, Irving," she scolded in March. "Lovable enough to charm the birds out of the trees and bad-tempered enough to have your throat slit at least once every week. I commend to you Dale Carnegie's book 'How to Win Friends and Influence People.' You and I should not only read it but study it and apply its ideas. Otherwise we'll wake up some fine morning and find ourselves friendless and maybe in a worse plight."[94]

They were no longer as much alike as Julia pretended. In fact, the eleven-year difference in their ages was becoming a chasm. Irving was juggling several careers — writing, teaching, and screenwriting. And whether she admitted it or not, Julia had all but retired. Irving was expecting his first child, Julia her first grandchild.

On April 19, 1937, Frida Peterkin gave birth to a son, William George Peterkin III. Julia wrote Irving the news. "You should see my little grandson. A queer stranger who keeps the whole Barrow household intent on his comfort yet is indifferent to all the attention he receives except when meal-time comes. I see no resemblance to anyone I know in his tiny features or his thick and too-long black hair which needs a barber's scissors. . . . I hope he will like living at Lang Syne, and be my very good friend. I'll try hard to win him." [95]

Joseph Fineman was born at the end of October, three days before Julia's fifty-seventh birthday. As Irving drifted away into fatherhood, Julia's threats grew ever more violent. "Maybe I'll induce the Ku Klux to tar and feather you; maybe I'll start writing dreadful anonymous letters about you to the *Trustees,* maybe I'll get somebody to burn up your house and kidnap your baby; maybe I'll find some nice man who will win Helene from you," she railed when he displeased her. [96] Julia was no more serious, of course, than when she had threatened to poison Irving's girlfriends or "scald" him for misbehavior. [97] But times had changed, and Irving was not amused by references to anti-Semitic violence.

By Christmas, Julia had recovered enough to hope that Irving's baby would be "a joy, a hope, a comfort, consolation, that makes up for all other lacks" — including, presumably, the lack of her own company. When Irving proposed meeting her in New York, she turned him down. The city seemed "like some enormous traction engine . . . that grinds and grinds people, anything that comes near its maw." [98] She resigned from the faculty of Bread Loaf and the editorial board of the Literary Guild, cutting her last ties to power in the world of ideas.

She said she was embarking on "a new cycle of living." In reality, she was coming back to the old Julia, who cared more about what her neighbors said than about book reviews and love affairs. "I tremble when I think of what might have been," she told Irving, speaking of both her writing and her sex life. "I've been spared so many consequences that my own stupidity might have brought about." [99]

Willie Peterkin was failing. Every few weeks brought another illness — malaria, pneumonia, kidney failure — each more frightening than the last. On Christmas Day 1937, Julia cooked her own dinner and ate it alone at the kitchen table. The faithful Wallace Heyward had taken a job cooking for work crews on the Santee-Cooper project, a "needless [government] undertaking," as Julia saw it, to "make miles of our great swamp into two enormous lakes" at a cost of $37.5 million. The project destroyed thousands of acres of hardwood forest and created hundreds of attractive jobs that "swallow[ed] up" the labor force. [100]

There were still more than a hundred black adults living on Lang

Syne, and at least ninety-six children.[101] "The cotton fields are a mass of bloom, the corn hangs heavy ears down from the stalks, the pigs and cattle thrive on lush pastures," Julia wrote to Tom Foster in July 1938. "The blacks 'shout' and sing for hours at a time."[102] But she had very little to do with the lives of those in the Quarters. She tried to view the change as a liberation, and in some ways it was. There were fewer people to pay at the end of the week, fewer who asked for help. "If I'd disappear from this earth it would make no real difference at all except to about two people who would have to readjust themselves to not having me answer when they call," she wrote cheerfully to Irving.[103]

Even Bill was threatening to leave. He talked about selling life insurance and interviewed for a job as farm manager on the Biltmore estate near Asheville, North Carolina.[104] In the end, he stayed close to his mother's doorstep, but the possibility of his departure was deeply unsettling to her.

Julia no longer wrote much in her letters about the plantation and its people — instead, she focused on books and ideas, on weddings and birthdays, the baby, her own activities. "We feel quite urban now with a power line and with paved roads and a moving picture house right in St. Matthews, only ten miles away," she wrote.[105] She poured all her creative energy into gentrified rural pursuits — raising sheep, breeding turkeys, making scuppernong wine. She redecorated the house from top to bottom and updated her wardrobe. And just as she had when she was a small child striving to please her grandfather, Julia made endless lists of ways to improve her character.

"More and more, I live to myself, keep to simple things, guard my peace," she informed Irving.[106] "New York and Bennington seem very far away. I can hardly remember either place."[107] Even so, she was hardly a hermit. In February 1938, Katharine and Marion Hepburn and their mother arrived to spend a week at Lang Syne. Friends and neighbors angled for invitations and drove by the farm looking hopeful. Julia took to Katharine at once, calling her "delightful, a perfect guest, simple, gentle, sensitive, intelligent." But she loathed Mrs. Hepburn, who was famous in her own right as a suffragist and, more recently, an outspoken advocate of birth control. Irving had once mentioned that Marion's mother reminded him of Julia. "Never have I met anyone who seemed more unlike what I think I am," Julia protested after a long weekend of being upstaged. "The father must surely be the parent who brought up those charming, good-mannered daughters, *not* this silly conceited woman. If I thought I were like her, I'd run jump out of the nearest window." [108]

At the end of the school year in 1938, Irving quit his job at Bennington and moved his family to Hollywood. Julia applauded his decision, yet carped behind his back to Thomas Foster that he was like most Jews in inviting punishment by "expecting and overly resenting" it.[109] Certainly Fineman had a tendency toward self-pity, a trait Julia had sometimes mocked and more often encouraged. But now he was almost paralyzed with horror at what was happening in Nazi Germany, and her irritable attempts to snap him out of it were tactless, to say the least. "Write to me whether or not I answer your letters, else I'll start a great anti-Jewish movement in these U.S. and select you as my personal target for mayhem, now that you've told me what mayhem is," she razzed him, recommending a healthy, middle-class routine as a remedy for his despair. "Be good, stop having colds. You eat too much. Watch your front too. Quit being so damned serious. Life is good. What if people are evil? You don't have to think about the bad ones so long as the good ones are," she wrote with a naive optimism belied by what was happening both at home and abroad.[110]

Her own life had narrowed to a vigil at Willie's bedside. "There's a strange loneliness about being in trouble, and also miserable selfishness," she reflected.[111] In October, Willie was admitted to the hospital, though his doctors held out little hope. For a few weeks he seemed better to Julia, and she thought he might recover. But on the day before Thanksgiving 1938, William George Peterkin died.

Julia was struck, she later recalled, with a bone-chilling realization — "I no longer come *first* with anybody." [112] It was true. Her son and her lover had started families of their own, edging her out of their lives. The plantation, once her private domain, was becoming a mechanized modern farm. She was no longer a writer, no longer a wife. Julia's loneliness — and selfishness — deepened.

CHAPTER 15

A Great White Column

S cores of people showed up at Willie's funeral. Some came to mourn, some to pay their respects, and some simply to mark the passing of "Cap'n," who had owned the fields as far as they could see and half the businesses in Fort Motte. One by one, they came up to tell Julia about things Willie had done for them. She heard from the widowed sisters and sisters-in-law he had supported, the nephews and brothers-in-law he had hired in hard times, the employees to whom he had loaned money and furnished credit, and the friends who had counted on him for advice.[1] Not so long ago, Julia had made fun of women who forgot their husbands' faults the minute they were widowed.[2] Now she was one of them. Willie became her hero, the perfect southern gentleman. She talked about his strength and integrity, his generosity and wisdom. He "stood between me and the hard things," she told Hudson Strode.[3]

Julia hated living alone. Shortly after the funeral she began walking across the fields to Belle Stuckey's house every morning. She always protested that she could only stay a minute, but Belle fed her breakfast, persuaded her to stay for lunch, and invited her to dinner. Before long she was staying all night, just as Belle had done when she changed families so many years before. "She's as good to me as any daughter could be," Julia told her cousin.[4]

Bill and Frida were another matter — their lives seemed out of control. Julia was suspicious of their friends, who were part of what was known at the time as a very "fast" crowd.[5] Frida, once a champion tennis player, had been depressed and irritable since William's birth and had gained a lot of weight. Twenty cocker spaniels had the run of the house; Frida watered them in an antique silver punchbowl. Bill took his father's death hard and turned to the bottle for solace. One day Frida showed up at Belle's kitchen door and demanded to see Julia. "Your son is drinking too much," she said.[6]

It was all more than Julia could handle. She didn't feel capable of coping with a depressed daughter-in-law, an alcoholic son, and a normal toddler on top of her own widowhood. She wanted to be taken care of, sheltered. She looked at the children of other women her age and felt she had been cheated.[7]

Julia's life as a widow seemed "queer and disturbed," with no focus except the crops.[8] She eventually moved back into her own house, but it was a rare occasion when she walked across the driveway to visit Bill and Frida.[9] She socialized mostly with wealthy friends who were content to make harmless small talk.

The world was losing interest in her doings; she found that she could go almost anywhere without making the news. When she attended the premiere of *Gone with the Wind*, in December 1939, she attracted little attention. She was glad to have her privacy back, but a little resentful, too. "I hate crowds," she complained to her friend Margaret Behrend, "and these crowds have seemed actually demented."[10] The crowds, of course, were cheering Margaret Mitchell, the world's new favorite southern writer.

Julia seemed to be heading for a tranquil old age out of the public eye, but on September 10, 1941, a tragedy laid her life open to the cold judgment of strangers. Like Helen West and Alma Ingraham, Frida Peterkin took her own life. Her suicide completed Julia's metamorphosis from secret-teller to secret-keeper, shattering the family circle so completely that Julia would feel compelled to defend Bill and William against the world. It removed the possibility that Julia herself would ever commit suicide. And it gave the white South Carolinians who had hated her books a final excuse to demonize her.

The days leading up to Frida's death were fevered and anxious. For what seemed like an eternity, America had been teetering on the brink of entering the European war and turning it into a world war. On September 5, a United States submarine escorting a British supply convoy was fired on by a German submarine. President Roosevelt compared the German nation to a rattlesnake poised to strike. The headlines loomed huge and black. People worried about bombing raids, Nazi spies, and surprise attacks, yet life went on as usual. There was a sense that something terrible was about to happen, and nothing to do but wait for it.

On the night of September 9, 1941, Bill Peterkin drove to Orangeburg to attend a meeting of the Lions Club. He returned home to find his wife in tears, clutching a loaded shotgun. She sobbed that someone had tried to break in and had slashed one of the window screens. Frida was supposed to leave the next morning for her parents' summer home near Hendersonville, North Carolina; now she insisted that she could not go. Bill called Mrs. Barrow to cancel the trip.

Early the next morning, he went out before breakfast to watch his men weigh cotton. When he returned, he couldn't find Frida. He asked the maid, Beulah Wine, if she had seen her; Beulah said she thought she had heard footsteps going up the stairs. He climbed up to the attic and saw a shape swinging from the rafters.

Bill screamed. Julia heard him and came running across the driveway. He pulled out his pocketknife and cut down the body, but Frida was dead.[11] He ran downstairs to look for William and found him eating crackers in his crib.

Bill called a friend, Murray Linnett, who in turn called the coroner. Bill and Murray tore the house apart looking for a suicide note. Instead, they found empty gin bottles, stashed in cupboards, behind rows of books, in every nook and cranny. Linnett looked under Frida's mattress and found a bottle of pills.

The news spread like wildfire. The question on everyone's lips, of course, was why Frida had done it. Why would the mother of a young child take her own life? Remembering Julia's Hedda Gabler, the gossips had a field day. People had *seen* Julia Peterkin convince a man to commit suicide, right there on the stage in Columbia. Julia was known to have been on the outs with Frida. It was a short step to the shocking conclusion that Julia had driven Frida to kill herself.

Another theory also blamed Julia, but in a more roundabout and typically southern way. It traced the tragedy to Julia's permissive racial and sexual attitudes. When Bill turned sixteen, the story went, his mother had presented him with a beautiful mulatto concubine to serve his sexual needs. The woman was dismissed when he married Frida. But Bill had fallen in love with his mistress, and he continued to see her. Frida killed herself because she had discovered their liaison.[12]

These stories were false, and Julia could have cleared her name simply by telling the truth: Frida had become addicted to alcohol and morphine. She may have started taking opiates to treat postpartum depression. People who encountered her after William's birth recall that she was withdrawn and uncommunicative, "almost catatonic."[13] But however she started, and for whatever reason, Frida seems to have ended up hooked on black-market morphine.

At one time, women were routinely given the opiate laudanum by their family doctors to treat "female trouble" and other ills. Medical attitudes changed in the 1920s and 1930s, and the opium trade was criminalized. There was a thriving underworld dedicated to supplying opiates, and morphine was easy to obtain, even in small towns. But when the outbreak of World War II cut off most of the major smuggling routes, the price went through the roof. By September 1941, all drugs derived from opium were fiendishly expensive and almost unobtainable.[14] No one will ever know for sure what caused Frida to kill herself. But morphine and alcohol withdrawal can cause depression, delirium, and finally suicide.

Julia would never forgive or forget the indignities of the next few days. Carloads of sightseers cruised through the driveway, craning their necks at the attic windows. The Episcopal priest refused to perform a funeral because Frida was a suicide. Frida's parents hired a private detective to look into her death. A local lawyer came to warn Bill that he was being followed. Federal narcotics agents arrived to investigate, though no charges were ever filed. Bill would spend the rest of his life trying to figure out what happened the night before his wife's death. Had someone really been harassing her? In the end, he concluded that the slashed screen had been cut from inside.[15]

Angry, hurt, and embarrassed as she was, Julia now had a purpose in life: mothering "the two Williams."[16] She clapped the shutters on her old life and turned her hand to the task. She explained as little as possible about Frida's death, even to her closest friends. Carl Sandburg heard about the tragedy more than a year after it occurred, from their mutual friend Fanny Butcher. "What I thought mostly was that there were no words and no angle of philosophy that you didn't already have at hand — but I would have liked to sit in silence or to walk in fog or mist with you," he wrote.[17]

Julia lavished on motherless William the fierce attention she had once spent on other men. Her letters to friends were of nothing but William — his toys, his friends, his illnesses. He was never allowed to play outside alone for fear that he would be kidnapped. She warned Bill constantly that he must not remarry because stepmothers were the worst plague on earth.[18]

Pearl Harbor sealed Julia in her isolation. Gasoline and tire rationing kept her close to home. An air force bombing range was set up near Murrells Inlet, and her summer cottage was hit by a stray shell. Had she been so inclined, she could have found abundant material for another novel; the Second World War, even more than the first, brought major changes to the plantation. The cabins emptied as black men joined the service, their wives got monthly checks, and single women left to take jobs in the defense industries. Faced with an acute shortage of labor, Bill shifted most of his land into hog production. Julia worried that he would be drafted and she would be left alone.[19] She no longer knew how to build fictional worlds that could help her transcend the real one.

"Time has grayed our heads, lined our faces, machines and fuel-oil fumes scent the fields, the grave-yard is larger," she wrote to Carl Sandburg.[20] Mary Weeks died in 1944, Henry Bellamann and Dr. Barrow in 1945.[21] Nineteen forty-six claimed Robert Adams and Lyle Saxon.[22] Like his father before him, William was sent off to boarding school. After almost four decades as a "practitioner," Laura Schneider renounced Christian Science and moved to Los Angeles, where she took up silversmithing and resumed her maiden name.[23] Irving Fineman was also in Los Angeles, and another old friend was in Carmel. Julia dreamed of going out West for a visit but felt harnessed to the farm.

She viewed her life as a series of boxes in which she had been confined. "When a compartment is filled," she wrote to Fineman in 1944, "it seems to shut up tight and shut us out, and all the others who were part of our days are separated from us because we are forced into another compartment where we flounder around until we adjust ourselves to utterly different circumstances and companions." People from other times occasionally wandered into her present life for brief, surreal visits, reminding her of the time when she "went to literary teas in N.Y.

and really believed publishers were honest." [24] Now the family and the farm were all that mattered.

The stillness Julia had conspired to cheat crept back to settle in the corners. William was away for most of the year; the cabins in the Quarters were emptying. Living alone in the Big House at Lang Syne, Julia and Bill behaved like an old married couple, bickering over every decision.

Julia would never recover her "social group" or find happiness in conformity. Most of the neighbors regarded her as eccentric, aloof, and even a little frightening. People remembered that she had once been famous — not so much because they had read her books as because she had famous friends. Everyone knew she had dined at the White House and had something to do with Ethel Barrymore. Katharine Hepburn's visit was something to tell the grandchildren about. Carl Sandburg still showed up occasionally, and his name, if not his poetry, was well known.[25] These associations gave Julia a certain luster, the patina of old brass. She cultivated a few young men with artistic interests and socialized with Bill's friends.[26] But no important new relationships kindled; no new sparks were struck.

The day William turned seventeen he enlisted in the navy. After training in Great Lakes, Michigan, he was posted to Hawaii. With his son grown up and gone away, Bill Peterkin, now fifty-two years old, embarked on a new life. Both he and his mother were much involved with the Murrells Inlet Protective Association, an environmental group formed to oppose coastal dredging. Bill's cousin, twenty-eight-year-old Genevieve "Sister" Chandler, was serving as the treasurer, and he began dropping by to give her a lift to meetings. The youngest daughter of Julia's second cousin, Genevieve had spent her childhood tagging along while her widowed mother, Genevieve Willcox Chandler, recorded Gullah songs and stories for the Federal Writers' Project. Now an employee of the Georgetown County Library, Sister had served overseas during the occupation after World War II and was passionate about local politics.

Soon Bill was materializing several times a week, ostensibly to discuss the progress of several lawsuits filed by the association. Genevieve found herself falling in love, though she knew Bill had more than one girlfriend. The situation distressed her. One day she told Bill that she was planning to move to Alaska. Bill, who had never even kissed her, proposed. Genevieve accepted.

Julia saw no reason why Bill should marry again. "My son will be an old man while you are still a young woman," she reminded Genevieve. "If you marry him, your life will end in tragedy. Bill is an alcoholic." [27] An acquaintance warned Genevieve that "that old woman" — Julia — would make her life a misery. An elderly man puzzled her by hoping she wouldn't "take the dope." Her sister, June Hora, wept. Belle Stuckey accused Bill of being in his second childhood. Only Mrs. Chandler was delighted. "He's the only man who's good enough for you," she told her daughter.[28]

One Monday morning in October, as Genevieve was leaving for work, Bill drove up to her house and said, "Sister, I've decided we're going to get married today! I'm not going to stand up and take the vows in front of people who can't be happy about it." They located a minister, invited Mrs. Chandler and Genevieve's roommate to serve as witnesses, and took their vows at Prince George Church. Then they headed for Lang Syne to break the news to Julia.

When they arrived, she was standing on the porch, staring grimly into the distance. The minister who performed the ceremony had called to see if the newlyweds had arrived safely. Genevieve burst out of the car and rushed up to hug her. Julia stood rigid, her arms at her sides, refusing to hug her back. Genevieve glanced up at the massive pillars behind her. Julia, it seemed to her, was "like a great white column." [29] Bill, attempting to break the ice, suggested they go for a ride. Without a word, Julia swept past Genevieve and took her accustomed place in the front seat, next to Bill. It was a harbinger of things to come.

Bill and Genevieve went back to Murrells Inlet so that Genevieve could serve out her notice at the library. When William came home on leave a couple of weeks later, the family gathered at Lang Syne. William took his father aside to tell him that he, too, was married, to Helen Inabinet, his childhood sweetheart from St. Matthews.

Julia was outraged. She summoned Belle Stuckey, who had moved to Columbia, and gathered the family around her. William and Helen were too young to get married, she said, and Bill must have the wedding annulled. Belle blamed Genevieve. "If you hadn't married his father, William never would have done this," she hissed. Julia tried to enlist Genevieve's sympathies, arguing that she must convince Bill to save William from a terrible mistake.

Finally Bill drew himself up and announced, "I want you both to remember that William is *my* son. I asked him last night when he had decided to marry Helen and he said 'in the fourth grade.' I will never interfere with a love that has been going on that long." Julia and Belle subsided. Bill sent William to bring his bride home.[30]

William and Helen went back to Hawaii with Bill's blessing, if not Julia's. In mid-November, Bill and Genevieve moved into the Big House with Julia. Bill had a home of his own, just across the lawn, but he had not lived in it since Frida died there, fifteen years earlier.

Julia did her best to make Bill's new wife uncomfortable. Though Genevieve was a devout Methodist, Bill and Julia, neither of whom ever went to church, convinced her to join the Episcopal church so that she and Bill would belong to the same denomination. Genevieve dutifully took instruction and set about preparing herself for the move. On the day before her confirmation, she, Julia, and Bill were seated with a table full of out-of-town guests. Julia suddenly announced that Genevieve was about to be confirmed. "Everyone who has read Freud knows," she continued, "that when a young woman gets interested in religion, either her sex life is lacking or there is a handsome young priest involved." Bill banged his knife on the table but did not say a word. Genevieve bit her tongue. She decided her mother-in-law was testing her, and she re-solved to make the grade.

Consistency had never been Julia's strong suit, and in old age she was shameless about reversing herself. "Now, Sister, it is every woman's pre-rogative to name her own child," she declared when Genevieve told her she was expecting. "You must be thinking about names." Lying in the hospital bed after delivering her son, whom she intended to call James Clark Peterkin after a relative she and Bill had in common, Genevieve looked up to see Julia looming over her. "Sister, your little boy will be named James Preston Peterkin," she announced. And so he was.[31]

Jim was what they used to call a "blue baby," and life at Lang Syne revolved around keeping him healthy. Julia was too unwell herself to carry much of the load, but she loved to hold and feed baby Jim.

William and Helen had a baby, too, Julia Elfrida Peterkin. When William was discharged from the navy, they all came home to Lang Syne. Soon Helen was expecting again. She produced a son and heir in 1957, William George Peterkin IV. While the little house across the driveway stood empty, everyone crowded into the Big House. It was a tight fit for seven people who did not always get along. Eventually Genevieve managed to convince Bill that they should move into the little house.

Tensions eased when the families spread out, but Julia continued to bait the younger women and play the households against each other. "It was divide and conquer in that family," Helen remembered. If Helen hurt Julia's feelings, she was off across the yard complaining to Sister and Bill. If Genevieve annoyed her by being a softhearted "fool," she ran to Helen and William for confirmation. She complained about all of them to Belle, who always took her side.[32]

But however much Julia chafed at their presence, Genevieve and Helen brought children and laughter back into her life. During afternoons spent sitting on a protected corner of the porch, they prompted her to reminisce. Sometimes Julia hinted at a racy past. Displaying the Oriental prints Carl Sandburg had sent to her, she pointed to two women playing tug-o-war with a string threaded through a mushroom. "That mushroom represents a penis," she told the incredulous Genevieve. She brought out Irving Fineman's pastel drawing of a naked red-haired woman. The artist, she said, had insulted her by implying that she was the subject. Sometimes she slipped money to unwed pregnant white girls through a minister and her hairdresser.[33]

Bill phased out cotton in favor of cattle, hogs, soybeans, millet, corn, and wheat. Hired crop dusters applied fertilizers and insecticides; there wasn't a mule on the place. Less than a dozen black men were employed in the fields to drive the trucks and tractors. When the government began offering subsidies through the Soil Bank to let the land lie fallow, Julia suggested they join. Bill insisted that they must continue farming in order to provide jobs. Occasionally Julia threatened to sell the farm, though she turned down several good offers. Helen felt that her talk about selling was just a way of keeping the whip hand.[34]

Trapped at home by failing health, Julia held her family hostage. Whenever William and Helen or Bill and Genevieve accepted an invitation, she was certain to take sick. Eventually they stopped going out. Bill bought a television set so that Julia could while away the hours. Elizabeth Darby, Willie's old flame, came over every afternoon to play Scrabble. On Thursdays, when Perry Como was on, she brought her suitcase and stayed overnight.

Julia always watched the news, and what she saw distressed her. On July 12, 1947, Judge J. Waties Waring had ruled that South Carolina must allow blacks to vote in primary elections. In 1950 came *Briggs v. Elliott*, a legal challenge to the concept of "separate but equal" established by *Plessy v. Ferguson* in 1896. Harry Briggs and his wife, Liza, filed suit on behalf of their five children, demanding that black schools in Clarendon County, South Carolina, be brought up to the standards of white schools. Attempting to head off integration, the governor, James F.

Byrnes, pushed through a $75 million bond issue to upgrade the state's black schools. He also convinced the legislature to authorize selling the public schools so that they could be reorganized as private institutions. *Briggs v. Elliott* was argued by Thurgood Marshall in Summerton, the town where Julia's sister Marian lived. In a two-to-one decision, the United States district court in Clarendon County upheld the school district's right to maintain separate schools. "Segregation is *per se* inequality," wrote Judge Waring, the lone dissenting voice. "It "must go and go now."[35] Marshall appealed the case to the Supreme Court, but in 1952, *Briggs v. Elliot* was remanded to the United States district court, from which Judge Waring had retired. The court ruled that Clarendon County had made adequate progress toward equalization. Marshall again appealed the case, and this time *Briggs v. Elliot* was tied in with four other desegregation suits brought by the NAACP Legal Defense and Educational Fund and heard as *Brown v. Board of Education.* On May 17, 1954, the Supreme Court decreed that school segregation was unconstitutional.[36]

Though one would hardly guess it from reading her books, Julia Peterkin was terrified of racial integration. She fretted that "outside instigators" were coming into the area posing as Bible salesmen and "stirring up unpleasantness among the people."[37] "Desegregation will cause trouble here," she wrote to Margaret Behrend in a shaky hand in 1956. "Neither race wants it."[38] The idea that her grandchildren might go to school with blacks was enough to make her cringe.[39] When she dropped her art, she dropped her sympathy for those who were oppressed. Julia lived out her last years indignant at the way the world had changed.

At last Julia's heart "grew tired of its work"; she could no longer climb the stairs. "I got out all your books," she wrote to Carl Sandburg one gloomy day, "looked at them, then built up a fire and read poems and poems, many more than once. Now I no longer feel apart from the world, shut away by the wet torrents outside."[40] But shut away she was, and largely by her own choice.

Julia was admitted to the Orangeburg hospital in February 1961, suffering from congestive heart failure. She came home for a few weeks, then had a relapse and returned. On August 1, she fell into a coma.

Bill was so unnerved by the prospect of losing his mother that he fulfilled one of her direst predictions: he became an alcoholic. In early August, he stooped to pick up a newspaper and pinched his sciatic nerve. He refused to go to the Orangeburg hospital for treatment because his mother was "dying there." Instead, he took to his bed and consumed large doses of Demerol. Early in the morning of August 10, Bill agreed to be admitted to the hospital. Julia died that afternoon without regaining consciousness.[41]

Unlike Willie's, Julia's was a small funeral, a hastily arranged graveside service in the Peterkin plot across from the Episcopal church. Few came to bid her good-bye. Ashleigh and Leah Mood were there, and Marian Burgess, but not Laura. Genevieve, Helen, and William, but not Bill, who had been sedated and put in traction. As was customary, the few black mourners stood outside the iron railing. The surrounding fields, planted in soybeans, shimmered in the heat.

Frida's body lay to Julia's right; Willie's to her left. Captain James Alexander Peterkin was nearby, resting under a patrician granite stone along with his wife, Agenora. All the Peterkin brothers were there, and the enigmatic James Crouch.

Mary Weeks and Lavinia Berry had been buried on Lang Syne, the place both regarded as home. Julia, however, was not. She was laid to rest neither on the plantation nor in the churchyard, but in a small enclosed space with her family.

In her prime, Julia had been strong and brave, a prophet who challenged white Southerners to confront their terrible hypocrisy. Her later life was less than heroic, and she leaves us with a disturbing paradox — a great artist who turned her back on everything she had stood for. Yet even if she could not stay true to her vision, we should hold onto it and remember her at her most daring. What was pain for her is art for us. Her writing glows and wounds with the flame of truth, timeless in its spare, steely elegance.

Epilogue

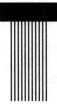rue to the old Indian woman's prophesy, and Vinner's, too, it was a strong woman who led Lang Syne into the era of integration. At great risk to herself and her family, Genevieve Chandler Peterkin campaigned for black voter registration and welcomed civil rights organizers to the plantation. She made sure that the few farm laborers who remained had window screens, modern kitchens, and bathrooms in their houses, and that their medical bills and burial expenses were paid. And she helped Bill see it as cause for rejoicing when someone who had once worked the Lang Syne cotton fields dropped by on his way to march with Jesse Jackson in Charleston.

Bill and Genevieve's son, Jim, was killed in a sailing accident off the coast of North Carolina when he was twenty years old. Wallace Heyward returned to his home in Murrells Inlet, where he continued to work for

Genevieve and Bill. He died of congestive heart failure on January 7, 1976, and was buried at Heaven's Gate Church. Bill and Genevieve retired to Murrells Inlet, and Bill died there in 1982.

Before they divorced in 1986, William and Helen Peterkin had three more daughters — Amy, Emily, and Laura. William remarried and now raises cotton and soybeans on Lang Syne plantation with his son, William George Peterkin IV. Helen Peterkin died of stomach cancer in 1988.

Irving Fineman divorced Helene after a long and acrimonious separation. After Julia's death, he tried to interest several publishers in producing a volume of her letters. He was told that no one was interested. But his own account of his affair with Julia was eventually made into a movie. In the late 1930s, he had written a screenplay based on *Lovers Must Learn.* A major studio bought the script, and every few years someone would take it out of a drawer, change the location, update the dialogue — and then shelve it again. In 1962, the year after Julia died, it was finally filmed as *Rome Adventure,* starring Suzanne Pleshette and Troy Donahue. Angie Dickinson — better known for her role as television's *Police Woman* — played the red-haired, cigarette-smoking, bitter vamp based on Julia Peterkin.

Late in life, Irving moved in with the writer Esther Hirschbein, widow of the noted playwright Peretz Hirschbein. Irving died in 1976 at a military hospital in Myrtle Beach, only a few miles north of Julia's beloved summer home in Murrells Inlet.

Descendants of the people who inspired Julia's books have their own tales to tell. Mary Weeks's grandson, William Henry Seabrook, is writing a memoir of life at Lang Syne; her great-great-nephew, Jackie Whitmore, is researching the family tree. By a strange chance, the day Jackie and I met was the day novelist Alex Haley died. As Jackie told stories about his remarkable clan — people I thought I knew well — I felt that I was talking to the man who could write the next *Roots.* For Jackie, as for many of his kin, Julia Peterkin's novels are disturbing because they rearrange the life stories of recognizable people. Yet he appreciates the books as a literary legacy of the sort few African American families have the luxury of accepting or repudiating.

Blue Brook plantation is a country of the mind, as real and unreal as Faulkner's Yoknapatawpha, Joyce's Dublin, or Shakespeare's London. The characters who inhabit it have lives of their own, apart from what actually happened. Some will say that Julia Peterkin stole her stories from people who possessed little else. But the world's great novelists have always been thieves who give us back ourselves.

Afterword: Searching for Julia

esearching this book was a great adventure that led me down many roads. Much of what has been written about Julia Peterkin is at best only half the truth, and Peterkin destroyed most of the thousands of letters she received during her lifetime. The members of her family were averse to writing things down, and the black people she described so expressively were, for the most part, illiterate. So whether or not she planned it that way, Julia's account of many events is all that survives, and her literary voice is so compelling that it resists contradiction.

Thomas Landess's 1976 biography, published as part of the Twayne American Authors series, proved a reliable guide to the milestones of Peterkin's public life, but I knew from the start that to dig any deeper, I would have to talk to people who had known her. There was a sense of urgency in my quest— Peterkin would have been 108 the year I began, and every month there were fewer people alive who could tell me what she was like. I started with Julia's daughter-in-law, Genevieve Peterkin, who is related by blood as well as by marriage to the Moods and the Peterkins. Genevieve shared with me an extraordinary fund of family stories and personal observations. Having decided that a biography was necessary, and that I was the one to write it, Genevieve never flinched or shirked, even when I made discoveries that distressed her. For years I double-checked every fact she told me, always to discover that her memory was almost photographic.

Genevieve put me in touch with Julia's surviving friends and relatives — Helen Peterkin, Beatrice Jefferson Stubbs, and Elizabeth Boatwright Coker, among others. She took me to see Julia Peterkin's nieces, Ann Neeley, Marian Barksdale, and Margaret Buie, who gave me Florence Mulligan's heartbreaking account of the death of Alma Mood along with a tape of their mother, Marian Mood Burgess, reminiscing about her childhood. They even let me ransack the top shelves of their closets in a fruitless search for Julia's wedding gown.

Mr. and Mrs. William G. Peterkin III graciously indulged my need to visit and revisit Lang Syne plantation. William identified family photographs, helped me understand what his beloved grandmother was like in old age, and tramped through many a snake-infested thicket to show me which buildings had stood where.

Meanwhile, I read everything I could find about the period and rounded up letters from numerous libraries. Noel Polk and Harlan Greene, fellow scholars who had each done research toward a biography of Peterkin, generously passed on the fruits of their labor, sparing me months if not years of searching. Then came a bolt from the blue. In the spring of 1988, I placed a query in the *New York Times Book Review* asking readers to respond with any information they had about Julia Peterkin. Almost immediately, I received a letter from Carolyn A. Davis, a librarian at Syracuse University, who asked if I would be interested in seeing hundreds of letters from Peterkin to Irving Fineman. I called Genevieve Peterkin to ask if Julia had ever mentioned anyone named Fineman. She thought for a minute and then said yes — he was the beautiful almond-eyed young man in Julia's box of photographs.

"Please send me copies of the letters as soon as possible," I wrote to Ms. Davis. She warned me that there were a lot. I said I didn't care. So she assigned a graduate student to the monumental task of copying the correspondence. Every few weeks a big box would arrive, filled with Julia Peterkin. Awaiting the birth of my daughter, Olivia, I lived through a decade of Peterkin's life as if it had been my own. I fell in love with Irving Fineman and hoped that Julia would run away with him, though I knew very well that she had not, and that he was not the kind of man to whom I would trust my heart. I suffered through her depressions, shared her triumphs, and even tried to imitate her style. With a grant from the National Endowment for the Humanities, I was eventually able to go to Syracuse and search the collection for other clues.

The Peterkin family had known nothing of Julia's affair with Fineman, and they were dismayed to learn that hundreds of her private love letters were housed in a public institution. Understandably, they would have preferred that her secrets stay secret forever. Yet they overcame their reservations to help me sort through the mass of information and disinformation.

By 1992 I had assembled twelve bulging file drawers of material about Peterkin's life and work. Still, a huge piece of the puzzle was missing — I had not managed to find anyone who could tell me much about Mary Weeks, Anaky Bryant, Lavinia Berry, and their kin. Then my friend Ted Rosengarten handed me a phone number for a college student named Jackie Whitmore who had approached him at a conference. I picked up the phone at ten that night, and didn't put it down until four the next morning.

It was clear to me in the first five minutes that Jackie was the real thing. We knew all the same people, though many of them had been dead for fifty years or more. I must have reeled off a hundred questions raised by Peterkin's writings; Jackie either knew the answers or promised to find out. He leaped up to consult a family tree on his wall that went back to Anaky and Frank Bryant. Some of the things he volunteered took my breath away. His grandmother was Lucinda Jackson, known to her friends as "Sing." The little girl who lost her eye to a rooster had died just the year before. Mary Weeks had left the plantation because of her daughter's anger over a newspaper photograph.

Jackie asked me questions, too. He had been trying — all his life, it seemed — to find out more about his family and the white woman who had turned them into characters in her fiction. I told him I was fairly sure that in her first drafts, Peterkin tended to use real names and record incidents without embroidering them. It was only in later versions that art and disguise reshuffled events and identities.

"Who were Bessie and Essie?" I asked as the night wore on into morning. "Ooooh, girl — how you know about *Bessie and Essie?*" Jackie demanded. "Julia Peterkin wrote about them," I replied. And we were off down another path, unraveling mysteries that had troubled both of us. I told him what was in Julia's unpublished papers, and he told me what his relatives had been telling him for the last twenty-three years. When Jackie didn't know the answer to a question, he was always careful to say so.

In the weeks that followed, Jackie went with me to see Ella Weeks Walker, Mary Heyward, and William Henry Seabrook, and he generally asked the questions. He tried to talk his older relatives into speaking with me directly. When some of them refused, he took my questions and came back with answers. Thus, many of the notes that are credited to "JW" refer to what Jackie gleaned from other people in the course of our joint research.

We combed the graveyards around Lang Syne, noting who was buried where. A black man and a white woman driving around the countryside together raise eyebrows around Fort Motte, but we were so absorbed in our quest that we hardly noticed. Nor did we pay much attention to the weather, even when we stopped to visit an old woman in the sandhills who was watching tornado warnings on her television. In the cemetery behind the Methodist church described in *Roll, Jordan, Roll*, we discovered Jackie's great-grandmother's grave, which he had never seen. Jackie almost cried. We moved on to another church, Jerusalem Baptist. Suddenly the sky turned pewter gray and we heard a sound like a freight train. We ran for the car and took off in the direction of Fort Motte. I could barely see to drive. Twigs and pine cones were pelting down along with the rain. Out of the murk a sign appeared — BRIDGE OUT. A chasm spanned only by rusty girders loomed in front of us.

We turned around as it started to hail. Jackie was shouting, but I couldn't hear him. The pines that lined the side of the road seemed to be bending double. One came down just in front of us, and I slammed on the brakes. The hailstones looked as big as plums. Behind us was the broken bridge, in front the fallen pine. Jackie decided we should brave the storm and try to move the tree.

I should have known we couldn't do it. Having lived through the aftermath of Hurricane Hugo, I know the weight of trees. Yet when the hail slackened, we got out of the car and shoved. Nothing happened. We were trapped. Jackie explored the area and found a road leading into a muddy field. Maybe we could skirt the tree and come out on the other side.

We bumped into the field without incident and sloshed our way around the fallen tree. But then there was a problem. Ditch all the way.

No trace of another access road. There *was* a place where the ditch was shallow, a rut instead of a culvert. Somehow Jackie convinced me that we had to jump it.

My Honda teetered atop a mound of blood red clay. Jackie hopped out and tried to create traction. I was afraid the car would shift and crush him under the wheels, so I made him get back in. "Jackie," I said, "do you think Julia Peterkin is looking down and laughing?"

"No," he shot back. "You know she ain't. She is lookin' *up*."

"You need to get all of us in a room together and ask, 'How did you hear this?'" Helen Peterkin warned me in 1988. Death, distance, and divorce made it impossible to follow her advice, but I asked my most important sources to read this book in manuscript and point out my errors. Without exception, they reported being confronted by facets of Peterkin's life they had known nothing about.

Most of the people who spoke with me were careful to explain their blind spots and biases; I seldom felt that their revelations were motivated by anger or spite. If an important point was at stake, I tried to find at least two sources who agreed on the facts. When one source contradicted another, I have noted the variants.

Peterkin seldom dated her personal correspondence and manuscripts, but in many cases it is possible to attribute approximate dates on the basis of internal evidence (a letter that is obviously a reply to another, dated letter or which alludes to datable events) or external evidence (a dated newspaper clipping that was attached or enclosed). Irving Fineman preserved almost all of his correspondence with Peterkin in the original envelopes, hence I have used the date of the postmark as the date of the letter. H. L. Mencken dated Peterkin's letters by year, probably several decades later when he was at work on *My Life as Author and Editor*. Many of these dates, given in brackets, are clearly inaccurate.

Ten years ago, when I started this book, a friend warned me that writing full time is the loneliest work on earth. I have found it to be just the opposite. Without the cooperation of Genevieve Peterkin, William Peterkin, and Jackie Whitmore, Julia's story could not have been told. I am profoundly grateful to the three of them.

Many others have also given me help and encouragement.

John C. von Lehe introduced me to his mother, the irrepressible Agenora von Lehe, who told me about the family life of the Drakes and the Peterkins. William George Peterkin IV shared family letters and pages from Julia Peterkin's scrapbook. A. K. Darby reminisced about life in Fort Motte and described the relationship between his mother and William Peterkin. Beatrice Jefferson Stubbs showed me her late husband's papers and described her impressions of Julia and Julius Mood. Mr. and Mrs. Ashleigh Mood filled me in on Julia's relationship with her half-brother, also named Ashleigh Mood. Helen Peterkin told me about growing up in St. Matthews and living at Lang Syne. Muriel Barrow Bell was kind enough to answer questions about her mother, Elfrida DeRenne Barrow, and her sister Elfrida Peterkin.

Elizabeth Boatwright Coker helped me understand Elfrida Peterkin's death and Julia's reaction to it. Thomas Foster wrote to me at length in answer to my many questions about Julia's stays in Bennington and his at Lang Syne. Joseph C. Fineman provided insights into his father's past and his parents' marriage. Mary Heyward recalled Mary Weeks and the other members of her family. William Henry Seabrook let me peek at his autobiography in progress. Dallas Griffin sent me genealogical records about the Adams family. Ellsworth Grant wrote to me about Julia's relationship with his late wife, Marion Hepburn Grant. Jenny Hane and Julian and "Pally" Wiles showed me how cotton was and is farmed around Fort Motte. Faith Rehyer Jackson, Helen Rosa, Pamela Playter, Sally Graham Vann, and Irene Yates helped flesh out my picture of Julia Peterkin.

Steve Hoffius made my research at the South Carolina Historical Society easy and pleasant, pointing me to important sources I would not otherwise have discovered. James Meriwether gave me a copy of the Peterkin play "Boy Chillen." David Haward Bain sent material from the Bread Loaf Writers' Conference, including pictures of Julia and copies of the daily newsletter, "The Crumb." Panthea Broughton Fischer put me in touch with Noel Polk, who lived up to the highest ideals of scholarship by sharing his hard-won research. Clark Center provided information about Hudson Strode. Oakley H. Coburn allowed me to examine the manuscript of *Scarlet Sister Mary* at Wofford College in Spartanburg, South Carolina; and Herbert Hucks Jr., also of Wofford, tracked down information about the Mood and Archer families. Ted Phillips regaled me with ancient gossip and trusted me with priceless photographs.

Judith Keller, William Clift, David Featherstone, Charles Hagan, Weston Naif, and Ron Pen deepened my understanding of Doris Ulmann and her relationship with Jack Niles. Philip Jacobs was extremely generous with his research into the details of Ulmann's life and death, and kindly allowed me to include material from his biography-in-progress. Sally Bingham let me read her play about Ulmann and Peterkin, *The Darkness and the Light.*

Veronica Gerald showed me how Julia Peterkin should be read aloud and initiated me into the African American culture of coastal South Carolina. Hariett Watson alerted me to Julian Meade's diverting account of Peterkin in *Adam's Profession and Its Conquest by Eve.* Jim Harrison searched the alumni files at Converse College and provided me with copies of what he found. Thomas Johnson sent me his files on the elusive Isaac Weston. Penelope Niven talked with me about Carl Sandburg, Belinda Rathbone about Walker Evans. Patty Gross of the McClellanville Branch, Charleston County Library, patiently filled my many requests for obscure information.

Bruce Kellner read my first five chapters and set me straight on many points. Shari Benstock and the late Bernard Benstock combed university libraries wherever they roamed for signs of Julia Peterkin. I am indebted to them for locating the original script of Dan Reed's dramatization of *Scarlet Sister Mary,* and for many years of friendship and wise advice.

Though Peterkin's personal papers and her collection of Doris Ulmann's photographs were safely stored at the South Carolina Historical Society by 1989, one of my greatest fears during Hurricane Hugo was that the family pictures owned by Genevieve Peterkin would be damaged or destroyed. Huddled in a Columbia hotel room with the wind howling outside, I took comfort from the fact that Lanie Youngman had made copies of these irreplaceable visual documents. The originals, as it turned out, barely escaped the storm. Everything in Genevieve's creekside sitting room was swept out to sea, including her mother's paintings, first editions of Peterkin's books, and snapshots of her late son, Jim. By some miracle, the older family photographs turned up dry on a closet shelf. Spurred to belated action by the accident of their survival, Genevieve and I had Paige Sawyer make high-quality negatives of every image. Bernadette Humphrey printed many of the photographs reproduced here. She also took over my responsibilities at the McClellanville Arts Center at times when the book required all my attention.

Harlan Greene brought a novelist's eye to the revision of the manuscript, and Chas Joyner a historian's. Billy Dinwiddie started out as my adviser on medical issues and ended as one of my most perceptive readers. Dale Rosengarten has been a constant source of inspiration and encouragement.

My greatest thanks go to Ted Rosengarten and Celia Patterson, who read and critiqued the manuscript in its many incarnations. They pushed me to do my best to live up to the demands of a great subject. My editor, Malcolm Call, has taken numerous delays in stride, with the admirable attitude, so rare these days, that a better book is always worth extra time.

Jo Luquire mothered Olivia while I chased Julia Peterkin. My parents, Dr. and Mrs. Paul H. Millar Jr., provided support and encouragement even when it seemed that I might never finish. And without the love and sacrifice of my husband, Dwight, I probably never would have.

Key to Abbreviations

Interviews and Correspondence

AKD	A. K. Darby
AM	Ashleigh Mood
AvL	Agenora von Lehe
BJS	Beatrice Jefferson Stubbs
EBC	Elizabeth Boatwright Coker
EWW	Ella Weeks Walker
GP	Genevieve Peterkin
HP	Helen Peterkin
JPN	Ann Neeley, Marion Barksdale, and Margaret Buie
JW	Jackie Whitmore
MH	Mary Heyward
MMB	Marian Burgess (interview recorded by her daughters)
TF	Thomas Foster
VG	Veronica Gerald
WGP	William G. Peterkin III
WGPIV	William G. Peterkin IV
WHS	William Henry Seabrook

Manuscript Collections

Letters written by and about Julia Peterkin are contained in scores of libraries and archives across the United States. Though I have tried to look at every available manuscript, I list here only the collections cited in the notes.

ABP	Albert Bigelow Paine papers, Henry Huntington Library, San Mateo, California
BM	Bobbs-Merrill papers, Lilly Library, Indiana University, Bloomington
CS	Carl Sandburg Collection, Rare Book Room, University of Illinois Library, Urbana; reprinted by permission of the Carl Sandburg Family Trust
ESS	Elizabeth Shepley Sargeant papers, Beinecke Rare Book and Manuscript Library, Yale University, New Haven, Connecticut
HLM	H. L. Mencken papers, Rare Books and Manuscripts Division, New York Public Library, Astor, Lenox and Tilden Foundations; reprinted by permission of the Enoch Pratt Free Library of Baltimore in accordance with the terms of the will of H. L. Mencken
HS	Hudson Strode papers, University of Alabama, William Stanley Hoole Special Collections Library, Tuscaloosa
IF	Irving Fineman papers, Syracuse University Library, Department of Special Collections, Syracuse, New York
JS	Joel Spingarn papers, Rare Books and Manuscripts Division, New York Public Library, Astor, Lenox and Tilden Foundations
LB	Lula Buck, courtesy of Eugenia Cutts

LS   Lyle Saxon papers, Special Collections, Howard-Tilton Memorial Library, Tulane University, New Orleans, Louisiana

MB   Bernard and Margaret Behrend collection, Special Collections, Clemson University Libraries, Clemson, South Carolina

PG   Paul Green papers, Southern Historical Collection, Library of the University of North Carolina at Chapel Hill

PPSSC Papers of the Poetry Society of South Carolina, The Citadel, Charleston

SCHS   Julia Peterkin papers, South Carolina Historical Society, Charleston

SCL   South Caroliniana Library, University of South Carolina, Columbia

SY   Stark Young papers, Humanities Research Center, the University of Texas at Austin

TMS   Thomas McAlpin Stubbs papers, courtesy of Beatrice Jefferson Stubbs

WW   Walter White papers, NAACP Administrative Files, Library of Congress Manuscript Division, Washington, D.C.

Books by Julia Peterkin

BA   *Black April*
BS   *Bright Skin*
GT   *Green Thursday*
PC   *A Plantation Christmas*
RJR   *Roll, Jordan, Roll*
SSM *Scarlet Sister Mary*

Notes

Preface

1. H. L. Mencken, "The Sahara of the Bozart," in *Prejudices, Second Series* (New York: Knopf, 1920), 137.
2. "The South Begins to Mutter," *Smart Set* 65 (August 1921): 138–44.
3. Mencken, "The Sahara of the Bozart"; and Mencken, "Confederate Strivings," *Baltimore Evening Sun,* May 16, 1921.
4. HLM, n.d.
5. Quoted in Emily Clark, *Innocence Abroad* (New York: Knopf, 1931), 224. See also BM, November 11, 1926.
6. "The Browsing Reader," *Crisis* 29 (December 1924): 81.
7. BM.
8. *The Spyglass: Views and Reviews 1924–1930,* ed. John T. Fain, 20–23 (Nashville: Vanderbilt University Press, 1963).
9. GP; Thomas McAlpin Stubbs, *Family Album: An Account of the Moods of Charleston, SC and Connected Families* (Atlanta: Curtis, 1943), 73–75.
10. GP; Julius Mood, "Dr. Mood Writes Recollections Grave and Gay of His Rich Life," *Columbia State,* December 17, 1933, 12A. For an account of Wade Hampton's activities in South Carolina and Laurens County, see Eric Foner, *Reconstruction: America's Unfinished Revolution, 1863–1877* (New York: Harper and Row, 1988), 573–75.
11. Quoted in Brooks Miles Barnes, "Southern Independents: South Carolina, 1882," *South Carolina Historical Magazine* 96 (July 1995): 231.
12. Peterkin joined the DAR in March 1906.
13. HLM, [1921].
14. Toni Morrison, *Playing in the Dark: Whiteness and the Literary Imagination* (Cambridge: Harvard University Press, 1992).
15. "Burton Quits Jury on Pulitzer Awards," *New York Times,* May 17, 1929. See also BM author files, and W. J. Stuckey, *The Pulitzer Prize Novels: A Critical Backward Look* (Norman: University of Oklahoma Press, 1981), 80–81.
16. Bobbs-Merrill sales records, collected in the 1970s by Noel Polk.
17. *RJR,* 87.
18. The limited edition is now worth thousands of dollars and is one of the most hotly collected photography books produced in the twentieth century.
19. GP; HP; WGP.
20. For example, Nancy M. Tischler, in *Black Masks: Negro Characters in Modern Southern Fiction* (University Park: Pennsylvania State University Press, 1969), claimed that Peterkin's characters are "pretty much in the minstrel tradition" and asserted that they are engaged in "constant razor-battles."
21. BM, September 4, 1927.
22. IF, May 24, 1937.
23. Harry Salpeter, "Studies in Color," *New York World,* July 10, 1927.
24. *BS,* 156.
25. BJS.

26. Quoted in Nicholas Lemann, *The Promised Land: The Great Black Migration and How It Changed America* (New York: Knopf, 1991), 363. For a cogent account of mechanization in the cotton fields, see pp. 3–7.

27. *SSM*, 170, 72.

A Note on the Language

1. Mason Crum, *Negro Life in the Carolina Sea Islands* (Durham: Duke University Press, 1940; rpt. New York: Negro Universities Press, 1968), 212. For an earlier example of this school of thought, see the foreword to *The Black Border*, by Ambrose Gonzales (Columbia: The State, 1922); and Reed Smith, *Gullah*, Bulletin of the University of South Carolina 190 (Columbia: University of South Carolina, 1926).

2. See, especially, Lorenzo Dow Turner, *Africanisms in the Gullah Dialect* (Ann Arbor: University of Michigan Press, 1949; rpt. New York: Arno, 1969).

3. Charles Joyner, *Down by the Riverside: A South Carolina Slave Community* (Urbana: University of Illinois Press, 1984), 223.

4. John Bennett to Yates Snowden, February 10, 1918, in *Two Scholarly Friends: Yates Snowden–John Bennett, Correspondence, 1902–1932*, ed. Mary Crow Anderson, 128 (Columbia: University of South Carolina Press, 1993).

Chapter One: Lang Syne

1. "Awful R.R. Wreck," *Sumter Herald*, June 5, 1903.

2. "What and Why I Have Written," SCHS; Peterkin also studied German and music.

3. A few years before, in December 1896, Julia's older sister Marian had worried that marrying during a blizzard would doom her marriage (MMB). For an account of superstitions concerning bad weather on the wedding day, see Newbell Niles Puckett, *Folk Beliefs of the Southern Negro* (Chapel Hill: University of North Carolina Press, 1926).

4. "A Pretty Wedding: Two Popular Young People Happily Married Wednesday Night," *Sumter Herald*, June 5, 1903; unpublished memoir by TMS.

5. Noel Polk, who did research for a biography of Peterkin in the early 1970s, recorded a 1974 interview with Margaret Thomas, who said that Julia Mood was once engaged to a man named Charles Kirby. Peterkin repeatedly referred to her "bastard lover" in the unpublished writings at SCHS. In one story, his name is Fred White, the real name of someone who painted a portrait of Julia in the late teens or early twenties.

6. "On a Plantation," SCHS.

7. AvL.

8. AvL. Records at SCHS show that Lang Syne, which then comprised about three thousand acres, passed from Augustine Smythe to Daniel Zimmerman in 1870, when the mortgage was foreclosed. In December 1877, the land was sold by the sheriff of Orangeburg County to Francis Pelzer, who evidently sold it to James Alexander Peterkin shortly thereafter.

9. GP; she heard the story from Sam Reid.

10. AvL; Drake genealogy.

11. "Recollections of Louisa Rebecca Hayne McCord (Mrs. Augustine T. Smythe), daughter of David J. and Louisa Cheves McCord, born August 10, 1845, died Jan. 8, 1928," MS in SCL, 77. The McCords did not end up in Hawaii, to Smythe's immense relief.

12. Last Will and Testament, Agenora Drake Peterkin.

13. GP.

14. Julius Mood, "Recollections Grave and Gay," 12A.

15. Stubbs, *Family Album*, 34, 35, 36, 38, 55. In the preface to his privately published historical novel *Kitty Mood's Cup*, Brainerd Cheney quoted McFarlane's obituary in the *Charleston City Gazette:* "Died at Sierra Leone on the 12th December, 1803, in the 80th year of his age." According to Stubbs, there was a church-sponsored colony for free Negroes in Sierra Leone, established in 1786.

16. Stubbs, *Family Album*, 22, 49.

17. Stubbs, *Family Album*, 38.

18. Stubbs, *Family Album*, 56; Henry Mood, "Sketches and Incidents in the Life of Rev. Henry M. Mood, A.M. of the South Carolina Conference, Written by Himself for the Perusal of His Own Family," copy courtesy of GP; the original is in the archives at Wofford College, Spartanburg, S.C. Francis Asbury Mood, "The Autobiography of Frances Asbury Mood," MS in SCL.

19. Stubbs, *Family Album*, 72–73.

20. Archer family records, Wofford College Archives.

21. Stubbs, *Family Album*, 72–73; Cheney, *Kitty Mood's Cup;* GP.

22. Julia Peterkin, "Seeing Things," *American Magazine* 105 (January 1928): 26–27, 115–16; rpt. in *The Collected Stories of Julia Peterkin*, ed. Frank Durham (Columbia: University of South Carolina Press, 1970).

23. GP; WGP.

24. "Seeing Things," 64; HP; GP.

25. HP; GP; WGP.

26. The fact that Julia wanted her father to deliver her baby, and that he agreed to do it, may be a manifestion of feelings that were "vaguely incestuous" (as Harlan Greene put it), but in an era when doctors were scarce and most women gave birth at home, it was fairly common for relatives to assist them. Medical literature of the period sheds little light on how doctors and laypeople felt about the ethics of such an arrangement.

27. HP; GP. William Peterkin Jr. was born on April 18, 1904. Julia's mother had died in April. Just as it had for T. S. Eliot, who called it "the cruellest month," April would come to signify both birth and death for Julia. Strangely, her future lover, Irving Fineman, also had an April birthday, and her grandson William Peterkin III would be born on April 19, 1937.

28. GP.

29. Eli Van de Warker, "The Fetich [*sic*] of the Ovary," *American Journal of Obstetrics* 54 (July–December 1906): 366–73.

30. Lawrence D. Longo, "The Rise and Fall of Battey's Operation: A Fashion in Surgery," in *Women and Health in America*, ed. Judith Walzer Leavitt, 270–83 (Madison: University of Wisconsin Press, 1984).

31. For contemporary accounts of Battey's operation, see also Robert Battey, "Address by Dr. Robert Battey, Rome, Ga.," *Transactions of the South Carolina Medical Association*, 39th session, April 23–24, 1889, 59–68; W. P. Chunn, "The Prevention of Conception," *Maryland Medical Journal* 32 (1894–95): 340–43; A. H. Ferguson, "Conservatism of Ovaries and Tubes," *New York Medical Journal* 78 (1903): 782–85; Norman E. Himes, *Medical History of Contraception* (New York: Schocken Books, 1936); W. Lindley, "Oophorectomy: Its Effect on the Mind and Nervous System," *California State Journal of Medicine* (1902–3): 84–86; C. Lockyer, "Complications Met with during and after Ovariotomy," *Practitioner* (London) 72 (1903): 629–56; and Emil Novak, "The Hormone Theory and the Female Generative Organs," *Surgery, Gynecology and Obstetrics* 9 (July–December 1909): 344, 350.

32. Peterkin was vague about the amount of time she spent in bed, saying variously a year, two years, a long time, or simply "years."

33. GP; HP.

34. SCHS, unpublished papers; AvL.

35. Older black women were called "Maum" as a term of respect, and younger women were addressed as "Sis" or "Sister."

36. GP; SCHS; JW.

37. AvL; GP. In her "Recollections" of Lang Syne, which span antebellum times, the Civil War, and Reconstruction, Louisa McCord Smythe said that "the army passed that way, burning many places as they went, but for some reason passed Lang Syne by" (SCL, 72). Willie Peterkin was too young to have been involved in the house fire.

38. "Seeing Things," 66. See also unpublished papers, SCHS. Samuel Gaillard Stoney wrote that

> when George Sterling wished to clear his title and make peace with the Congaree Indians, he found that he had to do business with a venerable squaw, a sort of female chief, who actually ran the tribe. She proposed that they enter into a partnership combining the rule of the tribe with the ownership of the plantation. Sterling held out for an independent property and got it; but the squaw then warned him that what he had obtained was "woman's land," that men could never rule it well or long. (*The Dulles Family in South Carolina* [Columbia: University of South Carolina Press, 1955], 3)

39. JW; GP.

40. EWW.

41. SCHS, 28–613–8; "Seeing Things."

42. All quotations are from "Venner's Sayings," *Poetry* 23 (November 1923): 59–67; and "Vinner's Sayings," *Poetry* 25 (February 1925): 240–43.

43. "Seeing Things," 68–69.

44. GP; SCHS. Part of the old house was eventually torn down; the remains, originally the library of the McCord house, were made into a house for the plantation foreman. This structure still exists but has been moved down the highway from Lang Syne.

45. "Seeing Things," 63–64; SCHS; Julian Meade, *Adam's Profession and Its Conquest by Eve* (New York: Longmans, 1937), and "Springtime Pilgrimage to the Gardens of Nine Women," *Good Housekeeping*, May 1938, 50–53, 154–63. Louisa McCord Smythe mentioned Daddy Champagne in her "Recollections."

46. "Venner's Sayings," 63. Many years later, DuBose Heyward and George Gershwin would use this line in the libretto for the folk opera *Porgy and Bess*.

47. SCHS.

48. See especially "Cooch's Premium," in "Imports from Africa," *Reviewer* 2 (January 1922): 200.

49. JW; SCHS; WHS. Mary Weeks's father, the overseer's son, was apparently murdered because of his involvement in Reconstruction politics.

50. Last Will and Testament of Agenora Drake Peterkin, AvL.

51. SCHS.

52. Various sources, published and unpublished, including "On a Plantation"; most famously quoted in *SSM*.

53. "Imports from Africa II," *Reviewer* 2 (February 1922): 253–55.

54. "Seeing Things," 65.

55. Both accounts appear among Peterkin's unpublished papers at SCHS. Estimates of how long Ellis Sanders stayed away vary; it may have been two years or it may have been three, as indicated in *RJR*. At any rate, he and Bina appear to have had two children together.

56. *RJR;* EWW; SCHS.

57. "A Wife," "Silhouettes," *Reviewer* 3 (June 1922): 1, 500; SCHS; JW. Hester and Jake did not live in the Quarters; their house still stands near Lang Syne.

58. "What and Why I Have Written," SCHS.

59. TMS, "Memo for Discussion with Dr. Frank Durham"; HP.

60. Stubbs, *Family Album,* 146; GP. One of Marian Mood Burgess's daughters puts this date at 1914, remembering that Laura was caught in Europe at the start of World War I (JPN).

61. HLM, n.d.; HP; GP.

62. "The Lower Berth," SCHS, 28–611–46.

63. SCHS.

64. MMB; JPN; GP; HP. In a tape made by her daughters, Marian Mood Burgess confirmed that Alma Mood asked her mother- and father-in-law to raise baby Julia instead of sending her home with her sisters.

65. SCHS; GP. The phrase is also used in *Black April,* where it refers to the character Breeze.

66. GP; JPN.

67. Stubbs, *Family Album,* 52.

68. GP.

69. Henry Mood, "Memoirs." For a fuller account of the evolving Methodist attitude toward slavery, especially in Charleston, see Margaret Washington Creel, *"A Peculiar People": Slave Religion and Community Culture among the Gullah* (New York: New York University Press, 1988), 140–41.

70. Stubbs, *Family Album,* 91.

71. BJS; JPN.

72. MMB; JPN.

73. "The Day of Judgment," unpublished dream recorded by Julia Mood as a child, owned by Genevieve Peterkin, dated Manning, December 18, 1888.

74. SCHS, 28−613−12.

75. CS, January 13, 1938; rpt. in *The Letters of Carl Sandburg*, ed. Herbert Mitgang (New York: Harcourt, Brace, and World, 1968), 357.

76. GP; HP; JPN.

77. GP.

78. GP.

79. GP; BJS; MMB.

80. GP; HP.

81. GP.

82. GP; VG.

83. GP. Wallace Heyward couldn't walk until he was four years old; his mother was said to have been pressured by the community to let him die in the woods when he was born. The doctor he saw was Shelton Horsely, a friend of Julius Mood's who treated many members of the Peterkin and Mood families.

84. HP; GP.

85. SCHS.

86. HLM, n.d.; SCHS.

87. SCHS. There are several accounts of Frank Hart's ordeal among Peterkin's unpublished papers at SCHS, the earliest a verse rendering. Julia told reporters that it was her father who cut off Hart's legs; BJS confirms this. "On a Plantation" (SCHS) contains another version that includes Hart's experiences in the hospital.

88. SCHS, 28−613−1.

89. "On a Plantation," SCHS. Other versions occur in *BA;* in "The Foreman," *Reviewer* 4 (July 1924): 286−94; and in Peterkin's unpublished papers at SCHS. EWW reports that people who lived on and around Lang Syne do not remember much about Frank Hart, though they do remember Charity. In a letter to her publishers written in 1926, Julia reported that "['April']'s wife's real name was Charity" (BM, November 29, 1926).

90. *BA,* 274.

Chapter Two: Cheating the Stillness

1. GP; JPN.

2. GP; John Andrew Huffman, "Elements of Historical Geography at Fort Motte, SC: A Geographic Perspective," MS dated 1970, SCL.

3. GP; SCHS.

4. John Hammond Moore, "South Carolina's Reaction to the Photoplay *The Birth of a Nation*," *Proceedings of the South Carolina Historical Association* 64 (1963): 30−40.

5. Mary White Ovington, *The Walls Came Tumbling Down* (New York: Harcourt, Brace, 1947), 166; E. David Cronin, *Black Moses: The Story of Marcus Garvey* (Madison: University of Wisconsin Press, 1955), 47; see also Edward Ayers,

Promise of the New South (New York: Oxford University Press, 1992); and Joel Williamson, *The Crucible of Race* (New York: Oxford University Press, 1984).

6. Walter B. Edgar, *South Carolina in the Modern Age* (Columbia: University of South Carolina Press, 1992), 2, 39.

7. Josiah Morse, "The Outlook for the Negro," *Sewanee Review* 28, no. 2 (April 1920): 152–59.

8. "On a Plantation," SCHS.

9. *BA*, 149.

10. Huffman, "Elements of Historical Geography."

11. Edgar, *South Carolina in the Modern Age*, 46.

12. Autobiographical fragment, SCHS.

13. Prospectus for the Waccamaw Hunt Club, published in Sumter, S.C., n.d., SCL; GP.

14. Both quotations appear in Charles Felton Pidgin, *Theodosia: First Gentlewoman of Her Time* (Boston: C. M. Clark, 1907). "A fair young queen" is from a poem written c. 1904 by Alexander Ormand (445); "wit and vivacity" is from James Parton, *The Life and Times of Aaron Burr* (Boston: Ticknor and Fields, 1867); "the best educated woman of her time and country" is from Virginia Tatnall Peacock, *Famous American Belles of the Nineteenth Century* (Philadelphia: Lippincott, 1901), 188.

15. Quoted in Margaret Farrand Thorp, "Altogether Doric: Louisa McCord," *Female Persuasion: Six Strong-Minded Women* (New Haven: Yale University Press, 1949), 203.

16. George Armstrong Wauchope, *The Writers of South Carolina* (Columbia: The State, 1910).

17. For another account of Louisa McCord, see Elizabeth Fox-Genovese, *Within the Plantation Household: Black and White Women of the Old South* (Chapel Hill: University of North Carolina Press, 1988), 253ff., 281.

18. Quoted in Jessie Melville Fraser, "Louisa McCord" (master's thesis, University of South Carolina, 1919), 9.

19. James B. Angell, *Reminiscences*, quoted in Thorp, "Altogether Doric," 198; and in Fraser, "Louisa McCord," 10.

20. Louisa McCord Smythe, "Recollections," 72, 81.

21. SCHS.

22. *BS*, 119.

23. GP; HP; AvL.

24. This account occurs in a number of sources. "Cheating the stillness" is from HLM, [1923].

25. SCHS; Marilyn Price Maddox, "The Life and Works of Julia Mood Peterkin" (master's thesis, University of Georgia, 1956).

26. AvL. Many years later, in 1930, Katherine Bellamann would publish a novel about jealousy called *My Husband's Friends*. Julia suspected that "I may perhaps be one of the characters. The villain, most likely" (IF, August 18, 1930); but there is no figure in the book who obviously resembles her.

27. Medora Field Perkerson, "Julia Peterkin — Author and Farmer," *Atlanta Journal*, April 28, 1940.

28. SCHS.

29. SCHS, 29–613–20. Bessie was born in October 1885 and is buried in Mt. Pisgah cemetery near Fort Motte.

30. SCHS, 28–613–20. AvL confirms that this account is true.

31. Town Theater Scrapbooks, SCL.

32. Town Theater Scrapbooks; PPSSC.

33. CS, January 5, 1921.

34. CS, January 25, 1921.

35. CS, January 28, 1921.

36. CS, telegram dated February 15, 1921; Penelope Niven, *Carl Sandburg: A Biography* (New York: Scribner, 1991).

37. Maddox, "Life and Works of Julia Mood Peterkin," 15.

38. CS, [1923 — misdated 1927?].

39. GP; CS, [1921].

40. CS, April 14, 1921.

41. CS, [1921].

42. Niven, *Carl Sandburg*, 373ff. AvL, born in the generation after Peterkin's, remembers being vaccinated as a girl.

43. HLM, March 28, 1922.

44. HLM, June 6, 1921.

45. HLM, [1921].

46. HLM, [1921].

47. HLM, June 6, 1921.

48. HLM, August 24, 1921.

49. SCHS.

50. HLM, [1921].

51. CS, January 5, 1921.

52. HLM to Ernest Boyd, quoted in William Manchester, *Disturber of the Peace: The Life of H. L. Mencken* (New York: Harper and Brothers, 1950), 159.

53. HLM, [1921].

54. H. L. Mencken, *My Life as Author and Editor* (New York: Knopf, 1991), 374.

55. Mencken, "Sahara of the Bozart," 136–54.

56. HLM, [1921].

57. Mencken, *My Life*, 373. See also Fred Hobson, *Mencken: A Life* (New York: Random House, 1993).

58. HLM, [1921].

59. SCHS.

60. "Nancy," SCHS.

61. SCHS, J. Berg Esenwein to JP, June 24, 1921. JW reports that the baby who lost her eye to the rooster, Maybell "Dode" Sanders, lived to a ripe old age and died in Columbia, S.C., in 1992. The baby's name is given in the story as Dode. Yet "Nancy" is apparently not a literal rendering of the situation. AvL says that the real Monroe Sanders married not Nancy but Bessie, one of Mary Weeks's bright-skinned daughters, and that he lived on the Robert Adams place, where one of his sons eventually became the foreman. Monroe was Ellis Sanders's uncle. The Sanders family had moved to Fort Motte from Newberry after the Civil War.

62. Two different letters to HLM, [1922–23].

Chapter Three: Cutting a Mouth

1. Emily Clark, *Innocence Abroad*, 213; HLM, n.d.
2. HLM, [1921].
3. Emily Clark, "Beginning the Second Volume," *Reviewer* 2 (October 1921): 37.
4. Emily Clark, *Innocence Abroad*, 7; H. L. Mencken, "Morning Song in C Major," *Reviewer* 2 (October 1921): 1–5.
5. "Mose," in "From Lang Syne Plantation," *Reviewer* 2 (October 1921): 6–9. It is not clear whether or not a child really poisoned his grandmother by mistake at Lang Syne. According to Peterkin's notes, the halfwit Dukkin once killed a cow when he sprinkled the toxic fertilizer nitrate of soda in a barnyard trough, but none of my sources recall that a woman ever died at Lang Syne after consuming nitrate of soda. Clearly, however, the possibility worried Peterkin. A character in "On a Plantation" (SCHS) frets that one day Dukkin will poison the spring and kill everybody on the place. JW reports that Dukkin lived on a nearby farm, not Lang Syne, and that his mother was a midwife named Olive Reese.
6. Mencken, *My Life*, 366–73.
7. HLM, [1922].
8. SCHS, 28–611–28.
9. "The Merry-Go-Round," *Smart Set* 46 (December 1921): 69–72.
10. John Andrew Huffman, "The Fort Motte Riot of 1896," MS dated 1976, SCL.
11. Peter Wood, *Black Majority: Negroes in Colonial South Carolina from 1670 through the Stono Rebellion* (New York: Knopf, 1974), 277.
12. Stubbs, *Family Album*, 94–95.
13. Louisa McCord Smythe, "Recollections," 82.
14. HLM, [1922].
15. Mencken, *My Life*, 373.
16. In the original manuscript, Julia also crossed out the name "Jesse" and substituted "Douglas," but Mencken did not make this change.
17. Frank Durham, "Mencken as Midwife," *Menckeniana* 32 (Winter 1969): 2–6.
18. January 11, 1922. See Emily Clark, *Ingenue among the Lions: The Letters of Emily Clark to Joseph Hergesheimer* (Austin: University of Texas Press, 1965), 48, 107.
19. Emily Clark, *Ingenue*, 41.
20. *Reviewer* 2 (January 1922): 198–200.
21. Gonzales, *The Black Border*, 72, 73, 78.
22. Gonzales, *The Black Border*, 78; translated by GP.
23. Gonzales, *The Black Border*, 72.
24. "Green Walnuts," in "Studies in Charcoal," *Reviewer* 2 (March 1922): 320–24.
25. "Roots Work," in "Studies in Charcoal," *Reviewer* 2 (March 1922): 327.
26. Harcourt papers, collected from the firm by Noel Polk in the 1970s.
27. Carl Sandburg to Alfred Harcourt, February 28, 1922, in Mitgang, ed., *Letters of Carl Sandburg*, 207.
28. Mencken, *My Life*, 288.
29. HLM, n.d.
30. HLM, April 1922.
31. CS, [1922].

32. HLM, April 25, 1922.

33. CS, n.d.

34. HLM, [1922].

35. HLM, [1922], four different letters.

36. HLM, n.d.

37. GP.

38. HLM, 1922.

39. Victor E. Gimmestad, *Joseph Hergesheimer* (Boston: Twayne, 1984), 1.

40. Mencken, *My Life*, 357.

41. Emily Clark, *Innocence Abroad*, 218.

42. Emily Clark, *Ingenue*, 59–60.

43. "The Right Thing," *Reviewer* 3 (April 1922): 386, 387.

44. James Alexander Peterkin, *Talks with the Cotton Farmer* (Charleston: Walker, Evans, and Cogswell, 1888), 29.

45. HLM, March 9, 1923.

46. HLM, n.d.

47. HLM, [1923].

48. H. L. Mencken, "The Usual Buncombe," *Smart Set* 67 (January 1922): 44.

49. HLM, n.d.

50. SCHS, 28–613–4.

51. SCHS; GP.

52. HLM, n.d.

53. H. L. Mencken, "Violets in the Sahara," *Baltimore Evening Sun*, May 15, 1922.

54. HLM, [1922].

55. "Poetry South," *Poetry* 20 (April 1922): 38.

56. "Notes," *Poetry* 20 (April 1922): 56–57.

57. "Poetry South," 41.

58. Peterkin's scrapbook, SCHS.

59. HLM, n.d.

60. "A Baby's Mouth," *Reviewer* 3 (May 1922): 440–42.

61. HLM, n.d.

62. Willie Snow Etheridge, "Julia Peterkin Learned to Know Negroes through 20 Years Study," 1930 clipping from an unidentified newspaper.

63. EWW. African American historian Veronica Gerald recalls hearing a similar tale at Brookgreen, along with another about a midwife cutting an anus. There really was a midwife called Maum Hannah at Lang Syne, but Peterkin used this name later for characters who are clearly modeled on Lavinia Berry.

64. SCHS, 28–613–1.

65. HLM, [1921].

Chapter Four: Poor Little Motherless

1. Emily Clark, *Innocence Abroad*, 217.

2. "Missy's Twins," *Reviewer* 3 (October 1922): 668–73.

3. Hunter Stagg, "Southern Woman Writes First Book," *Richmond Times-Dispatch*, September 28, 1924.

4. HLM, [1922].

5. Thomas McAlpin Stubbs, "Memo for Discussion with Dr. Frank Durham," MS owned by BJS.

6. "Missy's Twins," 673.

7. JPN. The unpublished poem "I've Never Had a Mother" (SCHS, 28–613–8) talks about how Julia's "mammy" helped her get through the pain of birthdays, which were ignored by her family. When I was copying a tape of Julia's sister Marian's voice at the College of Charleston, one of the technicians listened for a minute and cried, "Oh, that's Gullah!" It wasn't Gullah, exactly, but his reaction made me realize how much Julia and her sisters had been influenced by African American speech patterns.

8. SCHS; IF, n.d.

9. GP.

10. Gilda Varesi and Dolly Byrne, *Enter, Madame: A Play in Three Acts* (New York: Putnam, 1921).

11. Romeike clipping file, courtesy of Noel Polk.

12. Town Theater Scrapbooks.

13. HLM, n.d.

14. HLM, [1922], two different letters.

15. GP.

16. GP; HP.

17. See Emily Clark, *Innocence Abroad*, 216.

18. HLM, [1922?].

19. Mencken, *My Life*, 374.

20. HLM, [1923?].

21. GP.

22. See *RJR*, 213–16.

23. CS, [misdated 1927].

24. Edgar, *South Carolina in the Modern Age*, 49.

25. HLM, February 1923.

26. HLM, 1923. "God's Children" was later printed as a selection in Alfred A. Knopf's *Borzoi 1925*. In *Innocence Abroad* (214), Emily Clark maintained that the *Reviewer* never rejected one of Peterkin's manuscripts.

27. SCHS.

28. Florence Archer Mulligan, "Memories of Sister Alma Kennedy Archer Mood," unpublished memoir owned by JPN.

29. "The Girl Who Looked on Death," SCHS, 28–611–43. This appears to be a variant of a folk tale associated with Daisy Bank plantation, one of the old rice plantations along the North Santee River. In the original, a woman dies in childbirth and her husband buries mother and baby in a glass-topped coffin, the mother wearing a diamond bracelet. After a prominent family from the North buys the place to use as a hunting preserve, a young couple happens on the grave and the girl admires the bracelet. The boy smashes the glass and gets it for her. The girl becomes hysterical. People later report that the dead mother and child float just above the coffin, appearing to look for something. See Nancy Rhyne, *Touring the Coastal South Carolina Backroads* (Winston-Salem, N.C.: John Blair, 1992), 112–13.

30. See, for example, her letter to D. L. Chambers, January 12, 1929, BM; and autobiographical fragment, 28-613-12, SCHS.

31. See Stubbs, *Family Album.*

32. Letter to Chambers, January 12, 1929, BM: "My birth was in some way the cause of [my mother's] death. . . . I used to wonder if she held it against me."

33. GP.

34. SCHS.

35. "Venner's Sayings," *Poetry* 23 (November 1923): 59-67.

36. "Venner's Sayings," 62-67.

Chapter Five: **Green Thursday**

1. Peterkin seems to have preferred the spelling "Vinner," though in the first installment of "Vinner's Sayings" the name is spelled "Venner." On Berry's tombstone, the spelling is "Levina."

2. HLM, n.d. (two different letters).

3. Langston Hughes, *The Big Sea* (New York: Hill and Wang, 1940), 223.

4. Letter to Blanche Knopf, November 19, 1923 (Special Collections, Northwestern University Library, Evanston, Illinois). Evidently, Peterkin also read Waldo Frank's *Holiday,* a novel published in 1923. Accompanied by Toomer, Frank passed for black on a 1922 trip through the Deep South to collect material for the book. See Richard Barksdale and Keneth Kinnamon, *Black Writers of America* (New York: Macmillan, 1972), 475.

5. JS, n.d.

6. JS, n.d. Peterkin pumped Spingarn for information about Toomer and Frank.

7. Frank Durham, *DuBose Heyward: The Man Who Wrote* Porgy (Columbia: University of South Carolina Press, 1954), 28-29.

8. Quoted in Hollis Alpert, *The Life and Times of Porgy and Bess* (New York: Knopf, 1990), 24.

9. William H. Slavick, another of Heyward's biographers, said that the founders averted a "major crisis" by their "discreet silence" when Toomer joined the society; see Slavick, *DuBose Heyward* (Boston: Twayne, 1981), 23.

10. JS, February 23, 1923.

11. JS, n.d.

12. HLM, 1923; JS, n.d.

13. JS, n.d.

14. GP.

15. HLM, 1923.

16. H. L. Mencken in the Carl Sandburg papers, University of Illinois Library.

17. CS, n.d.

18. HLM; GP. Preston Mood died in January 1880. He was the editor of the *Clarendon Banner.*

19. HLM, June 27, 1923.

20. HLM, [1922]. See "Saving Souls," by Mencken's protégé Gerald W. Johnson, which appeared in *American Mercury* 3 (1924): 364-68, for a similar opinion on this subject.

21. HLM, [1923].
22. HLM, [1923?].
23. PG. For an account of Paul Green's publication of "Maum Lou," see John Herbert Roper, "Paul Green and the Southern Literary Renaissance," *Southern Cultures* 1 (1994–95): 84.
24. "Maum Lou," *Reviewer* 5 (January 1925): 30–32.
25. SCHS.
26. "Southern Imagination," SCHS.
27. HLM, [1924].
28. Emily Clark, *Innocence Abroad*, 222.
29. "Over the River," *Reviewer* 4 (January 1924): 84–96.
30. SCHS.
31. SCHS.
32. In one three-week period in 1925, more than one million acres of low country real estate changed hands; see Edgar, *South Carolina in the Modern Age*, 67.
33. Letter from Eulalie Salley, June 13, 1964, quoted in Louis Lee Henry, "Julia Peterkin: A Biographical and Critical Guide" (Ph.D. dissertation, Florida State University, 1965).
34. A letter from Walmsley is preserved in Peterkin's scrapbook, SCHS.
35. HLM, [1923?]. Peterkin was not alone in her reaction to Mrs. Knopf. Stories about her difficult personality abound.
36. HLM, [1924].
37. HLM, n.d.
38. JS, n.d.
39. "Venner's Sayings," 59–67.
40. October 4, 1924. Letter preserved in Peterkin's scrapbook, SCHS.
41. Bruce Kellner, *Carl Van Vechten and the Irreverent Decades* (Norman: University of Oklahoma Press, 1968), 195. (For a fuller account of this episode, I am indebted to a personal communication from Kellner.)
42. HLM, [1924].
43. *GT*, 145.
44. EWW.
45. *BS*, 137.
46. "Venner's Sayings," 59.
47. *GT*, 113.
48. *GT*, 188.
49. Stubbs, in *Family Album*, says it was a saw mill accident (99). Edwin Brogdon, a descendant, corrects this to a cotton gin accident.
50. GP.
51. GP; TMS; JPN.
52. *GT*, 155.
53. *GT*, 168.
54. GP; HP.
55. AvL remembers that Nannie and Ellis had one biological daughter, Lolly.
56. JW.
57. *GT*, 9.

58. *GT,* 22.

59. *GT,* 15–16.

60. *GT,* 20–24.

61. Robert Adger Law, "Mrs. Peterkin's Negroes," *Southwest Review* 14 (1929): 461.

62. *GT,* 47.

63. Julian Meade, "Julia Peterkin," *New York Herald Tribune Book Review,* January 17, 1933; Maddox, "Life and Works of Julia Mood Peterkin," 40.

64. HLM, [1924].

65. HLM, [1924].

66. CS, October 4, 1924.

67. HLM, n.d.

68. Peterkin was not the first white woman to write about her own life through the mask of black characters. Shari Benstock has theorized that Gertrude Stein did the same thing in 1909 when she wrote "Melanctha," transposing the story of her "failed affair" with May Bookstaver not only onto black culture but onto a hetero-sexual couple. See Benstock, *Women of the Left Bank: Paris, 1900–1940* (Austin: University of Texas Press, 1986).

69. HLM, [1925].

70. "Again a Serious Study of Negroes in Fiction," *New York Times Book Review,* September 28, 1924, 8.

71. Romeike clipping file, c. December 1924.

72. *Baltimore Evening Sun,* December 30, 1924, preserved in Peterkin's scrapbook, SCHS.

73. "A Thousand Dollar Throwdown," undated clipping from a Chicago newspaper, preserved in Peterkin's scrapbook, SCHS. Sandburg suggested that the jury should have split the prize four ways: among Sinclair Lewis (who had refused the prize), Christopher Morley for *Thunder on the Left,* Ruth Suckow for *Country People,* and Julia for *Green Thursday.*

74. "Mrs. Peterkin's Book Is Given N.Y. Review," *Columbia Record,* n.d., clipping in JP's scrapbook, page courtesy of WGPIV.

75. Henry Bellamann, [Review of *Green Thursday,*] *Columbia Record,* April 15, 1925.

76. HLM, dated 1924. Julia referred to the writer as "Mr. Moorman" in her correspondence with Mencken. Confusingly enough, however, the actual letter is preserved in JP's scrapbook, SCHS, and it is from Judge W. C. Benét.

77. Gerald W. Johnson, "Southern Image-Breakers," *Virginia Quarterly Review* 4 (1928): 511.

78. See note to "A Gullah Confession of Faith," by Ambrose Gonzales, *Yearbook of the Poetry Society of South Carolina,* 1923, PPSSC.

79. HLM, [1924].

80. JS, n.d.

81. HLM, [1924].

82. HLM.

83. CS.

84. HLM.

85. Edgar, *South Carolina in the Modern Age,* 56; Nancy Rhyne, *Touring the Coastal*

South Carolina Backroads (Winston-Salem, N.C.: John Blair, 1992), 42–443. Area roads were greatly improved by 1912.

86. Walter White, *The Fire in the Flint* (New York: Knopf, 1924), 279.
87. WW, December 9, 1924.
88. WW.
89. Walter White, *Rope and Faggot: A Biography of Judge Lynch* (New York: Arno, 1969).
90. WW.
91. Romeike clipping file, n.d.
92. Clipping in JP's scrapbook, pages courtesy of WGPIV.
93. Clipping, newspaper source unknown, provided by Noel Polk, n.d. Peterkin was pleased by the article — see HLM, 1924.
94. "Finely Wrought Stuff," rpt. in the *Columbia State*, December 7, 1924.
95. Barksdale and Kinnamon, eds. *Black Writers of America*, 484.

Chapter Six: Cross Purposes

1. JP told HLM that Willie was suffering from jaundice; she did not say what had caused the jaundice.
2. HLM, November 20, 1924.
3. Emily Clark, *Innocence Abroad*, 225–26.
4. *PC*, 24.
5. AvL.
6. *PC*, 25.
7. SCHS. In one sketch she called him "Fred White." In a later letter to a man named Fred Millet, she said that a Fred White had painted her portrait.
8. HLM.
9. HLM, n.d. Lois Stewart, an employee of Bobbs-Merrill, informed Noel Polk in a letter dated December 22, 1975, that Aley received a 2 percent royalty on manuscripts he brought in.
10. HLM, [1925].
11. CS, [February 1925]. James Weldon Johnson accurately summed up the unwritten racial codes of the period in his *Autobiography of an Ex–Colored Man* (New York: Sherman-French, 1912) when he said that it was considered perfectly proper for "the fairest lady in the South" to visit her cook's cabin to sit by a sickbed but not to enter the home of a black woman with money or education. Such a woman would no more think of doing such a thing, he claimed, "than she would think of going into a bar-room for a drink." In 1901, James K. Vardaman of Mississippi whipped crowds into a frenzy by telling them that President Theodore Roosevelt had invited Booker T. Washington to dine at the White House. Vardaman claimed that Roosevelt "had no more decency than to take a . . . d——d nigger bastard into his home, introduce him to his family, and entertain him on terms of absolute social equality" (see Nadine Cohodas, *Strom Thurmond and the Politics of Southern Change* [New York: Simon and Schuster, 1993], 24; and William F. Holmes, *The White Chief: James Kimble Vardaman* [Baton Rouge: Louisiana State University

Press, 1970], 99). Similarly, Mary White Ovington recalled attending an integrated 1904 dinner in New York at the Cosmopolitan Club. A reporter portrayed the gathering as a "miscegenation dinner" rife with sex and drinking (*The Walls Came Tumbling Down*, 52). As late as 1948, South Carolina governor Strom Thurmond sent a "routine" letter to the governor of the Virgin Islands, inviting him to visit the governor's mansion. When someone told him the governor was black, he replied, "I would not have written him if I knew he was a Negro. Of course, it would have been ridiculous to invite him" (Cohodas, *Strom Thurmond*, 188).

12. HLM, n.d.
13. HLM, [1925].
14. Letter in Peterkin's scrapbook, SCHS.
15. CS, March 9, 1925.
16. WW.
17. WW, February 16, 1925.
18. JP to Louis Bromfield, April 28, 1927, Ohio State University Libraries.
19. Letters in Peterkin's scrapbook, SCHS.
20. John Bennett to DuBose Heyward, quoted in Durham, *DuBose Heyward*, 74.
21. DuBose Heyward, "The New Note in Southern Literature," *Bookman* 61 (April 1925): 153–56.
22. HLM, 1924.
23. HLM, [1925].
24. In another version, he is an electrical engineer. Agenora Drake Peterkin's Marlboro County plantation was named Ellerslie.
25. "On a Plantation," SCHS.
26. In *White Women, Race Matters: The Social Construction of Whiteness* (Minneapolis: University of Minnesota Press, 1993), feminist scholar Ruth Frankenberg identified three historical stages of race consciousness in American white women. The first, "essentialist racism," is the simple belief that blacks are inferior. The second, "color and power evasiveness," involves denial and repression — white women politely claim to be "color-blind" and repudiate the idea that race matters, either to themselves or to their society as a whole. The third stage, "race cognizance," incorporates both a recognition of racial differences and a critique of racist social systems. Frankenberg points out that while all three attitudes are still current in America, it was in the early 1920s that essentialist racism began giving way to evasiveness. Race cognizance was largely confined to black separatists and black intellectuals.
27. HLM, May 10, 1925: "An artist came here and modeled my head and we talked a lot of that stuff. The rice-field experience. The drift-wood. Other things too. He thought we were all a bit off in our heads. Perhaps he's right. But I prefer being so to being the tea-table gossipy conventional female." See also an unsigned, undated student essay, Columbia Museum of Art; and Henry Bellamann's article about Weston in "The Literary Highway," *Columbia Record*, April 11, 1926. Surprisingly little is known about Weston, though copies of his larger-than-life bust of Peterkin are held at the Columbia Museum of Art and the South Carolina Historical Society. Wallace Heyward, Peterkin's cook, considered the sculpture all too

lifelike. "Miss," he once remarked to Genevieve Peterkin shortly after Julia's death, "dat 'ting goin' open e' mout' one day an' tell me what to do."

28. "The Foreman," *Reviewer* 4 (July 1924): 288–94.

29. DuBose Heyward encountered a similar dilemma while writing *Porgy*. The novel originally featured a white woman much like Helen West, but Heyward eventually took her out, vastly improving the novel (see Durham, *DuBose Heyward* and the manuscript of "Porgy" at SCHS). Years later, H. L. Mencken blandly summed up what was wrong with "On a Plantation" by saying simply that it was "badly organized and badly written" (*My Life*, 374).

30. HLM, May 16, 1925.

31. HP.

32. AKD, personal communication to the author.

33. HLM.

Chapter Seven: *Black April*

1. Binkie Kaminer was Bill Peterkin's first girlfriend, around 1918.

2. IF, June 16, 1930. See also IF, September 28, 1927, and June 19, 1930.

3. "Manners," *Reviewer* 5 (July 1925): 71–80.

4. SCHS.

5. Untitled clipping, *New York World*, April 21, 1925, preserved in Peterkin's scrapbook, SCHS.

6. HLM, May 19, 1925.

7. Sandy Island is one of the few places in America where children still go to school by boat. Until very recently it was threatened by development, but as of this writing an agreement has been reached to control access to the island.

8. *BA*, 22.

9. *BA*, 18.

10. AvL. See also the ledger from W. G. Peterkin's store, SCHS; JW.

11. *BA*, 16.

12. *BA*, 46.

13. EWW.

14. SCHS; Puckett, *The Magic and Folk Beliefs of the Southern Negro*.

15. *BA*, 247.

16. *BA*, 250.

17. *BA*, 248.

18. *BA*, 249.

19. Berton Roueché, *The Medical Detectives* (New York: Washington Square Press, 1980), 253–72. Mercury was also used to treat syphilis.

20. On July 26, 1923, Peterkin wrote to H. L. Mencken, "I'm convinced that to lose teeth is emasculating. Mr. Archibald Henderson will never be the same."

21. *BA*, 215.

22. *BA*, 267.

23. *BA*, 316.

24. For this information I am indebted to Dr. William Dinwiddie.

25. For a full discussion of this tradition, see Mel Watkins, *On the Real Side: Laughing, Lying and Signifying — The Underground Tradition of African-American Humor That Transformed American Culture, from Slavery to Richard Pryor* (New York: Simon and Schuster, 1994).

26. *BA*, 182. (In "On a Plantation," the frog-leg story is told by Lucy [Leacey].)

27. *BA*, 188–90. Peterkin told Chambers that a Mr. [Clifton] Furness from the Horace Mann School had been present on the night that "the preacher left 'not' out of the Ten Commandments" and could testify that the incident really occurred.

28. *BA*, 196.

29. *BA*, 197–98.

30. CS.

31. *BA*, 57. In inventing Blue Brook, Julia combined descriptions of Brookgreen, a coastal rice plantation, and Lang Syne, an inland cotton plantation.

32. *BA*, 157.

33. *BA*, 28.

34. IF, April 23, 1927.

35. SCHS, 28–613–1.

36. IF, December 28, [1925].

37. IF, n.d.

38. CS, n.d.

39. IF, n.d.

40. IF, n.d.

41. JW.

42. CS. Mary's behavior at Cicero's funeral is remembered differently by her family. According to Jackie Whitmore, she was so distraught that she had to be restrained from jumping into the grave. Family members also recall that when Cicero died, a tiny lizard was seen to run out of his ear.

43. BM, October 15, 1926.

44. Timothy D. Murray, "The Bobbs-Merrill Company," *Dictionary of Literary Biography* 46 (1986): 49–54.

45. BM, November 11, 1926.

46. BM.

47. Hudson Strode, *The Eleventh House* (New York: Harcourt Brace Jovanovitch, 1975), 139.

48. Strode, *Eleventh House*, 139–42.

49. BM, October 29, November 3, 1926. Though Hudson Strode would later charge that Bobbs-Merrill had nearly ruined Julia's first novel by inserting extraneous material, the Bobbs-Merrill files suggest that he was wrong. The material Strode cut was probably put there by Julia herself.

50. HLM, January 25, 1927.

51. HLM, January 25, 1927.

52. BM, March 8, 1927.

53. HLM, December 6, 1926.

54. CS, January 18, 1927.

55. BM, March 30, 1927.

56. BM.

57. Romeike clipping file, courtesy of Noel Polk. Ernest Rice McKinney, "The Bookshelf," *Chicago Defender*, April 23, 1927; and the *Chicago Broad Axe*, April 9, 1927.

58. BM, February 24, 1927.

59. Laurence Stallings, "*Black April*," *McCall's*, May 1927.

60. Romeike clipping file, October 23, 1927.

61. May 11, 1928, quoted in *Stark Young: A Life in the Arts, Letters, 1900–1962*, ed. John Pilkington (Baton Rouge: Louisiana State University Press, 1975), 270–71.

62. Romeike clipping file.

63. "Julia Peterkin," *Spyglass*, April 3, 1927, 23.

64. BM, February 27, March 8, 1927.

65. BM, March 1927.

66. BM, March 9, October 31, 1927.

67. BM.

68. W. T. Anderson, "Dead Tree Lumber," *Macon Telegraph* June 28, 1927.

69. Charles M. Puckett, "On a Carolina Plantation," *Saturday Review of Literature* 34 (March 19, 1927).

70. "Novels in Brief," *Nation* 649 (June 8, 1927).

71. John W. Crawford, "Hound-Dogs and Bible Shouting: Julia Peterkin's Fine Novel of 'Blue-Gum' Negroes Is Suffused with Life," *New York Times Book Review*, March 6, 1927, 5.

72. Edwin Clark, "Six Months in the Field of Fiction," *New York Times Book Review*, June 26, 1927, 5.

73. Romeike clipping file.

74. Romeike clipping file.

75. Alain Locke, "Negroes and Earth," *Survey* 58 (May 1, 1927): 173.

76. Quoted in Strode, *Eleventh House*, 156.

77. BM.

78. Eugene Gordon, "The Negro's Inhibitions," *American Mercury* 13 (February 1928): 165.

79. *Nigger Heaven* came out in July 1926, but it had already aroused controversy earlier in the summer because the inflammatory title was announced in the *Mercury* as a book forthcoming from Knopf. See Thadious M. Davis, *Nella Larsen, Novelist of the Harlem Renaissance: A Woman's Life Unveiled* (Baton Rouge: Louisiana State University, 1994), 208.

80. See *The Harlem Renaissance: A Historical Dictionary for the Era*, ed. Bruce Kellner (New York: Methuen, 1987), 263.

81. *Crisis* 31 (March 1926): 219.

82. "The Negro in Art: How Shall He Be Portrayed?" *Crisis* 31 (March 1926): 219.

83. *Crisis* 32 (September 1926): 238–39.

84. "Gullah," in *Ebony and Topaz: A Collecteana*, ed. Charles S. Johnson (New York: Opportunity, 1927).

85. Alain Locke, "Our Little Renaissance," in *Ebony and Topaz*.

86. *Crisis* 32 (October 1926).

87. BM, [March 1927].

88. Joel Williamson, *New People: Miscegenation and Mulattoes in the United States* (New York: Free Press, 1980), 96.

89. Ella Weeks Walker remembers a real mule named Julia working the fields at Lang Syne, many years after *Black April* was written. I asked who had named the animal — Julia, Willie, Bill, one of the farmhands? Mrs. Walker couldn't say. No matter who originated the joke, everybody seems to have thought it was funny, including Julia herself.

90. BM, [March 1927].

91. BM.

92. BM, March 1927.

93. BM, March 28, 1927.

Chapter Eight: *Scarlet Sister Mary*

1. BM, July 8, 1927.

2. BM, July 14, 1927.

3. IF, n.d.

4. BM, April 20, 1927.

5. "Seeing Things," *American Magazine* 105 (January 1928): 115–16.

6. BM, August 23, 1927 (to Chambers).

7. BM, JP to Anne Johnston, n.d. (c. March 1927).

8. BM, June 4 and 8, 1927 (to Chambers).

9. Strode, *Eleventh House,* 143–47.

10. See Wallace Stegner, *The Uneasy Chair: A Biography of Bernard DeVoto* (New York: Doubleday, 1974); and Strode, *Eleventh House.*

11. BJS.

12. IF, June 14, 1931.

13. See Sharon O'Brien, *Willa Cather: The Emerging Voice* (New York: Oxford University Press, 1987), 288–359.

14. Strode, *Eleventh House,* 141.

15. BM, August 12, 1927 (to Chambers).

16. WHS; MH; JW.

17. BM, January 22, 1927.

18. Dale Warren, "Doris Ulmann: Photographer in Waiting," *Bookman* 72 (October 1930): 138.

19. Salpeter, "Studies in Color"; JP to Henry Salpeter, July 29, 1927, Bennett-Peterkin papers, University of Virginia Library, Charlottesville; BM, August and September 1927.

20. BM, June 22, 1927.

21. BM, September 4, 1927.

22. "The Strange Disease of Pyorrhea," Romeike clipping file, courtesy of Noel Polk.

23. Romeike clipping file.

24. BM, May 1928; see also Harris Chewning, "A Secretary's Souvenir Now Rests in Wofford Library," *Sandlapper,* April 1975, 47–53.

25. *SSM,* 26, 270, 82.

26. *SSM,* 76.

27. *SSM,* 100–101.

28. *SSM,* 123.

29. *SSM*, 101.

30. *SSM*, 108, 159.

31. *SSM*, 248.

32. *SSM*, 248, 243, 245. The real Keepsie apparently belonged to Mary's sister, and he never lost a leg; JW.

33. *SSM*, 291.

34. *SSM*, 329. This scene echoes one of Julia's earliest published sketches, "Betsy." The tale is repeated in "On a Plantation" with the son who brings home the baby called Ellis and the grandmother Maum Anaky. According to JW, Mary's son Cicero did not bring home a baby — Anaky Bryant's grandson Edward did that.

35. *SSM*, 333, 335, 336, 337.

36. *SSM*, 339–40.

37. *SSM*, 343, 345.

38. SY, n.d.

39. *SSM*, 14.

40. JW. These same invented episodes offended black critic Sterling R. Brown, who characterized them as "lapses into condescension"; see Brown, *The Negro in American Fiction* (1938; rpt. New York: Arno, 1969), 121. A sketch at SCHS indicates that it was a woman named Leah who actually had twins and discovered a third baby in her bed (28–613–20).

41. BM, May 1938.

42. For an exhaustive account of such symbolism, see Susan Haskins, *Mary Magdalene: Myth and Metaphor* (New York: Harcourt Brace, 1994); and Anne Hollander, "A Woman of Extremes," *New Yorker*, October 3, 1994, 112–17.

43. JW.

44. MH; JW; WHS.

45. EWW.

46. MH; JW.

47. WHS.

48. BM, June 1928.

49. BM, June 1928.

50. GP.

51. Fraser, "Louisa McCord," 9–11.

52. Louisa McCord Smythe, "Recollections," 11.

53. JW points out that the Charity and Champagne who were alive in Julia's day were actually brother and sister.

54. Julia may have derived these names from the McCord-era slaves Mauma Juno and Paupa July.

55. See W. G. Peterkin Store account book and money order book, SCHS.

56. JW.

57. *SSM*, 26–27.

58. *SSM*, 236.

59. BM, 1928.

60. BM, July 1928.

61. BM, July 1928. Paperback editions published in the 1940s and 1950s showed a scantily clad Mary posed suggestively in the lighted doorway of her cabin.

62. BM.

63. BM, August 1928, September 24, 1928.

64. BM, August 1928.

65. Thadious Davis, in *Nella Larsen* (297), contended that *Scarlet Sister Mary was* a Literary Guild selection.

66. BM; WW.

67. BM, October 18, 1928.

68. Like Julia, Edward Clarkson Leverett Adams owned a plantation several miles south of Columbia, inhabited by almost four hundred blacks; several of his Gullah sketches had appeared in the *Reviewer.* His first book, *Congaree Tales,* appeared in 1927, and though less well known than any of Julia's books, received favorable attention from the black press. Adams was much in demand as a speaker, often performing dramatic readings in Gullah.

69. BM, October 19, 1928.

70. BM, October 1928.

71. HLM, April 12, 1928.

72. BM, May 1928.

73. Hobson, *Mencken,* 272−73.

74. HLM, n.d.

75. Hudson Strode, [Review of *Scarlet Sister Mary,*] *New York Herald Tribune,* October 28, 1928.

76. "Literary Highways," undated clipping, AvL.

77. Robert Chamberlain, "Julia Peterkin Writes Again of the Gullah Negroes," *New York Times,* October 21, 1928, 4.

78. Ellen Glasgow, "The Novel in the South," *Harper's* 140 (1928): 99.

79. Florence Loeb Kellogg, "A Black Mother Earth," *Survey* 61 (December 1, 1928): 313.

80. Bobbs-Merrill records collected by Noel Polk in the 1970s.

81. BM, December 25 and 28, 1928.

Chapter Nine: Gabriel's Harp

1. "Lone Survivor of Atrocity Recounts Events of Lynching," *New York Amsterdam News,* June 1, 1927; and "Blood-Thirsty Mob Lynches Three Members of One Family," *New York Sun,* October 8, 1926; rpt. in Ralph Ginzburg, *One Hundred Years of Lynchings* (Baltimore: Black Classic Press, 1962), 175−78.

2. White, *Rope and Faggot.*

3. NAACP press release, October 29, 1926, "Walter White Gets Names of Aiken, S.C., Lynchers," WW.

4. WW, October 20, 1928.

5. NAACP press release, September 12, 1925, signed James Weldon Johnson, WW.

6. Letter to Blondell Whaley from Walter White, October 10, 1925, WW.

7. NAACP files, letter from James A. Lowe, Winston-Salem, N.C., September 2, 1925, WW. Recounting the incident to her daughter-in-law years later, Peterkin said that Whaley was shot by two men from a moving vehicle as he stood in front of the train station.

8. Letter to Walter White from Governor Thomas G. McLeod, September 17, 1925, WW.
9. WW, October 27, 1928.
10. Quoted in W. J. Cash, *The Mind of the South* (New York: Random House, 1941), 248.
11. JW.
12. BM, June 1928.
13. AvL sets this incident much earlier, in 1918−19. GP; the phrase "negro million-aire" is from BM.
14. BM; WHS.
15. BM, December 1928.
16. Mary Schmidt Campbell, ed., *Harlem Renaissance: Art of Black America* (New York: Harry N. Abrams, 1987), 72.
17. "A Proudful Fellow," *Century* 116 (May 1928): 12−22.
18. IF, spring 1928.
19. IF, n.d.
20. BM, April 16, 1927.
21. IF, December 11, 1928.
22. IF, n.d.
23. IF, December 24, 1928.
24. AvL.
25. "The Ideal Woman for a Man-Made World," *Book League Monthly* 1 (March 1929): 5−10.
26. AvL; WGP.
27. When the stranger on the train asks for a kiss in "The Lower Berth" (SCHS), Julia thinks not only of her husband and son, but of someone called "the major" as well. Crouch was often referred to around Fort Motte as "Major" Crouch.
28. IF, May 23, 1929.
29. IF, May 23, 1929; see also BM, April 1929.
30. BM, March 30, 1929.
31. Stuckey, *The Pulitzer Prize Novels,* 80.
32. *New York Times,* May 6, 1926, 1.
33. Stuckey, *The Pulitzer Prize Novels,* 79. (Shortly afterward, the prize committee again changed the terms, restoring the emphasis on wholesomeness. But the Pulitzer is now given simply "for the best American novel published during the year.")
34. HLM, May 13, 1929.
35. BM, May 17 and 21, 1929.
36. BM files, May 21, 1929.
37. Jack O'Bar, "A History of the Bobbs-Merrill Company, 1850−1940" (Ph.D. dissertation, Indiana University, 1975). Gaffney was the hometown of W. J. Cash, who would later praise Julia in his groundbreaking study, *The Mind of the South.*
38. BM, June 15, 1929.
39. To Chambers, BM, June 16, 1929; BM and HLM, May 20, 1929; HLM, May 22, 1929.
40. AM.

41. BM, May 22, 1929.
42. O'Bar, "History of the Bobbs-Merrill Company."
43. BM, October 1, 1929.
44. "Whites Writing Up the Blacks," *Dial* 86 (January 1929): 29–30.
45. HLM.
46. *Good Housekeeping,* June 1930, 28–31, 170, 173, 174, 177, 178, 180, 183.
47. "The Diamond Ring," *Good Housekeeping,* June 1930, 183.
48. *Saturday Evening Post,* October 5, 1929, 5, 153, 154, 156.
49. JW.
50. BM, June 1, 1929.
51. BM, September 10, 1929.
52. Hudson Strode, *The Story of Bermuda* (New York: Random House, 1932).
53. Alma Reed, *José Clemente Orozco* (New York: Delphic Studios, 1932), 151.
54. Isadora Bennett, "Lang Syne's Miss," *Bookman* 69 (June 1929): 360.
55. Reed, *José Clemente Orozco,* 151.
56. IF, December 2, 1929.
57. IF, December 4, 1929.

Chapter Ten: One Lovely, Tempting Place

1. *RJR,* 198.
2. IF, December 2 and 4, 1929.
3. IF, December 1929. (She also told this story to Lyle Saxon.)
4. IF, December 11 and 10, 1929.
5. See J. Nelson Frierson, "Divorce in South Carolina," *The North Carolina Law Review* 9 (1930–31): 265–81.
6. IF, December 11, 13, and 14, 1929.
7. IF, December 14, 1929.
8. "A Plantation Christmas," *Country Gentleman* 94 (December 1929): 24, 86, 87. Peterkin's fellow South Carolinian Archibald Rutledge had published an essay of the same name in 1921, in a book called *Plantation Game Trails.*
9. *PC.*
10. AM; IF, December 23, 1929.
11. IF, December 23, 1929.
12. IF, n.d.
13. BM.
14. IF.
15. IF, January 27, 1930.
16. IF, June 12, 1930.
17. IF, January 27, 1930.
18. IF, n.d., January 27, 1930.
19. IF, February 11, 1930.
20. IF, February 20, 1930.
21. IF, February 16, 1930.
22. IF, February 12, 1930.
23. IF, February 16, 1930.

24. ABP, May 2, 1930.

25. IF, June 13, 1930.

26. IF, April 5, 1930.

27. IF, April 10, [1930].

28. IF, [spring 1930].

29. IF, February 25, 1930.

30. IF, [April 20], 1930.

31. IF, March 5, 1930.

32. IF, February 10, 1930.

33. "What I Believe," *Forum* 84 (July 1930): 48–52.

34. IF, May 9 and 16, 1930.

35. IF, May 16, 1930.

36. IF, June 27, 1929.

37. IF, June 24, 1929.

38. Warren, "Doris Ulmann: Photographer in Waiting," 132. See also "Julia Peterkin Lived before She Began to Write," *Boston Transcript*; rpt. *Columbia Sunday Record*, January 8, 1928.

39. IF, April 2, 1930.

40. IF, April 23, 1930.

41. IF, May 9, 1930.

42. IF, [April 20, 1930]. Fineman was a great fan of Woolf and probably called her attention to the piece.

43. "What and Why I Have Written," SCHS.

44. GP; *BS*; Stubbs, *Family Album*, 146.

45. Professor Monroe Smith, quoted in Stubbs, *Family Album*, 146.

46. GP tells the nun version; BJS the one involving malnutrition.

47. BJS.

48. GP.

49. IF, June 19, 1930. (A letter from Laura to Julia that I found tucked inside Henry Mood's memoirs in the Wofford College Archives bears out this conclusion. Written in the early 1920s, it implies that Willie's illnesses are all in his mind, and that Julia is to blame for indulging him.)

50. IF, n.d., May 5, 1930.

51. IF, June 6, 1930.

52. IF, July 9 and 6, 1930.

53. IF, [summer 1930].

54. IF, July 1930.

55. IF, September 19, 1930.

56. IF, July 13, 1930.

57. IF, September 20, 1930.

58. IF, September 25, 1930.

59. IF, August 4, July 9 and 26, 1930.

60. IF, July 20, 1930.

61. IF, September 19, 1930.

62. IF, September 25, 1930.

63. IF, September 20, c. June 12, 1930.

64. *Bookman* 72 (December 24, 1930), IF.

65. October 1930, 205.

66. IF, n.d.

67. IF, August 18, 1932; BM (to DLC), June 1930.

68. BM, June 21, 1930.

69. BM, June 22, 1930.

70. BM, c. June 21, 1930.

71. BM, June 23, 1930.

72. O'Bar, "History of the Bobbs-Merrill Company," 220–24.

73. BM, July 18, 1930.

74. BM, June 23, 1930.

75. IF, n.d., July 13, 1930.

76. SCHS, 28–612–9 and 28–612–10.

Chapter Eleven: A Stiff Masquerade

1. IF, February 3, 1931.

2. Waters would be nominated for an Academy Award in 1950 for her performance in the screen production of Carson McCullers's *The Member of the Wedding*.

3. Arnold Rampersad, *The Life of Langston Hughes*, vol. 1: *1902–1941, I, Too, Sing America* (New York: Oxford University Press, 1986), 191.

4. Margot Peters, *The House of Barrymore* (New York: Knopf, 1990), 133.

5. Peters, *House of Barrymore*, 134.

6. IF, March 25, 1930.

7. IF, March 25, 1930.

8. IF, n.d.

9. BM, March 30, 1930.

10. IF, August 18, 1930.

11. Peters, *House of Barrymore*, 179.

12. *Yearbook of the Poetry Society of South Carolina*, 1930, PPSSC.

13. Henry Bellamann, "*Scarlet Sister Mary*," *Columbia State*, November 30, 1930.

14. "Scarlet Sister Mary" typescript, Yale Collection of American Literature, Beinecke Rare Book and Manuscript Library, Yale University.

15. IF, August 5, 1930; BM, September 1930 (to Chambers).

16. IF, September 25, 1930.

17. Romeike clipping file.

18. Maddox, "Life and Works of Julia Mood Peterkin," 70–71.

19. Romeike clipping file.

20. Romeike clipping file.

21. BM, September 30, 1930.

22. Neal Gabler, *Winchell: Gossip, Power and the Culture of Celebrity* (New York: Knopf, 1995), 85.

23. Quoted in Gabler, *Winchell*, 111.

24. IF, n.d.

25. Strode, *Eleventh House*, 142.

26. IF, [October 1930].
27. *Washington Times,* October 14, 1930.
28. *New York Times,* n.d., Romeike clipping file.
29. *Washington Star,* n.d., Romeike clipping file.
30. IF, [October 1930].
31. *Durham (N.C.) Herald-Sun,* May 3, 1931. Julia herself may have contributed to Robeson's disenchantment. Around this time, the actor is said to have asked if he might come to live in the Quarters at Lang Syne, to get in touch with the soul of his people. Julia refused on the grounds that having a famous black actor around would disrupt the community (BJS and EBC).
32. BM, October 18, 1930.
33. IF, November 10, 1930.
34. IF.
35. IF, October 18, November 10, 1930.
36. IF, October 18, 1930.
37. Romeike clipping file.
38. IF, November 5, 1930.
39. *New York Telegraph,* n.d., Romeike clipping file.
40. "A Very Bad Evening," "A Very Bad Play," *New York Evening Post,* n.d., Romeike clipping file.
41. Robert Littel, *New York World,* November 26, 1930.
42. Romeike clipping file.
43. Marc Connelly, *The Green Pastures,* ed. Thomas Cripps (Madison: University of Wisconsin Press, 1979). Julia herself loved the play; *The Green Pastures* "delights my soul," she told Anne Johnston (BM, March 1930).
44. Henry Bellamann, *"Scarlet Sister Mary,"* *Columbia State,* November 30, 1930. This passage does appear in the typescript in the Yale Collection of American Literature. Julia's comments about Young and Bellamann are in IF, December 13, 1930.
45. Rampersad, *Life of Langston Hughes,* 1:191.
46. Hughes, *The Big Sea,* 228.
47. IF, December 3, 1930.
48. IF, medical records.
49. IF, January 14, 1931.
50. IF, January 1, 1931.
51. IF, n.d.
52. IF, January 26, 1931.
53. IF, February 9, 1931.
54. IF, February 16, 1930.
55. IF, March 23, 1931.
56. IF, March 25, 1931.
57. IF, n.d.
58. IF, March 28, April 23, 1931.
59. IF, April 28, 1931.
60. IF, April 28, 1931.

Chapter Twelve: **Bright Skin**

1. *Denver Post,* December 6, 1931, Romeike clipping file.
2. *Charlotte News,* July 30, 1933.
3. *Wilson Library Bulletin,* n.d., Romeike clipping file.
4. Quoted in "The Crumb," May 27, 1932.
5. IF, April 1931.
6. IF, April 28 and 2, 1931; n.d., c. May 1931.
7. Unattributed article reprinted from the *Calhoun Times,* owned by Eugenia Cutts.
8. GP.
9. GP.
10. BM, letter to Chambers, March 19, 1927.
11. GP.
12. I was astonished by the number of women who told me that Julia had played for their weddings.
13. IF, June 14, 1931.
14. IF, n.d., c. May 1931.
15. GP.
16. IF, n.d., July 10, 1931.
17. May 3, 1931, 16.
18. IF.
19. IF, August 16, 1931.
20. IF, August 18, 1931.
21. Frances Frost, *Woman of This Earth* (Boston: Houghton Mifflin, 1934), 13 (the book is dedicated to Irving Fineman); IF, September 14, 1931.
22. BM, August 14, 1931.
23. BM, October 15, 1931.
24. FF to IF, October 1, 1931.
25. IF, October 6, 1931.
26. IF, October 6, 1931.
27. IF, October 21, 1931; BM, October 18, 1931.
28. GP.
29. IF, n.d.
30. IF, November 24, 1931.
31. JP to George Shively, BM, October 20, 1931.
32. *BS,* 11.
33. *BS,* 22−23.
34. *BS,* 25.
35. *BS,* 94.
36. *BS,* 100.
37. *BS,* 106.
38. *BS,* 124.
39. *BS,* 132.
40. *BS,* 98.
41. *BS,* 228.

42. *BS*, 233.

43. *BS*, 232−33.

44. *BS*, 56.

45. Edgar T. Thompson, *Plantation Societies, Race Relations, and the South: The Regimentation of Populations* (Durham: Duke University Press, 1975), 40.

46. *BS*, 181−83.

47. *BS*, 135.

48. *BS*, 136.

49. *BS*, 308−9.

50. *BS*, 279−80.

51. *BS*, 316.

52. *BS*, 332.

53. *BS*, 342.

54. JW; MH. The *name* "Big Pa" seems to have come from William Sanders, Ellis's father, though it was a common designation for very old black men in South Carolina.

55. JW; AvL.

56. JW.

57. *BS*, 92.

58. JW.

59. GP.

60. Elizabeth Robeson recently suggested that Julia's mulatto heroine is a stand-in for Irving Fineman, who, because he was Jewish, would have been regarded by her relatives as a member of another race. See Robeson, "The Ambiguity of Julia Peterkin," *Journal of Southern History* 61 (November 1995): 761−862. Faith Rehyer Jackson, who knew both Fineman and Peterkin when they were teaching at Bennington College, believes that Julia was drawn to Fineman largely because his Jewishness made him seem exotic. Novelist Harlan Greene also called my attention to the fact that a Jew was "not quite white" to Julia's South Carolina "social peers."

61. For a contemporary account of estrogen therapy, see Charles Mazer and Leopold Goldstein, *Clinical Endocrinology of the Female* (Philadelphia: Saunders, 1930), 257.

62. In *Doris Ulmann, American Portraits* (Albuquerque: University of New Mexico Press, 1985), David Featherstone said that Peterkin swept Ulmann away for her health.

63. IF, December 24, 1931. See also Doris Ulmann to Cammie Henry, December 19, 1931, Northwestern State University of Louisiana, Watson Memorial Library, Cammie G. Henry Research Center, Federal Writers' Project, folder 121.

64. James W. Thomas, *Lyle Saxon: A Critical Biography* (Birmingham, Ala.: Summa, 1991), 50; LSC, December 8, 1928.

65. LSC, December 13, 1929.

66. To Chambers, BM, December 24, 1931.

67. IF, January 1, 1932. Julia told acquaintances in New Orleans that she was suffering from the flu.

68. IF, January 1, 1932.

69. IF, January 6, 1932.

70. IF, January 6, 1932.

71. IF, March 30, 1932.

72. IF, January 15, 1932.

Chapter Thirteen: *Roll, Jordan, Roll*

1. IF, January 15, 1932.

2. Figures for June 1932. George B. Tindall, *The Emergence of the New South, 1913–1945* (Baton Rouge: Louisiana State University Press, 1967), 354.

3. BM, April 1932.

4. BM, March 23, 1932.

5. BM, April 1, 1932.

6. Meade Minnigerode, *Lives and Times: Four Informal American Biographies* (New York: Putnam, 1925), 119, 120.

7. Edward T. James, ed., *Notable American Women: A Biographical Dictionary* (Cambridge: Harvard University Press, 1971), 1:270–72.

8. BM, June 27, 1932.

9. IF, March 31 and 30, 1932.

10. IF, February 4, 1932.

11. IF, March 1, 1932.

12. Town Theater Scrapbooks.

13. IF, March 1, 1932.

14. BM, April 1932.

15. IF, March 7, 1932.

16. IF, February 22, 1932.

17. John Chamberlain, "*Bright Skin,*" *New York Times,* April 10, 1932.

18. BM, c. April 10, 1932.

19. Gerald Bullett, "Notes on Fiction," *Nation* 134, no. 632 (June 1, 1932).

20. Archer Winsten, "The New Novels: *Bright Skin,*" *Bookman* 75 (1932): 107–8.

21. BM, April 24, 1932.

22. "Plantation Folk," *Saturday Review of Literature,* April 9, 1932.

23. BM, April 1932.

24. IF, December 17, 1932; BM, April 1932.

25. For discussions of the stereotype, see Penelope Bullock, "The Mulatto in American Fiction," *Phylon* 6 (1945): 78–82; and Jules Zanger, "The 'Tragic Octoroon' in Pre–Civil War Fiction," *American Quarterly* 18 (Spring 1966): 63–70.

26. To Shively, BM, March 1932.

27. BM, May 1932.

28. BM, June 8, 1932. Paul Robeson had first expressed interest in *Black April* in 1929, after he had starred in *Showboat* and was about to play Othello.

29. BM, June 10, 1932.

30. IF, April 20, 1932.

31. IF, May 31, 1932.

32. IF, May 31, 1932.

33. IF, May 31, 1932.

34. IF, May 31, 1932.

35. IF, n.d.; BM, 1932.

36. "The most prestigious address" — scrawled on the envelope of a letter to Willie, owned by Eugenia Cutts; BM, August 10, 1932.

37. BM, August 1932; IF, summer 1932; undated, unattributed clippings from Converse College alumni files.

38. BM, April 29, May 1 and 29, June 27, 1932.

39. BM, September 2, 1932; figures from Bobbs-Merrill records collected by Noel Polk in the 1970s.

40. Figures from Bobbs-Merrill records collected by Noel Polk in the 1970s; BM, December 6, 1932.

41. Isadora Bennett, "Lang Syne's Miss," 358.

42. IF, December 1932.

43. IF, July 30, 1931; BM, June 1934.

44. Romeike clipping file.

45. "The Art of Living," by Julia Peterkin, *Columbia State*, June 6, 1933. See also Rupert Fuller, "Julia Peterkin, Writer, Talks on Modern Topics," *Columbia State*, October 9, 1933.

46. Romeike clipping file.

47. October 1933. See Mildrid Seydell papers, boxes 26 and 29, Robert W. Woodruff Library, Emory University, Atlanta, Ga.

48. September 14, 1936, quoted in Pilkington, ed., *Stark Young*, 708.

49. This may have been Dr. Gregory Zilboorg, who by some accounts was the most famous psychoanalyst in New York in the 1920s. See Alpert, *The Life and Times of Porgy and Bess*, 84.

50. IF, June 26, 1930.

51. Tindall, *Emergence of the New South*, 379.

52. *Cleveland Plain Dealer, Washington Post*, September 13, 1933.

53. Andrew Lytle, "The Hind Tit," in *I'll Take My Stand* (rpt. Baton Rouge: Louisiana State University Press, 1977), 203.

54. Pilkington, ed., *Stark Young*, 110.

55. "Not in Memorium, but in Defense," *I'll Take My Stand*, 328.

56. *I'll Take My Stand*, 350.

57. *I'll Take My Stand*, 245.

58. IF, April 25, May 7, 1932.

59. IF papers; undated clipping sent to him by Frances Frost.

60. IF, letters from Frances Frost.

61. BM, August 28, 1932.

62. BM, September 6, 1932.

63. IF, September 23 and 30, 1932.

64. IF, September 23, 1932.

65. IF, September 23, 1932.

66. IF, October 26, 1932.

67. IF, November 3, 1932.

68. IF, November 30, 1932.

69. IF, February 10, 1933.

70. Quoted in Bettina Berch, *Radical by Design: The Life and Style of Elizabeth Hawes* (New York: Dutton, 1988), 52.

71. Elizabeth Hawes, *Fashion Is Spinach* (New York: Random House, 1938), 225.

72. Rampersad, *Life of Langston Hughes*, 1:226.

73. Rampersad, *Life of Langston Hughes*, 1:226. At Adams's home, Hughes was ushered in the front door, seated in the living room, and served food and drink. But Hughes's companion, a black physician from Columbia, sat outside while the two writers talked. When Hughes asked why, the doctor explained that if word got out that he had "gone through the front door [of a white man's house] as a guest," his hospital and his practice would be ruined.

74. IF, February 27, 1933.

75. IF, March 8, 1933.

76. IF, April 6, 1933.

77. IF, August 21, 1933, Elizabeth Hawes to IF.

78. IF, n.d. (Because it is separated from the postmarked envelope, it is also possible that this letter may refer to one of Frances Frost's many pregnancy scares.)

79. IF, n.d., March 8, 1933.

80. IF, January 9, 1934.

81. IF, c. March 23, 1933.

82. "Two Novelists Attend Party; Learn of Fame," *Chicago Daily Tribune*, March 8, 1933.

83. IF, March 28, 1933; JP to Chambers, BM, April 1, 1933; Mitgang, ed., *Letters of Carl Sandburg*, May 25, 1933, 293.

84. IF, March 28, 1933.

85. IF, April 6, 1933.

86. BM. "A Plantation Christmas" would be reprinted in *Scholastic Magazine* in 1935, and in *Good Housekeeping*, December 1960.

87. Ballou also published Henry Roth's *Call It Sleep*.

88. BM, May 1, 1933; IF, May 19, 1933.

89. IF, July 24, 1933.

90. See Ulmann's correspondence with Saxon in the Cammie Henry Research Center, Northwestern State University of Louisiana, especially the letters written in 1933.

91. For the details of this account of Ulmann's friendship with John Niles, I am indebted to Philip Jacobs and to participants in a seminar sponsored by the J. Paul Getty Museum in November 1994, including Ron Pen, David Featherstone, William Clift, Weston Naef, Judith Keller, and Charles Hagan. An edited transcript of the discussion appears as "Between Two Worlds: The Photographs of Doris Ulmann," in *In Focus: Doris Ulmann* (Malibu, Calif.: The J. Paul Getty Museum, 1996).

92. IF, August 5, 1933.

93. IF, August 15, 1933.

94. IF, September 2, August 15, 1933.

95. Romeike clipping file.

96. IF, August 29, 1933. The original title was *This Side of Jordan* (IF, August 15,

1933), a name that may have been discarded because it had already been used on a novel by Roark Bradford in 1929.

97. James Meriwether, "No Finer Collaboration," MS. Philip Jacobs notes that the limited edition is remarkably similar to Ulmann's earlier books about famous doctors and editors, and that Ulmann herself probably chose the printer, designed the book, and possibly even paid the bill.

98. Cammie Henry's copy of *Roll, Jordan, Roll* has an inscription from Lyle Saxon that identifies some of the photographs taken at Melrose in May 1931 — those on pages 12, 47, 5, 50, 64, and 67 of the trade edition; Melrose Collection, Cammie Henry Research Center, Northwestern State University of Louisiana.

99. BM, December 1933. Eight of Ulmann's plantation photographs were crisply reproduced in the Literary Guild of America's *Wings* magazine in September 1931, as illustrations to a feature on Roark Bradford.

100. *Nation* 137 (January 24, 1934): 106.

101. *RJR*, 9.

102. *BS*, 53.

103. John Chamberlain, "Books of the Times," *New York Times* December 15, 1933, 27.

104. Brown, *The Negro in American Fiction*, 122.

105. BM files.

106. *RJR*, 175, 180.

107. *RJR*, 180, 183.

108. *RJR*, 59.

109. Lyle Saxon, inscribing the book for his benefactor Cammie Henry, captioned the picture "Dan's Legs Being Polished by War Baby"; Cammie Henry Collection, Northwestern State University of Louisiana.

110. *RJR*, 84–87.

111. *RJR*, 87.

112. *RJR*, 53–54.

113. *RJR*, 194.

114. *RJR*, 199, 200.

115. *RJR*, 203, 204.

116. *RJR*, 131.

117. *RJR*, 229.

118. *RJR*, 232.

Chapter Fourteen: Smash-up

1. IF, June 16, 1934; November 14 and 27, 1933.

2. *South Carolina Poetry Society Yearbook*, 1930.

3. IF, October 17, 1933.

4. IF, December 8, 1933.

5. IF, December 16, 1933.

6. IF, January 31, 1934.

7. ESS, January 31, 1934.

8. IF, January 1934.

9. IF, January 12 and 22, 1934.

10. IF, January 16, 1934.

11. Telephone interview with Belinda Rathbone, author of *Walker Evans: A Biography* (Boston: Houghton Mifflin, 1995).

12. IF, January 16, 1934.

13. IF, January 23, 1934; ESS, January 21, 1934.

14. *BS;* IF, February 3, 1934.

15. Cohodas, *Strom Thurmond,* 37.

16. IF.

17. BJS. The Reconstruction Finance Corporation was already building a swimming pool and a park nearby.

18. WGP.

19. IF, February 3, 1934.

20. IF, January 12, 1934.

21. IF, n.d.

22. IF, March 1, 1935.

23. IF, March 14, 1935.

24. IF, March 6, 5, and 15, 1934.

25. IF, March 27, 1934.

26. IF, April 10, 1934.

27. IF, April 11, 1934.

28. IF, April 28, 1934.

29. IF, January 10, 1934.

30. IF, April 28, 1934.

31. IF, June 7, May 16, 1934.

32. IF, July 12 and 21, 1934. Inevitably, the gossip followed her back to South Carolina — one of Fineman's neighbors had a daughter who lived in Columbia.

33. IF, July 21, 1934.

34. Stegner, *Biography of Bernard DeVoto,* 122.

35. IF, August 22, 1934.

36. Romeike clipping file.

37. Julia claimed that she arranged to have the body stored in a vault until Doris's sister, Edna Necarsulmer, could get to New York from England. But Philip Jacobs reports that records from the cemetery indicate that Ulmann was buried immediately in the family mausoleum.

38. IF, August 30, 1934.

39. IF, September 3, 1934.

40. IF, October 4, 1934.

41. My account of the controversy over Doris Ulmann's will is based on original research done by Philip Jacobs in preparation for a biography of Ulmann, and on JP's account in her letter to IF.

42. JP to Lyle Saxon, September 12, 1934, Northwestern State University of Louisiana, Watson Memorial Library, Cammie G. Henry Research Center, Federal Writers' Project, folder 121.

43. "Like a dog," "dopey," and "lousy giglio" are from Uebler to Saxton, September 4, 1934.

44. Uebler to Saxon, two letters, September 4 and 10, 1934; and Saxon to Uebler, Sep-

tember 8, 1934, Federal Writers' Project, folder 121. At least two people managed to slip in, however: Albert Bigelow Paine and Doris's old boyfriend Arnold Koffler. See letters to Saxon from Peterkin and Paine (August 30, 1934) in Federal Writers' Project, folder 121.

45. JP to Saxon, September 21, 1934, Federal Writers' Project, folder 121, Cammie Henry Research Center, Northwestern State University of Louisiana.

46. IF, September 3, October 4, 1934.

47. IF, October 31, 1934. In fact, Doris's last will *was* eventually changed in favor of the Necarsulmers. On February 7, 1935, an Agreement of Settlement was filed in New York City between Niles, the Necarsulmers, the John C. Campbell Folk School, and the United States Trust Company of New York, resolving the controversy over the differences between the 1927 and 1934 wills (Philip Jacobs, unpublished chronology of Doris Ulmann's life). The assignment of copyright giving Julia the rights to the trade edition, executed June 16, 1935, is preserved among Peterkin's papers at SCHS.

48. IF, October 5, 1934.

49. IF, July 30, 1937. The friend was bookstore owner J. T. Gittman.

50. IF, September 6 and 28, October 4, 1934.

51. IF, March 1 and 23, 1934.

52. IF, May 8, 1935.

53. IF, April 7, 1935.

54. IF, April 16, 1935.

55. IF, April 20, May 8, 1935.

56. IF, n.d. Internal evidence dates this letter to spring 1935.

57. IF, April 7, May 8, 1935.

58. IF, June 21, 1935; GP.

59. IF, June 8 and 11, 1935.

60. IF, February 20, March 8, 1934.

61. IF, December 1934; BM, August 10, September 3, 1935.

62. Telegram in IF, October 8, 1935; IF, October 23, 1935.

63. IF, December 14, 1934.

64. IF, May 8, 1935.

65. IF, June 11, 1935.

66. IF, July 19, 1935.

67. IF, n.d., August 30 and 24, 1935.

68. "The Crumb."

69. "The Crumb."

70. "The Crumb."

71. IF, November 20, 1935.

72. IF, December 1935.

73. IF, September 18, 1935.

74. IF, n.d., March 27 and January 6, 1936.

75. IF, February, April 3, 1936.

76. IF, June 8, 1936.

77. *Washington Post,* July 12, 1936; rpt. in *"Gone with the Wind" as Book and Film,* ed. Richard Harwell (Columbia: University of South Carolina Press, 1983), 21.

Mitchell, who was a Peterkin fan, was ecstatic over Julia's review and wrote her a thank-you note. See Margaret Mitchell, *Gone with the Wind: Letters, 1936–1939,* ed. Richard Harwell, 46–47 (New York: Macmillan, 1976).

78. Margaret Mitchell, *Gone with the Wind* (New York: Macmillan, 1936).

79. IF, March 11, 1936.

80. BM, October 4, 1936.

81. "One Southern View-point," *North American Review* 244 (December 1937): 394.

82. LS, n.d., c. December 1937.

83. IF, March 11, 1936.

84. CS, n.d.

85. IF, May 18, 1936.

86. IF, 1936.

87. IF, July 1, 1936.

88. IF, February 19, April 12, 1937.

89. TF, letter to the author.

90. Maddox, "Life and Works of Julia Mood Peterkin," 92–93.

91. IF, February 19, 1936.

92. IF, March 17, 1937.

93. IF, May 11, 1937.

94. IF, March 13, 1937.

95. IF, April 30, 1937.

96. IF, December 4, 1937.

97. IF, January 9, 1934.

98. IF, December 30, September 21, 1937.

99. IF, May 11, 1937.

100. TF, July 11, 1938; GP; HP. That same year, Julia told a group of government agricultural agents that her writing had been "incidental" to the work of the farm. "A Woman Looks at the Agricultural Program," unpublished typescript, "An Address to the School for Extension Workers," held at Clemson, South Carolina, on August 23–27, 1937, Calhoun County Museum, Calhoun County Historical Commission history folder P.

101. Julia reported having 106 people screened for syphilis; 17 tested positive, including Lucinda Jackson. Ninety-six children attended Christmas festivities at the end of the year. IF, December 1937.

102. TF, July 11, 1938.

103. IF, January 6, 1938.

104. GP; HP.

105. IF, July 30, 1937.

106. IF, July 30, 1937.

107. IF, October 19, 1937.

108. IF, February 19, 1938.

109. TF, July 11, 1938.

110. IF, June 21, 1938.

111. IF, November 14, 1938.

112. SY, January 17, 1939; HP.

Chapter Fifteen: A Great White Column

1. GP.
2. IF, August 30, 1930.
3. HS, n.d.
4. Letter to Lula Buck, n.d., owned by Eugenia Cutts.
5. EBC; GP.
6. HP.
7. Letter from JP to Bill Peterkin, owned by GP.
8. MB, September 1940.
9. See a letter from Ben Robertson dated March 6, 1939, Ben Robertson papers, folder 38, Special Collections, Robert Muldrow Cooper Library, Clemson University.
10. MB, December 15, 1939.
11. GP. (JW heard from his grandmother that one of the hands was called in to do the actual cutting.)
12. These rumors were still making the rounds in 1981, when Richard Haymaker published *A Blossom of the Night-Blooming Cereus* (Chicago: Adams Press), a novel narrated by a man whose wife commits suicide when she discovers that her husband has been seduced by a mixed-race woman with the tacit approval of his mother. According to novelist and historian Harlan Greene, Haymaker told staff members at the South Carolina Historical Society that his book was inspired by the life of Julia Peterkin. (It also has echoes of DuBose Heyward's *Mamba's Daughters.*) Descriptions of the house, especially the library, sound like Lang Syne. But the mother is an opera singer, the son a voluble musician and art critic, and his wife, who shoots herself in the head, the extremely pious and sheltered daughter of a bishop.
13. HP; GP; TF.
14. David Courtwright, *Dark Paradise: Opiate Addiction in America before 1940* (Cambridge: Harvard University Press, 1982), 6, 59.
15. TF, letter to the author; GP. In a rare interview a few years before her death, JP talked about Frida's death to Marilyn Price Maddox, a student working on a master's thesis at the University of Georgia. A member of the family "who wishes to remain anonymous" told her that private detectives were hired to investigate Frida's death (Maddox, "Life and Works of Julia Mood Peterkin," 94–95). Almost everyone I interviewed about Julia Peterkin reported hearing rumors that Frida had a drug problem and that Julia had somehow provoked her death.
16. MB, September 29, 1941.
17. July 14, 1943; Mitgang, ed., *Letters of Carl Sandburg,* 415.
18. GP; HP.
19. MB, June 9, 1943; GP.
20. CS, November 16, 1945.
21. Bellamann amazed his friends by producing a best-seller late in life. In 1940 he published the melodramatic *Kings Row,* which, even more so than Fineman's *Lovers Must Learn,* may be based on what the author knew about Julia Peterkin's

life. Like *Black April*, it features a double amputation; the patient's name is Drake, which, as Harlan Greene points out, was old Agenora Peterkin's maiden name. AKD, who grew up near Fort Motte, confirms that Bellamann drew on "Lang Syne experiences" for the plot of *Kings Row*. In Bellamann's version, a beloved town doctor cuts off a young (white) man's healthy legs to prevent him from marrying his daughter. Ronald Reagan starred in the movie version, waking after the horrific surgery to utter his signature line, "Where's the rest of me?"

22. Thomas, *Lyle Saxon*.
23. HP; GP.
24. IF, April 4, 1944.
25. He had moved to a farm called Connemara near Hendersonville, N.C.
26. One of them was John Askling, a professional indexer who first met her on her trip west in 1934. For many years he visited Lang Syne every Christmas. Julia eventually fell out with him when she discovered that the handsome young men he brought with him were not really his nephews.
27. GP. AvL confirms this story.
28. GP.
29. GP.
30. GP.
31. GP. For a written account of this incident, see South Carolina Hall of Fame Acceptance Speech, January 1994, rpt. in *Brookgreen Journal* 24, no. 1 (1994): 11.
32. GP; HP.
33. GP; HP.
34. GP; HP.
35. Cohodas, *Strom Thurmond*, 233. See also Tinsley Yarbrough, *A Passion for Justice: J. Waties Waring and Civil Rights* (New York: Oxford University Press, 1987).
36. See Michael D. Davis and Hunter R. Clark, *Thurgood Marshall: Warrior at the Bar, Rebel on the Bench* (New York: Birch Lane Press, 1992).
37. Irene L. Neuffer, "An Unforgettable Whim," undated clipping, Converse College alumni files.
38. MB, January 3, 1956.
39. GP; HP.
40. CS, March 2, 1953.
41. GP.

Bibliography

Works by Julia Peterkin

"From Lang Syne Plantation" ["Teaching Jim," "Mose"]. *Reviewer* 2 (October 1921): 6–9.

"The Merry-Go-Round." *Smart Set* 66 (December 1921): 69–72.

"Imports from Africa" ["Cat-fish," "Cooch's Premium," "The Ortymobile," "The Plat-Eye," "Betsy"]. *Reviewer* 2 (January 1922): 197–200.

"Imports from Africa II" ["Finding Peace," "Cholera," "Cato," "Uncle Bill," "A Sketch"]. *Reviewer* 2 (February 1922): 253–59.

"Studies in Charcoal" ["Green Walnuts," "Roots Work"]. *Reviewer* 2 (March 1922): 319–27.

"The Right Thing." *Reviewer* 3 (April 1922): 383–88.

"A Baby's Mouth." *Reviewer* 3 (May 1922): 437–42.

"Silhouettes" ["A Wife," "A Crutch"]. *Reviewer* 3 (June 1922): 500–503.

"Missy's Twins." *Reviewer* 3 (October 1922): 668–73.

"From a Plantation." *Reviewer* 3 (July 1923): 925–31.

"Venner's Sayings" ["Green Thursday," "The Wind," "Gifts," "Two Kinds of Love," "Boy-Chillen," "Men," "Warning," "Greed of the Ground," "Advice," "Prayer from Lang Syne Plantation"]. *Poetry* 23 (November 1923): 59–67.

"Over the River." *Reviewer* 4 (January 1924): 84–96.

"The Foreman." *Reviewer* 4 (July 1924): 286–94.

"Daddy Harry." *Reviewer* 4 (October 1924): 382–83.

Green Thursday. New York: Knopf, 1924.

"Maum Lou." *Reviewer* 5 (January 1925): 17–32.

"Vinner's Sayings" ["Pray, Chile, Pray," "Somebody Gwine Dead," "You Can' Belongst to Nobody," "Winter," "When You Go Walkin' Out," "Ol' Mens Runnin' Roun'," "No Need Fo' Mark Grabe"]. *Poetry* 25 (February 1925): 240–43.

"Manners." *Reviewer* 5 (July 1925): 71–80.

"Whose Children?" In *The Borzoi 1925; Being a Sort of Record of Ten Years of Publishing,* ed. Alfred A. Knopf, 155–64. New York: Knopf, 1925.

"The Sorcerer." *American Mercury* 4 (April 1925): 441–47.

Black April. Indianapolis: Bobbs-Merrill, 1927.

"Gullah." In *Ebony and Topaz: A Collecteana,* ed. Charles S. Johnson. New York: Opportunity, 1927.

"Negro Blue and Gold." *Poetry* 31 (October 1927): 44–47.

Scarlet Sister Mary. Indianapolis: Bobbs-Merrill, 1928.

"Seeing Things." *American Magazine* 105 (January 1928): 26–27, 115–16.

Review of *Southern Exposure,* by Peter Mitchel Wilson. *Saturday Review of Literature,* January 14, 1928.

"A Proudful Fellow." *Century* 116 (May 1928): 12–22.

[Autobiography]. In *On Parade: Caricatures by Eva Herrmann,* ed. Erich Posselt, 114–18. New York: Coward-McCann, 1929.

"The Ideal Woman for a Man-Made World." *Book League Monthly* 1 (March 1929): 5–10.

"Heart Leaves." *Saturday Evening Post,* October 5, 1929, 5, 153, 154, 156.

"Greasy Spoon." *Ladies' Home Journal,* October 1929, 5, 139, 141.

"A Plantation Christmas." *Country Gentleman,* December 1929, 24, 86, 87.

"Santy Claw." *Ladies' Home Journal,* December 1929, 20–21, 163, 165.

"The Diamond Ring." *Good Housekeeping,* June 1930, 28–31, 170, 173, 174, 177, 178, 180, 183.

"What I Believe." *Forum* 84 (July 1930): 48–52.

"Ashes." *Golden Book* 13 (June 1931): 51–55.

"Old Uncle Mose." *New York Herald Tribune Magazine,* November 22, 1931.

Stories of the South: Old and New. Chapel Hill: University of North Carolina Press, 1931.

"The Bright Crown of the Year." *New York Herald Tribune Magazine,* December 25, 1932.

Bright Skin. Indianapolis: Bobbs-Merrill, 1932.

"Boy-Chillen." In *One-Act Plays for Stage and Study,* ed. Zona Gale, 3–15. New York: Samuel French, 1932.

"The Art of Living." *Columbia State,* June 6, 1933.

Roll, Jordan, Roll. New York: Robert O. Ballou, 1933.

A Plantation Christmas. Boston: Houghton Mifflin, 1934.

"A Plantation Christmas." *Scholastic,* December 14, 1935, 4–6.

Review of *Gone with the Wind. Washington Post,* July 12, 1936. Reprinted in *Gone with the Wind as Book and Movie,* ed. Richard Harwell, 21–23. Columbia: University of South Carolina Press, 1983.

"One Southern View-point." *North American Review* 244 (December 1937): 394.

"Ashes." *Ellery Queen's Mystery Magazine,* March 1954, 81–89.

"Conjuration" and "The Bury League" (reprinted from *Roll, Jordan, Roll*). In *The Book of Negro Folklore,* ed. Langston Hughes and Arna Bontemps, 102–13. New York: Dodd, Mead, 1958.

"A Plantation Christmas." *Good Housekeeping,* December 1960, 54–55.

The Collected Short Stories of Julia Peterkin. Ed. Frank Durham. Columbia: University of South Carolina Press, 1970.

"The Red Rooster" and "Son" (reprinted from *Green Thursday*). In *A Tricentennial Anthology of South Carolina Literature, 1670–1970,* ed. Richard James Calhoun and John Caldwell Guilds, 340–55. Columbia: University of South Carolina Press, 1970.

Secondary Sources

A.M. "Plantation Tales." *St. Paul News,* October 28, 1924.

Aaron, Daniel. *Writers on the Left: Episodes in American Literary Communism.* New York: Columbia University Press, 1992.

Abrahams, Roger D. *African Folktales.* New York: Pantheon, 1983.

———. *Afro-American Folktales: Stories from Black Traditions in the New World.* New York: Pantheon, 1985.

Adams, E. C. L. *Congaree Sketches*. Chapel Hill: University of North Carolina Press, 1927.

———. *Tales of the Congaree*. Ed. and intro. Robert G. O'Meally. Chapel Hill: University of North Carolina Press, 1987.

"Again a Serious Study of Negroes in Fiction." *New York Times Book Review*, September 28, 1924.

Alderman, Edwin Anderson, et al. *Library of Southern Literature*. Atlanta: Martin and Hoyt, 1929.

Allen, Frederick Lewis. *Only Yesterday: An Informal History of the 1920s*. New York: Harper, 1931.

Allen, Hervey. "The Low Country Speaks." *Saturday Review of Literature*, March 14, 1925.

Allston, Susan Lowndes. *Waccamaw in the Carolina Low Country*. Charleston: Walker, Evans, and Cogswell, 1935.

Alpert, Hollis. *The Barrymores*. New York: Dial Press, 1964.

———. *The Life and Times of Porgy and Bess*. New York: Knopf, 1990.

Anderson, Jervis. *This Was Harlem*. New York: Farrar, Straus and Giroux, 1981.

Anderson, Mary Crow. *Two Scholarly Friends: Yates Snowden—John Bennett, Correspondence, 1902–1932*. Columbia: University of South Carolina Press, 1993.

Andrews, William L. "Miscegenation in the Late Nineteenth-Century American Novel." *Southern Humanities Review* 13 (Winter 1979): 13–24.

"Appointed to Bennington College Faculty." *New York Times*, September 6, 1936.

"Appointed to Faculty, Bennington College, Vermont." *New York Times*, June 29, 1936.

Atkinson, J. Brooke. "The Play." *New York Times*, November 26, 1930.

"An Author Goes on Stage." *New York Times*, April 10, 1932.

"Author of *Scarlet Sister Mary* Pleased with Town Theater Plan." *Columbia State*, September 15, 1929.

"Awful R.R. Wreck." *Sumter Herald*, June 5, 1903.

Ayers, Edward. *Promise of the New South*. New York: Oxford University Press, 1992.

Baker, Ernest A., and James Packman. *A Guide to the Best Fiction*. London: Routledge, 1932. 232–33.

Ball, John C., and Carl D. Chambers, eds. *The Epidemiology of Opiate Addiction in the United States*. Springfield, Ill.: Charles C. Thomas, 1970.

Barksdale, Richard, and Keneth Kinnamon, eds. *Black Writers of America*. New York: Macmillan, 1972.

Barrymore, Ethel. *Memories: An Autobiography*. New York: Harper and Brothers, 1955.

Basso, Hamilton. "Letters in the South." *New Republic* 83 (June 19, 1935): 161–63.

Battey, Robert. "Address by Dr. Robert Battey, Rome, Ga." *Transactions of the South Carolina Medical Association*, 39th session, April 23–24, 1889. 59–68.

Beach, Joseph Warren. *The Twentieth-Century Novel: Studies in Technique*. New York: Century, 1932. 232–33.

Beatty, Richmond Croom. *Contemporary Southern Prose*. Boston: Heath, 1940. 313–20, 597–614.

Bellamann, Henry. "*Green Thursday,* Julia Peterkin, Is an Extraordinary Achievement." *Columbia Record,* November 24, 1924.

———. "Julia Peterkin's New Novel." *Columbia State,* April 10, 1932.

———. "Literary Highway." *Columbia State,* January 20, 1933.

———. [Review of *Green Thursday.*] *Columbia Record,* April 15, 1925.

———. "*Scarlet Sister Mary.*" *Columbia State,* November 30, 1930.

Bennett, Isadora. "Lang Syne's Miss." *Bookman* 69 (June 1929): 357–66.

Benstock, Shari. *Women of the Left Bank: Paris, 1900–1940.* Austin: University of Texas Press, 1986.

Berch, Bettina. *Radical by Design: The Life and Style of Elizabeth Hawes.* New York: Dutton, 1988.

Berliner, Louise. *Texas Guinan: Queen of the Night Clubs.* Austin: University of Texas Press, 1993.

Bingham, Sallie. "The Darkness and the Light." Unpublished play.

"*Black April.*" *Outlook* 145 (April 6, 1927): 443.

"Black Beauty." *Time,* January 1, 1934.

Bokinsky, Caroline. "Names of Julia Peterkin's Characters." *Names in South Carolina* 28 (Winter 1981): 11–12.

Bonn, Thomas L. *Undercover: An Illustrated History of American Mass Market Paperbacks.* New York: Penguin, 1982.

Botkin, B. A. *Folk-Say: A Regional Miscelany.* Norman: University of Oklahoma Press, 1930.

Bradbury, John M. *Renaissance in the South: A Critical History of the Literature, 1920–1960.* Chapel Hill: University of North Carolina Press, 1963.

Brickell, Herschel. "Books on Our Table." *New York Evening Post,* September 25, 1924.

———. "Books on Our Table." *New York Evening Post,* March 14, 1925.

———. "The Literary Awakening in the South." *Bookman* 66 (1927): 138–43.

———. "On the Old Plantation." *North American Review* 237 (February 1934): 189.

———. "A Pagan Heroine: Scarlet Sister Mary." *Saturday Review of Literature* 5 (November 3, 1928): 318.

———. "Plantation Folk." [Review of *Bright Skin.*] *Saturday Review of Literature* 28 (April 9, 1932).

"*Bright Skin.*" *Times (London) Literary Supplement,* June 23, 1932.

Brown, Sterling. "Arcadia, South Carolina." *Opportunity: A Journal of Negro Life* 12 (February 1934): 59, 60.

———. "Negro Character as Seen by White Authors." *Journal of Negro Education* 2 (1933): 179–203.

———. *The Negro in American Fiction.* New York: Arno, 1969.

Bullett, Gerald. "Book Notes." *New Republic* 71 (June 29, 1932): 189.

———. "Notes on Fiction." *Nation* 134 (June 1, 1932): 632.

Bullock, Penelope. "The Mulatto in American Fiction." *Phylon* 6 (1945): 78–82.

Burns, James MacGregor. *Roosevelt: The Soldier of Freedom, 1940–1945.* New York: Harcourt Brace Jovanovich, 1970.

Burton, E. Milby. *South Carolina Silversmiths, 1690–1860.* Charleston, S.C.: Charleston Museum, 1942.

"Burton Quits Jury on Pulitzer Award." *New York Times,* May 17, 1929.

Cady, Edwin, ed. "Studies in the Bobbs-Merrill Papers." *Indiana University Bookman,* March 8, 1967.

Calverton, V. F. "The Bankruptcy of Southern Culture." *Scribner's* 99 (1936): 294–98.

Campbell, E. "Literary Husband, Wife: Two Writers Like Tanglewood." *Winston-Salem (N.C.) Journal,* December 20, 1963.

Campbell, Mary Schmidt, ed. *Harlem Renaissance: Art of Black America.* New York: Abrams, 1987.

Canby, Henry Seidel. "Notes of a Rapid Reader: *Black April.*" *Saturday Review of Literature* 3 (April 16, 1927): 725.

Cash, W. J. "The Mind of the South." *American Mercury* 18 (1929): 191.

———. *The Mind of the South.* New York: Random House, 1941.

Chamberlain, John. "Books of the Times." *New York Times,* December 15, 1933.

———. "*Bright Skin.*" *New York Times,* April 10, 1932.

———. "Julia Peterkin Writes Again of the Gullah Negroes." *New York Times,* October 21, 1928.

———. "The Negro as Writer." *Bookman* 70 (February 1930): 601–11.

Cheney, Brainard. "Can Julia Peterkin's Genius Be Revived for Today's Black Mythmaking?" *Sewanee Review* 88 (January–March 1972): 173–79.

———. *Kitty Mood's Cup.* Washington, D.C.: Burr Oak, 1985.

Chewning, Harris. "A Secretary's Souvenir Now Rests in Wofford Library." *Sandlapper,* April 1975, 47–53.

Chunn, W. P. "The Prevention of Conception." *Maryland Medical Journal* 32 (1894–95): 340–43.

Clark, Edwin. "Six Months in the Field of Fiction." *New York Times Book Review,* June 26, 1927, 5.

Clark, Emily. *Ingenue among the Lions: The Letters of Emily Clark to Joseph Hergesheimer.* Ed. and intro. Gerald Langford. Austin: University of Texas Press, 1965.

———. *Innocence Abroad.* New York: Knopf, 1931.

———. "Negro Life on a South Carolina Plantation." *New York Herald Tribune Books,* April 10, 1932.

———. [Review of *Black April.*] *New York Herald Tribune,* April 17, 1927.

Clay, Edward. "The Negro in Recent American Literature." *American Writers Congress* (New York: International, 1935), 145–53.

Coates, Carroll. "Julia Peterkin: Her Novels Still in Style." *Columbia State* and *Columbia Record,* May 8, 1966.

Cohodas, Nadine. *Strom Thurmond and the Politics of Southern Change.* New York: Simon and Schuster, 1993.

Coker, Elizabeth Boatwright. "Our Julia." MS.

Collins, Mary. "Winthrop Gives Diplomas to 321 at Commencement: Mrs. Julia Peterkin Delivers Commencement Address at Rock Hill." *Spartanburg Herald,* June 6, 1933.

Colson, Amanda. "Ahead of Her Time: Peterkin Wrote Realistically of South She Saw." *Sumter Item,* July 22, 1990.

Connelly, Marc. *Green Pastures*. Ed. and intro. Thomas Cripps. Madison: University of Wisconsin Press, 1979.

Cooper, Wayne F. *Claude McKay: Rebel Sojourner in the Harlem Renaissance*. Baton Rouge: Louisiana State University Press, 1987.

Corbin, Laura. "Wofford Has Manuscript of Winning Novel." *Spartanburg Herald*, December 14, 1976.

Couch, W. T. "American Peasants." *Virginia Quarterly Review* 10 (October 1934): 637–38.

————, ed. *Culture in the South*. Chapel Hill: University of North Carolina Press, 1935.

————. "Reflections on the Southern Tradition." *South Atlantic Quarterly* 35 (1936): 284–97.

"Courage Applauded: Gaffney Newspaper Prints Story Banned as Immoral." *Gaffney Ledger*, February 18, 1967, 24.

Courtwright, David. *Dark Paradise: Opiate Addiction before 1940*. Cambridge: Harvard University Press, 1982.

Crawford, John W. "Hound-Dogs and Bible Shouting: Julia Peterkin's Fine Novel of 'Blue-Gum' Negroes Is Suffused with Life." *New York Times Book Review*, March 6, 1927, 5.

Creel, Margaret Washington. *"A Peculiar People": Slave Religion and Community Culture among the Gullahs*. New York: New York University Press, 1988.

Cripps, Thomas. *Slow Fade to Black: The Negro in American Film, 1900–1942*. New York: Oxford University Press, 1977.

Cronin, E. David. *Black Moses: The Story of Marcus Garvey*. Madison: University of Wisconsin Press, 1955.

Crum, Mason. *Gullah: Negro Life in the Carolina Sea Islands*. Durham: Duke University Press, 1940.

Cullen, Countee. *Color*. New York: Harper, 1925.

Dabney, Virginius. *Liberalism in the South*. Chapel Hill: University of North Carolina Press, 1932.

Davidson, Donald. "The 45 Best Southern Novels for Readers and Collectors." *Publishers' Weekly* 127 (April 27, 1935): 167–76.

————. "A Meeting of Southern Writers." *Bookman* 74 (January–February 1932): 494–96.

————. *The Spyglass: Views and Reviews, 1924–1930*. Ed. John T. Fain. Nashville: Vanderbilt University Press, 1963. 20–23.

Davis, Joe Lee. *James Branch Cabell*. New York: Twayne, 1962.

Davis, Michael D., and Hunter R. Clark. *Thurgood Marshall: Warrior at the Bar, Rebel on the Bench*. New York: Birch Lane Press, 1992.

Davis, Thadious M. *Nella Larsen, Novelist of the Harlem Renaissance: A Woman's Life Unveiled*. Baton Rouge: Louisiana State University Press, 1994.

Day, Dorothy. *The Long Loneliness*. New York: Harper and Brothers, 1952.

Daykin, Walter I. "Negro Types in American White Fiction." *Sociology and Social Research* 22 (1937): 45–52.

Devereaux, Anthony Q. *The Rice Princes*. Privately printed by the *Columbia State*, n.d.

Dickson, Frank. "Remembering Old Lang Syne." *State Magazine*, January 25, 1987, 6.

Dolmetsch, Carl R. *The Smart Set: A History and an Anthology.* New York: Dial Press, 1966.

Downes, Randolph Chandler. *The Rise of Warren Gamaliel Harding, 1865–1920.* Columbus: Ohio State University Press, 1970.

Duberman, Martin. *Paul Robeson.* New York: Knopf, 1988.

Du Bois, W. E. B. "The Browsing Reader." *Crisis* 29 (December 1924): 89.

———. "Criteria of Negro Art." *Crisis* 32 (October 1926): 290–97.

———. *Encyclopedia of the Negro.* New York: The Phelps Stokes Fund, 1945.

Durante, Jimmy, and Jack Kofoed. *Night Clubs.* New York: Knopf, 1931.

Durham, Frank. *DuBose Heyward: The Man Who Wrote* Porgy. Columbia: University of South Carolina Press, 1954.

———. *DuBose Heyward's Use of Folklore in His Negro Fiction.* The Citadel Monograph Series, no. 2. Charleston, S.C.: The Citadel, 1961.

———. "Julia Peterkin: The Art of Writing." *Carolinian* 45 (March 1932): 6, 8.

———. "Mencken as Midwife." *Menckeniana* 32 (Winter 1969): 2–6.

———. "The Rise of DuBose Heyward and the Rise and Fall of the Poetry Society of South Carolina." *Mississippi Quarterly* 19 (Winter 1965–66): 66–78.

———. "South Carolina's Poetry Society." *South Atlantic Quarterly* 41 (April 1953): 277–85.

E.A.M. "Writers of Today in South Carolina." *Columbia State*, April 2, 1934.

E.L. [Review of *Green Thursday.*] *Chicago Federated Press Bulletin*, November 29, 1924.

Edgar, Walter B. *South Carolina in the Modern Age.* Columbia: University of South Carolina Press, 1992.

Egerton, John. *Speak Now against the Day: The Generation before the Civil Rights Movement in the South.* New York: Knopf, 1994.

Erenberg, Lewis A. *Steppin' Out: New York Nightlife and the Transformation of American Culture, 1890–1930.* Westport, Conn.: Greenwood Press, 1981.

"Ethel Barrymore Has Peterkin Novel Play." *New York Times*, June 14, 1929.

"Ethel Barrymore to Act Tonight." *New York Times*, November 25, 1930.

"Ethel B. Colt in Stage Debut." *New York Times*, September 26, 1930.

F.B. "*Scarlet Mary* a Rich Picture of Negro Life." *Chicago Daily Tribune*, December 1, 1928.

Fain, John Tyree, and Thomas Daniel Young, eds. *The Literary Correspondence of Donald Davidson and Allen Tate.* Athens: University of Georgia Press, 1974.

Fauset, Jessie. *Plum Bun.* Boston: Beacon Press, 1990.

Featherstone, David. *Doris Ulmann, American Portraits.* Albuquerque: University of New Mexico Press, 1985.

Ferguson, A. H. "Conservatism of Ovaries and Tubes." *New York Medical Journal* 78 (1903): 782–85.

Fergusson, Francis. "Miss Ethel Barrymore in Blackface." *Bookman* 72 (January 1931): 514–15.

Field, E. P. "Who's Who in the Golden Book." *Golden Book* 13 (June 1931): 4.

Fineman, Irving. *Lovers Must Learn.* New York: Longmans, 1932.

————. *This Pure Young Man.* New York: Longmans, 1930.

————. "Wormsloe Revisited after 30 Years." *Savannah Morning News,* November 29, 1964.

Fisher, Rudolph. "The Caucasian Storms Harlem." *American Mercury* 11 (August 1927): 393–98.

Foner, Eric. *Reconstruction: America's Unfinished Revolution, 1863–1877.* New York: Harper and Row, 1988.

Fox-Genovese, Elizabeth. *Within the Plantation Household: Black and White Women of the Old South.* Chapel Hill: University of North Carolina Press, 1988.

Frankenberg, Ruth. *White Women, Race Matters: The Social Construction of Whiteness.* Minneapolis: University of Minnesota Press, 1993.

Fraser, Jessie Melville. "Louisa McCord." Master's thesis, University of South Carolina, 1919.

Frazier, Annie C. M. "The South Speaks Out." *Sewanee Review* 35 (1927): 313–24.

Friedman, Lawrence J. *The White Savage: Racial Fantasies in the Postbellum South.* Englewood Cliffs, N.J.: Prentice-Hall, 1970.

Frierson, J. Nelson. "Divorce in South Carolina." *North Carolina Law Review* 9 (1930–31): 264–81.

Frost, Frances. *Woman of This Earth.* Boston: Houghton Mifflin, 1934.

Fuller, Rupert. "Julia Peterkin, Writer, Talks on Modern Topics." *Columbia State,* October 9, 1933.

Gabler, Neal. *Winchell: Gossip, Power and the Culture of Celebrity.* New York: Knopf, 1995.

Gaines, Francis Pendleton. *The Southern Plantation: A Study in the Development and Accuracy of a Tradition.* New York: Columbia University Press, 1924.

Gatewood, Willard B. *Preachers, Pedagogues, and Politicians: The Evolution Controversy in North Carolina, 1920–1929.* Chapel Hill: University of North Carolina Press, 1966.

Genovese, Eugene. *Roll, Jordan, Roll: The World the Slaves Made.* New York: Pantheon, 1974.

Gimmestad, Victor E. *Joseph Hergesheimer.* Boston: Twayne, 1984.

Ginzburg, Ralph. *One Hundred Years of Lynchings.* Baltimore: Black Classic Press, 1962.

Glasgow, Ellen. "The Novel in the South." *Harper's* 143 (1928): 93–100.

Gloster, Hugh M. *Negro Voices in American Fiction.* Chapel Hill: University of North Carolina Press, 1948.

Gonzales, Ambrose E. *The Black Border: Gullah Stories of the Carolina Coast.* Columbia, S.C.: The State, 1922.

Gordon, Eugene. "The Negro Press." *American Mercury* 8 (June 1926): 207–15.

————. "The Negro's Inhibitions." *American Mercury* 13 (February 1928): 159–65.

Grantham, Dewey W. *The South in Modern America: A Region at Odds.* New York: HarperCollins, 1994.

Green, Paul. "A Plain Statement about Southern Literature." *Reviewer* 5 (January 1925): 71–76.

"*Green Thursday.*" *Christian Advocate*, January 2, 1925.

"*Green Thursday.*" *Vogue*, November 1924, 10.

"*Green Thursday* and *Porgy.*" *Raleigh News and Observer*, October 18, 1925.

Gregorie, Anne King. *History of Sumter County, South Carolina.* Sumter, S.C.: Library Board of Sumter County, 1954.

Groves, J. A. *The Alstons and Allstons of North and South Carolina.* Atlanta: Franklin, 1901.

Guinan, Texas. "How to Keep Your Husband out of My Nightclub." *Liberty*, April 30, 1932, 50–51.

H.B. [Herschell Brickell.] "Books on the Table." *New York Evening Post*, March 14, 1923.

Hackett, Alice Payne. *Sixty Years of Best Sellers, 1895–1955.* New York: Bowker, 1956.

Halper, Albert. "Whites Writing Up the Blacks." *Dial* 86 (January 1928): 29–30.

Hart, Lynn Taylor. "Once Banned, Books by Julia Peterkin Treasured." *Georgetown Times*, January 11, 1984, 3A, 6B.

Hatcher, Harlan H. *Creating the Modern American Novel.* New York: Farrar and Rinehart, 1935. 140–51.

Havemeyer, Louisine. *From Sixteen to Sixty: Memoirs of a Collector.* New York: privately printed for the family of Mrs. H. O. Havemeyer and the Metropolitan Museum of Art, 1961.

Hawes, Elizabeth. *Anything but Love.* New York: Rinehart, 1942.

———. *Fashion Is Spinach.* New York: Random House, 1938.

Haymaker, Richard E. *A Blossom of the Night-Blooming Cereus.* Chicago: Adams Press, 1981.

Hemmingway, Theodore. "Beneath the Yoke of Bondage: A History of the Black Folks in South Carolina." Ph.D. dissertation, University of South Carolina, 1976.

Hemphill, J. C. *Men of Mark in South Carolina.* Washington, D.C.: Men of Mark Publishing Company, 1907.

Henry, Louis Lee. *Julia Peterkin: A Biographical and Critical Study.* Ann Arbor, Mich.: University Microfilms, 1966.

Herrick, Robert. "A Study in Black." *New Republic* 57 (December 26, 1928): 172.

Herskovits, Melville. *The Myth of the Negro Past.* Boston: Beacon Press, 1958.

———. "Negro Art: African and American." *Social Forces* 5 (December 1926): 291–98.

Heyward, Dorothy. "Porgy's Native Tongue — A Dissertation on Gullah, the Negro Language of the Play." *New York Times*, December 4, 1927.

Heyward, DuBose. *Brass Ankle.* New York: Farrar and Rinehart, 1931.

———. *Mamba's Daughters.* New York: Literary Guild, 1929.

———. "The New Note in Southern Literature." *Bookman* 61 (April 1925): 153–56.

———. *Porgy.* New York: Doran, 1925.

Hibbard, Addison. "Literature South — 1924." *Reviewer* 5 (January 1925): 52–58.

Hill, Herbert, ed. *Anger and Beyond: The Negro Writer in the United States.* New York: Harper and Row, 1966.

Himes, Norman E. *Medical History of Contraception.* New York: Shocken Books, 1936.

Hobson, Fred. *H. L. Mencken: A Biography.* New York: Random House, 1994.

———. *Serpent in Eden: H. L. Mencken and the South.* Baton Rouge: Louisiana State University Press, 1974.

Holmes, William F. *The White Chief: James Kimble Vardaman.* Baton Rouge: Louisiana State University Press, 1970.

Holsey, Albon L. "Learning How to Be Black." *American Mercury* 16 (April 1929): 421–25.

Hubbell, Jay B. *The South in American Literature, 1607–1900.* Durham, N.C.: Duke University Press, 1954.

Huffman, John Andrew. "Elements of Historical Geography of Fort Motte, SC." MS, dated 1972, in the South Caroliniana manuscript collection, University of South Carolina.

———. "The Fort Motte Riot of 1896." MS, dated 1976, in the South Caroliniana manuscript collection, University of South Carolina.

———. "Negro Insularity at Fort Motte, SC: A Geographic Perspective." MS, dated 1970, in the South Caroliniana manuscript collection, University of South Carolina.

Huggins, Nathan Irvin, ed. *Voices from the Harlem Renaissance.* New York: Oxford University Press, 1976.

Hughes, Langston. *The Big Sea.* New York: Hill and Wang, 1940.

———. *Fine Clothes to the Jew.* New York: Knopf, 1927.

———. *I Wonder as I Wander: An Autobiographical Journey.* New York: Rinehart, 1956.

Hughes, Langston, and Zora Neale Hurston. *Mule Bone: A Comedy of Negro Life.* Ed. and intro. George Houston Bass and Henry Louis Gates Jr. New York: HarperCollins, 1991.

Ikonné, Chidi. *From Du Bois to Van Vechten: The Early New Negro Literature, 1903–1926.* Westport, Conn.: Greenwood Press, 1981.

J.R. "Fiction Notes." *New Republic* 51 (June 29, 1927): 157.

James, Edward T., ed. *Notable American Women: A Biographical Dictionary.* 3 vols. Cambridge: Harvard University Press, 1971.

Johnson, Charles, Edwin Embree, and Will Alexander. *Collapse of the Cotton Tenancy.* Chapel Hill: University of North Carolina Press, 1935.

Johnson, Gerald W. "The Congo, Mr. Mencken." *Reviewer* 3, nos. 11 and 12 (July 1923): 887–93.

———. "Critical Attitudes North and South." *Social Forces* 2 (May 1924): 575–79.

———. "The Horrible South." *Virginia Quarterly Review* 11 (April 1935): 201–17.

———. "Saving Souls." *American Mercury* 1 (1924): 364–68.

———. "Southern Image-Breakers." *Virginia Quarterly Review* 4 (1928): 508–19.

———. "The South Takes the Offensive." *American Mercury* 2 (May 1924): 70–78.

Johnson, Guy. "The Negro Migration and Its Consequences." *Social Forces* 2 (May 1924): 404–8.

————. "Race Prejudice and the Negro Artist." *Harper's* 157 (1928): 769–76.

Johnson, James Weldon. *Autobiography of an Ex–Colored Man.* New York: Knopf, 1927.

————. *Black Manhattan.* New York: Atheneum, 1969.

Jones, Theodore M. "South Carolina History Makers — Julia Peterkin." *Columbia Sunday Record,* July 19, 1931.

Joyner, Charles. *Down by the Riverside: A South Carolina Slave Community.* Urbana: University of Illinois Press, 1984.

Judge, J. "*Roll, Jordan, Roll* a Social Document." *Savannah Morning News,* January 7, 1934, 6B.

"Julia Peterkin." *Carolinian,* May 1939, 8, 31.

"Julia Peterkin Glad She's Off for Plantation." *New York Herald Tribune,* May 30, 1933.

"Julia Peterkin in Europe." *New York Evening Post,* August 15, 1925.

"Julia Peterkin in New York." *Columbia State,* June 2, 1933. Reprinted from *New York Herald Tribune.*

"Julia Peterkin Is College Favorite." *Lantern* (Limestone College, Gaffney, S.C.), March 15, 1937.

"Julia Peterkin, Novelist, Was 80." *New York Times,* August 12, 1961.

"Julia Peterkin's *Bright Skin.*" *Columbia State,* April 10, 1932.

Kelley, Welbourn. "Plantation Lore: *Roll, Jordan, Roll.*" *Saturday Review of Literature* 10 (December 30, 1933): 377, 382.

Kellner, Bruce. *Carl Van Vechten and the Irreverent Decades.* Norman: University of Oklahoma Press, 1968.

————, ed. *The Harlem Renaissance: A Historical Dictionary for the Era.* New York: Methuen, 1987.

Kellogg, Florence Loeb. "A Black Mother Earth." *Survey* 61 (December 1, 1928): 313–14.

Kinney, James. *Amalgamation! Race, Sex, and Rhetoric in the Nineteenth-Century American Novel.* Westport, Conn.: Greenwood Press, 1985.

Knopf, Alfred A. *The Borzoi 1925; Being a Sort of Record of Ten Years of Publishing.* New York: Knopf, 1925.

————. "Reminiscences of Hergesheimer, Van Vechten, and Mencken." *Yale University Library Gazette,* April 1950, 157–65.

Kreyling, Michael. *Author and Agent: Eudora Welty and Diarmud Russell.* New York: Farrar, Straus and Giroux, 1991.

Kunitz, Stanley J., and Howard Haycraft, eds. *Twentieth Century Authors.* New York: Wilson, 1942. 1096–97.

L.W. "*Green Thursday.*" *Boston Evening Transcript,* November 1, 1924.

Landess, Thomas. *Julia Peterkin.* Boston: Twayne, 1976.

Landrum, J. B. O. *History of Spartanburg County.* Atlanta: Franklin, 1900.

Latimer, Dean, and Jeff Goldberg. *Flowers in the Blood: The Story of Opium.* New York: Franklin Watts, 1981.

Latimer, Margery. "Superstition." *New York Herald Tribune Books,* December 14, 1924.

Lauder, Ernest McPherson. *A History of South Carolina, 1865–1960.* Columbia: University of South Carolina Press, 1973.

Law, R. A. "Mrs. Peterkin's Negroes." *Southwest Review* 14 (1929): 455–61.

Leaming, Barbara. *Katharine Hepburn.* New York: Crown, 1995.

Lemann, Nicholas. *The Promised Land: The Great Black Migration and How It Changed America.* New York: Knopf, 1991.

Lindley, W. "Oophorectomy; Its Effect on the Mind and Nervous System." *California State Journal of Medicine* (1902–3): 84–86.

"Literary Leaders Talk of Profession." *New York Times,* August 30, 1936.

Littlefield, Daniel. *Rice and Slaves: Ethnicity and the Slave Trade in Colonial South Carolina.* Urbana: University of Illinois Press, 1991.

Locke, Alain. "Negroes and Earth." *Survey* 58 (May 1, 1927): 172–73.

———. "The Negro Speaks for Himself." *Survey* 52 (April 15, 1924): 71–72.

———, ed. *The New Negro.* New York: Atheneum, 1968. 29–44.

Lockyer, C. "Complications Met with during and after Ovariotomy." *Practitioner* (London) 52 (1903): 629–56.

Loggins, Vernon. *I Hear America.* New York: Crowell, 1937. 195–219.

Longo, Lawrence D. "The Rise and Fall of Battey's Operation: A Fashion in Surgery." In *Women and Health in America,* ed. Judith Walzer Leavitt, 270–83. Madison: University of Wisconsin Press, 1984.

Loveman, Amy. "Books of the Spring II." *Saturday Review of Literature* 8 (April 23, 1932): 684.

Maddox, Marilyn Price. "The Life and Works of Julia Mood Peterkin." Master's thesis, University of Georgia, 1956.

Markey, Morris. "New Books in Brief Review: *Black April.*" *Independent* 118 (May 21, 1927): 544.

Martin, Tony. *Literary Garveyism: Garvey, Black Arts and the Harlem Renaissance.* Dover, Mass.: Majority Press, 1983.

Mazer, Charles, and Leopold Goldstein. *Endocrinology of the Female.* Philadelphia: Saunders, 1933.

McCord, Louisa Rebecca Hayne. "Recollections of Louisa Rebecca Hayne McCord (Mrs. Augustine T. Smythe), daughter of David J. and Louisa Cheves McCord, born August 10, 1845, died January 8, 1928." MS, South Caroliniana Library, University of South Carolina.

McKay, Claude. *Home to Harlem.* New York: Harper, 1928.

McKay, Nellie Y. *Jean Toomer, Artist: A Study of His Literary Life and Work, 1894–1936.* Chapel Hill: University of North Carolina Press, 1984.

McKinney, Ernest Rice. "The Bookshelf." *Chicago Defender,* April 3, 1927.

McMinn, George R., and Harvey Eagleson. *College Readings in the Modern Short Story.* New York: Ginn, 1931. Foreword and pp. 102–13, 461.

Meade, Julian. *Adam's Profession and Its Conquest by Eve.* New York: Longmans, 1937.

———. *I Live in Virginia.* New York: Longmans, 1935.

———. "Julia Peterkin." *New York Herald Tribune Book Review,* January 17, 1933.

———. "Springtime Pilgrimage to the Gardens of Nine Women Who Wield a Spade as Well as a Pen." *Good Housekeeping,* May 1938, 50–53, 154–63.

Mencken, H. L. *The Diary of H. L. Mencken.* Ed. Charles A. Fecher. New York: Knopf, 1989.

———. "God Help the South." In *Prejudices, Second Series.* New York: Knopf, 1927. 141–44.

———. "Morning Song in C Major." *Reviewer* 2 (October 1921): 1–5.

———. *My Life as Author and Editor.* Ed. and intro. Jonathan Yardley. New York: Knopf, 1993.

———. [Review of *Green Thursday.*] *Baltimore Evening Sun,* December 20, 1924.

———. "The Sahara of the Bozart." In *Prejudices, Second Series.* New York: Knopf, 1920. 136–38.

———. "The Second Blooming." *Baltimore Evening Sun,* February 21, 1925.

———. "Violets in the Sahara." *Baltimore Evening Sun,* May 15, 1922.

Meriwether, James B., ed. *South Carolina Women Writers.* Proceedings of the Reynolds Conference, University of South Carolina, October 24–25, 1975. Spartanburg, S.C.: Reprint Company, 1979.

"Mess." *New Yorker* 6 (May 24, 1930): 13.

Milbank, Caroline Rennolds. *New York Fashion: The Evolution of American Style.* New York: Abrams, 1993.

Miller, Robert M. "The Attitudes of American Protestantism toward the Negro, 1919–1939." *Journal of Negro History* 41 (July 1956): 215.

Millet, Fred B. *Contemporary American Authors.* New York: Harcourt, Brace, 1944. 44, 51, 117, 525–26.

Minnigerode, Meade. *Lives and Times: Four Informal American Biographies.* New York: Putnam, 1925.

Mitchell, Margaret. *Gone with the Wind: Letters, 1936–1949.* Ed. Richard Harwell. New York: Macmillan, 1976.

Mitgang, Herbert, ed. *The Letters of Carl Sandburg.* New York: Harcourt, Brace, and World, 1968.

Monroe, Harriet. "The Old South." *Poetry* 22, no. 2 (May 1923): 89–92.

———, ed. "This Southern Number." *Poetry* 20 (April 1922): 31–49, 56–57, 114–15.

Mood, Francis Asbury. "The Autobiography of Francis Asbury Mood." MS in the South Caroliniana Library, University of South Carolina.

Mood, Henry. "Sketches and Incidents in the Life of Rev. Henry M. Mood, A.M. of the South Carolina Conference, Written by Himself for the Perusal of His Own Family." Unpublished papers, courtesy of Genevieve Peterkin.

Mood, Julius. "Doctor Mood Writes Recollections Grave and Gay of His Rich Life; Went through Burning of Columbia." *Columbia State,* December 17, 1933, 12A.

Moore, John Hammond. "South Carolina's Reaction to the Photoplay *The Birth of a Nation.*" *Proceedings of the South Carolina Historical Association* 64 (1963): 30–40.

Morrison, Toni. *Playing in the Dark: Whiteness and the Literary Imagination.* Cambridge: Harvard University Press, 1992.

Morrow, Lenna Vera. "Folklore in the Writings of Julia Peterkin." Master's thesis, University of South Carolina, 1963.

———. "A Social Interpretation: South Carolina." *Social Forces* 4 (June 1926): 690–701.

Mott, Frank Luther. *Golden Multitudes; The Story of Best-Sellers in the United States.* New York: Macmillan, 1947.

"Mrs. Bones." *New Yorker* 6 (December 6, 1930): 35.

"Mrs. Peterkin and a Play — Or, How It Came to Pass That Miss Barrymore Is Acting Scarlet Sister Mary." *New York Times*, November 23, 1930.

"Mrs. Peterkin, President of Converse College Alumnae Association, Presides at Reunion and Reads 'Vina's Sayings.'" *Spartanburg Herald*, May 29, 1927.

"Mrs. Peterkin to See Play." *New York Times*, September 28, 1930.

"Mrs. Peterkin on Southern Writers." *Columbia State*, May 14, 1933.

"Mrs. Peterkin Will Place Cornerstone for Gymnasium." *Columbia State*, March 1, 1938.

Mulkins, Dora. "*Green Thursday.*" *New York International Book Review*, January 1925.

Murray, Timothy D. "The Bobbs-Merrill Company." *Dictionary of Literary Biography: American Literary Publishing Houses, 1900–1980*, 49–54. Detroit: Gale, 1986.

Musto, David. *The American Disease.* New Haven: Yale University Press, 1975.

"The Negro in Art: How Shall He Be Portrayed? A Symposium." *Crisis* 32 (September 1926): 238–39.

Nelson, John Herbert, ed. *Contemporary Trends: American Literature since 1914.* New York: Macmillan, 1933. 225–27, 483.

Neuffer, Irene L. "An Unforgettable Whim: A Last Visit with Julia Peterkin." Undated clipping, Converse College Alumni files.

"A New Spirit." *Raleigh News and Observer*, October 18, 1925.

Newby, I. A. *Black Carolinians: A History of Blacks in South Carolina from 1895–1968.* Columbia: University of South Carolina Press, 1973.

Newman, Frances. "*Green Thursday.*" *Atlanta Journal*, December 14, 1924.

Nicholls, Cassie. *Historical Sketches of Sumter County: Its Birth and Growth.* Sumter, S.C.: Sumter County Historical Society, 1975.

Niven, Penelope. *Carl Sandburg: A Biography.* New York: Scribner, 1991.

Noggle, Burl F. "With Pen and Camera: In Quest of the American South in the 1930s." In *The South Is Another Land: Essays on the Twentieth-Century South*, ed. Bruce Clayton and John A. Salmond, 187–204. Contributions in American History 124. New York: Greenwood Press, 1987.

"Not Yet in the Nature of Man." *Columbia State*, March 10, 1929.

Novak, Emil. "The Hormone Theory and the Female Generative Organs." *Surgery, Gynecology and Obstetrics* 9 (July–December 1909): 344–50.

"Novels in Brief." *Nation* 124 (June 8, 1927): 649.

O. Henry Memorial Award Prize Stories of 1930. New York: Doubleday, Doran, 1930.

O. Henry Memorial Award Prize Stories of 1925. New York: Doubleday, Page, 1926.

O'Bar, Jack. "A History of the Bobbs-Merrill Company, 1850–1940." Ph.D. dissertation, Indiana University, 1975.

O'Brien, Michael. *The Idea of the American South, 1920–1941.* Baltimore: Johns Hopkins University Press, 1979.

O'Brien, Sharon. *Willa Cather: The Emerging Voice.* New York: Oxford, 1987.

O'Donnell, George Marion. "Portrait of a Southern Planter: 1920–1932." *American Review* 3, no. 5 (October 1934): 608–20.

Odum, Howard W. "The Discovery of the People." *Social Forces* 4 (December 1925): 414–17.

——. *Folk, Region, and Society: Selected Papers of Howard W. Odum.* Chapel Hill: University of North Carolina Press, 1964.

——. "Lynching, Fears, and Folkways." *Nation* 133 (December 30, 1931): 719–20.

——. "A More Articulate South." *Social Forces* 2 (September 1924): 730–35.

——. *The Negro and His Songs.* Chapel Hill: University of North Carolina Press, 1925.

——. *Race and Rumors of Race.* Chapel Hill: University of North Carolina Press, 1944.

——. *Rainbow Round My Shoulder: The Blue Trail of Black Ulysses.* Indianapolis: Bobbs-Merrill, 1928.

——. "Regional Portraiture." *Saturday Review of Literature* 6 (July 27, 1929): 1–2.

——. *Social and Mental Traits of the Negro.* New York: Columbia University Press, 1910.

Oliver, John B. *Victim and Victor.* New York: Macmillan, 1928.

Overton, Grant. *The Women Who Make Our Novels.* New York: Dodd, Mead, 1928. 257–61.

Ovington, Mary White. *The Walls Came Tumbling Down.* New York: Harcourt, Brace, 1947.

Paine, Gregory. *Southern Prose Writers.* New York: American Book Company, 1947. i–cxvii.

Parler, Mary Celestia. "*Black April* Reviewed." *Anderson, South Carolina Independent* (Converse College Library Files).

Parsons, Alice Beal. "High Heads." *Nation* 128 (January 9, 1928): 47–48.

Pearson, E. E. "Book Table." *Outlook* 145 (April 6, 1927): 443.

Perkerson, Medora Field. "Julia Peterkin — Author and Farmer." *Atlanta Journal Sunday Magazine,* April 28, 1940.

Peterkin, James Alexander. *Talks with the Cotton Farmer.* Charleston, S.C.: Walker, Evans, and Cogswell, 1888.

Peters, Margot. *The House of Barrymore.* New York: Knopf, 1990.

Pettee, Frank. "Black Sorrow." *Chicago Evening Post,* January 16, 1925.

Phifer, Mary Hardy. "Julia Peterkin Winner of the Pulitzer Prize." *Holland's,* September 1929.

Phillips, Ulrich Bonnell. "The Economics of the Plantation." *South Atlantic Quarterly* 2 (July 1903): 231–36.

——. "The Plantation as a Civilizing Factor." *Sewanee Review* 12 (July 1904): 257–67.

——. "The Slave Labor Problem in the Charleston District." *Political Science Quarterly* 22, no. 3 (September 1907): 416–39.

Pidgin, Charles Felton. *Theodosia: The First Gentlewoman of Her Time.* Boston: C. M. Clark, 1907.

Pilkington, John, ed. *Stark Young: A Life in the Arts, Letters 1900–1962*. 2 vols. Baton Rouge: Louisiana State University Press, 1975.

Pinckney, Darryl. "The Honorary Negro." *New York Review of Books*, August 18, 1988.

Potter, Joan, with Constance Claytor. *African-American Firsts*. Elizabethtown, N.Y.: Pinto Press, 1994.

"A Precious Book." *St. Louis Globe-Democrat*, January 4, 1925.

"A Pretty Wedding: Two Popular Young People Happily Married Wednesday Night." *Sumter Herald*, June 5, 1903.

Puckett, Newbell Niles. *Folk Beliefs of the Southern Negro*. Chapel Hill: University of North Carolina Press, 1926.

Puckette, Charles M. "On a Carolina Plantation." *Saturday Review of Literature* 34 (March 19, 1927).

Racine, Philip N. *Spartanburg County: A Pictorial History*. Virginia Beach, Va.: Donning, 1980.

Rampersad, Arnold. *The Life of Langston Hughes*. Volume 1: *1902–1941, I, Too, Sing America*. New York: Oxford University Press, 1986.

Raper, Arthur F. *Preface to Peasantry: A Tale of Two Black Belt Counties*. Chapel Hill: University of North Carolina Press, 1936.

———. *The Tragedy of Lynching*. Chapel Hill: University of North Carolina Press, 1933.

Raper, Arthur, and Ira Reid. *Sharecroppers All*. Chapel Hill: University of North Carolina Press, 1941.

Rascoe, Burton, and Groff Conklin, eds. *The Smart Set Anthology*. New York: Reynal and Hitchcock, 1934. xiii–xliv, 726–31.

Rathbone, Belinda. *Walker Evans: A Biography*. Boston: Houghton Mifflin, 1995.

Reed, Alma. *José Clemente Orozco*. New York: Delphic Studios, 1932.

———. *Orozco!* New York: Oxford University Press, 1956.

"Reminders of Past." *Sumter Daily Item*, October 15, 1969.

[Review of *Green Thursday*.] *Atlanta Journal*, December 14, 1924.

[Review of *Green Thursday*.] *New York Times*, September 28, 1924.

[Review of *Green Thursday*.] *San Francisco Chronicle*, November 16, 1924.

[Review of *Green Thursday*.] *Time*, September 29, 1924.

[Review of the *Richmond Reviewer*.] *Columbia State*, November 23, 1924.

[Review of "Venner's Sayings."] *New York Evening Post*, February 7, 1925.

"The Reviewer." *Raleigh News and Observer*, August 16, 1925.

Rhyne, Nancy. *Touring the Coastal South Carolina Backroads*. Winston-Salem, N.C.: John F. Blair, 1992.

Richardson, Eudora Ramsay. "The South Grows Up." *Bookman* 70 (January 1930): 545–50.

"Rising Tide of Prejudice." *Nation* 122 (March 10, 1926): 247.

Robeson, Elizabeth. "The Ambiguity of Julia Peterkin." *Journal of Southern History* 61 (November 1995): 761–862.

Rodney, Walter. "Upper Guinea and the Significance of the Origins of Africans Enslaved in the New World." *Journal of Negro History* 54 (October 1969): 327–45.

Rollins, Hyder E. "The Negro in the Southern Short Story." *Sewanee Review* 24 (1916): 42–60.

Roper, John Herbert. "Paul Green and the Southern Literary Renaissance." *Southern Cultures* 1 (1994–95): 75–89.

Roueché, Berton. *The Medical Detectives*. New York: Washington Square Press, 1980.

Saint-Amand, Belle T. "Chatelaine of 'Lang Syne.'" *Wilmington (N.C.) State*, April 2, 1934. Reprinted from the *Columbia State*, April 14, 1929.

Salpeter, Harry. "Studies in Color." *New York World*, July 10, 1927.

————. "A Thousand-Dollar Throwdown, in Which Case Sandburg Writes Pointedly about Sinclair Lewis' Refusal of the Pulitzer Prize." n.p., n.d. Peterkin's scrapbook, SCHS.

"Says Harlem Tries to Sing Slump Away." *New York Times*, April 16, 1932.

Scarborough, Dorothy. "Julia Peterkin's Gullahs Sit for Their Portrait." *New York Times*, January 7, 1934.

"Scarlet Sister; Red Apples." *Time*, December 1, 1930, 28.

Schorer, Mark. *Sinclair Lewis: An American Life*. New York: McGraw-Hill, 1961.

Schuyler, George S. "The Van Vechten Revolution." *Phylon* (Fourth Quarter 1950): 342–67.

Scott, Anne Firor. *The Southern Lady: From Pedestal to Politics*. Chicago: University of Chicago Press, 1970.

Scott, Mary Wingfield. "The Provincetown Players Invade Broadway." *Reviewer* 1 (February 15, 1921): 15–19.

Scruggs, Charles. *The Sage in Harlem: H. L. Mencken and the Black Writers of the 1920s*. Baltimore: Johns Hopkins University Press, 1984.

Sessions, William A. "The Land Called Chicora." *Southern Review* 19 (Autumn 1983): 736–48.

"Seventy-one Seniors Receive Degrees . . . Mrs. Peterkin Receives Recognition." *Spartanburg Herald*, May 31, 1927.

Shaw, Charles G. *Night Life: Vanity Fair's Intimate Guide to New York after Dark*. New York: Day, 1931.

Shealy, Ann. *The Passionate Mind: Four Studies Including "Julia Peterkin: A Souvenir."* Philadelphia: Dorrance, 1976.

Singal, Daniel Joseph. *The War Within: From Victorian to Modernist Thought in the South, 1919–1945*. Chapel Hill: University of North Carolina Press, 1982.

Singh, Amritjit. *The Novels of the Harlem Renaissance: Twelve Black Writers, 1923–1933*. University Park: Pennsylvania State University Press, 1976.

Sitwell, Osbert. "New York in the Twenties." *Atlantic Monthly*, February 1962, 38–43.

Slavick, William H. *DuBose Heyward*. Boston: Twayne, 1981.

Smith, Reed. *Gullah*. South Carolina Bureau of Publications, Bulletin 190. Columbia: University of South Carolina, 1926.

————, ed. *South Carolina Ballads*. Cambridge: Harvard University Press, 1928.

Smythe, Louisa Rebeccah Hayne McCord. "Reminiscences of Her Life at Pendleton, Columbia, Charleston, and Fort Motte, with Anecdotes of Servants . . ." MS, South Caroliniana Library, University of South Carolina.

Stackhouse, Eunice Ford. "Julia Mood Peterkin." In *South Carolina's Distinguished Women of Laurens County*, ed. Marguerite Tolbert, Irene Dillard Elliott, and Dr. Will Lou Gray. Columbia: Bryan, 1972. 104–5.

Stagg, Hunter. "Southern Woman Writes First Book: Julia Peterkin's *Green Thursday* Is Novel of Rare Promise." *Richmond Times-Dispatch*, September 28, 1924.

Stallings, Laurence. "*Black April*." *McCall's* 54 (May 1927): 24.

———. "*Green Thursday*." *Saturday Review of Literature* 1 (October 11, 1924): 186.

———. "Julia Peterkin and Realism." *New York World*, April 21, 1925.

———. "The Other Side of Jordan — *Green Thursday*, Negro Character Sketches, Are Spirituals in a Magic Prose." *New York World*, November 16, 1924.

"Stand on Politics Told by Authors." *New York World*, October 4, 1928.

"Stays at Home during Premiere." *Columbia State*, September 20, 1930.

Stegner, Wallace. *The Uneasy Chair: A Biography of Bernard DeVoto*. New York: Doubleday, 1974.

Stein, Hannah. "Would Rather Cook Than Write." *Brooklyn Daily Eagle*, July 7, 1929.

Stevenson, John W. "Julia Mood Peterkin, '97: The Only South Carolina Writer to Receive the Pulitzer Prize." *Converse College Bulletin* 91 (July 1980): 1–2.

Stoney, Samuel Gaillard. *The Dulles Family in South Carolina*. Columbia: University of South Carolina Press, 1955.

Stott, William. *Documentary Expression and Thirties America*. New York: Oxford University Press, 1973.

"Strange Disease of Pyorrhea." *Dallas Times*, October 1, 1927.

Street, James H. *The New Revolution in the Cotton Industry*. Chapel Hill: University of North Carolina Press, 1957.

Strode, Hudson. *The Eleventh House*. New York: Harcourt Brace Jovanovitch, 1975.

———. [Review of *Scarlet Sister Mary*.] *New York Herald Tribune*, October 28, 1928.

———. *The Story of Bermuda*. New York: Random House, 1932.

Stubbs, Thomas M. *Family Album: An Account of the Moods of Charleston, SC and Connected Families*. Atlanta: Curtis, 1943.

Stuckey, W. J. *The Pulitzer Prize Novels: A Critical Backward Look*. Norman: University of Oklahoma Press, 1981.

Sylvester, Robert. *No Cover Charge: A Backward Look at the Night Clubs*. New York: Dial Press, 1956.

Taggard, E. K. "Julia Peterkin of 'Lang Syne.'" *Scholastic* 27 (December 14, 1935): 6.

Tante, Dilly, ed. *Living Authors: A Book of Biographies*. New York: Wilson, 1931. 318–20.

Tate, Allen. "Random Thoughts on the 1920s." *Minnesota Review* 1 (Fall 1960): 45–56.

Tebbel, John. *Paperback Books: A Pocket History*. New York: Pocket Books, 1964.

"Ten Best Books." *Huntington (W.Va.) Advertiser*, January 18, 1925.

[Theatrical Notes.] *New York Times*, September 25, 1930.

Thomas, James W. *Lyle Saxon: A Critical Biography*. Birmingham, Ala.: Summa Publications, 1991.

Thompson, Edgar T. *Plantation Societies: Race Relations and the South.* Durham: Duke University Press, 1975.

———. "The Planter in the Pattern of Race Relations in the South." *Social Forces* 19 (December 1940): 244–68.

Thompson, H. Dean, Jr. "Minerva Finds a Voice: The Early Career of Julia Peterkin." Ph.D. dissertation, Vanderbilt University, 1987.

Thorp, Margaret Farrand. "Altogether Doric: Louisa McCord." In *Female Persuasion: Six Strong-Minded Women.* New Haven: Yale University Press, 1949.

Thurman, Wallace. *Infants of the Spring.* Plainview, N.Y.: Books for Libraries Press, 1972.

———. "Negro Artists and the Negro." *New Republic*, August 31, 1927, 37–39.

Tischler, Nancy M. *Black Masks: Negro Characters in Modern Southern Fiction.* University Park: Pennsylvania State University Press, 1969.

Turner, Lorenzo Dow. *Africanisms in the Gullah Dialect.* Ann Arbor: University of Michigan Press, 1949.

Ulmann, Doris. "Portrait Photographs of Fifteen American Authors." *Bookman* 70 (September 1929–February 1930): 410.

van Cleve, Kit. "Julia Peterkin: Lost and Good Riddance." *Crisis* 83 (August–September 1976): 235–38.

Van de Warker, Eli. "The Fetich of the Ovary." *American Journal of Obstetrics* 54 (July–December 1906): 366–73.

Van Doren, Carl, ed. *Modern American Prose.* New York: Literary Guild, 1934. 817–22, 934.

Van Vechten, Carl. *Nigger Heaven.* New York: Knopf, 1925.

Vance, Rupert P. *All These People: The Nation's Human Resources in the South.* Chapel Hill: University of North Carolina Press, 1945.

———. "Cotton Culture and Social Life and Institutions of the South." *Publications of the American Sociological Society* 23 (1929): 51–59.

———. *Human Factors in Cotton Culture: A Study in the Social Geography of the American South.* Chapel Hill: University of North Carolina Press, 1929.

Varesi, Gilda, and Dolly Byrne. *Enter, Madame: A Play in Three Acts.* New York: Putnam, 1921.

Waldron, Edward E. *Walter White and the Harlem Renaissance.* Port Washington, N.Y.: Kennikat Press, 1978.

Walker, Marianne. *Margaret Mitchell and John Marsh: The Love Story behind* Gone with the Wind. Atlanta: Peachtree, 1993.

Warren, Dale. "Amid the Sylvan Haunts of Peterborough." *Boston Evening Transcript*, September 3, 1927.

———. "Doris Ulmann: Photographer in Waiting." *Bookman* 72 (October 1930): 129–44.

———. "Julia Peterkin: Impressions and a Conversation." *Boston Evening Transcript*, December 24, 1927, 1.

———. "Julia Peterkin Lived before She Began to Write." *Boston Transcript.* Reprinted in the *Sunday Record* (Columbia, S.C.), January 8, 1928.

———. [Review of *Bright Skin.*] *Boston Transcript*, November 1, 1924.

———. [Review of *Scarlet Sister Mary.*] *Boston Transcript*, November 10, 1928.

Warren, Robert Penn. "Not Local Color." *Virginia Quarterly Review* 8 (1932): 153–60.

———. "Some Don'ts for Literary Regionalists." *American Review* 8 (December 1936): 142–56.

———. *A Southern Harvest.* Boston: Houghton Mifflin, 1937.

Wasson, Ben. "Jingling in the Wind . . . *Scarlet Sister Mary.*" *Outlook and Independent* 150 (November 21, 1928): 1212.

Watkins, Mel. *On the Real Side: Laughing, Lying and Signifying — The Underground Tradition of African-American Humor That Transformed American Culture, from Slavery to Richard Pryor.* New York: Simon and Schuster, 1994.

Watkins, T. H. *The Great Depression: America in the 1930s.* Boston: Little, Brown, 1993.

Watson, James Frake. "Descendents of Zachariah Alford Drake of Marlboro County, S.C." Unpublished monograph, dated August 1981.

Wauchope, George Armstrong. *The Writers of South Carolina.* Columbia: The State, 1910.

Wells, Betty Jean. "Regionalism and Fictional Art in the Writings of Julia Mood Peterkin." Master's thesis, Vanderbilt University, 1963.

Wells, Dicky. *The Nightclub People.* Boston: Crescendo, 1971.

White, Walter. *The Fire and the Flint.* New York: Knopf, 1924.

———. *Flight.* New York: Negro Universities Press, 1969.

———. *Rope and Faggot: A Biography of Judge Lynch.* New York: Arno, 1969.

Williams, Mrs. M. Dial. "Father and Mother of Julia Peterkin Recalled by One Who Knew Them." *Spartanburg Herald,* n.d.

Williamson, Joel. *The Crucible of Race.* New York: Oxford University Press, 1984.

———. *New People: Miscegenation and Mulattoes in the United States.* New York: Free Press, 1980.

———. *William Faulkner and Southern History.* New York: Oxford University Press, 1993.

Wilson, Edmund. "Night Clubs." *New Republic,* September 9, 1925, 71.

"Winners of the Pulitzer Prizes and Scholarships in Letters and Journalism." *New York Times,* May 13, 1929.

Winsten, Archer. "The New Novels: *Bright Skin.*" *Bookman* 75 (1930): 107–8.

"Winthrop Hears Julia Peterkin." *Columbia State,* June 6, 1933.

Wintz, Cary D. *Black Culture and the Harlem Renaissance.* Houston: Rice University Press, 1988.

"A Woman Speaks to Women." *Columbia State,* June 7, 1933.

Wyatt, Euphemia van Rensselaer. "The Drama . . . *Scarlet Sister Mary.*" *Catholic World* 132 (January 1931): 462–63.

Wynn, William T., ed. *Southern Literature.* New York: Prentice-Hall, 1932. 238–44, 494.

Yarbrough, Tinsley E. *A Passion for Justice: J. Waties Waring and Civil Rights.* New York: Oxford University Press, 1987.

Yates, Irene. "A Collection of Proverbs and Proverbial Sayings from South Carolina Literature." *Southern Folklore Quarterly* 11 (September 1947): 187–99.

———. "Conjures and Cures in the Novels of Julia Peterkin." *Southern Folklore Quarterly* 10 (June 1946): 137−49.

Yearbook, The Poetry Society of South Carolina, 1921−59.

Young, Stark. "Dialect and the Heart." *New Republic* 55 (May 30, 1928): 45−46.

———. *Heaven Trees.* New York: Scribner, 1926.

———. *Immortal Shadows: A Book of Dramatic Criticism.* New York: Octagon, 1973.

———. "*Scarlet Sister Mary* Dramatized by Dan Reed from Novel by Julia Peterkin; Ethel Barrymore Theater, November 25, 1930." *New Republic* 65 (December 10, 1930): 101−2.

———. *So Red the Rose.* New York: Scribner, 1934.

———. *A Southern Treasury of Life and Literature.* New York: Scribner, 1937. v−viii, 574−83.

Zanger, Jules. "The 'Tragic Octoroon' in Pre−Civil War Fiction." *American Quarterly* 18 (Spring 1966): 63−70.

Index

Abortion, 60, 69–70, 217

Adams, E. C. L., 136, 216, 290 (n. 68), 300 (n. 73)

Adams, Elizabeth Peterkin ("Lizzie"), 3, 6, 10

Adams, Robert, 10, 78, 79, 145–46, 250, 276 (n. 61)

Adams family, 93

Africa, 90; traditions of, 163

African Americans: folk practices and beliefs of, 102–3; folk humor of, 105; poetry of, 117; fiction of, xi, 150; spirituals of, 224

Agee, James, 220

Agrarians, 212, 213

Aiken, S.C., 140–41

Alabama, 23, 164, 165, 212

Alabama, University of, 111

Alaska, 251

Aley, Maxwell, 86, 109, 110, 207, 283 (n. 9)

Aley, Ruth, 86, 121, 126

Allen, Hervey, 47, 48, 63

All God's Chillen Got Wings (O'Neill), 72

Alliance Française, 97

All Quiet on the Western Front (Remarque), 148

Alsberg, Henry B., 237

Alston, Joseph, 203

Alston, Theodosia Burr, 25, 202–3

Alston family, 4, 24, 25, 44, 210

Amelia Township, S.C., 3

American Association of University Women, 114

American Magazine, 122

American Mercury, xv, 68, 71, 89, 115, 126

Anderson, John, 181

Anderson, Maxwell, 207

Anderson, Sherwood, ix, 116, 200, 241

Anderson, W. T., 114

"Andrea del Sarto" (Browning), 173

Angola, 198

April, significance of, for Julia Peterkin, 271 (n. 27)

Archer family, 6, 58, 166

Arkansas, xv

Arrowsmith (Lewis), 148

"Ashes," 77–78, 80

Asheville, N.C., 182, 244

As I Lay Dying (Faulkner), 206

Askling, John, 306 (n. 26)

Asparagus, 165

Atherton, Gertrude, 113

Atlanta, Ga., 211

Atlanta Journal, 82

Atlantic Monthly, 94

Austen, Jane, 104

Autobiography, 89, 122

"Baby's Mouth, A," 48–49, 71

Back to Africa movement, 194

Bahamas, 242

Ballou, Robert O., xiv, 219, 220, 240, 300 (n. 87)

Baltimore, Md., 33, 229

Baltimore Sun, 31, 47

Bancroft, Caroline, 186

Bank of Fort Motte, 22

Bank holiday, 217

Barrow, Craig, 188, 191, 227, 228, 230

Barrow, Elfrida DeRenne (Mrs. Craig), 188, 191, 227, 228, 248

Barrow, Elfrida DeRenne (Mrs. William G. Peterkin Jr.). *See* Peterkin, Elfrida DeRenne Barrow

Barrow family, 242, 250

Barrymore, Ethel. *See* Blythe, E. M.

Barrymore, John, 208

Barrymore, Lionel, 178, 208

Baruch, Bernard, 237

"Bastard lover," 2, 85, 89, 270 (n. 5)

Battey's operation, 7, 272

Beaufort, S.C., 221

Beaumont (Texas) Enterprise, 113

Beethoven, 27, 165, 216

Behrend, Margaret, 247, 255

Bellamann, Henry, 27–29, 30, 31, 32, 47, 49, 78, 79, 86–87, 93, 131, 137, 170, 181, 206, 236, 241, 250, 305 (n. 21)

Bellamannn, Katherine, 28, 87, 170, 275 (n. 26)

Ben, 133–34

Benét, W. C., 282 (n. 76)

Bennett, Isadora. *See* Reed, Isadora Bennett

Bennett, John, xx, 63

Bennington College, 213–14, 215, 216, 230, 232, 234, 244, 245; Peterkin teaches at, 241–42

Benstock, Shari, 282 (n. 68)

Bermuda, 153, 183–84

Berry, Bob, 28, 55

Berry, Champagne, 10, 273, 289 (n. 53)

Berry, Hagar, 28

Berry, Lavinia ("Maum Vinner"), xii, 8–9, 10, 15, 17, 18, 21, 27, 30, 33, 39, 44, 49, 51, 52, 55, 56, 57, 59, 60, 61, 72, 73, 87, 117, 133, 221, 256, 257, 278 (n. 63), 280 (n. 1)

Berry, Paul, 28, 44–45

Best Short Stories, 89

"Betsy," 40, 289 (n. 34)

Beverly Hills Hotel, 208

Big Sea, The (Hughes), 182

Biltmore estate, 244

Birth of a Nation (Griffith), 22

Black April, x, xi, xiv, xvi, 19, 92, 95, 103, 106–8, 112–15, 118, 120, 121, 122, 123, 125, 126, 127, 134, 188, 196, 205, 209, 224, 273 (n. 65), 274 (n. 89), 286 (n. 49), 306 (n. 21); dramatization of, 159, 162, 176, 180, 206, 240, 298 (n. 28)

Black Border, The (Gonzales), 40

Blacker the Berry, The (Thurman), 150

Blease, Coleman, 22, 67, 142

Blossom of the Night-Blooming Cereus, A (Haymaker), 305 (n. 12)

Blue Brook plantation, xvi, 89, 103, 107, 258, 286 (n. 31)

Blythe, E. M., 176, 177, 178, 179, 180, 181, 182, 183, 206, 208, 251

Bobbs, Julian, 149

Bobbs-Merrill Company, x, xiv, 86, 109, 110, 111, 112, 122, 126, 127, 135, 136, 137, 145, 149, 171, 172, 178, 180, 190, 209, 210, 214, 240, 283 (n. 9), 286 (n. 49)

Boll weevil, 23, 36, 67, 107, 108, 202

Bontemps, Arna, 117

Book League of America, 136

Book League Monthly, 146

Bookman, 88, 171, 205

Book of the Month Club, 135, 136, 220

Bookstaver, May, 282 (n. 68)

Borzoi 1925, 89, 279 (n. 26)

Boston, 62; books banned in, xiii, 149

Boston, 147

Boston Evening Transcript, 131

Boulder, Col., 208

Bourke-White, Margaret, 220

Boyd, Ernest, 159

Bradford, Roark, 181, 301 (n. 96)

Brasstown, N.C., 233

Brawley, Benjamin, 116

Bread Loaf Writers' Conference, 232, 237, 238, 241, 243

Brentano's best-seller list, 120

Brickell, Herschell, 137, 206

Bridge over San Luis Rey (Wilder), 148

Briggs, Harry, 254

Briggs, Liza, 254

Briggs v. Elliott, 254–55

Bright Skin, xiii, xiv, xv, xvi, 165–6, 190, 192–201, 204, 209, 210, 211, 212, 213, 214, 218, 221, 222

Broaddus, John, 227, 228, 229, 230, 232, 238

Broadway, 178, 181, 182

Brogdon, Edwin, 281 (n. 49)

Bromfield, Louis, 148

Brookgreen plantation, xvi, 24, 25, 26, 71, 81, 102, 203, 210, 286 (n. 31)

Brown, Sterling R., 222, 289 (n. 40)

Brown Fellowship Society, 5

Browning, Robert, 173

Brown v. Board of Education, 255
Bryant, Anaky, 10, 133, 197, 289 (n. 53)
Bryant, Frank, 197
Bryant, James "Bully," 10, 28, 134
Bryant, Rudy Mae ("Kutch"), 131–32, 198
Buckhead Creek, 3
Buerger's disease, 105
Bullett, Gerald, 205
Burgess, Marian Mood, 13, 15, 21, 57, 59, 75, 160, 255, 256, 270 (n. 3), 273 (nn. 60, 64), 279 (n. 7)
Burgess, Plumer, 15, 21
Burlington, Vt., 190, 214
Burr, Aaron, 25, 203
Burton, Richard, 147
Butcher, Fanny, 232, 236, 250
Byrnes, James F., 254

Cabell, James Branch, 36, 44, 84
Cable, George Washington, xx
Caius Gracchus (McCord), 25
Calcium arsenate, 24
Calder, Alexander, 215
Caldwell, Erskine, 220
Calhoun County, S.C., 9, 141, 187
Call It Sleep (Roth), 300 (n. 87)
Camden, S.C., 64
Cane (Toomer), 63
Cane River, 199
Cape Hatteras, 203
Carl Brandt agency, 190
Carmel, Calif., 250
Carnegie, Dale, 242
Carter, Robin, 12
Cash, W. J., 291 (n. 37)
Castration, female, 7, 272
Castration, male, 185, 214, 239
"Cat-Fish," 40
Cather, Willa, ix, 71, 110, 124
Catholic Church, 167
Catholic Worker, 207
Central of Georgia Hospital, 227
Century, 144
Chain gangs, 209

Chamberlain, John, 205, 222
Chamberlain, Robert, 137
Chambers, D. Laurance, 110, 111–12, 113, 114, 118, 119, 120, 123, 126, 127, 132, 133, 135, 136, 137, 138, 142, 143, 144, 145, 147, 149, 153, 155, 171, 172, 176, 179, 187, 192, 199, 200, 203, 205, 206, 209, 214, 218, 219, 237, 240, 286 (n. 27)
Chan, Charlie, 110
Chandler, Genevieve Willcox, 251–52
Charleston, College of, 5, 237
Charleston, S.C., 4, 5, 14, 17, 29, 54, 63, 88, 118, 153, 170, 182, 257, 273 (n. 69); race riot in, 22
Charleston News and Courier, 22, 186; on lynchings, 141
Charleston Poets, 48
Chekhov, Anton, 206
Cherokee Times, 149
Cheseboro, Frank, 38
Cheseboro, Hester, 12, 78, 111, 198, 273 (n. 57)
Cheseboro, Jake, 12, 273 (n. 51)
Chesnut, Mary Boykin, 26
Chesnutt, Charles W., 116
Cheves, Langdon, 25
Chicago, Ill., 134, 162, 218; race riots in, 22, 30, 62
Chicago Broad Axe, 112
Chicago Daily News, 28, 113
Chicago Defender, 82, 112
Chicago Poems (Sandburg), 29
Chicago Theater, 218
Chicago Tribune, 232
Chicago World's Fair, 186
Chicora College, 27
Children of Strangers (Saxon), 200, 240
Children's Hour, The (Hellman), 235
Chippewa Square, 191
Christian Century, 171
Christian Science, 13, 167, 198, 250
Circumcision, 239
Citadel, The, 54
Civil Rights movement, 195, 257

Civil War, xii, 3, 5, 8, 16, 67, 88, 198, 276
Clansman, The (Dixon), 22
Clarendon Banner, 280 (n. 18)
Clarendon County, S.C., 254−55
Clark, Edwin, 115
Clark, Emily, 35, 36, 39, 44, 47, 54, 57,
   68, 83−84, 279 (n. 26)
Clark family, 70
Cleveland, Ohio, 178
Cleveland News, 178
Cleveland Plain Dealer, 178, 181
Cockfighting, 207
Collins, George, 38
Colorado, University of, 208
Colt, Ethel Barrymore, 177, 179
Colt, Russell, 179
Columbia, S.C., xii, xviii, 5, 22, 27, 29,
   30, 31, 53, 59, 80, 81, 87, 114, 121, 123,
   131, 135, 136, 191, 192, 216, 230, 239,
   252, 276, 290 (n. 68)
Columbia Female College, xii, 166
Columbia Hotel, 204
Columbia Record, 79, 80, 131, 142, 181
Columbia Stage Society, 28
Columbia State, 40, 80, 102, 114, 121, 135,
   141; on lynchings, 22
Columbia Town Theater, 31, 53, 159,
   204, 211
Columbia University, 147, 167
Columbus, Ohio, 178
Commodore Hotel, 55
Communism, 212−13
Communist Party, American, 212
Como, Perry, 254
Confederate government, 6
"Confession, The," 69−70, 196
Congaree Indians, 272 (n. 38)
Congaree River, 3, 135
Congaree Tales (Adams), 216, 290
   (n. 68)
Connelly, Marc, 181
Connemara farm, 306 (n. 25)
Conrad, Joseph, 110
Converse College, 166
"Cooch's Premium," 40, 131
Copland, Aaron, 124

Cos Cob, Conn., 86
Cosmopolitan Club, 284 (n. 11)
Cosmopolitan Publishing Company, 171,
   199
Cotton, 3, 23, 135, 165, 254, 258, 270
   (n. 26), 286 (n. 31); prices of, 12, 21,
   24, 56, 202
Country Gentleman, 150, 157
Country People (Suckow), 282 (n. 73)
Crawford, John, 114
Crisis, 64−65, 116, 117
Crouch, Charlotte Adams Peterkin, 145
Crouch, James, 21, 145−47, 160, 172, 201,
   256, 291 (n. 27)
Crowninshield, Frank, 63
Crum, Mason, xix
"Crutch, A," 224
Cullen, Countee, 116, 117

"Daddy Harry" (Clark), 84
Daisy Bank plantation, 279 (n. 29)
Dallas Times, 126
Daniel, 185
Darby, Buck, 95
Darby, Elizabeth, 95−96, 133, 181, 254
Darby, May, 236
Daufuskie Island, 198
Daughters of the American Revolution,
   xii, 9, 269 (n. 12)
Davidson, Donald, xi, 113, 212
Davis, Jefferson, 46
Day, Dorothy, 207
"Day of Judgment, The," 274 (n. 73)
DeBow's Review, 26
Delphic Studios, 153
Denver Post, 186
Depression, 179, 186, 189, 191, 209, 217,
   220
DeVoto, Bernard, 232
Dewey, John, 187
Diabetes, 105
Dial (Halper), 150
Dialect, 43. *See also* Gullah
"Diamond Ring, The," 150−51
Dickinson, Angie, 258
Dixon, Thomas, 22

Documentaries, 220
Dodsworth (Lewis), 148
Donahue, Troy, 258
Doris Ulmann Foundation, 233
Dos Passos, John, 241
Dostoevski, Feodor, 206
Double Dealer, 47
Drama (Orozco), 154, 173
Dreiser, Theodore, 187, 241
Duane Hotel, 220
Dublin, Ireland, 258
Du Bois, W. E. B., x, 82, 116, 118
Duke University, xix
Dunbar, Paul Laurence, 117
Durham, Frank, 63

Early Autumn (Bromfield), 148
Eaton, Allen, 219
Ebony and Topaz, 117
Eddy, Mary Baker, 167
Einstein, Albert, 187
Elbow Beach Hotel, 184
Eliot, T. S., 71, 110, 271 (n. 27)
Ellerslie plantation, 284 (n. 24)
Ellis, Havelock, 88
Ellison, Ralph, 150
El Paso, Texas, 209
Emancipation, xvii
Enter, Madame (Varesi), 52−54
Esenwein, J. Berg, 33−34
Estrogen, 161, 199
Evangelists, 67
Evans, Walker, 220, 228

Father Divine, 194
Faulkner, William, 150, 200, 206, 208,
    240, 241, 258
Fauset, Jessie, xi, 116, 117, 150
Federal Writers' Project, 237, 251
"Finding Peace," 11−12
Fine Clothes to the Jew (Hughes), 216
Fineman, Helene Hughes, 235−39, 241,
    242, 243, 258
Fineman, Irving, 98, 108, 109, 144−45,
    154, 155, 156, 157, 158, 159, 160, 161,
    162, 163, 165, 166, 168, 169, 170−71,

172, 176, 178, 179, 180, 182, 183, 184,
    185, 187, 188, 189, 190, 191, 192, 200,
    201, 204, 205, 207, 208, 211, 212, 213,
    214, 215, 216, 217, 218, 219, 220, 226,
    227, 228, 229, 230, 231, 232, 234, 235,
    236, 237, 238, 239, 240, 241, 242, 243,
    244, 245, 250, 254, 258, 271, 293
    (n. 42), 296 (n. 21), 297 (n. 60), 302
    (n. 32), 305 (n. 21)
Fineman, Joseph, 243
Fire in the Flint, The (White), 81
First Church of Christian Science, 168
Fisher, Rudolph, 150
Fitzgerald, F. Scott, x
"Flies, The," 224
"Folklore Corner," 103
Folly Beach, S.C., 237
Fontanne, Lynne, 215
"Foreman, The," 94, 105, 274 (n. 89)
Forrest, Belford, 204
Fort Motte, S.C., 3, 6, 22, 30, 34, 45, 70,
    97, 112, 132, 133, 135, 140, 172, 179,
    191, 218, 236, 246, 276 (n. 29), 291
    (n. 27), 306 (n. 21); riot in, 38
Fort Motte Guard, 38
Fortnightly Club, 66, 67
Forum, 163
Foster, Thomas, 241, 244, 245
France, 97, 168−69, 191
Frank, Waldo, 280 (n. 4)
Frazier, Marie Brown, 115
Freedmen's Bureau, xii
"Free school," 18
Freud, Sigmund, 253
"From Lang Syne Plantation," 36
Frost, Frances, 189, 190, 191, 192, 204,
    207, 208, 213−14, 215, 216, 217, 227,
    228, 235, 236, 237, 242, 300 (n. 78)
Frost, Robert, 238
Fugitive, xi, 47, 113
Furness, Clifton, 286 (n. 27)

Gaffney, S.C., 149, 291 (n. 37)
Galsworthy, John, 40
Garland, Robert, 181
Garvey, Marcus, xiii, 22, 194

Geiger, Essie, 10, 11, 28, 130, 142–43, 198
Geiger, Robert, 143, 198
Georgetown, S.C., 17
Georgetown County Library, 251
Georgia, 23
Georgia Poetry Society, 188
Gerald, Veronica, 278 (n. 63)
Gershwin, George, 273 (n. 46)
Gish, Dorothy, 215
Gittman, J. T., 114, 136, 303 (n. 49)
Gittman's bookstore, 79
Glasgow, Ellen, 137
Glover, Sammy, 198
"God's Children." *See* "Whose Children"
Gone With the Wind: the novel, 239; the movie, 247
Gonzales, Ambrose, 40–41, 75, 80, 114
Gooden, Jessie, 38
Good Housekeeping, 150, 153
Gordon, Eugene, 115
Graham, Martha, 204
"Greasy Spoon, The," 151–52
Great Lakes, Mich., 251
"Greed of the Ground," 60
Green, John, 44–45
Green, Paul, 84, 94, 175, 281 (n. 23)
Greene, Harlan, 297 (n. 60), 305 (n. 12), 306 (n. 21)
Green Pastures, The (Connelly), 181
Green Thursday, x, xiv, 72–82, 85, 86, 88, 89, 92, 94, 98, 106, 112, 114, 122, 134, 187, 196, 205, 212, 222, 224, 282 (n. 73)
Greenville, S.C., 145
"Green Walnuts," 41–42, 44
Greenwich Village, 72, 199
Griffith, D. W., 22
Groves, J. A., 25
Guest, Edgar, 122
Guinan, Texas, 163, 218
Guinea, 107
Gullah, xix–xx, 4, 34, 40–41, 52, 72, 74–75, 114, 115, 117, 177, 179, 251, 279 (n. 7), 290 (n. 68); and gender, 78
"Gussie's Twins," 69

Haley, Alex, 258
Halper, Albert, 150
Hamilton, Alexander, 203
Hampton, Wade, xii, 3, 269 (n. 10)
Handicrafts of the Southern Highlands (Eaton), 219
Harcourt, 64
Harcourt, Alfred, 42, 43, 72
Hard-Boiled Virgin, The (Newman), 124
Harlem, xiii, 22, 63, 116, 117, 135, 144, 192, 194, 196, 197, 198, 205
Harlem Renaissance, xi, 118, 182
Harris, Joel Chandler, xx, 113
Hart, Charity, 18–19, 36, 274 (n. 89), 289 (n. 53)
Hart, Frank, 18–20, 27, 94, 95, 105, 274 (n. 87)
Hart, Frank, Jr., 19
Havana, Cuba, 147
Havemeyer, H. O., 167
Havemeyer, Louisine, 167–68
Hawaii, 3, 251, 253, 271 (n. 11)
Hawes, Elizabeth, 215–16, 227
Haydn, Franz Joseph, 167
Haymaker, Richard, 305 (n. 12)
Hear, Ye Sons (Fineman), 226
Hearst Corporation, 171, 199
"Heart Leaves," 151–52
Heaven's Gate Church, 258
Hedda Gabler (Ibsen), 204, 248
Hellman, Lillian, 235
Hemingway, Ernest, x, 241
Henderson, Archibald, 285 (n. 20)
Hendersonville, N.C., 248, 306 (n. 25)
Henry, Cammie, 199, 301 (nn. 98, 109)
Hepburn, Katharine, 215, 242, 244–45, 251
Hepburn, Katharine Houghton, 244
Hepburn, Marion, 242, 244–45
Hergesheimer, Joseph, 39, 40, 44, 83–84
Heyward, Dorothy, 124
Heyward, DuBose, 29, 47, 48, 63, 64, 87, 88, 112, 116, 117, 123, 124, 136, 148, 175, 273 (n. 46), 280 (n. 9), 305 (n. 12)
Heyward, Mary, 132
Heyward, Noonie, 17

Heyward, Wallace, 17, 18, 43, 134, 223, 229, 230, 243, 257–58, 274 (n. 83), 284 (n. 27)
Hill, Sheriff, 141
Hirschbein, Esther, 258
Hirschbein, Peretz, 258
Hitler, Adolph, 218
Holiday (Frank), 280 (n. 4)
Hollywood, 208, 245
Home Correspondence School, 33
Home to Harlem (McKay), 143, 150
Hopkins, Arthur, 162, 177, 180
Hora, June, 252
Horace Mann School, 286 (n. 27)
Horsely, Shelton, 44, 274 (n. 83)
Houghton Mifflin Company, 126, 145, 218
Howard, Sheriff, 140
How to Win Friends and Influence People (Carnegie), 242
Hughes, Helene. *See* Fineman, Helene Hughes
Hughes, Langston, 63, 116, 117, 182, 216, 218, 300 (n. 73)
Huntington, Archer Milton, 210
Hurricanes: Hugo, xviii; of 1893, 16; of 1928, 135
Hurston, Zora Neale, ix, 117

I Believe: The Personal Philosophies of Certain Eminent Men and Women of Our Time, 187
Ibsen, Henrik, 204
"Ideal Woman for a Man-Made World, An," 146
Illinois, University of, 98, 162
I'll Take My Stand, 212–13
"Imports from Africa," 40, 47
Inabinet, Helen. *See* Peterkin, Helen Inabinet
In Abraham's Bosom (Green), 176
Independent, xi, 115
Influenza, 18, 22
Integration, 254–55, 257
Internal Revenue Service, 209
Invisible Man (Ellison), 118, 150

"I've Never Had a Mother," 279 (n. 7)
"I've Never Touched Your Hand," 108

Jackson, Caleb, 134
Jackson, Faith Rehyer, 297 (n. 60)
Jackson, Jesse, 257
Jackson, Josh, 134
Jackson, Lucinda ("Sing"), 229–30
James, Henry, 93
Jester, Ralph, 215
Jim Crow laws, 23
John C. Campbell Folk School, 233, 303 (n. 47)
Johnson, Charles S., 117
Johnson, Gerald W., 80, 237, 280 (n. 20)
Johnson, James Weldon, 82, 116, 150, 283 (n. 11)
Johnston, Anne, 125–26
Jones, Katie, 221
Joyce, James, 258
Joyner, Charles, xx
Juilliard School of Music, 86
Julia the mule, 119, 288 (n. 89)
Jung, Carl, 211–12
Jurgen (Cabell), 36

Kaminer, Binkie, 97–98, 285 (n. 1)
Kaminer, Blanche, 27, 97–98
Keitt, 70
Kellner, Bruce, 116
Kennedy, John Pendleton, 222
Kentucky, 219
Kings Row (Bellamann), 305–6 (n. 21)
Kipling, Rudyard, 115
Kirby, Charles, 270 (n.5)
Knopf, Alfred A., x, 43, 68, 69, 78, 81, 85–86, 89, 96, 101, 109, 110, 145, 171, 187, 279 (n. 26), 287 (n. 79)
Knopf, Blanche, 71, 72, 85–86, 96, 101, 112, 281 (n. 35)
Koffler, Arnold, 169–70, 303 (n. 47)
Ku Klux Klan, 22, 39, 65, 67, 81, 87, 112, 218, 239, 243

Ladies' Home Journal, xv, 150, 152
Lancelot and Guinevere, 174

Lang Syne plantation, x, xii, xiii, xvi,
    xvii, xviii, xx, 1, 3–4, 6, 8, 9, 10, 15,
    16, 17, 18, 19, 21, 22, 23, 25, 26, 27, 29,
    30, 31, 33, 39, 44, 48, 54, 55, 56, 57,
    60, 64, 65, 69, 71, 73, 77, 82, 84, 85,
    87, 102, 109, 111, 122, 123, 125, 131,
    132, 134, 137, 139, 142, 143, 149, 154,
    157, 159, 160, 162, 163, 165, 166, 168,
    177, 187, 189, 191, 198, 200, 202, 208,
    209, 210, 212, 215, 216, 217, 221, 223,
    227, 228, 229, 230, 232, 234, 236, 242,
    243, 244, 251, 252, 253, 256, 257, 270
    (n. 8), 272 (nn. 37, 44), 273 (n. 57),
    274 (n. 89), 277 (n. 5), 278 (n. 63),
    286 (n. 31), 288 (n. 89), 295 (n. 31),
    305 (n. 12), 306 (nn. 21, 26)
Lang Syne School, 237
Larsen, Nella, xi, 150
Laudanum, 249
Laurel Hill plantation, 24
Law, Robert Adger, 78
Lay, George, 149
Leacey, Lucy, 17, 98, 286 (n. 26)
Leprosy, 105
Lescaut, Manon, 174
Let Us Now Praise Famous Men (Evans),
    220
Lewis, Sinclair, ix–x, 42, 43, 116, 148,
    241, 282 (n. 73)
Library of Congress, 203
Light in August (Faulkner), 206
Lindbergh kidnapping, 205
Linnett, Murray, 248
Literary Digest, 44
Literary Guild of America, 135, 136, 243,
    290 (n. 65), 301 (n. 99)
Literary Review, 115
Locke, Alain, 115, 116, 117, 118
Logan, Minnie, 131, 135, 198
London, England, 258
Long, Huey, 228
Long Island, N.Y., 198
Longmans-Green novel contest, 158–60,
    168, 230
Look Homeward, Angel (Wolfe), 150
Los Angeles, Calif., 250

Louisiana, 23, 63
Lovers Must Learn, 191–92, 200, 227,
    258, 305 (n. 21)
"Lower Berth, The," 291 (n. 27)
Lowman, Bertha, 140
Lowman, Clarence, 140
Lowman, Demon, 140
Lowman, Samuel, 140–41
Lurçat, Jean, 216
Lynching, xvii, 22, 38, 64, 82, 88,
    139–42
Lytle, Andrew, 212–13

McClendon, Rose, 175, 182
McCord, Louisa, 25–26, 133, 227
McCord family, 3, 28, 271 (n. 11), 272
    (n. 44), 289 (n. 54)
McCullers, Carson, 294 (n. 2)
McDermott, William, 178
MacDowell, Marian, 123–24, 189
MacDowell Colony, 124–25, 144, 227
McFarlane, Alexander, 5, 271 (n. 15)
McKay, Claude, 143, 150
McKinney, Ernest Rice, 112
McLeod, Thomas G., 140–41
Macon Telegraph, 114
Maddox, Marilyn Price, 305 (n. 15)
*Magic and Folk Beliefs of the Southern
    Negro*, 103
Main Street (Lewis), 42
Malaria, 16, 67, 162, 243
Malcolm X, xiii
Mamba's Daughters (Heyward), 136, 148,
    305 (n. 12)
Mann, Thomas, 71, 110, 241
"Manners," 98–100, 102
Manning, S.C., 59, 66
Marbury, Elisabeth, 175–76, 207
Marlboro County, S.C., 3, 284 (n. 24)
Marshall, Thurgood, 255
Mary Magdalene, 131
Maugham, Somerset, 177
"Maum Ann," 67
"Maum Lou," 67, 224, 281 (n. 23)
"Maum Patsy," 2, 52, 59, 279 (n. 7)
"Maum Vinner." *See* Berry, Lavinia

Medea, 146

"Melanctha" (Stein), 282 (n. 68)

Melrose plantation, 199, 221, 223, 301
(n. 98)

Melton, William D., 45

Member of the Wedding, The
(McCullers), 294 (n. 2)

Memphis, Tenn., race riot in, 22

Memphis Commercial Appeal, xvii

Mencken, H. L., x, xii, 29, 31–33, 34,
35, 36, 37, 39, 42, 43, 45, 46, 47, 48,
49, 50, 51, 54, 55, 57, 62, 63, 64, 65,
66, 67, 68, 71–72, 73, 78, 79, 83, 84,
85–86, 87, 89, 92, 95, 96, 101, 110,
112, 116, 123, 136, 142, 148, 149, 187,
280 (n. 20)

Mendum, Georgie Drew, 177

Menorah Journal, 98

"Merry-Go-Round, The," 37–39, 139

Methodism, 5, 14, 273

Metropolitan Life Insurance Company,
147

Mexico, 23, 209

Micah, 170

Middlebury, Vt., 232

Migration, xvii, 23, 56, 143

Millet, Fred, 283 (n. 7)

Mind of the South, The (Cash), 291
(n. 37)

Miss Eastway's Sanitarium, 192, 236

Mississippi, 23

"Missy's Twins," 50–51, 52, 56, 69, 72,
77, 117

Mitchell, Margaret, 211, 239–40, 247,
304 (n. 77)

Mobile, Ala., 164, 221

Mona Lisa, The, 172–74

Monroe, Harriet, 31, 59, 62, 89

Monteleone Hotel, 199

Montgomery, Mabel, 237

Mood, Alma Kennedy Archer (mother),
1, 13, 271 (n. 27), 273 (n. 64), 280
(n. 32); death of, 57–59; marriage
of, 58

Mood, Ashleigh (half-brother), 13, 65,
66, 75, 78, 119, 256

Mood, Ashleigh (nephew), 149

Mood, Emma, 161

Mood, Henry, xii, 4, 5, 13, 14, 15, 66, 166,
188, 273 (n. 64), 293 (n. 49)

Mood, Janie Brogdon (stepmother), 2,
13, 75, 98, 160

Mood, John, 4, 5, 6

Mood, Julius (cousin), 118

Mood, Julius (father), xii, xvi, 1, 4, 5, 7,
13, 14, 15, 18, 19, 24, 38, 39, 44, 57, 59,
66, 70, 71, 75, 78, 79, 80, 85, 94, 118,
147, 158, 160, 161, 168, 173, 188, 214,
215, 231, 271 (n. 26), 274 (n. 83, 87);
marriage of, 58; reaction to *Black
April* of, 119–20; death of, 239

Mood, Laura (grandmother), xii, 52, 273
(n. 64)

Mood, Laura (sister). *See* Schneider,
Laura Mood

Mood, Leah, 65, 75, 118, 256

Mood, Lula (aunt), 119

Mood, Margaret Ethel, 65

Mood, Preston, 65–66, 280 (n. 18)

Mood family, 4, 14, 59, 65, 93, 212, 274
(n. 83)

Mood Infirmary, 2, 19, 75

Morley, Christopher, 282 (n. 73)

"Morning Song in C Major," 36

Morphine, 249

Morrison, Toni, ix, xii

Morse, Josiah, 23

Mt. Pisgah cemetery, 276 (n. 29)

Mulattoes, folklore of, 119

Mules, 119, 254, 288 (n. 89)

Mulligan, Florence, 57–58

Mumford, Lewis, 159, 187

Murrells Inlet, S.C., 15, 17, 24, 81, 169,
172, 190, 203, 221, 250, 252, 257, 258

Murrells Inlet Protective Association, 251

Museum of Modern Art, 153

My Husband's Friends (Bellamann), 275
(n. 26)

Myrtle Beach, S.C., 81, 169, 258

Nachitoches, La., 199

"Nancy," 33, 74

Nashville, Tenn., 47, 113, 212
Nathan, George Jean, 37, 43, 68, 89
Nathan, Robert, 113
Nation, xv, 114, 126, 205
National Association for the Advancement of Colored People (NAACP), 42, 64, 81, 117, 140–41, 222; Legal Defense and Education Fund, 255
National Negro Development Union, 141
National Urban League, 82
Native Son (Wright), 118
Nazi Germany, 245
Necarsulmer, Edna, 233, 234, 302 (n. 37)
Necarsulmer, Evelyn, 233
Necarsulmer, Henry, 233
Necarsulmer family, 303 (n. 47)
"Negro In Art: How Shall He Be Portrayed?" (Du Bois and Fauset), 116
"Negro's Inhibitions, The" (Gordon), 115
Nelson, Alice Dunbar, 117
Newberry, S.C., 276
New Deal, 229
Newman, Frances, 82, 124
New Masses, xv, 126, 207
New Negro, The (Locke), 117
New Orleans, La., 47, 199–200, 209, 221
New Republic, xv, 113, 124, 126
New York City, 13, 22, 33, 55, 62, 63, 71, 72, 86, 87, 88, 97, 109, 126, 141, 142, 143, 144, 153, 159, 160, 162, 163, 165, 167, 168, 170, 180, 184, 191, 207, 209, 215, 227, 230, 231, 232, 233, 235, 243, 244, 284 (n. 11); opening of *Scarlet Sister Mary* in, 181
New Yorker, 190, 215
New York Evening Journal, 181
New York Evening Post, 137
New York Herald Tribune, 137, 187, 211, 220
New York Post, 181
New York Telegram, 181
New York Times, xii, 63, 137, 180, 189, 205, 222
New York Times Book Review, 79, 114, 115
New York World, 82, 141, 178

Nigger Heaven (Van Vechten), 116, 143, 287 (n. 79)
Nigger to Nigger (Adams), 136
Niles, John Jacob, 219, 233–34, 235, 303 (n. 47)
Nitke, Maurice, 177
North Carolina, 219
North Carolina, University of, 84

Oaks plantation, 24
O'Brien, E. J., 89
Odum, Howard, 112
Old South, 212, 213
"Old Women, The" (Pinckney), 100
Oliver, John, 147
O'Neill, Eugene, x, 72, 159, 176
"On a Plantation," 89–96, 101, 103, 109, 274 (n. 87), 277 (n. 5), 286 (n. 26), 289 (n. 34)
Oophorectomy, bilateral. *See* Battey's operation
Opium trade, 249
Opportunity, xv, 82, 126
"Opportunity" dinners, 117
Orangeburg, S.C., 142, 181, 215, 255
Orangeburg Lions Club, 114, 248
Orozco, José Clemente, 153–54, 173–74
"Ortymobile, The," 40
Othello, 298 (n. 28)
"Our Little Renaissance" (Locke), 117
Outer Banks of North Carolina, 25
"Outlook for the Negro," 23
"Over the River," 68–69, 72, 224, 225
Ovington, Mary White, 284 (n. 11)

Page, Thomas Nelson, xx, 78, 113
Paine, Albert Bigelow, 161, 303
Paris, 1, 97, 167, 184, 215
"Parisite," 215
Paterson, Isabel, 180
Pearl Harbor, 250
Pelzer, Francis, 270 (n. 8)
PEN, 86
Penn School, 177
Pentecost, 73
Perkins, Frances, 228

Peterboro, N.H., 123, 125–26, 144, 189

Peterkin, Agenora Drake, 3, 10, 11, 256, 284 (n. 24), 306 (n. 21)

Peterkin, Amy, 258

Peterkin, Edward, 145

Peterkin, Elfrida DeRenne Barrow, 188–89, 239, 242, 253, 256, 305 (n. 15); suicide of, 247–50

Peterkin, Emily, 258

Peterkin, Genevieve Chandler ("Sister"), 189, 198, 251–54, 256, 257, 258, 285 (n. 27), 290 (n. 7)

Peterkin, Helen Inabinet, 252, 254, 256, 258

Peterkin, James, 10

Peterkin, James Alexander, 3, 6, 9, 38, 39, 45, 256, 270 (n. 8)

Peterkin, James Preston (Jim) (grandson), 253, 257

Peterkin, John, 10

Peterkin, Julia Elfrida, 253

Peterkin, Julia Mood: wedding of, xii, 1–3; birth of, 2, 280 (n. 32); education of, 2; engagement of, 2; first job of, 3; honeymoon of, 6; pregnancy of, 6; birth of son by, 7; castration of, 7; postpartum depression of, 7–8, 9; gardening of, 9–10; marriage of, 12–13; childhood of, 13; piano lessons of, 27; sexual relationship with Irving Fineman of, 163; college education of, 166; relationship with sister Laura of, 166–67; psychotherapy of, 211–12; death of, 256

Peterkin, Laura, 258

Peterkin, Preston, 6, 9, 10

Peterkin, W. G. (Willie) (husband), xii, 1, 3, 6, 7, 8, 9, 10, 12–13, 16, 21, 24, 26, 27, 30, 43, 44, 45, 51, 54, 55, 56, 66, 73, 79, 83, 95, 108, 109, 132, 133, 139, 145, 147, 156, 162, 169, 172, 181, 182, 189, 202, 207, 210, 214, 216, 227, 228, 229, 230, 231, 237, 239, 241, 242, 243, 245, 246, 256, 272 (n. 37), 283 (n. 1), 288 (n. 89), 293 (n. 49)

Peterkin, William George, Jr. (Bill)

(son), xvii, 8, 12, 16, 21, 27, 43, 44, 46, 48, 51, 54, 55, 64, 78, 113, 125, 133, 149, 181, 187–88, 189, 196, 210, 222, 239, 244, 245, 247–49, 250, 251, 253, 254, 255, 256, 257, 285 (n. 1), 288 (n. 89); birth of, 7; wedding of, 191; remarries, 252; death of, 258

Peterkin, William George, III (grandson), xiv, xvii, 247, 248, 249, 250, 251, 254, 256, 258, 271; birth of, 242; marriage of, 252–53

Peterkin, William George, IV, 253, 258

Peterkin family, 8, 11, 78, 130, 132, 198, 256, 274 (n. 83)

Philadelphia, Pa., 62

Pinchback, P. B. S., 63

Pinckney, Josephine, 63, 100

"Plantation Christmas, A," 157, 161, 218

"Plat-Eye, The," 40

Pleshette, Suzanne, 258

Plessy v. Ferguson, 254

"Plum Blossoms," 74

Plum Bun (Faucet), 150

Poetry, 31, 62, 89, 188, 216; "Southern Number," 47

"Poetry South" (Allen and Heyward), 47

Police Woman, 258

Polk, Noel, 270 (n. 5), 283 (n. 9)

Porgy (Heyward), 88, 118, 175

Porgy and Bess (Gershwin and Heyward), 273 (n. 46)

Pound, Ezra, 110

Powell, Willie, 198

"Prayer from Lang Syne Plantation," 60–62

"Prejudices," 31

Preston, Keith, 113

"Pretend," 16

"Prig's Progress," 171

Prima Donna, 146

Prince George Church, 252

"Proudful Fellow, A," 144, 174

Provincetown Playhouse, 72, 159

Publishers Weekly, 147

Puckett, Newbell Niles, 103

Puckette, Charles, 114

Pulitzer, Joseph, 148
Pulitzer Prize, xiii, 78, 79, 147, 148–49, 150, 153, 206, 218, 282 (n. 73), 291 (n. 33)
Pyorrhea, 126

Quicksand (Larsen), 150

Rabies, 183
Race riots of 1919, 22
Racial conflicts, 103
Racial violence, 23, 139
Racism, 284 (n. 26)
Ransom, John Crowe, 212, 238
Rasputin, 208
Reagan, Ronald, 306 (n. 21)
"Recollections of Sister Alma Kennedy Mood" (Mulligan), 58
Reconstruction, xii, 3, 32, 38
Reconstruction Finance Corporation, 218, 302 (n. 17)
Redshirts, xii
Reed, Alma, 153–54, 173
Reed, Daniel, 28, 29, 52, 53, 93, 159, 162, 176, 177, 180, 181, 207, 234, 240
Reed, Isadora Bennett, 28, 29, 159, 207
Reels, 30
Reese, Dukkin, 27, 277 (n. 5)
Reese, Olive, 277 (n. 5)
Reid, Sam, 270 (n. 9)
Remarque, Erich Maria, 148
Reviewer, x, xiv, 35, 36, 37, 39, 41, 43, 44, 47, 48, 50, 51, 57, 84, 94, 100, 188, 219, 224, 279 (n. 26), 290 (n. 68)
Reynaud's syndrome, 105
Rice, 16, 25, 71, 286 (n. 31)
Richmond, Va., x, 35, 44, 83
Ridge, Albert, 180
Ridgeland, S.C., 227
"Right Thing, The," 44, 56
Rinehart, Mary Roberts, 110
Robeson, Elizabeth, 297 (n. 60)
Robeson, Paul, 72, 159, 180, 206, 240, 295 (n. 31), 298 (n. 28)
Robinson, Edwin Arlington, 124

"Robot Field Hands Successfully Invade Southland," xvii
Rock Hill, S.C., 71, 210
Roll, Jordan, Roll, xiv, 219–25, 240, 269 (n. 18), 273 (n. 55), 301 (n. 98), 303 (n. 47)
Rome, Italy, 98
Rome Adventure, 258
Romeo and Juliet, 174
Roosevelt, Eleanor, xvii, 228, 229, 237
Roosevelt, Franklin Delano, 217, 218, 228, 229, 237, 248
Roosevelt, Theodore, 283 (n. 11)
Roots (Haley), 258
"Roots Work," 42, 44, 221, 224
Roth, Henry, 300 (n. 87)
Russell, Bertrand, 187
Rutgers, 72
Rutledge, Archibald, 292 (n. 8)

Sacco-Vanzetti case, 147
"Sahara of the Bozart," 31
St. Helena Island, 177
St. Louis, Mo., race riot in, 22, 62
St. Luke's Episcopal Church, Paris, 167
St. Matthews, S.C., 141, 244, 252
Salivation, 104
Salpeter, Harry, 126
"Sam Dickerson" (Gonzales), 40–41
Sams, Stanhope, 121–22, 126
Sandburg, Carl, x–xi, 15, 28, 29, 30, 31, 32, 42, 43, 46, 47, 49, 54, 55, 56, 59, 64, 65, 72, 78, 79, 81, 82, 87, 106, 109, 110, 112, 122, 133, 198, 216, 218, 240, 249, 250, 251, 254, 255, 282 (n. 73)
Sandburg, Margaret, 31
Sanders, Bessie, 10, 11, 28, 130, 276 (n. 61)
Sanders, Ellis, 12, 75–76, 183, 198, 221, 273, 276, 281 (n. 55), 297 (n. 54)
Sanders, Lolly, 281 (n. 55)
Sanders, Martha, 10, 221
Sanders, Maybell "Dode," 77, 276 (n. 61)
Sanders, Monroe, 276 (n. 61)
Sanders, Nannie, 12, 75–76, 198, 221, 281 (n. 55)

Sanders, William ("Big Pa"), 297 (n. 54)

Sandy Island, 101, 107, 285 (n. 7)

Santee-Cooper project, 243

"Santy Claw," 151–52

Saratoga Springs, N.Y., 183, 208

Sargeant, Elizabeth Shepley, 124–25, 211

Sartoris (Faulkner), 150, 206

Saturday Evening Post, 150, 152

Saturday Review of Literature, 114

Savannah, Ga., 182, 188, 191, 227, 228

"Saving Souls," 280 (n. 20)

Saxon, Lyle, 199, 200, 219, 234, 240, 250, 292 (n. 3), 301 (nn. 98, 109)

Scarlet Sister Mary, xiii, xiv, xvi, xviii, 125, 127–38, 147, 155, 186, 187, 192, 205, 209, 224, 290 (n. 65); wins Pulitzer Prize, 148; serialization of, 149; "feather-weight airplane edition," 149; the play, 175–82, 206, 207

Schneider, Andreas, 167–68, 173

Schneider, Laura Mood (sister), 1, 2, 13, 55, 57, 59, 75, 160, 166, 167–68, 198, 250, 256, 273 (n.60), 293 (n. 49)

Scopes "monkey trial," 92

Scranton, Pa., 233

Seabrook, William Henry, 125–26, 132, 258

"Seeing Things," 122–23

Segregation, 22, 195, 240, 254–55

Shadow-Shapes, 124

Shakespeare, William, 258

Share Cropper's Union, 212

Shaw, George Bernard, 176

Sherman, General William Tecumseh, xii, 8

Shively, George, 172, 178, 179, 201, 207

Showboat, 298 (n. 28)

Shubert, Jacob, 177, 178

Shubert, Lee, 176, 177, 178

Shuffle Along, 63

Sikelianos, Mme, 153

Simon and Schuster, 187

Sinclair, Upton, 147

Skipworth, Alison, 208

Slavery, xv, xvii, xix, 4, 5, 8, 14, 16, 26, 38, 85, 133–34, 213, 273 (n. 69)

Smallpox, 18, 31, 276 (n. 42)

Smalls, Ed, 143

Smalls Paradise, 143

Smart Set, x, 31, 32, 35, 37, 39, 43, 46

Smith, Reed, 88, 93, 102

Smoke and Steel, 29

Smythe, Augustine, 26, 270 (n. 8)

Smythe, Louisa McCord, 133, 271 (n. 11), 272 (n. 37), 273 (n. 45)

Snowden, Yates, 88, 212

Society for the Preservation of Spirituals, 177

Soil Bank, 254

Somme, Battle of the, 118

"Sophisms of the Protective Policy" (Bastiat), 25

"Sorcerer, The," 89

Sound and the Fury, The (Faulkner), 150, 206

South Carolina: racial attitudes in, xi, xv, 79–80, 87, 88, 113, 283–84 (n. 11), 300 (n. 73); economy of, 70; divorce laws in, 156

South Carolina, University of, 23, 45, 52, 88, 102

South Carolina Democratic Party, 229

South Carolina Federation of Women's Clubs, 126

South Carolina Legislature, 5, 23, 218

South Carolina Poetry Society, 29, 47, 63, 80

South Carolina Press Association, 147

South Carolina Supreme Court, 140

"Southern Imagination, The," 67–68

Southern Literary Messenger, 26

Southern Quarterly Review, 26

Southern renaissance, xi, 68

Southern womanhood, cult of, 100

Southern Women's National Democratic Organization, 209

Soybeans, 210, 254

Spartanburg, S.C., 27, 63, 166

Spingarn, Amy, 64, 86–87, 93

Spingarn, Joel, x, 42, 43, 64–65, 72, 78, 86–87, 93, 112, 116, 142, 280 (n. 6)
Sprunt, Jim, 172
Stallings, Laurence, 79, 80, 82, 100, 112, 206, 208
Standard English, xx, 52, 74
Staten Island, N.Y., 220
Stein, Gertrude, 282 (n. 68)
Sterling, George, 272 (n. 38)
Stevens, Wallace, 71
Stewart, Lois, 283 (n. 9)
Stock market crash, 153, 158
Stoney, Frances Frost. *See* Frost, Frances
Stoney, Samuel Gaillard, 176, 227, 272
Strode, Hudson, 110–11, 115, 124, 125, 135, 137, 153, 177, 183, 184, 189, 234, 246, 286 (n. 49)
Strode, Thérèse, 111, 153, 183
Stubbs, Thomas McAlpin, 51
Stuckey, Belle Taber, 27, 109, 247, 252–53, 254
"Studies in Charcoal," 41
Suckow, Ruth, 282 (n. 73)
Suicide, 136, 172–75; apparent, of Preston Mood, 66; Julius Mood considers, 161, 214; Julia Peterkin considers, 215, 231; Frida Peterkin's, 248–50
Summerton, S.C., 21, 255
Sumter, S.C., 1, 7, 13, 18, 19, 54, 119, 158, 168, 231
"Sunday, A," 76
Sunday, Billy, 45, 67
Sunnyside, 15, 170
Survey, 137
Survey Graphic, 117
Swallow Barn (Kennedy), 222
Synge, John Millington, 82
Syphilis, 18, 285 (n. 19), 304 (n. 101)

Taber, Charles, 38
Taber, Mary Belle Peterkin, 6, 27
Tate, Allen, 212
"Teaching Jim," 75
Tennessee, 219
Their Eyes Were Watching God (Hurston), 118

This Pure Young Man (Fineman), 144–45, 158, 159, 170; receives Longmans-Green prize, 168
Thomas, Margaret, 270 (n. 5)
Thompson, Edgar T., 194
Three Mountains, 237
Thunder on the Left (Morley), 282 (n. 73)
Thurman, Wallace, xi, 118, 150
Thurmond, Strom, 284 (n. 11)
Tilting tournaments, 222
Time, 149, 171, 180
Toomer, Jean, 63–64, 87, 150, 280 (nn. 4, 6, 9)
Torches Flare, The (Young), 113
Tours, France, 97
Trevor, Claire, 215
Tristan and Iseult, 174
Tuberculosis, 18; of Alma Archer, 58; of Andreas Schneider, 168
Tulsa, Okla., race riot in, 22
Turgenev, Ivan, 42, 82, 206
Twain, Mark, 75
Typhoid fever, 110

Uebler, George, 192, 199, 233–34
Ulmann, Doris, xiv, 153–54, 160, 161, 163–65, 169, 170, 179, 183, 184, 189, 192, 199, 200, 204, 210, 216, 219, 220, 221, 222, 232–34, 235, 301 (n. 97), 302 (n. 37), 303 (n. 47)
Undset, Sigrid, 71
United Daughters of the Confederacy, xii, 46, 81
United States Department of Agriculture, 23
Urbana, Ill., 162–63
"Usual Buncombe, The" (Mencken), 46

Vacaville, Calif., 127
Vanderbilt family, 205
Vanderbilt University, xi
Van Doren, Dorothy, 221
Vanity Fair, 63
Van Vechten, Carl, 113, 116, 143
Vardaman, James K., 283 (n. 11)
Varesi, Gilda, 52

Veneer mill, 210, 239
"Venner's Sayings," 89, 156
Victim and Victor (Oliver), 147
Viking Press, 214
"Vinner's Sayings," 60, 62
"Violets in the Sahara," 47
Virgin Mary, 131
Virginia, University of, 54
Vogue, 79

Waccamaw Hunt Club, 70
Waccamaw Neck, 16, 17
Waccamaw River, xvi, 16–17
Wadmalaw Island, S.C., 41
Walker, Alice, ix
Walker, Ella Weeks, 48, 102
Walls of Jericho, The (Fisher), 150
Walmsley, James Eliot, 71
"Walter Winchell on Broadway," 178
"Wanted: A Negro Novelist," xi
Wappingers Falls, N.Y., 170
Waring, J. Waties, 254–55
"Warning" (Frost), 190
Warren, Dale, 126, 131, 180, 218, 234
Warren, Robert Penn, 212
Washington, Booker T., 283 (n. 11)
Washington, D.C., 179
Washington Post, 240
Washington Star, 180
Washington Times, 179
Watch Night, 84, 224
Waters, Ethel, 175, 294 (n. 2)
Webb, Beatrice, 187
Weeks, Brudge, 198
Weeks, Cicero, 110, 286 (n. 42), 289
    (n. 34)
Weeks, Jabez, 10, 273 (n. 49)
Weeks, Mary (Mary Bryant), xiii, xvii,
    xviii, 10, 11, 12, 15, 17, 27, 28, 30, 32,
    33, 36, 39, 40, 48, 49, 64, 94, 110, 125,
    126, 127, 130–33, 135, 142, 198, 221,
    229, 250, 256, 258, 273 (n. 49), 276
    (n. 61), 286 (n. 42), 289 (n. 34)
Weeks, Virginia, 198
West, Mae, 176
West, Nathaniel, 215

Weston, Isaac, 87, 93, 284 (n. 27)
Whaley, Blondell, 142
Whaley, V. H. "Pink," 141–42, 290 (n. 7)
"What I Believe," 163, 187
Wheatley, Phillis, 117
Whitaker, Miller, 142
White, Fred, 270 (n. 5), 283 (n. 7)
White, Walter, xi, 81, 86, 87–88, 116,
    118, 135, 136, 140–42, 146, 150, 222
White House, 251, 283 (n. 11)
White supremacy, xvi, 4, 93, 195
Whitmore, Jackie, xvii, xviii, 133, 258
"Whose Children," 56–57, 89, 279
    (n. 26)
"Wife, A," 224
Wilder, Thornton, 148, 218
Williams College, 241
Williamson, Joel, 119
Wilson, Edmund, 215
Wilson, Woodrow, 22
Wilson Library Bulletin, 186
Winchell, Walter, 178, 179, 216, 220, 232
Wine, Beulah, 248
Wings, 301 (n. 99)
Winsten, Archer, 205
Winter Park, Fla., 215
Winthrop College, 71, 210–11
Wizard of Oz, The (Baum), 110
Wolfe, Thomas, 150, 240
Woolf, Virginia, 165, 293 (n. 42)
Works Progress Administration, 237
World War I, xvii, 22, 118, 124, 143, 273
    (n. 60)
World War II, xvii, 250
Wright, Charlton, 80, 142

Yaddo Writers' Colony, 183, 208
Yankees, 239–40
Yoknapatawpha County, 258
You Have Seen Their Faces (Bourke-
    White and Caldwell), 220
Young, Stark, 113, 130, 181, 207, 211, 212,
    213

Zilboorg, Gregory, 299 (n. 49)
Zimmerman, Daniel, 270 (n. 8)

Susan Millar Williams lives in
McClellanville, South Carolina,
where she is the executive director
of the McClellanville Arts Council.
Her writing has been published in
Nation and *Southern Review*.

CPSIA information can be obtained
at www.ICGtesting.com
Printed in the USA
LVHW051552010520
654850LV00009B/119

9 780820 332505

A Devil and a Good Woman, Too is the award-winning biography of a remarkably talented, enigmatic southern woman whose fiction about rural African Americans drew on her own emotional traumas and family scandals. A white plantation mistress who vowed to "write what is, even if it is unpleasant," Julia Peterkin produced five books that revolutionized American literature, including the Pulitzer Prize–winning novel *Scarlet Sister Mary*. In the 1920s, Peterkin wrote stark, powerful stories that earned the praise of W. E. B. Du Bois, Langston Hughes, Carl Sandburg, and H. L. Mencken. But for reasons explored in this biography, she chose to stop writing at the height of a brilliant career and retreat to a provincial life rather than follow her characters as they moved away from the plantation.

Susan Millar Williams teaches American literature and creative writing at Trident Technical College in Charleston, South Carolina. Her writing has been published in the *Nation* and the *Southern Review*.

"Williams makes a convincing argument for [Peterkin's] singularity as a woman and, more important, for the resurrection of her work." —*Publishers Weekly*

"An exceptional piece of work." —Louis D. Rubin Jr.

"A work to be read and remembered. Highly recommended." —*Choice*

"A well-researched account of Peterkin's life, almost as readable as a good novel." —*Atlanta Journal-Constitution*

"Remarkable . . . A triumph of dedicated research and imaginative insight." —*South Carolina Historical Magazine*

ISBN-13: 978-0-8203-3250-5
ISBN-10: 0-8203-3250-X

9 780820 332505   90000

The University of Georgia Press
ATHENS, GEORGIA 30602   WWW.UGAPRESS.ORG

Cover design: Mindy Basinger Hill   Cover image: Photograph of Julia Peterkin in a leopard-skin coat. South Carolina Historical Society.